MW00995488

Managing Performance through Training & Development

Monica Belcourt
Associate Professor
Atkinson College, York University

Philip C. Wright
Associate Professor
Hong Kong Baptist University

Alan M. Saks
Associate Professor
Atkinson College, York University

Monica Belcourt, Series Editor

1120 Birchmount Road
Scarborough, Ontario M1K 5G4
www.nelson.com
www.thomson.com

Canadian Cataloguing in Publication Data

Belcourt, Monica Laura, date
        Managing performance through training & development

2nd ed.
(Nelson Canada series in human resources management)
Includes bibliographical references and index.
ISBN 0-17-616648-3

1. Employees – Training of.   I. Saks, Alan M. (Alan Michael), 1960–   .
II. Wright, Phillip Charles.   III. Title.   IV. Series.

HF5549.5.T7B45 2000   658.3′124   C99-932923-5

Executive Editor	Tim Sellers
Marketing Manager	David Tonen
Project Editor	Mike Thompson
Production Editor	Tracy Bordian
Production Coordinator	Hedy Later
Art Director	Angela Cluer
Interior Design	Julie Greener
Cover Design	Anne Goodes
Senior Composition Analyst	Zenaida Diores
Printer	Webcom

Printed and bound in Canada
1   2   3   4   03   02   01   00

To my son, Brooker Belcourt, who has the best qualities of a learner:
curiosity, intelligence, focus, and patience.
— M.B.

To Sara and Kenneth,
who make my life interesting,
stimulating, and challenging.
— P.W.

To Kelly, who makes it all worthwhile.
— A.M.S.

BRIEF CONTENTS

DETAILED CONTENTS

Chapter 3: Needs Analysis: Approaches and Methods 43

Chapter 4: Strategic Goal Setting   77

Chapter 5: Program Design   97

CHAPTER 6: OFF-THE-JOB TRAINING METHODS   133

CHAPTER 7: ON-THE-JOB TRAINING METHODS   157

Chapter 11: Training Programs   265

Chapter 12: Management Development   297

CHAPTER 13: EQUITY IN TRAINING   323

CHAPTER 14: ORGANIZATIONAL LEARNING   343

INDEX   365

ABOUT THE SERIES

One resource in organizations can't be easily imitated or duplicated by competitors: human resources. The management of this resource makes the difference between a mediocre organization that meets some goals and a superior organization that surpasses its objectives. We see and feel the result of the management of this asset in our daily lives, as consumers of services offered by employees who have been trained to provide this service. As students entering professions, we need to know about career development strategies and company recruitment practices. Thus, the effective management of human resources touches not only the employees and managers of the organizations, but all those with whom they interact. Knowledge of this field is critical, and so Nelson Thomson Learning has published a series of texts dedicated to those managers and human resource professionals who are responsible for people.

In addition to this book, texts in the *Nelson Series in Human Resources Management* include:

- *Occupational Health & Safety*
- *Recruitment and Selection in Canada*
- *Compensation in Canada: Strategy, Practice, and Issues*
- *Strategic Human Resources Planning*
- *Research, Measurement, and Evaluation of Human Resources*
- *An Introduction to the Canadian Labour Market*

The *Nelson Series in Human Resources Management* is important for many reasons. Each book in the series (except for *Compensation*) is the first Canadian text in the area. Human resource practitioners in Canada must work with Canadian laws, Canadian statistics, Canadian policies, and Canadian values. This series serves these needs. The series also represents the first time that practitioners have access to a standardized guide to the management of the various HR functional areas. This one-stop resource will prove useful to anyone involved in the management of people.

The publication of this series signals that the HR field has advanced to the stage where theory and applied research guide practice. Because the HR field is still emerging and new tools and methods are being invented, the theory and research are being supplemented with common methods shared among Canadian HR professionals. The books in this series cover the dominant HR functional areas and are based on applied HR research. This research is supplemented with examples of best practices used by Canadian companies who are leaders in the HR area. Each text identifies the process of managing and implementing HR strategies, thus serving as an introduction to the functional area for the new student of HR and as a validation manual for the more experienced HR practitioner. Cases, exercises, discussion questions, and supporting references contained at the end of each chapter provide opportunities for further discussion and analyses.

As you read the texts, I hope you share the excitement of learning about the field of human resources management, which observers say will be the most important management area in the next decade.

Monica Belcourt
SERIES EDITOR
JANUARY 2000

ABOUT THE AUTHORS

MONICA BELCOURT

Professor Belcourt is an associate professor of Human Resources Management in the Department of Administrative Studies, Atkinson College, York University. She holds a B.A. in psychology from the University of Manitoba, an M.A. in organizational psychology from York University, an M.Ed. in adult education from the University of Ottawa, and a Ph.D. in administration from York University. She is a certified human resources professional (CHRP).

Dr. Belcourt has extensive experience in human resources management as director of personnel for CP Rail, manager of employee development for the National Film Board, manager of consumer services for the Quebec Region of Consumer and Corporate Affairs, personnel administrator for the Federal Government, and as a consultant. Serving as a director on boards such as CIBC Insurance and the Human Resources Professionals Association of Ontario has given her a strategic perspective on the HR function. In addition, she has received more than $360 000 in research grants and has published more than 70 articles and books on human resources and entrepreneurship. She is founding director of the Human Resources Research Institute of the Human Resources Professionals Association of Ontario. The HRRI promotes HR research by giving awards for best theses and dissertations, and by funding research. HRRI disseminates research studies to HR professionals through the Research Forum in the *HR Professionals* magazine, through the *HRM Research Quarterly*, and the Applied Research Stream at the HRPAO annual conference. Dr. Belcourt is series editor of the *Nelson Canada Series in Human Resources Management*, and is the lead author of *Managing Human Resources*, Second Canadian Edition. She is a frequent commentator on HR issues for CTV, Canada AM, CBC, *The Globe and Mail*, the *Canadian HR Reporter*, and other media.

PHILIP C. WRIGHT

Philip C. Wright, an associate professor in the Department of Management at the Hong Kong Baptist University, spent nine years in the Faculty of Administration at the University of New Brunswick in Fredericton, where he held the rank of full professor. Dr. Wright has taught or completed consulting contracts in 10 countries in Asia, North America, and Eastern Europe, in the process working in seven different M.B.A. programs.

Dr. Wright received a B.A. (Hons.) from Bishop's University, a M.Ed. from the University of Toronto, an M.A. from Wilfrid Laurier University, a M.Sc. from the University of Guelph, and a Ph.D. from Penn State University. He has been made a fellow of the Institute of Personnel and Development (UK) and of the Canadian Institute of Management, where, for 13 years, he held the volunteer post of academic dean. He has published more than 100 refereed and professional papers, written six books, and completed several monographs. Dr. Wright has been associate editor of the *Journal of European Industrial Training* for more than 10 years.

ALAN M. SAKS

Alan Saks is an associate professor of Human Resources Management in the Department of Administrative Studies, Atkinson College, York University. He earned a B.A. in psychology at the University of Western Ontario, an M.A.Sc. in industrial-organizational psychology from the University of Waterloo, and a Ph.D. in organizational behaviour and human resources from the University of Toronto.

Prior to joining York University, Professor Saks was a member of the Department of Management in the Faculty of Commerce and Administration at Concordia University in Montreal. Training is one of his major areas of research, and he has published more than a dozen articles on training and the transfer of training, as well as on other subjects in human resources including recruitment, job search, and the socialization and work adjustment of new employees. Professor Saks's research has been published in journals such as the *Journal of Applied Psychology, Personnel Psychology, Academy of Management Journal, Journal of Organizational Behavior,* and the *Journal of Vocational Behavior.* Professor Saks is currently on the editorial board of the *Academy of Management Journal, Journal of Organizational Behavior, Journal of Vocational Behavior,* and the *International Journal of Selection and Assessment.* He is the editor of the *HRM Research Quarterly,* and is the chair of the Applied Research Stream of the Human Resources Professional Association of Ontario. In addition to this text, Professor Saks is the author of *Research, Measurement, and Evaluation of Human Resources,* which is also part of the *Nelson Series in Human Resources Management.*

PREFACE

The Western world is going through a period of adjustment as profound and as far-reaching as the Industrial Revolution that ended almost a century ago. The last great spirit of industrialization lasted almost 300 years, but the present revolution (couched in terms like *globalization*) is proceeding at a pace that astonishes even those who spend their professional lives predicting change and developing change management programs. It is against this background of chaos and rapid industrial and human displacement that this text is written.

This is a book about Canada. Like anything else in our work world, training and development is facing fundamental restructuring. Trainers and the managers who employ them will need to rethink the philosophies, missions, and roles surrounding all human development activities, otherwise their functions will cease to be credible in a corporate world that is asking for proof of value-added. We hope that the second edition of this text, the only one on the market to address these issues grounded in Canadian facts and philosophy, will guide those involved in performance management to prove that training activities do make a difference.

This book is part of the *Nelson Series in Human Resources Management*, which examines the functional areas of human resources management. The purpose of the series is to profile the best thinking and research in the human resources (HR) field, while demonstrating how each functional area is related to overall HR strategy. Training and development is one such area, a subsystem within the human resources management function. For example, information from human resources planning, job analyses, and performance appraisals drives the type of training to be developed. Legislation and programs in employment equity and safety determine new types of training. In these ways, training and development can be seen to be tightly integrated with other HR areas.

In this second edition, we welcome a new author, Alan M. Saks, who has an excellent reputation as a researcher and author in organizational behaviour and human resources management, especially in training. I also want to acknowledge the contribution of Philip Wright, who has moved to Asia to delight business students there with his knowledge, experience, and unique perspectives on the world.

STRUCTURE OF THE BOOK

We begin this book with chapters that develop the theme that training is an investment, and that this investment in human capital must be managed. Chapter 1 introduces the strategic importance of training. This chapter offers the first of many Canadian facts, practices, and stories in the text. Chapter 2 outlines the roles and responsibilities of those in human resources development (HRD). Readers learn about how to position the training function, how to manage it, and how to increase its credibility throughout the organization. The next nine chapters identify the key steps in the process of training, that is, the steps most likely to result in an effectively trained workforce.

The process starts with the delineation of the need for training, accomplished through needs analyses at three levels (Chapter 3). Once these needs have been established, the next step is the setting of measurable goals that have been aligned with the strategy of the organization (Chapter 4). These quantifiable goals allow trainers to determine if training is the best solution. Throughout the text, the emphasis is that training is an expensive solution and not always the most effective option for improving performance. These ideas about investment, positioning, and analysis serve as a springboard for one of the primary intellectual threads woven throughout the text: it is not training activity that is important, but employee effectiveness. Hence the title of this book focuses on managing *performance*, not *performers*.

Chapter 5 on program design, has been extensively rewritten, with the goal of providing the reader with a step-by-step guide to the actual design of a training course. The trainer can then choose the best training method (Chapter 6), based on what was learned in the objectives and design chapters. Not all learning in organizations takes place in classrooms, so we have devoted a chapter (7) to those activities that managers and performance experts can use on the job to increase employee knowledge and skills.

Obviously, the ultimate goal of all training and development is the transfer of the new skills or knowledge to the job. Chapter 8 provides trainers, trainees, and their managers with the tools to ensure that newly learned abilities are applied on the job. Of course, both managers and trainers want to know if the training was effective. Did the trainees learn, apply that learning to their jobs, and did this make any difference to organizational results? Methods for answering these questions are outlined in Chapter 9 on evaluation. The loop is closed by costing the training intervention (Chapter 10).

We have introduced a new chapter in this edition of this text, to introduce the reader to the types of training courses that Canadian organizations are conducting. An examination of various types of training programs is presented in Chapter 11. The development of managers is of principal concern to organizations. Because management development differs in time and focus from other training efforts, it is the focus of a separate chapter (Chapter 12).

Trainers must be aware that some training and development methods may have the unintended effect of systematically excluding the designated groups from participating, and so we have provided a number of prescriptions in Chapter 13 to ensure that training and development is equitable. The final chapter (Chapter 14) moves to a macro level of learning. One of the most significant changes impacting training (besides technology) is the concept of the learning organization. In this chapter, which is new to the second edition, we discuss what this concept means, and how to create, capture, and diffuse organizational knowledge.

Each chapter begins with a description of the key learning within the chapter to orient the reader. A summary of these key points is provided at the end of the chapter. Minicases, discussion questions, and exercises, with supporting references, are included to allow students the opportunity to analyze and to apply the theory. A running case encourages students to build their skills systematically and coherently.

Acknowledgments

As most authors do, we have used not only our own thoughts and experiences, but we have also drawn on the experiences and published work of a large number of practitioners and academicians throughout North America and Europe.

We wish to thank our reviewers: Brad Hill (St. Lawrence College), Susan FitzRandolph (Ryerson Polytechnic University), Robert Gawreluck (Grant MacEwan Community College), and Hermann Schwind (St. Mary's University). Each one contributed to this text by lending us their expertise and by taking the time to share experiences and to make insightful comments.

Similarly, we would like to express our appreciation to our many colleagues who have given freely of their expertise through their research and publications. In particular we wish to thank our colleagues in the academic community who have contributed their research and thinking to advancing the field: Robert Haccoun, Gary Latham, Greg Irving, Ron Monroe, Indira Somwaru, Alain Gosselin, Len Karakowski, Nina Cole, A. R. Elangovin, and Gerard Seijts.

We are grateful to the team that helped to develop and produce this text. The authors wish to acknowledge the entrepreneurial spirit of Peter Jackson, the acquisitions editor at Nelson Thomson Learning who first recognized the need for a Canadian series in human resources management. We especially appreciate the support of Tim Sellers, Executive Editor, who for many years has been an enthusiastic support of the Series. We thank our production team: Mike Thompson, who has done an outstanding job of managing this project, and Tracy Bordian, who worked carefully to ensure a quality product.

Our greatest indebtedness, however, is to our families. The craft of authorship takes time, energy, and emotion, often at the expense of those whose lives we share. To them: Michael, Marc, and Brooker Belcourt; Sarah and Kenneth Wright; and Kelly Saks.

Monica Belcourt
YORK UNIVERSITY

Philip C. Wright
HONG KONG BAPTIST UNIVERSITY

Alan M. Saks
YORK UNIVERSITY

1

A MODEL
OF TRAINING

THE WORLD OF TRAINING

Imagine that you are a newly hired employee for a major Canadian company. You have been carefully selected for your knowledge and skills, as well as for your ability to learn and to adapt to changing conditions. Before starting the job, you receive reading material from the company about its history, mission, products, and services. Upon arrival at your workplace, you are invited to attend a three-day formal orientation program that covers benefits, company structure, and operations. However, most of the time is spent training you in company processes and your job responsibilities. Your supervisor then spends one pre-arranged hour every day listening to you and coaching you.

Because you are working as part of a team responsible for a territory, you receive off-the-job training in team-building, problem identification, and conflict resolution. In addition, your team spends several hours per week discussing ways to improve the quality of the company's products. Every member of the team is trained in facilitation skills. As a group, you identify a need for better ways to handle customer complaints. Using an action learning model, your team proposes an innovative solution that wins a national award from your professional association.

Given the fast pace of your organization, you find that you are having problems managing all your projects. The training facilitator suggests a multimedia training program in project management, which you can use at your work station and learn during company-scheduled training breaks. You are accustomed to learning independently, as most job-specific training is given by the company online, through the use of electronic performance support systems. The company also encourages you to attend university in the evening to complete your degree and reimburses your tuition.

You are selected by your team to be its representative in an international companywide organization development effort to improve service quality. All representatives are sent to Germany to analyze competitor practices and benchmark the best. This trip is preceded by a training workshop in benchmarking service performance standards. The trip is beneficial to you because your career goal is to become vice president of marketing, and international experience is a job requirement (along with the degree). Your employer supports you in your career goals, and you, in turn, are committed to helping the organization meet its goals.

A fantasy of the future? No, this scenario is fairly typical of large Canadian companies that believe that investing in employees through continual training and learning opportunities gives them a strategic advantage in the marketplace and ensures their survival and profitability. The executives of these organizations have learned that human capital investments pay off not only for the organization but in higher wages and job growth for employees.

CHAPTER GOALS

This book will introduce you to the exciting world of performance management through training and development. After reading this chapter, you should be able to

- understand the meaning of the terms *performance management, training,* and *development*
- list the organizational, employee, and societal benefits of training
- describe training in Canada
- describe three models of training and discuss their differences
- outline a systems approach to training

PERFORMANCE MANAGEMENT

For a long time, managers have been mouthing the cliché that "people are our greatest asset." Indeed, Dofasco's company slogan is "Our product is steel; our strength is people." People *are* an organization's greatest asset. Increasingly, research evidence is showing that the effective management of human resources results in higher profits and productivity, as well as enhanced employee well-being (Belcourt, 1996–97). Training not only builds capabilities, it creates commitment. Employees are aware of the investments made in them, and they reciprocate by working harder and smarter.

Of course, training is not a silver bullet and cannot accomplish these gains without an alignment with other human resource management systems. High-performance work systems (HPWS) consist of aligned HR practices and policies (such as linking rewards to performance) that enable organizations to achieve superior productivity from employees. (You can go to <**www.nelson.com**> to read about how to manage human resources effectively through the implementation of high-performance work systems.) Training and development are an integral component of these HPWS, and their use enables organizations to achieve their goals. All these systems (staffing, appraisal, compensation, and training) enable the organization to manage performance more effectively.

Performance management is a process of establishing performance expectations with employees, designing ways to improve that performance, and monitoring the success of these interventions. This process signals to employees what is really important in the organization, fixes accountability for behaviour and results, and helps to improve performance (Gosselin, Werner, & Hall, 1997). Performance management is not a single event, such as a performance appraisal or a training program.

Training is just one of the ways that performance can be improved. **Training** refers to the acquisition of knowledge, skills, and abilities that results in improved performance in the current job. Training usually implies a short-term focus on acquiring skills in a formal, off-the-job learning environment. Most of you have experienced this type of training; your company may have sent you to a workshop to learn a software package like Excel, or to learn how to deal with a hostile client. The goal was to help you to do your current job better.

Human resources development focuses on the acquisition of knowledge and attitudes that may be required in the long-term achievement of individual career goals and corporate objectives. The goal is to prepare you for future jobs or responsibilities. The training may consist of longer programs such as a leadership course, but this would be in addition to job rotation, coaching, and other assignments. The goal is usually to prepare employees for managerial careers. You can read more about management development in Chapter 12.

From an organizational perspective, the development of human resources refers to the process of assessing the abilities of employees, and to the preparation of programs that enable employees to achieve their full potential and meet organizational objectives. Obviously, training and development are intertwined within a larger system of performance management. The creation of an organizational environment conducive to optimum performance is a fundamental first step in the process of a performance management system that

performance management the process of establishing performance expectations with employees, designing ways to improve that performance, and monitoring the success of those interventions

training the acquisition of knowledge, skills, and abilities that results in improved performance

human resources development the acquisition of knowledge and attitudes to facilitate the achievement of career goals and corporate objectives

develops employees. All systems are concerned with the goal of improving organizational effectiveness through the improvement of human resources.

We look next at the benefits organizations, employees, and society experience when individuals are trained.

The Importance of Training

Companies that invest in the training of their employees reap many benefits. But so do the employees themselves and the society in which they live. This section describes some of the benefits of training.

Organizational Benefits

1. Facilitate strategy Organizations want to survive, and then to prosper. Training can help organizations achieve these goals. Organizations can be successful by training employees to be competent and motivated to work toward organizational goals. High-performance organizations (those reporting excellent financial performance over the past three years) integrate training into strategy, and communicate this strategy to employees. Nontraditional training, such as mentoring and job sharing, and increased access to formal training play a large role in corporate success (Bailey, 1998).

Most organizations recognize the benefits of a trained workforce; the others may not realize the costs of *not* training. Most organizations do not measure their human assets, or even begin to estimate the costs associated with a poorly trained workforce. Manufacturing companies, for example, have good cost accounting systems for measuring scrap material and work that must be redone, but do not assess in quantifiable terms the cost of incompetent employees who necessitate this work.

Take quality control as one example of how training can have an impact on goal achievement. Canadians rate quality as the most important factor in purchase decisions, so for many organizations, a good strategy is to produce high-quality products. Small and medium-sized organizations spend an average of 30 percent of payroll and 75 percent of all their quality control spending on checking the quality of work and fixing work errors. They could shift this money to training people to not make errors in the first place and achieve significant savings (*The Training Report*, 1998).

Furthermore, the ability to handle the challenges of changes in the environment and in technology is enhanced, as well as the capacity to cope with competition (Coravan, 1995). As many executives are realizing, "our ability to learn has become the heart of our ability to compete" (Greco, 1997). Product cycle times, the period in which a product is invented, put on the market, and becomes obsolete, have decreased from five years to three to one to six months. Innovative firms spend twice as much on training as others (Baldwin &

Johnson, 1995). In a world defined by economic competitiveness, employees' abilities are the international currency. Employers realize that the best competitive tactic is to ensure that employees are highly skilled and competent.

Not only manufacturing environments use training to meet strategic ends. In the service sector, Alimentation Couche Tard Inc., Canada's second-largest convenience-store operator, uses training as a strategic tool to grow its stores under company labels such as Provi-soir, Winks, and Red Rooster. Couche Tard invests twice as much as the national average (3.6 percent of payroll versus 1.6 percent) in training its employees in customer service, management, and merchandising (Millan, 1997).

2. INCREASE PRODUCTIVITY AND PROFITS   There is a calculable benefit in training employees. Trained employees can do more work, make fewer errors, require less supervision, have higher morale, and have lower rates of attrition (Bowsher, 1990). In a 1998 survey conducted by the American Management Association, companies that expanded their training programs showed gains in productivity and larger operating profits (Adams, 1999). Other studies find that a 10 percent increase in training produced a 3 percent increase in productivity over two years (Mandel, 1993). Those companies that invest more heavily in training ($900 per employee versus $275 per employee) are more successful and more profitable. These companies spend up to 6 percent of payroll on training, but they achieve 57 percent higher sales per employee, 37 percent higher gross profits per employee, and a 20 percent higher ratio in market-to-book values. Study after study finds that companies with a strong commitment to training have higher revenues, profits, and productivity growth than firms that carry out less training (Betcherman, Leckie, & McMullen, 1997).

3. ATTRACT AND RETAIN EMPLOYEES   Training can be used by organizations to ensure that they are the employer of choice. Furthermore, training will help keep valuable employees on the job. For example, Canada currently has about 20 000 vacant information technology (IT) jobs, and so employers must develop retention strategies to keep the employees they want. IT workers look first at employers who are committed to a learning environment, and those companies should be spending significantly more than 1 percent of payroll on training (Lister, 1998).

In another study, 99 percent of the respondents said that there are job areas in which training would be useful to them, and in which training decreases their willingness to jump to another company (Schaaf, 1998). Indeed, training as a staffing tool is so successful that 90 percent of employers use training and development opportunities to attract potential employees, and 94 percent use training to keep employees. Training is the number one attraction and retention tool. An organization that fails to train will find itself increasingly dependent on the external labour market to fill positions.

4. REDUCTION OF FRAUD   A study of 1200 organizations worldwide reports that almost half were defrauded in the past year, and 84 percent of the frauds were committed by employees. Training in ethics and control systems can have a major impact on the incidence of fraud (*The Training Report*, 1998).

5. LEARNING TO LEARN   We know that children who are raised in a home environment that values educational achievement are more successful than others. Likewise, there is increasing evidence that employees who work for corporations that have a strong commitment to education, training, development, and learning (i.e., have a strong learning culture) are more motivated to learn and use that learning on the job (Belcourt & Saks, 1997).

INDIVIDUAL BENEFITS

At a personal level, trained people may find themselves enjoying the intrinsic and extrinsic benefits of training. Employees exhibit greater confidence in the performance of their job. They describe feelings of increased usefulness and belonging in the organization, and they seek out opportunities to fully exploit their new skills and abilities (Garavan, Costine, & Heraty, 1995). Extrinsic benefits include increased earning capabilities (due to increased skills and improved productivity), improved marketability, greater security of employment, and enhanced promotion prospects. Half a dozen studies done in the late 1980s conclude that company-sponsored training programs boost workers' wages by 4 percent to 11 percent over the long run (Mandel, 1993). For example, graduates of a computer-training program increased their earning power dramatically, according to a study published in *The Training Report* (1998).

Who benefits the most when an employee is trained—the company or the employee? Revenue Canada argued that the employee does, and suggested that employees who undertake an employer-funded MBA program at a cost of $54,000 be required to pay taxes on this "benefit." Employers appealed, stating that the MBA should be considered a training expense, part of the cost of developing human capital. In a knowledge-based society, companies have to invest continually in employees (Church, McCarthy, & Pitts, 1997).

SOCIETAL BENEFITS

Many organizations offer literacy and numeracy training if employees failed to obtain them through regular education channels. This training, which enables employees to function more effectively in their daily lives, has societal benefits. These workers are more likely to be able to read instructions for assembling their children's toys or to add up a car-repair bill. They are more likely to be able to find other work if their employer closes a plant. The federal government spends more than $11 billion annually on education and training,

TRAINING TODAY 1 The Union Perspective on Training

Advocates for employees have suggested that training is used strategically to facilitate workplace restructuring to the detriment of employees. To cut labour costs and make the workforce lean and flexible, management needs the cooperation of the workers. Management wants employees to divulge their intimate knowledge of their jobs and to encourage them to generate ideas on ways to streamline production and increase productivity by eliminating waste. But the intimate knowledge of how work is done is a source of power in the workplace.

The message to the workers is confusing. They are trained to become empowered (knowledge workers, co-managers, team players) while also being trained to be multifunctional flexible cogs in the system. Continual improvement training is one way to appropriate worker knowledge and control over work processes.

Training has changed. Until the late 1980s, new workers were given short training courses to enable them to start work, then they could advance through the technical training system to work up the internal job ladder. The job classification system represents another source of collective power. The shift in training occurred when workers were trained to be flexible, thus undermining the contractual work rules of seniority and job classifications. Under the former system, workers could, using seniority and experience, bid for jobs of their choice, protect themselves from injury and layoffs, and manoeuvre themselves into desirable jobs. Now, workers have little control over their mobility. Learning has become, for employees, a process of continually intensifying their work and increasing productivity. All work energies are devoted to maintaining or increasing the firm's competitive position, and people do whatever jobs are necessary, even at the sacrifice of their personal interests and careers, to maintain that competitive edge. Workers complain that their jobs are a series of separate repetitive tasks, divided among groups of workers on an assembly line, resulting in training for parallel low-level jobs. Workers who were drawn to teamwork were disillusioned by management's inability to deliver on democracy.

Workers are multiskilled (union view: multitasking with bits of former jobs), flexible (union view: being assigned to jobs and having to ask the boss for permission to transfer), and value teamwork (union view: altitudinal restructuring of the workforce to undermine the union). The official position of the CAW (Canadian Auto Workers) is to reject the corporate agenda for workplace training and negotiate for more job-related training, on company time, for everyone, which will enhance career development and mobility.

Source: K. Hadley. (1994). Working lean and mean: A gendered experience of restructuring in an electronics plant. Unpublished dissertation, University of Toronto.

---

because it sees a strong link between an educated workforce and a high-wage economy. In Quebec, employers are required to invest 1 percent of all payroll on training. How well people live depends on how well they learn (Geis, 1991). Employees who have taken company-sponsored training report using their new skills to better manage their personal lives.

So far, we have discussed only the benefits of training. Are there negative aspects? For a view of training as a tool to disempower workers, see the union perspective in Training Today 1 box.

Having established the importance of training, we turn now to an examination of the training industry in Canada.

TRAINING FACTS IN CANADA

Trying to get a good picture of the training industry in Canada is difficult. No one organization, such as a professional training association, surveys Canadian companies to determine their overall training patterns. Such a survey is conducted annually in the United States (Industry Report, 1999). It is tempting to simply use the American statistics and apply the one-tenth rule (our population of 30 million is about one-tenth of the American population of about 300 million). So, for example, we know that U.S. organizations spend about $62.5 billion a year on formal training. Should we extrapolate and say Canadian companies spend $6 billion? But we know from previous surveys that Canadian companies spend less (maybe about half) of what American firms spend (Larson & Blue, 1991). We also know that the American survey covers only organizations with more than 100 employees, and only calculates formal training, and does not include the cost of employee time off the job. So even the American figure of $62 billion might be an underestimation. Given all these cautions, we think a fair estimate of the money spent by Canadian companies on training is about $4 billion.

The American survey is worth studying because we tend to lag behind the Americans in human resource management practices by about two to four years. We monitor their data to see trends, such as the increasing use of training delivered by computers (14 percent), the increasing percentage of training delivered by outside contractors (one-third), and the percentage of computer-training courses (33 percent). Overall, U.S. training budgets are increasing, trainer salaries are rising, and there is a dramatic surge in spending on outside courses. If we follow U.S. trends, then these facts represent entrepreneurial opportunities for Canadian trainers. Indeed, we are starting to become recognized for our expertise in training software. Canada has a global reputation for high-class technology training in such key industries as transportation, entertainment, health care, petroleum, engineering, and forestry. With the help of Industry Canada and the Department of International Trade, the training industry is being promoted here and abroad. There are 400 training companies in Canada, most less than 10 years old.

The facts about training in Canada, which have been compiled from many surveys, are summarized in the Training Today 2 box. These figures will enable you to compare your organization and experience against others.

The statistics in Training Today 2 are interesting for reasons other than benchmarking your situation against national averages. For example, a quick glance shows that those with advanced skills and positions receive even more skill training. Curiously, those working in the education sector receive the least amount of training, perhaps due to the high levels of education necessary to qualify for jobs. In other words, the government and the employee have assumed the costs of their education, and this survey of employer-sponsored education does not capture this. Labour market factors often affect the amount

TRAINING TODAY 2 Training in Canada: The Facts

INDIVIDUAL TRAINING FACTS

- 5.8 million Canadian adults are enrolled in education and training activities
- men spend about 108 hours per year on learning; women spend about 98 hours per year on learning
- about 37 percent of Canadians between the ages of 25 and 44 are engaged in learning activities
- 57 percent are studying for career reasons, 29 percent for personal reasons, and 14 percent for both
- 66 percent of learners are employed full-time, 12 percent work part-time, and 21 percent are unemployed
- 59 percent of those studying earn more than $60,000 annually compared with 21 percent who earn less than $21,000

CORPORATE TRAINING FACTS

- 1.6 percent of payroll is spent on training (note that the benchmark for highly productive companies is 6 percent of payroll)
- $850 is spent per employee
- the average Canadian worker receives 7 hours of training annually
- average days on training per management employee: 4.4; for sales, 3.3; for clerical, 2.8; for production, 5.1; for service, 3.7; and for trades, 5.3
- there is one training and development specialist for every 170 employees

- the most popular training subject for Canadian employees is health-and-safety training; orientation was the next most common type of training
- the transportation, communication, public utilities, and oil and gas sectors spend the most; the education sector spends the least
- older and senior people get more training; younger people get less
- 95 percent of employees with a university degree received formal training from their employer, while 66 percent of those with high school or less received formal training
- bigger companies spend more proportionately than smaller companies
- about half of Canadian companies expect training budgets to increase
- those rated as one of the 100 best companies to work for in Canada spend the most on training per employee

Sources: Human Resource Development Canada. (1998). *Canada's adult learners and learning technologies.* Ottawa: Office of Learning Technologies, Author; Beach, B.K. (1998). The Canadians are training, the Canadians are training. *Training & Development 52* (2); Little, B. (1997, June 13). Training splits into haves and have-nots. *The Globe and Mail,* p. B9; MacDonald, G. (1997, February 13). Growth prompts more training. *The Globe and Mail,* p. 4; Betcherman, G., Leckie, N., & McMullen, K. (1997). *Training for the new economy.* Ottawa: Canadian Policy Research Networks, <www.cprn.com>; Saigue, J.P. (1996). Focus on competencies: Training and development practices, expenditures, and trends (Report 177-96). Ottawa: Conference Board of Canada.

and type of training available to employees, as will be discussed in the next section on the environmental influences on training.

THE ROLE OF THE ENVIRONMENT IN TRAINING

Training and development are imbedded within environmental and organizational contexts. They flow from these contexts. Training and development are not isolated activities independent of the surrounding environment and organization, as will be re-enforced throughout the text.

Environmental influences such as legislation, the economic climate, demographics, and social values will have an impact on the organization. For example, if a competitor introduces a lower-priced product, the organization will have to decide whether to match the competitor's actions or compete in other ways, such as providing superior service. This strategic decision will in turn affect costs, the ability to pay employees, or the necessity to train and reward employees for effective performance.

Some key environmental factors that are driving the training industry include the following.

GLOBAL COMPETITION   The relatively low Canadian dollar has made it attractive for Canadian companies to export. Our multilingual, multinational population has made establishing an international base a much easier task, aided by our peacekeeping reputation. About 70 to 85 percent of the Canadian economy is affected by global competition.

TECHNOLOGY   The computer has an impact on every job. Much training is about computers and is delivered electronically. Rapidly changing software requires continual updating of employee skills. Furthermore, the economy is moving from touch labour to knowledge workers, whose tools are technology and whose currency is new information.

RESTRUCTURING OF THE LABOUR MARKET   The number of people working part-time and on contract work has doubled over the past decade. This contingent workforce has to be managed differently. Indeed, there are indications that organizations are treating their core employees to luxuries such as permanent employment, full benefits including profit sharing, and intensive training. Training is used as the lure to catch and keep the high-value candidates. The contingent workforce is managed as it always has been: no job security, no benefits, and no training. Furthermore, we are seeing a trend toward the virtual office, which means an increased reliance on technology and different management skills to facilitate the work of these virtual employees.

RESTRUCTURING OF THE ORGANIZATION   Organizations are flatter, with fewer management levels. Employees are expected to become co-managers (empowered) and need to be trained in problem solving, decision making, team work, and so on.

CONTINUAL CHANGE   While many complain about the constant churning of employees and having to react to sudden switches in strategy, many recognize and embrace the shifts. For example, one worker was scared and shocked the first time she was downsized, taking it as a condemnation of her competence. The second time, she recognized the termination for what it was: a change in the firm's direction. She anticipated the third restructuring and used her buy-out to return to school for advanced training. Managing change becomes a normal part of the job.

External changes in the environment are not the only factors that influence training. Internal organizational changes also have an impact.

THE ORGANIZATIONAL CONTEXT OF TRAINING

Training and development are influenced not only by external factors but also by events within the organization. Training and development should be tightly integrated within an organizational context dedicated to improving performance. Strategy is the most important factor influencing training and development. If the strategy is to grow the organization as rapidly as possible, then employees need to be trained in the management of mergers, acquisitions, joint ventures, and international ventures. All these growth components necessitate the building of new skills, and training may be one way to do this. Additionally, the profitability of the company influences the degree to which an organization can afford to invest in training. The structure of the organization affects how training is practised, as will be seen in Chapter 2 on the training function.

Training should be integrated not only within the larger organizational context but within the HR web of activities. The objective of the human resources management (HRM) function is to attract, motivate, develop, and retain employees in a safe, equitable environment. HRM accomplishes these objectives through the provision of counsel and services in HR planning, organization design and job analysis, compensation and benefits, recruitment and selection, orientation, training and development, performance appraisal, industrial relations, health and safety, employment equity, and HRM information systems. Each function should feed information into a related subsystem, such as training. For example, if a new performance appraisal system is implemented to increase employee productivity, then managers need training in the conduct of performance evaluations, and the output of these systems has to be fed into the training department to identify training needs resulting from performance gaps.

Training needs to be closely aligned with other HRM activities for several reasons. First, there is a need for every unit to do more with less, and this efficiency can be achieved by eliminating redundancies. For example, there should not be separate systems for recording information about performance evaluations and attendance at training programs. Second, every department is pushing to become more strategic, more business oriented. This means treating the entire business process as the unit of analysis, not just the employee. Performance problems may be the result of poor selection, or bad job design, or the wrong incentives, or lack of skills. It is important for training professionals to work with other HR professionals to determine the most appropriate solution to the performance problem.

Now that human resources are recognized as strategic assets, managers are paying attention to the practices of human resources management. At the

Sony Technology Centre, managers are trained to hire using a competency-based approach. They are trained to develop performance plans and conduct performance reviews, and attack performance problems (Caudron, 1998). Trainers become partners not only with the managers in this scenario, but with the other HR specialists in staffing and appraisal.

Progressive companies value this tight link between the environment, the organization, and the development of human resources. To illustrate, take the case of INTEC (a pseudonym for a real company), an international equipment company (Summers & Summers, 1997). The parent company and key customers were planning to expand their overseas business. The labour market was not able to provide candidates with the requisite KSA (knowledge, skills, and abilities), nor were the schools able to supply qualified graduates. The aging of INTEC's workforce put additional pressure on the company to find enough qualified employees to achieve its objectives. INTEC was unable to buy these skills on the open labour market, so it adopted a build strategy. The business plan led to an analysis of jobs, which in turn translated to skill-building training. (You can read how INTEC did the needs analysis in Chapter 4).

External and internal changes influence organizational strategy, the way human resources are managed, and the way that training and development is approached.

MODELS OF TRAINING AND DEVELOPMENT

A frequent criticism of the human resource management field is that there is no theory to guide us in our thinking about ways to manage employees effectively. Training is no different. Training is a pragmatic specialty, where theory develops from practice; trainers are developing new approaches, such as the learning organization or coaching, and then professors (academics) are writing about these approaches, attempting to embed the practice into a theory. So we do not really have theories of training as much as we have typical approaches to training. We take the best practices from practitioners and develop models. Here are three such models.

THE PERFORMANCE MODEL

performance model
a system in which productivity is increased by correcting gaps in employee performance by increasing their KSAs

The most common and more traditional approach to training is to focus on increasing the knowledge, skills, and abilities (KSA) of employees. The goal is to increase the productivity or performance of employees by correcting the gap between how employees are doing the job and how they should be doing the job. Learning (and training) is centred on the development of individual skills and knowledge, based on current business practices. This perspective rests on the assumption that the KSA of today will be needed tomorrow, or that future KSA are fairly predictable. Employees are trained to fill current job-based deficiencies. Performance gaps are identified through systematic needs analysis.

The approach is problem centred: a training need is identified and a training solution is applied.

The training professional is the subject matter expert, and is the person most skilled at delivering training, primarily in a classroom environment. Learning is transmitted to employees from trainers. Attempts to link the training of individual employees to organizational performance in most organizations are minimal. Additionally, employees are encouraged to ascertain their own training needs, or managers may reward employees by arranging training courses for them.

This performance approach is a valid method when used according to a system of best practices. These include needs analysis, the establishment of learning objectives, the choice of the most valid training methods, and an assessment of results. These steps form the basis of this text, and are an approach used by most organizations. The weak link in the chain is the connection between training and corporate objectives, established by measuring that the training did in fact enhance both employee and departmental performance.

The next model attempts to strengthen the association between training and corporate performance by starting with strategy.

THE STRATEGIC MODEL

A second and concurrent approach to training states that human resources development initiatives should be aligned with key organizational objectives and visions. Instead of starting with the employee as the consumer of training, many organizations look at the organization, or a department within, as the customer. Each department or unit has goals, derived from corporate strategies and visions.

Strategy gets the organization from here to there (Wickens, 1987). What is an organization's purpose, its goals? How does it achieve its strategy? Organization strategies determine the types of training required by groups of employees. The strategy determines the learning objectives. For example, if the strategy is to provide inexpensive fast food (McDonald's strategy), then labour costs must be minimized to keep product and service costs low. The human resources (HR) strategy is to compensate at minimum wage. This means hiring people with very few skills who are willing to work for low wages. This strategy also results in high turnover among employees who move to better-paying jobs. Because employees have few skills and turnover is high, jobs are designed to be routine and simple. What are the training implications of such a strategy? Employees have to be trained rapidly and often. Training courses at McDonald's are on site (usually in the basement), delivered electronically, and can be completed within an hour. A new employee can be effective immediately, and thousands can be trained annually.

In a relatively predictable environment, training can be matched with business strategies to enhance production. Trainers may be subject matter experts, but more often they are seen as business consultants. They work

strategic model the alignment of training and development objectives with organizational strategy

strategy refers to the development of the organization's mission, objectives, and action plan

closely with management, and understand intimately the goals of the department and the methods used to achieve those goals. For example, auto manufacturers pair trainers and plant managers to create and customize training programs specific to the needs of the plants. These plant managers are very concerned with getting the most out of their training dollars, as this money could be allocated elsewhere in the plant.

Trainer consultants with a strategic focus are knowledgable about business, process improvements, and change management tools, and they know many ways to achieve performance goals. They pay attention to reducing costs, shortening product cycle times, improving quality, and measuring improvements in these areas. For example, trainers in this model would not just teach customer service but would be able to create a culture of customer focus, including being market driven, reducing bureaucracy, and improving efficiencies through job redesign. The trainer becomes a business partner, a change agent, and internal consultant. The goal is to facilitate the achievement of the strategy, which may also involve closing performance gaps as outlined in the performance approach to training.

Training may not take place in the classroom, but might take the form of workshops on the plant floor, or teaching managers how to coach, or commissioning software to deliver just-in-time (JIT) job knowledge. Training becomes the tool for continual improvement and alignment with corporate objectives. In the Apple corporate training department, trainers are permanently assigned to business units to exchange information about the strategic direction of the business unit. Target, an operator of retail stores, uses managers to deliver training (Olian & Durham, 1998). In other companies, all employees are trained in business skills, so that even machine operators know how to read financial statements. Training hours are not tracked; the ability of an employee to meet business objectives is tracked.

But with increasing turbulence in the environment, businesses no longer want to lock into strategies and training programs. Executives are uncertain of what the future holds. They do know that they cannot predict the future much beyond one year, so they want employees who are skilled and flexible. They feel the need to create development systems that not only train people to acquire knowledge and manage change, but also train them to create knowledge, value change, and pursue opportunities for new business. Thus, we see a movement to an opportunistic model in which the learning organization plays a central role.

THE LEARNING MODEL

learning model a system in which an organization is transformed for future needs through coalitions of employees who create knowledge

In an unpredictable and turbulent environment, executives recognize the need for the continual transformation of their organizations. Learning is the means to achieve that goal and to exploit opportunities as they arise or are envisioned by employees. Employees learn to build on collective wisdom, and to go beyond standard frames of reference to envision what the organization could become. Action learning is the principal tool to "learn to learn." The goal is not to become better at well-understood and routine activities (i.e., continual improvement) but to generate innovations and create new ways of doing things. The knowledge is created, not transferred from a textbook or a trainer. Employees are assembled in learning coalitions with the goal of either solving business problems or anticipating and capitalizing on future trends. The participants in a learning coalition use their own experiences and their abilities to think outside the box to envision a different future. Most of these learning activities take place in corporate universities. Indeed, at Motorola University, the new business development offices are right next door. The corporate university is seen as the base of knowledge creation, and serves as an incubator for the entrepreneurial activities of the company (Baldwin, Danielson, & Wiggenhorn, 1997). The concept of the learning organization is fully developed in Chapter 14. See Table 1.1 for a summary of the ways in which organizations manage their performance through learning activities.

TABLE 1.1 PERFORMANCE MANAGEMENT MODELS

STAGE/FACTOR	PERFORMANCE	STRATEGIC	LEARNING
Focus	individuals	teams, units	organizations
Environment	stable	relatively predictable	uncertain, turbulent
Goals	employee productivity, close performance gaps	achieve strategies, work together effectively	exploit opportunities, prepare for an unknown future
Trainer's role	subject matter expert	performance facilitator	change agent, knowledge creator
Learning location	classroom	office/plant	corporate university
Interaction	student/teacher one-way knowledge transfer	teams two way: knowledge acquisition	learning coalition knowledge creation and implementation
Pedagogy	training	multiple options	action learning
Solution	performance evaluation	strategic	competitors and environmental changes
Trigger	learning	imperatives	survival
Evaluation	performance	goal attainment	new business

Source: Adapted from Baldwin, T. T., Danielson, C., & Wiggenhorn, W. (1997). The evolution of learning strategies in organizations: From employee development to business redefinition. *Academy of Management Executive 11* (4), 46–49

A SYSTEMS APPROACH TO PERFORMANCE MANAGEMENT THROUGH TRAINING AND DEVELOPMENT

systems approach
a series of steps designed to improve performance and facilitate strategic ends

We identified three models of training, the first two dealing with performance improvement of individuals, groups, or organizations. We now turn to a systems approach to performance management through training and development, which will be the focus of the book in the remaining chapters. We devote an entire chapter to the exploration of the third model, the learning organization, as it is an emerging model.

Training is a process—a series of steps designed to improve performance and facilitate strategic ends. The training and development process deals principally with performance management for individual employees and work groups. The cycle starts with current performance and ends with improved performance.

THE PERFORMANCE CULTURE

The first step is to establish a performance culture. The starting point can be strategy, whereby managers look for ways to build employee capabilities and facilitate the achievement of the corporate strategy. Or the starting point could be a performance problem that is making it difficult for the employee or the department to achieve its goals or meet standards. Either way, there must be signals that performance is important, it will be assessed, and that managers and employees have a responsibility to meet performance objectives and will be accountable. If performance objectives cannot be met, then an analysis of the performance problem must be conducted. This all sounds very formal. In many companies, particularly smaller organizations, the problem analysis starts with an *itch;* an *itch* is something in the organization that is not quite right or is of concern to someone. Perhaps customer complaints are too high, quality is low, market share is being lost, or employees are frustrated by management or technology. If some part of the organization itches, or is not satisfied with the performance of individual employees or departments, then the problem needs to be analyzed. Part of the performance culture is a learning culture. A **learning culture** can be defined as one in which knowledge and skills acquisition are highly valued and the application of new ideas and skills on the job is rewarded (Belcourt & Saks, 1997). The learning culture is important because employees know that any training they receive will be valued, and efforts will be made to ensure that they can implement newly acquired KSA on the job.

learning culture an organizational climate in which knowledge and skills acquisition are highly valued and their application in the job is rewarded

Whether the starting point is as subtle as an itch or as overt as a change in strategy, the skills of the training professional are needed to determine how best to meet the desired objectives. A critical step in the systems approach is an analysis to determine if training is the best solution.

A needs analysis is performed to determine the difference or gap between the way things are and the way things should be. In this step the questions asked include

- What is the employee/department/organization supposed to be doing?
- What do employees/teams need to achieve success?
- How is that success measured?
- What is the gap between their current performance and the measure of success?

Based on the data collected from employees or corporate documents, the performance objectives for closing the gap are written. The setting of objectives—or measurable goals—to improve the situation and reduce the gap are derived directly from the needs analysis. Before training is determined to be the best solution to the problem, alternatives to this very expensive option must be assessed. The solution to the performance gap might be feedback, incentives, or other interventions. The needs analysis, the setting of objectives, and the consideration of alternatives force the trainers to focus on performance improvement, not the delivery of a training program.

Training is only one solution—and not necessarily the best one—to performance problems. How can we close that gap in the most efficient and effective ways? What are the alternatives to a very expensive training solution?

If training is the solution, a number of factors must be considered in the development of the course or program. Using the objectives as guidelines, the course designer determines the best training methods for achieving those objectives. At this point, the program must be costed. In this way, the trainer can decide if the solution is worth the cost of solving the problem.

After the program has been implemented, the key questions become: Did the program accomplish its objectives? Was the gap reduced? Was it worth it? Methods can be used to evaluate the effectiveness of training. Costing exercises enable the trainer to compare delivery methods to achieve efficiencies without sacrificing effectiveness. Principles of equity must be incorporated into the design to ensure fair access and treatment of employees. The purpose of all training and development efforts is ultimately to improve organization performance.

THE PLAN OF THE BOOK

STRUCTURE

This book starts with an overview of training, looking at the benefits of training employees, training facts, models of training, and a systems approach to training, which guides the development of the text content. Chapter 2 examines the role of the trainer and the training function. Issues such as the role of the trainer as an internal consultant and outsourcing the training function are addressed. Chapter 3, on needs analysis, is the most important chapter in the text because the assessment of the need for training is the cornerstone of any training system. This chapter offers a variety of methods used to identify performance gaps. Before any project can be implemented to improve performance, we need to know exactly what we are attempting to accomplish. This can be done through the establishment of objectives, goals for the intervention, or learning objectives. We discuss objective setting in Chapter 4. We then turn to the design of the training program in Chapter 5. Finally, in Chapter 6 we look at the core of the training system, the training methods. An array of off-the-job training methods, including the lecture, behavioural modelling, and the case method are described. But not all training takes place in classrooms; we examine in Chapter 7 how performance is improved through on-the-job training methods, including coaching and job aids. Chapter 8 can be seen as an overview chapter, concerned with optimizing the transfer of newly acquired knowledge, skills, and abilities to the job.

After we have done everything possible to ensure that the training program is effective, we need to measure just how effective it was. The evaluation of training is presented in Chapter 9. Training programs are expensive, and we walk you through the costing process in Chapter 10.

The next two chapters deal with specific training programs. Types of training programs, including technical courses and literacy programs, are discussed in Chapter 11, and management development programs are outlined in Chapter 12. Principles of equity must be incorporated into training and development programs to ensure fair access and treatment of designated groups. These are discussed in Chapter 13. Many managers are embracing the concept of the learning organization, but are struggling with the management of such a process. We outline the principles, practices, and problems of the learning organization in Chapter 14.

CHAPTER FEATURES

Each chapter is structured to help you learn. Each chapter starts with learning objectives: what we expect you to know after reading the chapter. The chapter content is followed by a summary and by a listing of the key terms you should remember. A new feature in this edition is the inclusion of a running case, which allows students to build skills in the development of a training program. The running case is introduced in Chapter 5, "Program Design," and is featured in Chapters 6 through 10. We then hope to engage you in debate and application of the content (to enhance learning, of course!) and invite you to complete the questions, exercises, and cases found at the end of each chapter.

Summary

This introductory chapter stressed the importance of viewing training as an investment in human capital. The organizational, individual, and societal benefits of training were listed. We concluded with a picture of training in Canada today. Training is part of a larger HR strategy that in turn is dependent on the strategy of the organization and the influence of the environment. Three models of training were outlined: performance, strategic, and learning. A systems approach to performance management starts with a performance management culture and moves through the identification of needs, the development of objectives, the planning of the intervention, and the evaluation of the effectiveness of the intervention.

Key Terms

human resources development   3

learning model   14

learning culture   16

performance management   3

performance model   12

strategic model   13

strategy   13

systems approach   16

training   3

Exercises

1. There are three sources of funding for training and education: the public sector (governments using taxpayers' dollars), the private sector (businesses using shareholders' money) or you, using your after-tax dollars. Who should pay for training? Debate this question with two other students, each taking a different position and defending that perspective. Try to support your points by quoting surveys, which you can find by accessing the following databases: **CBCA** and **ABI Inform** from your university or college electronic library. CBCA will identify articles like "The training wheels of government go flat" in *The Globe and Mail*, Saturday April 13, 1996, p. D4.

2. Private organizations are said to benefit from training because trained employees give them a competitive advantage and even make the companies more innovative. How does this apply to the public sector? What do you think are the organizational benefits to a public company or a volunteer organization?

3. To learn about how Canada compares to other countries in its education and training, go to <**www.nald.ca/nls. htm**>, the Web site for the National

Literacy Secretariat in Ottawa. Locate Literacy Skills for the Knowledge Society, where you can learn how formal learning declines with age, who pays for the training of men and women, and how much time Canadians spend hitting the books compared to about a dozen other countries. Using this information and the information provided in the text, describe what Canadians do well and where we could improve.

CASE: MANAGING PERFORMANCE AT AVENOR

Avenor is a pulp and paper company based in Montreal, Quebec. In 1993, Avenor was owned by Canadian Pacific. The company was not profitable, and was having difficulty surviving. As James Merchant, vice president HR for Avenor stated, "in 1993, we were technically bankrupt." The HR team, in an effort to survive, used performance management as a key driver of the turn-around strategy. The purpose, principles, and process of the new performance management system were introduced in 1994, during a meeting with 60 managers.

Phase I started with the HR team talking with managers and employees about their core responsibilities, and then setting annual performance objectives. About 1000 employees were trained to conduct performance appraisals. In addition, HR designed a performance management guidebook, a step-by-step reference manual for managers and their employees. Managers conducted their first performance appraisals immediately after the training.

Phase II consisted of reviewing the degree to which performance objectives were met, diagnosing performance problems, and determining performance bonuses. The HR department trained a network of line and HR professionals as facilitators to provide support to managers. The three-day course built new skills in facilitation, the elements and tools of performance management, and the methods to train new employees in the process.

Phase III provided another interim assessment of performance, and ensured that managers were providing performance feedback. Nicole Halle, corporate director of HR reports that, currently, the performance management system is well understood by all employees, and some locations have integrated it into their management practice. More training for managers in coaching and feedback is needed. Halle says, "instill a culture first [of performance management], and fine-tune the instruments later. Position performance management as a communication tool between managers and employees, as a continuous process, rather than an annual event."

The financial results have shown the wisdom of this approach. In 1997, Canadian Pacific Enterprises had a 16.5 percent return on equity, up from 9.1 percent ROE in 1993.

Sources: Adapted from Avenor Annual Reports, 1993–1998; Performance management spurs corporate turn-around. (1998). The Training Report 1 (2), 16; Canadian Pacific Annual Reports, 1993–1997.

QUESTIONS

1. Describe how Avenor aligned their training program with strategy and other HRM initiatives.

2. Is Avenor's approach strategic or performance driven?

REFERENCES

Adams, M. (1999). Training employees as partners. *HR Magazine 44* (2), pp. 64–70.

Baldwin, J.R., & Johnson, J. (1995). Human capital development and innovation: The case of training in small and medium-sized firms [research paper series]. *Statistics Canada and the Canadian Institute for Advanced Research 74.*

Baldwin, T.T., Danielson, C., & Wiggenhorn, W. (1997). The evolution of learning strategies in organizations: From employee development to business redefinition. *Academy of Management Executives 11* (4), 46–49.

Bailey, G. Training as a recruitment tool. (1998). *HR Focus 75* (7), 11–12.

Belcourt, M . Making a difference, and measuring it with the five Cs. (1996–97). *Human Resource Professional* (December–January 1997), 20–24.

Belcourt, M., & Saks, A.M. (1997). Effects of pretraining activities and a learning culture on the transfer of training. *Canadian Learning Journal* (December), 10–11.

Betcherman, G., Leckie, N., & McMullen, K. (1997). *Developing skills in the Canadian workplace*. Ottawa: Canadian Policy Research Networks.

Bowsher, J. (1990). Making the call on the CEO. *Training and Development Journal* (May), 65–66.

Caudron, S. (1998). Integrate HR and training. *Workforce* (May), 89–93.

Church, E., McCarthy, S., & Pitts, G. (1997, March 27). Tax issue poses tough question. *The Globe and Mail*, p. B14.

Garavan, T.N., Costine, P., & Heraty, N. (1995). *Training and development in Ireland: Context policy and practice.* Dublin: Oak Tree Press.

Gosselin, A., Werner, J., & Hall, N. (1997). Ratee preferences concerning performance management and appraisal. *Human Resource Development Quarterly 8* (4), 315–333.

Greco, J. (1997). Corporate home schooling. *Journal of Business Strategy 18* (3), 48–52.

Harris, D.M., & DeSimone, R.L. (1994). *Human resource development.* Toronto: Dryden Press.

Industry report 1999: An overview of employee training in America. (1999). *Training 36* (10), 37–81.

Larson, P.E., & Blue, M.W. (1991). *Training and development 1990: Expenditures and policies* (Report 67–91). Ottawa: Conference Board of Canada.

Lister, T. (1998). *Study on recruitment and retention of hi-tech employees.* Toronto: PricewaterhouseCoopers.

Management development slashes quality control costs. (1998). *The Training Report 1* (2), 5.

Mandel, M. (1993, February 22). Jobs, jobs, jobs. *Business Week,* p. 76.

Millan, L. (1997, September 26). King of the corner store. *Canadian Business,* pp. 101–104.

Olian J.D., & Durham, C.C. (1998). Designing management training and development for competitive advantage. *Human Resource Planning 21* (1), 20–31.

Schaaf, D. (1998). What workers really think about training. *Training 35* (9), 59–66.

Summers, T.P., & Summers, S.B. (1997). Strategic skills analysis for selection and development. *Human Resource Planning 20* (3), 14–19.

Training, technology key to the fight against fraud. (1998). *The Training Report 35* (10), 3.

Wickens, P. (1987). *The road to Nissan.* London: MacMillan.

Women get big income boost after computer training. (1998). *The Training Report 35* (10), 2.

2

POSITIONING, MANAGING, AND MARKETING THE TRAINING FUNCTION

CHAPTER GOALS

Training, the diffusion of work-related knowledge, skills, and attitudes from person to person, from person to group, or even from generation to generation, has been part of both organizations and societies for more than 1000 years. Only recently, however, have we progressed beyond learning by watching others, or learning through trial and error. Despite the existence of apprenticeships and other vocational learning opportunities, it was not until World War II that formal industrial-training activities became widespread throughout Western societies.

In this chapter, we will discuss the training function. After reading this chapter, you should be able to

- effectively position a training function within an organizational hierarchy
- understand the issues in managing the training function
- advise managers on the advantages and the disadvantages of outsourcing a training function
- understand the relationship between training and "the trainer as a consultant"
- design training programs, taking ethical factors into account

POSITIONING THE TRAINING FUNCTION

Based on the assumption that people are a valued and an appreciating (versus a depreciating) asset, human resource (HR) considerations should be incorporated into strategic decision making. Without adequate attention to human resource management (HRM) functions (including training), long-term organizational goals can be placed in jeopardy. At the Travelers Corporation, for example, "top management committed extensive … [funding toward training] after corporate training officials demonstrated that the company's strategic goals would be unattainable without timely, cost-effective training" (Casner-Lotto, 1989, p. 5).

Further, companies such as National Cash Register (NCR) are anchoring their HR strategies in their mission statements, allowing the HRD function to depart from the traditional passive role and enter the mainstream of corporate planning and decision making. Management support for HRD is slowly increasing as training in many large companies is positioned at, or near, the vice-presidential level (Garavan, 1991; Garavan, Costine, Heraty, 1995).

A *full-service* training organization in a large company might be centralized and organized into a series of divisions. By separating the HRD function from the personnel management unit or department, access to the highest levels of decision makers is made easier (see Figure 2.1).

Of course, smaller firms would have much less elaborate structures. As well, it appears that government-supported vocational education is the most significant system of formal training for most small employers. The small-business community will have to overcome its reluctance to pay the often higher training costs associated with improved technology, given the need to upgrade basic workplace skills (Lichenstein, 1992). Even in the smallest organizations, training should either be positioned near the top or, if there is no formal training function, HRD considerations must be made part of the strategic planning process.

Developing this strategic emphasis is impossible without the increased involvement of line personnel in the training function. Traditionally a weak subunit within a weak personnel organization, HRD now commands the attention of managers at all levels. Indeed, one study finds that, in 71 percent of companies surveyed, training departments are no longer the prime initiators of training. Instead, the role is shared with line management (McKibben, 1991; Burrows, 1996).

ORGANIZING THE TRAINING FUNCTION

Given the increased importance of developing human assets and the relatively recent line involvement in training, considerable debate has been generated about how the HRD function should be organized. Of primary importance is

FIGURE 2.1 THE STRUCTURE OF A FULL-SERVICE TRAINING ORGANIZATION

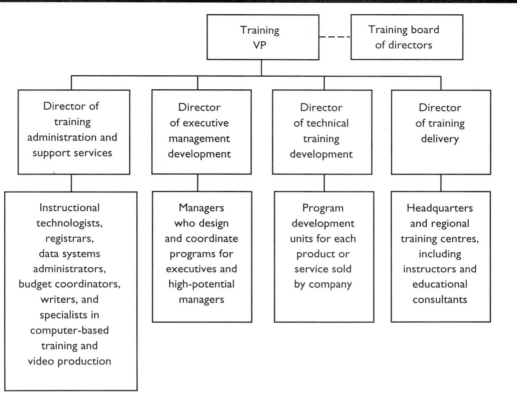

Source: London, M. (1994). *Managing the training enterprise.* San Francisco: Jossey-Bass, p. 65. Reprinted by permission.

the **centralization/decentralization** controversy. While management in some organizations have found it more efficient to centralize training efforts, others have tried a decentralized approach. British Columbia Telephone (BCTel), for example, created a model city to train employees, while Control Data Corp. used a somewhat decentralized training program aimed at keeping decision making close to the customer (Gerber, 1987; Lee, 1988). Each system had advantages and disadvantages, so in some cases training policy was set centrally but delivery was controlled regionally. The best approach depends on an individual organization's need and on the type of training being delivered. Hence, Johnson Controls and BCTel used learning centres, while San Diego County in California, with 13 000 employees, operated a decentralized training function. In this instance, the potential advantages of centralization (control, economy of scale, consistency of content, commonality of values, superiority of design and presentation) are sacrificed for customization, ownership, and local budget control (Tovar, Rossett, & Carter, 1989).

centralization the positioning of the training function within the organization's headquarters

decentralization the positioning of the training function within each business unit

staff employees who provide services to the organization

line employees responsible for the marketing and production of an organization's goods and services

Another important trend concerns the trainer's traditional status as **staff**, rather than as a **line** professional. Some experts suggest that trainers relinquish their staff status by accepting assignments in specific departments and working directly with line personnel as part of a managing team, so that training better reflects company needs (Harrison, 1997). Indeed, Zemke (1987) went one step further, reporting on a successful training approach in which at least half the staff were not professional trainers but line managers cycling through the training department as part of their career development plan.

Involvement with line managers can become very intense, giving the training a broader mandate based on human resources performance, rather than human resources development (Fierstein, 1988; Arcelus & Wright, 1993). This scenario is based on Gilbert's (1978) early work in human competence engineering. In human competence engineering, training is but one activity that focuses on what employees do to further organizational goals. The training department becomes the performance management department, in which approximately 80 percent of the effort is spent fixing the environment and 20 percent training the employee, with a focus on creating world-class performance, no matter what has to be done to get there (Arcelus & Wright, 1993; Maglitta, 1997). A more detailed discussion of the "trainer as consultant" can be found later in the chapter.

Thus far, we have not drawn an organization chart to show the "correct" structure of a training department, since every organization is different and this variety should be reflected in training organization design. Whatever formal structure prevails, however, it should revolve around some key concepts. We have discussed the overriding centralization/decentralization issue. To this background, we have added the concept that line managers can and should be included in every step of training design, delivery, marketing, analysis, and evaluation. As well, the training function should report to a position close to the centre of power, so that input into the strategic planning process is assured. Finally, it has been suggested that HRD might be organized around a much broader role that focuses on HR results.

Whatever the final configuration, the organization chart must indicate how training interacts with the other HRM functions. The idea is to create a corporate entity whose members, at all levels, spontaneously learn and innovate in ways that promote the well-being and mission of the organization (Bencivenga, 1997). Organizations are changing rapidly, and suggesting appropriate structures can be difficult. HRD, however, has been described as an "organizational fishbowl" that must focus on the organization's most pressing business needs in a manner that leads the way in terms of management style and employee empowerment (Kahnweiler, 1991).

Where training fits within the organizational matrix, then, is not important, as long as the function can influence organizational direction in both a strategic and a day-to-day sense. Every organization is unique; what works in one may fail completely in another. The task is to design structures that either allow trainers to participate directly in achieving corporate goals, or (if there is no formal training function, as in smaller organizations) to use training as a tool that accomplishes the same ends. The location of training on the organization chart is less important than assigning responsibility to either managers or staff trainers for the development of employee knowledge and skills.

MANAGING THE TRAINING FUNCTION

Based on ever more complex business environments, the complexity of HRD, and the necessity of integrating this function into the broad range of HRM activities, managing training requires skills far beyond technical knowledge and the ability to present learning sessions. The training manager must

- learn training (as a discipline) well and keep up with trends in both the discipline and the manager's industry
- learn about the informal power structure in the organization and carefully build a power base
- understand and concentrate on the organization's mission, culture, and core competencies
- cultivate widespread management support for training activities
- handle resistance creatively
- develop credibility by modelling effective behaviours
- learn to work within the cultural and the political limitations imposed by the organization (Kirby & Ginzel, 1989; Burack, 1991)

As Warshauer (1990) indicates, the ability to play organizational **politics** is often just as important to a trainer as technical expertise. With these skills, the training manager must do two things: plan and integrate training (or performance improvement) into the very fibre of the firm, and create a training team capable of meeting the organization's HRD needs. These processes are complicated further by the trend to involve line personnel in training and by the rate of change in most corporate environments (Filipczak, 1996; Blickstein, 1996).

politics the informal power structure within the organization

As organizations must plan strategically, so too must the training manager or individual responsible for HRD. The key concept is to operate as if internal contacts (e.g., internal departments) are paying customers (which they may be) by developing a strategy-to-practice model that meets their real (as opposed to perceived) needs. This approach will avoid the problem described by the following conversation.

> **Line supervisor:** "Did you see the personnel department's new training catalogue? I can't believe the number of programs offered. You'd never know we're supposed to be cutting budgets!"

Manager: *"Yeah, not only are there a lot of programs, but I'd like to know what "Advanced Oral Presentations" and "Managing Your Boss" have to do with getting the job done. They never asked me what skills my people really need. It makes me wonder if we could get better services from people outside the organization. And who knows, it might cost less!" (McDermott & Emerson, 1991, p. G1).*

When conversations like this one occur—Sebrell (1990) calls this the "student's return quotient"—it is almost certain that the person responsible for training has failed to develop an appropriate strategy that links training to business needs.

Credible plans are difficult to develop, however, if a training management system is not in place. The training manager can obtain access to performance information through methods described in the next chapter.

Training programs should result from employee–manager analyses that identify precise needs, which then might be met by either internal or outsourced programs. The better the database, the more likely it is that appropriate management decisions will be made.

Aside from decision-making data, training managers require a system for analyzing and reporting activities. The maintenance of trainee records, training histories, customized learning opportunities, schedules, and course and material inventories is a routine, but necessary, activity. As well, the system should be able to handle registrations for in-house courses, outsourced programs, public seminars or classes, and self-study (Sebrell, 1989). To this inventory might be added the capacity to track individual career development and learning plans. Software is available that can do all these things.

THE TRAINER AS CONSULTANT

As the pace of change accelerates and competitive forces continue to decrease profit margins, the practice of setting aside monies for improving productivity through training is being questioned. Although the North American faith in the value of education certainly has "permeated" corporations for many years (Odiorne, 1987), it is now becoming clearer that between 70 and 80 percent of productivity improvements can be found in the job environment, culture, or process, not in the people who do the work (Wright, 1994a). As suggested earlier in this chapter, then, managers should be concerned with performance, not with performers (Wright & Geroy, 1997a).

If one accepts the idea (known to organizational development practitioners for many years) that the environment is of paramount importance, allocating funds specifically for training will be viewed with suspicion (Wright & Geroy, 1997b). Training budgets tend to beget training—and training is aimed at between 20 and 30 percent of the performance-improvement possibilities. Similarly, training departments, even if their programs are evaluated on a strict cost–benefit basis, tend to justify their existence through training.

Does this concept mean that training is not a justified business activity? Not at all. What is being suggested is that management should take a much broader approach that focuses on performance improvement, accepting the necessity to train only as part of an overall commitment to improve work performance. In one large bakery, for example, cakes came down a conveyer on the operator's right; the operator picked up a cake, decorated it, and placed it on a quality-check conveyer on the left. As efficient as that may sound, the left-hand conveyer was too high—the operator tended to throw the cakes onto the higher finished-goods conveyer to avoid standing up each time. The impact on quality was predictable. Successive attempts by management to train the operators failed, and there was constant friction between the production and quality control departments. In this case, money spent lowering the conveyer would not only improve quality but would create a better work climate as well.

There are many similar situations in both the private and the public sectors. Coping with them requires an adaptation of the trainers' role to that of internal consultant, with a mandate and a budget to search out and to improve performance in any way possible. Ideally, an **internal consultant** would have to prove that his or her services were cost-effective. Funds would be directed to areas of greatest potential benefit. If this area happened to be training, training would be conducted. If other activities promised greater returns, monies would be steered away from the training function (Wright & Geroy, 1999).

internal consultant a trainer, employed full-time by the organization, who provides solutions to performance problems

Such a system would have to focus on problems; spending money to treat symptoms (as many organizations do) would result in insufficient performance improvement to support the consultant's expenses. This trend to organizational problem analysis would greatly improve management's understanding of the overall corporate/organizational culture, enabling all sectors of the enterprise to make sounder decisions (Stolovitch & Keeps, 1992). Problems are identified by studying the work environment, by asking the question, "What prevents individuals from doing a good job?" Should this question be asked at all levels in the organization, the answer may indeed be "inadequate training," or it could be "poor ventilation," "poor support systems," or any combination of factors. The key is to discover the real problems and to eliminate them (Wright & Geroy, 1997a). The next chapter presents a method to do this.

To make a consultant-based system work, the system must become part of the organization's culture (Wright & Geroy, 1997a); the system must be introduced with the greatest care. The actual steps involved in altering corporate value systems have been well documented and need not be repeated in detail here (for example, see Carnall, 1995). Some common pitfalls, however, should be considered. First, it is essential that all levels in the organization be involved in the program. A top-down approach will most certainly encourage failure.

Second, the consultant must be trusted by both line managers and staff. A well-known, high-profile individual should be chosen, preferably from inside the company. Third, this individual should report to someone at a very senior level in the organization so as to afford the consultant some protection from organizational politics and to lend prestige to the position (Wright, 1994b).

How can a consulting focus affect the traditional training department? The answer depends on the environment and on the skills of the trainer. If training is found to be a necessary part of improving performance, or if training is obviously necessary to organizational survival (e.g., training temporary sales staff before Christmas), a consulting focus may have little effect on the training function. If the trainer has sufficient knowledge and prestige to work as a consulting specialist, however, he or she can play a vastly more important role in the organization. Conversely, should training professionals not be able to cope with this broader definition of productivity improvement, they could well find themselves redundant to the organization's needs (Wright & Kusmanadji, 1994).

In essence, the job will evolve toward counselling management in managing change and solving performance problems. It will entail working with line managers at all levels as a facilitator, identifying key individuals (sources of power), and creating links that bring about significant change, leading to measurable productivity or quality improvements or both. In personnel terms, the task will become one of more effectively integrating the members of the organization in pursuit of the objectives of the organization. Whether training is involved will be irrelevant.

Outsourcing Training

outsourcing contracting outside the organization to have work done that was formerly done by internal employees

Well-staffed in-house training departments often are a luxury reserved for larger organizations and even then meeting all the demands internally for training can be difficult. Consequently, in many organizations, **outsourcing** increasingly is a solution (Pickard, 1998).

Arrangements with outside vendors can range from the development, delivery, and evaluation of training on project-by-project contracts to the outsourcing of all human resource development activity. Often, core or technical concepts, such as orientation, training on internal systems, and specialized product-knowledge courses are kept in-house, while more generic skills and knowledge training, such as selling techniques and basic supervisory training, might be outsourced to a private agency (Cohen, 1996; Morrall, 1996). In 1998, about one-third of all course design and delivery was outsourced (Industry Report, 1999).

The essential issues to consider when deciding whether to use internal or external training providers concern the availability of a supplier with an approach, a culture, and values close to the strategic direction in which the purchaser wants to proceed. If, for example, management's strategic focus is on becoming more entrepreneurial, a provider could be selected and the responsibility for winning new business would rest with the training designers or deliverers. Should the strategic thrust be on becoming more "people-friendly," a supplier that prides itself on treating its own people well should be chosen (Hardingham, 1996).

Re-engineering and downsizing likely will continue as managers continue to focus on cost-effectiveness. The human resources management function (including training) is already outsourced more often than any other part of business, and this will also likely continue. The keys to successful outsourcing fall into three categories:

1. using strategic analysis
2. selecting the provider
3. managing the relationship

As suggested previously, there are certain functions that are best retained. The key to determining which functions to outsource lies in an analysis of the organization's strategy (Embleton & Wright, 1998).

Outsourcing usually involves a long-term relationship that requires the supplier and the purchaser to work closely together, so the choice must be made with care. First, a supplier profile needs to be identified, as a match between corporate cultures is important. Then, a request for information needs to be circulated, describing the outsourcing requirements in detail, including scope and objectives. As well, on-site visits that focus on people, cultural fit, and administrative processes should be used to choose the final candidates. Once a choice is made, both management teams must negotiate a mutually beneficial contract. Remember too, that all finalists should be treated professionally; they may be needed in the future (Foster, 1996).

Managing the outsourcing agreement will require not only time and effort, but different management skills. There needs to be transparency, that is all employees need to know what is happening, or morale will suffer. Existing employees within the training function need to be accommodated. They may even join the supplier on this project, but again, morale is the key issue. If the training function is to be downsized because of outsourcing, employees in other areas of the organization may feel that they are next (Embleton & Wright, 1998). In fact, "it doesn't take long for the survivors to channel that emotion [fear] into two counter-productive streams: retaliation and self-defense" (Navron Assoc., 1996). Outsourcing needs to be handled with care and sensitivity.

To outsource parts or all of the training function then, managers must consider the company's strategy, culture, workforce skills and competencies, and future directions for both training and the industry. No magic switch can preserve employ morale; managers will benefit most, however, by taking steps to ensure that the human cost of outsourcing is minimized ("Effective downsizing," c. 1996; Embleton & Wright, 1998).

Managing Stakeholders

Whether one is managing a large training department or operating a small business, it is essential to identify and, when appropriate, to utilize services provided by stakeholders. These services may or may not consist of training.

The term **stakeholder** refers to those institutions or associations that have an established interest in training and development. These stakeholders include governments at all levels, unions, associations, employers, and educational institutions. Their interests lead these parties to research the employment market to determine the need for training. They then develop programs for funding and supplying training. The goal of these programs is to ensure that the right number of trained workers are ready for available jobs.

Working with governments, unions, professional associations, and other stakeholders can save an organization both time and money, as they can offer literacy, software, and soft-skills training; identify qualified workers and offer relocation assistance; develop apprenticeship programs; offer outplacement services for those unable or unwilling to train; offer adaptive services for those with special needs; and so on.

Governments

Government-sponsored training programs are delivered by community colleges, employers, private agencies, schools, community-based organizations, and government departments. Funded clients include immigrants, people with physical and mental disabilities, towns seeking assistance for former employees of a closed factory, young school dropouts in need of job-search skills, or employers seeking to upgrade staff.

The money is spent not only on training and development programs, but also on income support, child care, transportation, and other subsidies. Programs and legislation change constantly (Johnson, 1998), but monies spent by all levels of government directly on training are estimated to be $4 billion annually. Any manager interested in training needs to become familiar with the various funding sources so that the cost of corporate training can be offset, where possible, by these government-sponsored programs.

Unions

Unions combine forces with other stakeholders to provide training to decrease the effects of restructuring within their trades and to modernize their member's skills. A typical program uses funds generated by employee pay deductions to set up training funds, so that the employer and the union can work together. As well, federal and provincial governments often contribute.

PROFESSIONAL ASSOCIATIONS

Associations, like the Human Resources Professionals Association of Ontario, provide training for their members. This training includes courses that lead to formal certification and informal courses on topics of interest to members. This program is typical of most trade and professional associations. In addition, most associations educate their members through newsletters and annual conferences.

In Canada, more than 100 association-sponsored certification programs are being delivered to approximately 30 000 students (Wright, 1997). Not all associations that deliver programs for their members are professional associations. For example, organizations such as The Native Women's Association and the YWCA deliver training in life skills, job upgrading, and job readiness on a contract basis for governments and sometimes for individuals.

EDUCATIONAL INSTITUTIONS

Educational institutions offer training and development programs beyond their basic mandates of primary, secondary, and post-secondary schooling. Most universities have a noncredit continuing education department. Some school boards play an active role in community development by assisting employers, unions, and communities with labour-market adjustments such as plant closures and downsizing.

The knowledgable HRD manager not only plans and manages internal stakeholders but utilizes the services and funding available from a wide variety of stakeholders. Partnerships with various agencies and organizations become part of the training system. The partnerships can be formed and ended, however, as the training needs of an organization evolve in anticipation of or in response to changes in the environment.

THE TRAINING BUDGET

During the last five decades, expenditures on training throughout North America have grown steadily. In 1998, more than $62 billion was spent on formal workplace training in the United States (Industry Report, 1999).

Justification for this massive spending has required a fundamental change in management's thinking. In the past, training often was seen as an unnecessary expense. The myth of training suggested that trainers were always the last hired and the first fired. Although one can still find organizations in which this tradition is followed—allowing training budgets to fluctuate with profit levels—there is now an unmistakable trend toward viewing human resource development (HRD) as an investment. Where this change in attitude has occurred, trainers can play a more proactive role in managing the organization (Harrison, 1997).

The idea that training budgets are always the first to be cut in recessionary times does not appear to apply to the past decade. In studies on the state of training in mid-sized Canadian companies, for example, there appears to have been either stable or increased funding allocated to training (McIntyre, 1992; Benson, 1997). In the United States, training budgets have increased about 25 percent since 1993 (Industry Report, 1998). However, smaller organizations are more likely to cut their training budgets than large organizations, which have accepted the fact that training plays a key part in the attainment of strategic goals.

It is still wise, however, to expect close scrutiny of the training budget and to be prepared to defend it. The importance of HRD expenditures should be explained long before the formal budgeting process begins. Aid can be solicited from allies outside the HRD function. Another method is to find less-expensive methods of training and to link these savings to cost reductions of goods and services. Of course, a sophisticated, believable cost–benefit analysis system, combined with an effective reporting structure, is the best defence against budget cuts (Phillips, 1991; Blickstein, 1996). For example, Royal Bank trainers were able to prove the effectiveness of their training programs in the language that executives understand (dollars and cents) and had their training budgets increased significantly.

From a budget-management viewpoint, one must not ignore those who suggest that training should be (or should attempt to be) self-financing. There are two main avenues of revenue enhancement. The HRD function can work on a *chargeback* basis, whereby internal budget transfers are made when other units send their people for training, or outside clientele can be actively solicited. This latter activity turns the HRD department into a possible profit centre (Fazio, 1988; Long, 1990).

The advantages of these cost-recovery or chargeback systems are that, in general, they are viewed favourably by upper management, and the learning programs offered to internal clients, of necessity, must be relevant (Hequet, 1991). As well, the extra income—if not matched with comparable budget cuts—can be used to improve the training environment.

Conversely, what the clients think they need may not be compatible with corporate strategy and short-term plans. As well, the search for profitability may siphon energy and talent away from HRD's main role, that of orchestrating strategic culture change (Burack, 1991; Hequet, 1991).

MARKETING THE TRAINING FUNCTION

HRD professionals frequently fail to demonstrate the value of what they do. As a result, many trainers labour in obscurity. The failure of HRD to sell itself is well known (Lookatch, 1991).

Credibility has to become the operational objective for all training professionals. Part of this process involves traditional marketing activities performed internally, such as selecting a target market, analyzing market needs, and developing the capability to address these needs.

To operate effectively, however, the training manager must establish the mission of the training unit or function. In smaller organizations, the same process should occur, but the task will fall to either the CEO or to another senior manager. While creating a training mission, the following questions need to be asked:

1. Why does the training function exist?
2. Who are its customers or stakeholders?
3. Why is training valuable to these customers?
4. How does the stated purpose of the training function relate to #3 above?
5. How will the purpose or function of the training unit change in the future?

This process suggests that the training manager adopt an organization-wide consultative approach so that the mission is acceptable to the various internal clients and stakeholders (Garavan et al., 1995).

Another issue that must be addressed when marketing the training function concerns the development of measurement techniques so that trainers can speak the quantitative (profit and loss) language of senior managers (Nachshen, 1987; Lookatch, 1991). Strategic alliances must also be formed, beginning with the president or CEO. One of the most important tasks for a newly appointed training manager may be to bring senior managers (and other individuals with influence) on side (Gerber, 1988). While most HRD directors complain that their CEO is not interested in employee education programs, many CEOs indicate that they do not hear from their training directors (Bowsher, 1990). This internal selling process, then, must be planned as carefully as any other facet of departmental management.

Which is more expensive, training or ignorance? The training profession, or the training craft, is still coping with the radical changes in corporate needs and expectations caused by global restructuring and the increased need to be competitive. This chapter has suggested how the training function should be positioned and managed to cope with rapid change and the intense need to transform corporate cultures into true learning organizations. Because the field is changing so rapidly, we have avoided "how to" prescriptions. Rather, we have presented concepts and, where possible, alternative views. This approach should provide the student or the practitioner with sufficient background to analyze individual, unique work environments and to develop appropriate HRD structures that can cope with constant change.

THE ETHICS OF TRAINING MANAGEMENT

Ethical dilemmas in our society range from broadly based macro issues to (no less important) day-to-day management situations. In 1997, Warr spoke of an "underclass" that was being denied training, because "for many people at work there is little opportunity for the acquisition of new skills and knowledge," especially among older employees and those who work part-time. Similarly, the growing wage gap between skilled and unskilled workers reported by Lynch (1995) has not narrowed (Weiss, 1998).

What are the ethical dilemmas faced by trainers? Trainers must monitor not only how they train, but what they train. The Internal Revenue Service in the United States, for example, has been accused of abusing the taxpayer (Herman, 1997). No doubt, IRS trainers have performed well in training tax specialists in the art of collecting taxes according to a set of impersonal standards, but should the focus have been on these particular standards (Nilson, 1998b)? Indeed, the zealous application of these "standards" has led the agency into disrepute (Broder, 1997). Are trainees behaving in an ethical fashion if their training gradually destroys the organization's reputation? This is an example of one of the broader ethical questions faced by trainers.

A more everyday dilemma arises when trainers are asked to conduct training, often by powerful senior managers. Should stress management courses be provided, even though the trainer knows that the sources or causes of the stress have not been addressed? Suppose a senior manager insists upon courses in the latest fad-of-the-month management technique; what is the ethical response? Faced with these challenges, and the normal concern for self-preservation, we argue that many trainers will relent and run the courses without comment. Indeed, they may have no other choice, but the damage to the training function and to the organization can be severe.

If the training function has been placed at or near the top of the organization, however, then the trainer can approach this problem differently, pointing out that training effectiveness is likely to be limited and the costs substantial. By appealing to good business sense (i.e., the effect on performance and on profitability), many of these inappropriate requests can be rejected.

By having input into strategic and mission design, trainers (or at least their senior managers) help to guide corporate direction, and they can design the human development function with ethical implications in mind. Given the widespread interest in business ethics and in ethical management practices and employee conduct, can business ethics be taught to managers and employees (i.e., can behaviour be changed through training)?

Does the trainer restrict himself or herself to the teaching of business ethics? Not according to Carolyn Nilson, editor of the *Training and Development Yearbook, 1998*:

Along with the current search for relevant performance indica-
tors, today's businesses are looking for contemporary and mean-
ingful standards of corporate conduct and personal
skill-standards that reflect the corporation's role and potential for
contribution in people's lives, in communities, and in national
and global economies. Trainers often get involved in the develop-
ment of courses and programs about mission statements and cor-
porate values; they often facilitate discussion about corporate
standards in employee orientation programs and in management
training programs. (p. 5.24)

The trainer should be involved in more than the creation of appropriate standards, however, as training and developmental activities must be designed to combat ageism, sexual bias, racism, and a host of other inequities. Access must be monitored and curricula and methodologies developed, for example, that allow for maximum participation. This process might include literacy classes and the provision of basic training. Conversely, the management development process needs to address the glass ceiling concept, so that women and minorities can move into every part of the organization.

Ethical dilemmas and moral problems can be complex and vague. Ethics courses, then, should not advocate one best way to approach specific ethical problems, nor should they promote formulas for thinking through problems. Instead, ethical training can add value to the moral environment of a firm and to relationships in the workplace by

- developing a match between company and employee values
- helping employees to deal with potential unethical behaviour of superiors or colleagues
- enabling employees to deal with systems, either formal or informal, that encourage unethical behaviour

The teaching of business ethics should not promise to provide solutions to complicated problems involving morality and ethical behaviour; employees can be made aware of the boundaries between behaviour that is ethically correct and behaviour that is not. As well, the trainer can help employees to search out unintentional ethical blind spots and to establish forums in the workplace for discussing morality and corporate social responsibility (Weiss, 1998).

Indeed, perhaps Handy's (1998) concept of "proper selfishness" is an appropriate ethical position for trainers to adopt. Handy suggests that organizations survive only as long as they make the world a better place, not only through their products and services, but by helping employees to be fulfilled and by helping to find answers to social problems. In other words, trainers need to look beyond economic wealth toward creating a better, more decent civilization.

Summary

Training as we know it today became widespread during World War II. Because expenditures have risen sharply since then, an unmistakable trend toward the view that training is an investment that must compete with other activities for funding has emerged.

In sophisticated organizations, however, training is part of the strategic plan, and trainers are now behaving more proactively or even becoming consultants to management. Whether centralized or decentralized, training is no longer a weak subunit; it commands the attention of all levels of management, so much so that line managers are becoming more and more involved.

There is no correct HRD structure, then, as long as the training function can influence the direction in which the organization is heading. This responsibility probably requires that training be positioned near the top of the organization.

Managing the training function will also require new skills. Not only must the training manager of the future have excellent presentation skills, high-level expertise in conflict resolution and networking will be necessities. Similarly, the ability to speak the language of top management must be combined with the abilities to manage staff, develop budgets, and market the training function both internally and externally.

KEY TERMS

centralization   25
decentralization   25
internal consultant   29
line   26

outsourcing   30
politics   27
staff   26
stakeholder   32

EXERCISES

THE DAY THEY HIRED JENNY

"Great course, Sam!" they chorused as they trooped out the door and headed for the parking lot.

Sam Harris, a veteran trainer with Flotation Ltd., a manufacturer of life jackets and other flotation devices, smiled as he gathered his notes together.

He had just finished two hours of wise-cracking and slightly off-colour story-telling as he worked his way through the third session of a human relations course for supervisors. "Keep 'em happy" was Sam's motto. Give the troops what they want, keep your enrollments up, and no one will complain.

Sam was good at it, too! For 20 years, he had earned an easy living, working the politics, producing good numbers (of trainees) for the top brass to brag about ("we give each employee up to 26 hours of training every year!"), and generally promoting his small training group as a beehive of activity.

Everybody knew Sam; everybody loved Sam. His courses were such fun. He had no trouble convincing managers to send their people. He put out a little catalogue with his course list every year in January. He hadn't had a cancellation in more than 10 years. Some managers said that training was the best reward they had. Now, only three years from retirement, Sam intended to coast comfortably into pension land. All his favourite courses had long been prepared; all he had to do was to make adjustments here and there and create some trendy titles.

But times were changing. Elsewhere, someone was thinking differently.

"And I need somebody to take a close look at our training function."

Sitting in the president's office, Jenny Stoppard, the newly hired vice president of human resources, wondered what he meant. Flotation Ltd. had a reputation as a company with a well-trained workforce.

"We need to increase our productivity per person by 50 percent over the next three years," the president continued. "And you are going to spearhead that effort. Yes, we spend a lot on training. Yes, we cycle people through a lot of courses. But I'm not satisfied with the bottom line. I know that while Dad was president he swore by old Sam–said he was the greatest. I don't know anymore. Maybe a whole new approach is needed. Anyway, I want you to take a close look at Sam's operation."

Later in the day, the president called Sam into his office.

"Sam, I want you to meet Jenny Stoppard. I've just hired her as vice president of human resources. She's your new boss, Sam. I think the next three years are going to be very exciting around here, and Ms. Stoppard is going to be a key player in the drive to increase our competitiveness. I want you to do everything in your power to cooperate with her."

QUESTIONS

1. Comment on Sam's approach to training. Would you want him working for your company? Why, or why not?
2. What skills of a trainer has Sam not developed?
3. Compare Sam's traditional measures of training with the president's ideas.

REFERENCES

Arcelus, F.J., & Wright, P.C. (1993). On the implementation of CIM in small manufacturing firms. *Technology Analysis and Strategic Management 6* (4), 403–413.

Bencivenga, D. (1997). Employers and workers come to terms. *HRMagazine* (June), pp. 91–97.

Benson, G. (1997). Is training different across the border? *Training and Development* (October), 57.

Blickstein, S. (1996). Does training pay off? *Across the Board 33* (6), 16–20.

Bowsher, J. (1990). Making the call on the CEO. *Training and Development Journal 44* (5), 64–66.

Broder, J.M. (1997, October 11). Clinton presents proposals to improve IRS *New York Times*, p. A9.

Burack, E. H. (1991). Changing the company culture—The role of human resource development. *Long Range Plan 24* (1), 88–95.

Carnall, C. (1995). *Managing change in organizations* (3rd ed.). London: Prentice Hall.

Casner-Lotto, J., & Associates. (1989). *Successful training strategies.* San Francisco: Jossey-Bass.

Cohen, A. (1996). Is outsourcing necessary? *Sales & Marketing Management 148* (9), 44.

Cohen, S. L. (1989a). Managing human-resource data: Information, please. *Training and Development Journal 43* (7), 28–35.

———. (1989b). Managing human-resource data: Keeping your data clean (part 2). *Training and Development Journal 43* (8), 50–54.

———. (1989c). Managing human-resource data: Applying the data base. *Training and Development Journal 43* (9), 65–69.

Embleton, P., & Wright, P. (1998). A practical guide to successful outsourcing. *Empowerment in Organizations 6* (3), 94–106.

Effective downsizing: a compendium of lessons learned for government organizations. (c. 1996). The National Academy of Public Administration. Internet: <www.clearlake.ibm.com/alliance/cluster/rs/downsize.html>.

Fazio, R.A. (1988). Beyond bureaucracy: Riding the new wave in HR. *Personnel 65* (2), 28–35.

Fierstein, J. (1988). Let's get rid of the training department. *Training 25* (6), 63–66.

Filipczak, B. (1996). Who owns your OJT? *Training 33* (12), 44–49.

Foster, E. (1996). Outsource sense. *Info World 8* (37), 14–16.

Garavan, T., Costine, P., & Heraty, N. (1995). *Training and development in Ireland: Context, policy, and practice.* Dublin: Oak Tree Press.

Garavan, T. N. (1991). Strategic human resource development. *Journal of European Industrial Training 15* (1), 17–30.

Gerber, B. (1987). It's a whole new ball game at B.C. Tel. *Training 24* (1), 75–81.

———. (1988). The care and feeding of trainers. *Training 25* (8), 41–46.

———. (1989). "Rewarding and recognizing trainers. *Training 26* (11), 35–41.

Gilbert, T. F. (1978). *Human competence: Engineering worthy performance.* New York: McGraw-Hill.

Handy, C. (1998). *The hungry spirit.* New York: Broadway Books.

Hardingham, A. (1996). Improve an inside job with an outside edge. *People Management 2* (12), 45–46.

Harrison, R. (1997). Financial giants taking training into big league. *People Management 3* (13), 47.

Hequet, M. (1991). Selling in-house training outside. *Training 28* (9), 51–56.

Industry report 1999: Training budgets. (1999). *Training 36* (10), 44.

Johnson, D. (1998). Preparing for the information age economy. *Canadian HR Reporter 11* (16), 4.

Kahnweiler, W.M. (1991). HRD and empowerment. *Training and Development 45* (11), 73–76.

Kirby, P., & Ginzel, L. (1989). Look smarter in your first training job. *Training and Development Journal 43* (8), 69–72.

Lee, C. (1988). Where does training belong? *Training 25* (2), 53–60.

Lichenstein, J. (1992). Training small-business employees: Matching needs and public training policy. *Journal of Labor Research 13* (1), 23–40.

Long, R.F. (1990). Protecting the investment in people—Making training pay. *Journal of European Industrial Training 14* (7), 21–27.

Lookatch, R.P. (1991). HRD's failure to sell itself. *Training and Development 45* (7), 47–50.

Lynch, L.M. (1995). The growing wage gap: is training the ensure? *Economic Policy Review 1* (1), 54–59.

Maglitta, J. (1997, August 25). Train in vain? *Computer World*, pp. 80–81.

McDermott, L.C., & Emerson, M. (1991). Quality and service for internal customers. *Training and Development Journal 45* (1), 61–64.

McIntyre, D. (1992). Training budgets weather the recession. *Canadian Business Review 19* (2), 33–34, 37.

McKibben, J. (1991). When training becomes part of the job. *Industrial Society* (March), 16–17.

Morrall, K. (1996). Bringing training in-house. *Bank Marketing 28* (8), 43–47.

Nachshen, B. (1987). The value of training in dollars and cents. *Computerworld 21* (14), 69–76.

Navron Associates. (1996). *Caring for survivors of organizational downsizing: Part 1.* New York: Author, 1–3.

Nilson, C. (1998a). Standards for virtual communities. In Nilson, C. (Ed.), *Training and development yearbook 1998* (p. 5.27). Paramur, NJ: Prentice Hall.

———. (1998b). Research summary. In Nilson, C. (Ed.), *Training and development yearbook, 1998* (pp. 4.48–4.49). Paramus: Prentice Hall.

Odiorne, G. (1987). *The human side of management.* Lexington: Lexington Books.

Phillips, J.J. (1991). Measuring the return on HRD. *Employment Relations Today 18* (3), 329–342.

Pickard, J. (1998). Externally yours. *People Management 4* (15), 37.

Sebrell, B. (1989). A training management system. *Computerworld 23* (15), 134.

———. (1990). Calculating training quality. *Computerworld 24* (24), 120.

Stolovich, H., & Keeps, E. (Eds.). (1992). *Handbook of human performance technology.* New York: National Society for Performance and Instruction.

Tovar, R.T., Rossett, A., & Carter, N. (1989). Centralized training in a decentralized organization. *Training and Development Journal 43* (2), 62–65.

Warr, P. (1997). [As quoted in] Underclass is denied training opportunities. *People Management 2* (1), 12–13.

Warshauer, S. (1990). Setting the stakes for success. *Training and Development Journal 45* (4), 26–31.

Weiss, J.W. (1998). *Business ethics.* Orlando: Harcourt Brace & Company.

Wright, P. (1994a). A policy alternative to externally-sponsored management development and skills training programs. *Journal of Small Business and Entrepreneurship 11* (3), 49–59.

———. (1994b). The cultural mosaic. In Prior, J.K. (Ed.), *The Governor handbook of training and development* (2nd ed.) (pp. 113–120). Aldershot, NC: Governor.

Wright, P.C. (1997). Certification: an answer to our skills shortage [special section—Learning for the workplace]. *Canadian HR Reporter 10* (10), 13–16.

Wright, P., & Kusmanadji, K. (1994). The strategic application of TQM principles to human resources management. *Training for Quality 1* (3), 5–14.

Wright, P.C., & Geroy, G.D. (1991). *Experience, judgement, and intuition: Qualitative data-gathering methods and aids to strategic planning.* Bradford: MCB University Press.

———. (1997a). *Human competence engineering versus the training myth.* Working paper 97-009, University of New Brunswick, Fredericton, N.B.

———. (1997b). *Human competency engineering profiles: A tool for the OD practitioner.* Working paper 91-010, University of New Brunswick, Fredericton, N.B.

———. (1999). *Changing the mindset: The training myth and the need for world-class performance.* Working paper 99013, Dept. of Management, Hong Kong Baptist University.

Zemke, R. (1987). Bill Yeomans: Making training pay at J.C. Penney. *Training 24* (8), 63–64.

3

....

NEEDS ANALYSIS: APPROACHES AND METHODS

CHAPTER GOALS

Needs analysis is the cornerstone of the process of training and development. Needs analysis is concerned with the gaps between actual performance and desired performance. When a gap exists, there are many solutions to this performance problem. This chapter explains how to determine if training is the best solution.

After reading this chapter, you should be able to

- define needs analysis
- describe why the diagnosis of needs is important
- list the four steps in the diagnostic process
- explain how organizational analysis can be done by discussing strategy, the environment, benchmarking, and culture
- delineate the six steps in job analysis
- define competencies and give examples

- outline the four steps in employee analysis, illustrating the process with the aid of the needs analysis decision tree
- discuss data-collection methods, including general methods of documentation, and discuss sampling issues and data-collection problems

PERFORMANCE PROBLEMS

Managing employees who are unable to meet performance objectives requires a lot of managerial time and attention. Personnel problems can be frustrating. One reason is our failure to take the time to analyze the causes of poor performance. We search for simple solutions such as "he has a poor attitude," or "she lacks motivation." These explanations of human behaviour do not provide us with tools to correct performance problems.

An analysis of poor performance must include a description of the employee's ineffective performance or behaviour. Most managers, when discussing employee performance problems, start with a psychological description of the cause: "lazy," "poor attitude." Managers should start with a description of the behaviour or performance ("reports are late," "does not follow directions") and then move to an assessment of the environment in which this behaviour is occurring. The employee with the poor attitude may be handing in assignments late (the behaviour) because there are positive consequences for doing so. The employee may be delaying submitting reports because it gets the boss's attention. Or maybe the employee has to wait for others to provide input to the report, and staff allocation is beyond that employee's control. Sending this employee to a motivation course would not change the performance. Thus, an effective analysis of performance problems must include both the employees and their environments.

needs analysis the identification of gaps or deficiencies in employee or organizational performance

Needs analysis refers to those methods designed to identify gaps or deficiencies in employee or organizational performance. For a review of various models of needs assessment, consult Moore and Dutton (1987), Sleezer (1992), Lewis and Bjorkquist (1992), and McClelland (1995). The goal of needs analysis is to identify the differences between what is and what is desired or required. When dealing with managers, don't use the term "needs analysis"; just call it "understanding the performance problem."

The way to spot these performance gaps is to solicit information from those who are affected by the performance problem. A needs analyst collects information from key people within an organization about the organization, the jobs, and the employees to determine the nature of the performance deficiencies (Pace, Smith, & Mills, 1991). This information identifies the problem, which is simply the difference between the way the work is being done and the most cost-effective way of doing it. In the simplest terms, needs = required results – current results (Kaufman, 1991).

We will be discussing several methods for identifying these gaps, but first we start with the reasons why we should conduct needs analysis.

The Importance of Needs Analysis

There are three good reasons why organizations should take a proactive stance in the diagnosis of training needs: to establish a performance base line, to meet legal obligations, and to help employees remain employable.

Establishing Base-Line Performance

The first reason to conduct needs analysis is to establish a base line of performance against which improvements can be measured. This base-line information allows trainers to

- determine what the trainee already knows
- estimate the cost of the present performance
- identify what the employee needs to know
- design a program to train the employee in deficient areas only
- prepare measurable learning objectives
- test for increases in knowledge and skills
- conduct a cost–benefit analysis of the program

To quote Hobbs (1990, p. 17), "an ounce of analysis is worth a pound of programming."

Legal Considerations

Some employers have a legal responsibility to assess worker knowledge and skills in areas regulated by the government. Government agencies have responsibility for either the industry or for issues across industries. In Canada, an example of a regulatory agency responsible for an industry (or a vertical agency) is that of the Ministry of Transportation, which regulates the standards and certification of public-transportation workers. A horizontal agency that regulates issues across sectors would be the Ontario Workplace Health and Safety Agency, which is concerned with occupational health and safety. Employers are legally bound to ensure that specific employees are certified. These regulatory agencies must be provided with evidence that designated employees have been pre-tested, or trained and tested, to meet regulations. The data provided by a good needs analysis would meet these requirements.

Moral Obligations

Some argue that employers have a moral obligation to assess the needs of employees to reduce the impact of skill obsolescence (Wexley & Latham, 1991). A recent trend in employee relations suggests that large companies have a responsibility to their employees, even to the point of assisting them to find jobs in the event of layoffs and providing them with training to ensure their employability. Unions are demanding that workers have the right to be part of a needs-identification program to determine if the skills being taught are really necessary to do the job. These factors provide strong arguments for conducting regular and objective assessments of training needs.

Some other cited benefits of needs analysis include generating consensus on the need for training so that it is supported; developing the case that training is needed, and raising the profile and credibility of the training department (Caravan, Costine, & Heraty, 1995). Managers need objective data when diagnosing problems, and needs analysis allows them to gather insights and feedback about the nature of the problem.

THE DIAGNOSTIC PROCESS

There are a number of ways to measure performance problems and potential training needs. Figure 3.1 outlines the needs-analysis process that we will be discussing in this chapter. The process starts with a problem. If the performance problem is important, stakeholders are consulted and gathering information about the problem is conducted in three general ways: an organizational analysis, a job analysis, and an employee analysis.

We start with step one in the diagnostic process: the concern that something is wrong.

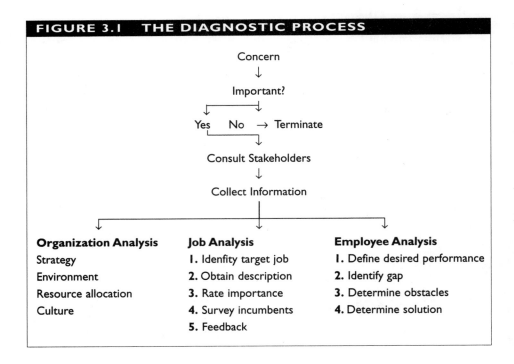

FIGURE 3.1   THE DIAGNOSTIC PROCESS

Concern
↓
Important?

Yes   No   → Terminate
↓
Consult Stakeholders
↓
Collect Information

Organization Analysis
Strategy
Environment
Resource allocation
Culture

Job Analysis
1. Idenfity target job
2. Obtain description
3. Rate importance
4. Survey incumbents
5. Feedback

Employee Analysis
1. Define desired performance
2. Identify gap
3. Determine obstacles
4. Determine solution

STEP ONE: A CONCERN

The process of identifying training needs originates slowly and informally with a concern. This concern is sometimes called an *itch* or a *pressure point*, something that causes managers to notice it. This concern might be as subtle as noticing that employees are treating customers in an abrupt manner, or observing that employees are spending a lot of time asking one another for help with a new system. Others spot concerns by recognizing a shift in regular activities, such as an increase in defective parts, accidents, or complaints (Mills, Pace, & Peterson, 1989). Sometimes the pressure comes from the external environment, as legislation regarding employee relations is changed, or the competition introduces a highly popular service feature. At IBM, one needs-identification program began with the CEO's comment that about 10 percent of all complaints addressed to him involved client dissatisfaction with IBM's handling of telephone calls (Estabrooke & Foy, 1992).

STEP TWO: ITS IMPORTANCE

After a concern has been raised, the next step is to determine if the concern is central to the effectiveness of the organization. The training manager must be aware of the strategic orientation of the organization. The goals, plans, introduction of products and services, changes in technology, practices, and regulations should be clear. Human resource (HR) policies must be linked with the strategic directions of the company. The training strategy should boost the organization's competence to achieve its goals (Carr, 1992). In IBM's case, one strategic goal was customer satisfaction, and further analysis revealed that 70 percent of all customer contact was by telephone (Estabrooke & Foy, 1992). The complaints about telephone calls had to be taken seriously because the concern was central to the effectiveness of the organization.

Another important concern is saving money. Does current performance cost the company in lost productivity or dissatisfied customers? If the performance problem is important, then there must be some way to demonstrate that correcting the problem will result in increased productivity or client satisfaction. A concern is important (i.e., worthy of further exploration and analysis), if it has an impact on outcomes that are important to the organization.

STEP THREE: THE STAKEHOLDERS

The next step in the needs-analysis process is to involve the principals who have a vested interest in the process and outcome (Geroy, Wright, & Caffrey, 1989). Interventions in organization systems have the same ripple effect as throwing a stone in a pond. The designers of needs analyses must recognize that development programs operate within organizations that consist of individuals with their own beliefs and attitudes. Support from key players in the organization is necessary from the beginning of the needs-analysis process.

At a minimum, top management should understand the rationale for the needs analysis. Training analysts must obtain agreement on why the needs assessment is being done and who will be involved. Managerial expectations must be clarified (Goldstein, 1993). Likewise, other stakeholders, such as employees or their collective representatives, should be consulted. At IBM, interviews with employees revealed that they believed they treated customers courteously, and that the managers were antagonistic about learning telephone skills (Estabrooke & Foy, 1992). The attitude was, "just train the secretaries and switchboard operators," even though managers and even financial analysts were receiving calls from customers. The trainers at IBM worked hard to obtain agreement and support from employees on the need for a full analysis. Management sent out a strongly worded message to employees that there was a problem and that together they were going to fix it. Indeed, the manager of U.S. operations made telephone effectiveness one of five key measures of effectiveness. (The others included profit and revenue measures.)

Cooperation, communication, and trust are critical variables in the success of any intervention (Glaser & Taylor, 1973). All stakeholders must buy into the diagnostic phase to ensure that the data collection will result in accurate information and that they have a vested interest in the success of the program. The linking of the training plans to business strategy and the involvement of key stakeholders resulted in dramatic improvements in customer satisfaction at IBM.

The environment (i.e., managers and organizational culture) must support any intervention. Actions that managers can take to support the assessment of needs will be outlined in Chapter 8.

STEP FOUR: DATA COLLECTION

The next stage in the determination of needs involves the documentation of the concern through the collection of information from a variety of sources. Three sources of information are the *organization*, the *job*, and the *employee*. The next section includes a definition of each source and the procedures for conducting a needs analysis within each group. That segment is followed by a presentation of data-collection methods, which are generic to any analysis of organizational or human performance. These analyses lead to the identification of macrotraining and microtraining needs. See Figure 3.2 for an explanation of these terms.

ORGANIZATIONAL ANALYSIS

organizational analysis
a study of an
organization's strategy,
environment, key
indicators, and culture

Organizational analysis is the study of the entire organization: its strategy, its environment, its key indicators, and its culture. An understanding of each of these components will provide information useful not only for the identification of training needs but also for the probability of the successful transfer of the training to the workplace.

FIGURE 3.2   MACROTRAINING AND MICROTRAINING
                      NEEDS

Macro- and Microtraining Analysis: The identification of macrotraining needs occurs when the entire organization, a whole department, or substantial numbers of employees need training. The example of IBM, cited earlier, would be considered a macrotraining needs analysis because 150 000 employees were affected. By comparison, a microtraining need exists for just one person or a very small group of people. A personnel analyst who needs to know how to use a software package in HR planning would be considered a case of a microtraining need. Similarly, a group of 10 sales representatives who needed to master a computerized reporting system would be regarded as a case of microtraining. Training for just a few people could be accomplished through a self-study program, an external course, or individual coaching.

STRATEGY

Most organizations have broad objectives, which may be stated as visions ("uncompromising dedication to quality"), goals ("the number-one software business in Canada"), or market share ("40 percent of market share through the introduction of new products"). These broad statements trickle down to specific goals and objectives for each department or unit, and reflect an organization's plan for survival, growth, adaptation, profitability, and so on. Because the business environment constantly changes, this is an ongoing planning process.

The process of relating training needs to corporate strategies can be understood through a concrete example. Pepsi Cola had a strategic objective of the development of talented people (Schuler, 1992). The goals generated from this objective included empowering employees, developing the necessary broad skills, and building career opportunities. The training programs resulting from these goals included changing the corporate culture (empowerment); detailed HR planning, which resulted in specific training programs; and a four-week leadership program.

Corporate strategies are also intertwined with the environment of the organization.

ENVIRONMENT

Organizations exist within societies that have complex mores, laws, and regulations that influence the operation of businesses and public agencies. Training programs are often a direct result of government regulations (as seen in the earlier example of safety regulations), or attitudes (e.g., managers need to understand the nature and effects of sexual harassment). Large organizations such as Ontario Hydro, which are in the public eye, are often the leaders in the development of programs to meet both public expectations and government regulations.

Besides this regulatory influence, organizations are conscious of the strategies of competitors. The nature of the training program can be a direct result of an organization's attempt to establish a new market niche.

The environment is dynamic and uncertain. New technologies, inventions, recessions, and trade agreements may profoundly affect not only the content of the training but the employees' receptivity to being trained.

BENCHMARKING

benchmarking the continual process of measuring quantitative and qualitative organizational factors, and comparing them to past performance or competitors' performance

Benchmarking is the continual process of measuring quantitative and qualitative organizational factors to compare against performance in previous years or against acknowledged competitors. Benchmarking is part of an operational audit to measure efficiencies and effectiveness in production and service. Managers are always monitoring organizational information, such as number of units produced, percentage of defective products, accidents, complaints, scrap levels, and so on. Any variance in these ratios from the expectations or the standards of the company could be the basis for an analysis. Obviously, inefficiencies could be the result of many factors, and the solutions could even exclude training. A thorough analysis will help in identifying causes and resolutions.

Monitoring the flow of HR also provides much information for training purposes. Increases in turnover, hiring, transfers, and promotions often precipitate training programs. HR planning is the process of anticipating the need for employees with particular skills for expected jobs. By linking training plans with HR plans, organizations can prepare employees for new assignments, promotions, and so on to meet the organization's needs.

Organizational resources, including profitability and viability, will affect the organization's reaction to the introduction of change programs. Does the organization have the resources (money, time, and expertise) to do training if it is warranted?

CULTURE

culture the collective attitudes of employees toward work, supervision, and company goals, policies, and procedures

Organizations consist of more than buildings, equipment, and paper. They are social entities. The people within the buildings have feelings, attitudes, and values. The **culture** of an organization refers to the collective attitudes of its employees toward work, supervision, and company goals, policies, and procedures (Bass & Vaughn, 1966). Employees also have opinions about such intangible systems as communication and decision making. These attitudes are learned and are affected by the experiences of the employee within the organization. Socialization agents and trainers must first be aware of these attitudes before attempting to change them.

Pace et al. (1991) suggest that the perceptions of employees can be measured along two dimensions or levels. The first level of assessment deals with attitudes of employees toward organizational systems, such as communication and decision making. This analysis, termed **functional analysis**, focuses on the processes used to achieve organizational goals. Decision making, communication, and delegation styles are examples of processes used in organizations. The achievement of these goals is measured and, by correlation, the processes are evaluated. The implication is that outputs can be increased by changing process inputs. For example, if communication patterns can be changed from closed to open, then turnover or client complaints might be reduced.

The second dimension is that culture can be interpreted by the analyst in a highly subjective way. This **interpretive analysis** relies heavily on the abilities of the analyst and uses talk as the primary data-collection method. Organization talk centres on three types of messages: accounts, stories, and metaphors. The explanations people give for their behaviour are accounts. An answer to a query about a poor sales record provides analysts with useful information about both an individual and the corporate practices and milieu.

Stories are the equivalent of legends or parables in modern society. The verbal re-creation of an event allows employees to learn the organization's norms and practices. For example, that a top executive made a favourable (and unexpected) decision on a proposal as he headed out to a golf game becomes translated by employees into an insight about how decisions are really made in the company.

Metaphors allow the employees to project a picture of their real feelings about work. Statements such as "this place is a zoo" provides the analyst with a snapshot of overwork, chaos, and a lack of structure and control. During coffee breaks, employees may complain that working in the organization is like riding an elevator: lots of ups and downs; someone is always pushing your buttons; sometimes you get the shaft but what really bothers you are the jerks (Pace et al., 1991). These metaphors, stories, and accounts are a rich source of employees' real perceptions.

Mining these attitudes, either through a functional or interpretive analysis, provides extremely valuable information. Asking employees what would help them make a stronger contribution to the organization or what is preventing them from working to capacity are questions whose answers contribute important data for organizational improvement.

Air Canada conducted an organizational culture survey. They assessed 20 different culture dimensions including rewards and recognition, management effectiveness, and job satisfaction (Dolan & Schuler, 1994). This perceptual information is critical because employee performance may be deficient as a result of culture, not ability.

Once the strategy, environment, benchmarks, and culture of the organization have been assessed, the information gathered could be used to design a change program. Further information can be collected by examining jobs and employees.

functional analysis the assessment of employee attitudes about organizational processes

interpretive analysis the evaluation of employee attitudes through the analysis of accounts, stories, and metaphors

Job Analysis

job   a group of related activities, duties or tasks

task   the smallest unit of work

job analysis   the process of obtaining information about a job by determining the duties, tasks, and activities involved

Let us review the terms used to describe jobs, before we discuss how to do a job analysis. A **job** consists of a number of related activities, duties, or tasks. A **task** is one of those activities. A task is the smallest unit of behaviour studied by the analyst and describes the specific sequence of events necessary to complete a unit of work. A **job analysis** results in a list of the activities or work operations performed on the job and the conditions under which these activities are performed (Goldstein, 1993). A job analysis reveals the tasks required for a person to perform a job.

Six steps are involved in a job analysis:

1.   Identifying the target jobs.

2.   Obtaining a job description.

3.   Rating the importance of each dimension and the frequency of the performance of each task.

4.   Surveying a sample of job incumbents.

5.   Analyzing and interpreting the information.

6.   Getting feedback on the results.

1. IDENTIFYING THE TARGET JOBS.   After an examination of records of production and organizational culture, determine which jobs have a performance gap. More than a job title is required here. For example, the title *associate* often describes quite different types of jobs, depending upon the department or level within any organization. These target jobs may be identified by managers.

job description statement of the tasks, duties, and responsibilities of a job

2. OBTAINING A JOB DESCRIPTION.   A **job description** lists the specific duties carried out through the completion of several tasks. In large organizations, most positions have a description of the tasks and minimum qualifications required to do the job. If this description has not been updated within the last year, consult with both the manager and several employees in the position (subject-matter experts) to obtain a current listing of tasks and qualifications. The job description should contain a summary of the major duties of the job, a listing of these duties, and the conditions under which they are performed. All tools and specialized knowledge should be listed.

An example of a job description for a manager is contained in Figure 3.3. After preparing a job description, the list of duties should be reviewed with subject-matter experts, managers, or job incumbents in interviews or focus groups. The analyst wants to develop a list of tasks to be performed; the knowledge, skills, and abilities needed to perform those tasks; a list of necessary tools, software, or equipment; and an understanding of the conditions under which the job is to be performed. You can see that the result looks very much like a job description, with job specifications. (A job specification is a statement of the knowledge, skills, and abilities of the job holder).

FIGURE 3.3 JOB DESCRIPTION MANAGER

- Administers, directs, and coordinates all activities needed for the department to carry out its objectives.
- Coaches, directs, and assists employees in the performance of their duties.
- Prepares written reports regarding activities of the department; acts as a lobbyist for organizational resources; provides feedback to upper management and employees on progress toward goals.
- Prepares departmental budgets; monitors financial performance of the department.

Creating job descriptions and making lists of tasks and duties does have its downside. Critics argue that jobs change too rapidly and these lists are quickly out of date. Most job analysts prefer to develop a list of competencies. A **competency** is a cluster of related knowledge, skills, and abilities that forms a major part of a job and that enables the job holder to perform effectively (Parry, 1998). Competencies are behaviours that distinguish effective performers from ineffective performers. Competencies can be knowledge, skills, behaviour, or personality traits. (Most analysts prefer not to use personality traits such as "charisma," and instead want to describe the behaviour underlying the trait.)

Examples of competencies for managers include setting goals and standards, coaching, making decisions, and organizing. As you can see, competencies are very similar to skills. But skills can be very specific, such as "negotiate a collective agreement," whereas competencies are generic and universal: "win agreement on goals, standards, expectations, and time frames." The Banff Centre for Management has developed competency profiles for senior leaders so that they can assess needs and then train (MacNamara, 1998). An example taken from their profile is listed in Table 3.1.

competency a cluster of related knowledge, skills, and abilities that enables the job holder to perform effectively

TABLE 3.1 A COMPETENCY PROFILE FOR SENIOR LEADERS

Core Competency	ability to obtain buy-in of key stakeholders to new directions
Level 1	communicates new directions so that everyone affected knows the new directions
Level 2	leads team through discussions and research to identify key new themes and goals that everyone can accept and use
Level 3	key stakeholders are consulted and have input to direction setting
Level 4 behaviours	all stakeholders are engaged in a process to rewrite the new directions in terms that relate specifically to their roles

Source: MacNamara, D. (1998, November 16). Learning contracts, competency profiles the new wave in executive development. *Canadian HR Reporter*, pp. G8–G10.

Most lists of competencies are simply wish lists; they are lists of different skills that managers think are important to the job. The usefulness of these lists has to be tested or validated. In other words, do people who have these competencies perform better than those who don't? One company decided that preparing wish lists of competencies (i.e., traits, skills, behaviours) was a waste of time. Instead, they set about to prepare a valid list of competencies for their company.

The first step was to interview managers, using behaviourally based questions, to solicit their perceptions of the competencies that make for effective management at the supervisory level. The managers described 130 competencies. Two research experts analyzed the list and reduced the list of competencies to 84 items, grouped into 14 categories, which were then tested on the supervisors. The categories included: *technological leadership, managing people, innovation,* and *client relations.* An example of observable behaviour under the category client relations was: "tunes into clients—involves them, listens to them, anticipates future needs, wants products to meet these needs."

The Profile Development Questionnaire, made up of this list, was then sent to every supervisor, and to subordinates, peers, and managers (the supervisors' bosses). Each was asked to rate the extent to which the supervisor performed each of the 84 competencies. Two months later, the same people were asked to rate how important these competencies were to the work of the supervisor in that company. As a result of all this work, 14 items have emerged as the competencies that lead to success in the company.

HR professionals can now use this list to recruit, select, evaluate, and train employees.

Source: Adapted from Raelin, J. A., & Sims, A. (1995). From generic to organic competencies. *Human Resource Planning 18* (3), 24–33.

The goal is to develop competencies that are teachable (i.e., we can observe them and describe them). If these competencies are then associated with effective performance, we can use them as a base to increase the effectiveness of individual employee's on-the-job work behaviour. Competencies can then be used instead of job descriptions. The Training Today 1 box describes how one company developed a competency model for its managers in a high-tech environment.

3. RATING THE IMPORTANCE OF EACH DIMENSION AND THE FREQUENCY OF THE PERFORMANCE OF EACH TASK. The group interviews suggested in the previous step could be used to generate these ratings.

4. SURVEYING A SAMPLE OF JOB INCUMBENTS. Using the position description, develop a questionnaire or structured interview asking the managers and employees in the specific jobs to rate the importance of tasks and the competency with which they are performed.

An example of this type of survey is given in Figure 3.4. A supervisor could complete the survey for each employee as an additional check on validity. Two additional sections should be included in the survey (Nowack, 1991). The first includes demographic information such as tenure in the job, location, and so on. The second section assesses the organization's climate by

FIGURE 3.4   SAMPLE JOB-ANALYSIS SURVEY

For each of the following areas of skill, knowledge, and ability, please make two ratings. Looking at your own job, assess the importance of the task by circling a number from I (not important) to 5 (very important). Then, consider your own level of competence in that task and rate it from I (not at all competent) to 5 (extremely competent).

Job Task	Importance	Competence
Knowledge: ability to explain technical information to co-workers.	I 2 3 4 5	I 2 3 4 5
Control: ability to develop procedures to monitor and evaluate activities.	I 2 3 4 5	I 2 3 4 5
Planning: ability to schedule time, tasks, and activities efficiently.	I 2 3 4 5	I 2 3 4 5
Coaching: ability to provide verbal feedback to assist in the development of more effective ways of handling situations.	I 2 3 4 5	I 2 3 4 5

asking questions about attitudes regarding barriers to productivity and change, job satisfaction, work motivation, perceptions of managers, and so forth.

5. ANALYZING AND INTERPRETING THE INFORMATION.   Quantify the information by conducting some elementary statistical analyses. Identify those tasks that are important, frequently performed, and rated as low in ability. Statistical software packages can assist in this task and can be used for more complex analyses. Comparisons between groups may reveal additional important information. Job incumbents may rate their own performance highly, while their managers may feel that the employees are not working up to standard. New employees may feel that there are no barriers to optimum performance, while those with several years of service may perceive problems. Landey and Vasey (1991) found that experienced police officers spent less time in traffic activities, and more in non–crime-related tasks than recent recruits, validating the need to collect background information on respondents. Conducting a training course without understanding the participants and the environment may result in less-effective learning and transfer of skills to the workplace.

6. GETTING FEEDBACK ON THE RESULTS.   One route to preparing the organization for change is to provide small groups of managers and employees with feedback about responses to the survey. This feedback encourages employees to talk about areas of strengths and weaknesses and to propose solutions to problems. By owning the problem and generating the solution, employees may be more willing to change their behaviours.

Texas Instruments developed job-role profiles to analyze and document current job requirements, project future needs, and provide training in skills gaps (Overmeyer-Day & Benson, 1996). They identified 43 jobs within the information technology group and developed critical skills requirements for each job. They use these profiles for self-assessments, career development, skills inventories, and training. The entire process is handled by a computer database.

EMPLOYEE ANALYSIS

employee analysis
the process of studying employee behaviour to determine whether performance meets standards

A third focus of analysis is on the person performing the work. Although overlaps between the three areas of analysis occur, each plays a distinctive role. The analysis of the organization provides information about its strategies and culture, about its norms and standards. The job analysis contributes details about the tasks and the relevant knowledge, skills, and abilities needed to perform selected jobs. **Employee analysis** is the process of studying employee or workgroup behaviour to determine if the performance meets the work standards. A standard is the desired level of performance—ideally the quantifiable output of a specific job (Hobbs, 1990).

Defining standards of performance differs from describing tasks, which was a step in the analysis of jobs. A task might read "to process incoming mail." The standard would be to sort 500 pieces of mail within one hour, with less than a 0.05 percent error rate. Standards are expressed in terms of time, units, dollars, completions, and so on.

One way to determine standards of performance is to study those employees who perform exceptionally well. A star or exemplary performer is an employee who consistently performs above the standard (Hobbs, 1990). Bell Labs studied both stars and average performers (Froiland, 1993). They developed a checklist of 60 to 80 work strategies, compared the two groups of performers, and determined that the stellar performance was due to nine strategies. Bell Labs then developed objective descriptions of these strategies and trained the average performers.

Another way to determine the most efficient way of working is to conduct studies such as time–motion studies. The analyst can also assist the manager in determining the standards by asking questions such as, "When you envision the work being done properly, what does the worker do? When you praise or correct an employee's work, what specific tasks are you discussing? What would you like them to be doing that they are not doing?" (Laird, 1985). Standards can be generated by asking a series of questions about extremely effective and ineffective performance, a process similar to the development of a Behaviourally Anchored Rating Scale (BARS) appraisal form (see Table 3.2).

In employee analysis, the competencies of individual employees are assessed. Employee analysis answers these questions: How well does the employee perform? Who, within the organization, needs training? What kind of training do they need?

TABLE 3.2 BEHAVIOURALLY ANCHORED RATING SCALES (BARS) KEY COMPETENCY: SERVICE

5 Excellent Performance

Incumbent will study customer-profile information cards; observe and greet customers; refer to interesting features of the merchandise related to customer-profile characteristics; ask specifically for a reaction, and offer a suggestion.

4 High Performance

Incumbent will approach customers, inquire if they have noted a special feature, and offer assistance.

3 Competent Performance

Incumbent will observe customers entering and offer assistance.

2 Needs Improvement

Incumbent will observe customers entering and approach, if customer asks for assistance.

1 Ineffective Performance

Incumbent will engage in personal calls, lengthy breaks, or busy work to avoid customer contact.

A four-step process should help answer these questions:

1. Define the desired performance.
2. Identify the gap between desired and actual performance.
3. Determine the obstacle to effective performance.
4. Determine a solution.

1. DEFINE THE DESIRED PERFORMANCE. The first step is to establish measures of performance. These norms will be important in the needs analysis, during training, and in evaluating effectiveness after training.

2. IDENTIFY THE GAP BETWEEN DESIRED AND ACTUAL PERFORMANCE. Sources of data on gaps include performance appraisals, managerial requests for training, work samples, observations, self-assessments of competencies, and formal tests. CIBC uses formal tests to determine competencies of financial advisers (Trainor, 1998). Results from the "Financial Advisor Skills and Capabilities Assessment" are used by employees to gain self-awareness and to prepare a developmental plan. More objective sources might be found in records of output, complaints, accidents, rejects, lost time, maintenance hours, and equipment efficiency. The employee's performance can be compared with industry norms or with that of other workers.

The thinking work of executives is much harder to measure than the psychomotor work of lower-level employees. Managerial measurements include organizational goals such as return on equity or increase in customers. Another approach is to measure the processes managers use to achieve goals, rather than the goals themselves. Goals such as market share may be influenced by factors such as the recession or competitor actions, which are beyond the control of the manager. Managerial processes such as delegation and control (see job description) are assumed to be a good substitute.

Wexley and Latham (1991) outline three types of measures used to assess employee performance: behavioural measures, economic measures, and proficiency tests. **Behavioural measures** are based on managerial or peer observations of performance. As such, they are subject to the biases inherent in human judgment:

behavioural measures
managerial or peer observations of employee performance

- the halo effect (the tendency to rate an employee highly on all characteristics because one characteristic, such as honesty, is rated highly)
- first impressions (the error of making snap judgments based on impressions received at a first meeting)
- similarity effect (the tendency to evaluate highly people similar to the person doing the rating in ethnicity or gender)
- contrast effect (the tendency to compare workers against each other, rather than against standards)

There are techniques for training managers to overcome this subjectivity through the use of structured behavioural rating scales. (See Table 3.2 for an example.)

economic measures
objective and quantitative measures of employee performance

Economic measures refer to the quantitative aspects of performance. Records of waste, sales, accidents, market share, and so on provide objective evidence of accomplishment. This source is useful for jobs such as factory workers or sales representatives, but pose problems for the measurement of professional or managerial jobs where process is important.

proficiency tests formal or simulated tests to measure employee performance

Proficiency tests consist of sampling job performance through the use of formal tests (typing tests or safety knowledge exams) or simulated tests (managerial assessment centres or sales-calls role plays). These tests provide objective information that can be compared to norms. The tests may not reflect actual performance on the job, where every factor cannot be controlled. The ringing of telephones or the anger of a real customer may derail effective performance. However, these three measures usually provide better information than that provided by self-assessment.

Forecasting future needs is problematic. One approach is to compare the performance of recently hired workers to that of experienced workers, and to identify training needs of new employees.

3. DETERMINE THE OBSTACLE TO EFFECTIVE PERFORMANCE. Performance weakness may be the result of deficiencies in execution, not deficiencies in skill or knowledge. Sometimes, the gap is the result of the worker not knowing about the standard, not receiving adequate feedback about performance relative to the standard, and not being rewarded for meeting the standard. Lack of feedback about current performance is often the reason for continuing poor work. Supervisors take good performance for granted, reasoning that the employee is paid to do it anyway. However, feedback can enhance performance. Some guidelines to the effective use of feedback include:

- Be specific. Define the performance objective by stating "We expect all associates to greet customers within 30 seconds of their appearance," or "You must get the complaint ratio below 1 percent."

- Be positive. State performance expectations positively. We would rework the previous example to read "Customer satisfaction at 99 percent," or "I expect you at work at 7:55," rather than "Don't be late."

A wide range of potential barriers to effective performance is presented in Table 3.3.

TABLE 3.3 BARRIERS TO EFFECTIVE PERFORMANCE

Human
Lack of knowledge
Lack of skills
Lack of motivation
Counterproductive reward systems
Group norms
Informal leaders
Organizational political climate

Technical
Poor job design
Lack of tools/equipment
Lack of standardized procedures
Rapid change in technology

Information
Ill-defined goals/objectives
Lack of performance measurements
Raw data, not normative or comparative data
Resources suboptimized
Ineffective feedback

Structural
Overlapping roles and responsibilities
Lack of flexibility
Lack of control systems

Source: Adapted from Chevalier, R.D. (1990). Analyzing performance discrepancies with line managers. *Performance and Instruction 29* (10). Reprinted by permission.

4. DETERMINE A SOLUTION. If you consider all the barriers to performance cited in Table 3.3, only the first two (lack of skills and knowledge) suggest a training remedy.

The solution to poor performance is not always training. Saying "I've got a training problem" is like going to the doctor and saying you have an aspirin problem (Mager & Pipe, 1970). Training, like aspirin, is a solution, not a problem. Mager and Pipe have developed a decision tree to assist in determining if training is the solution (see Figure 3.5). Let us review the branches in this decision tree.

After the performance deficiency is noted, the manager must decide if the problem is worth spending either time or money to correct. For example, a manager may be irritated by employees who wear their hair shoulder length, but having short hair will make absolutely no difference to productivity or other measures of effectiveness. The exception might be in a manufacturing environment, where long hair would pose a safety hazard (solved easily by wearing a head covering).

If, however, the performance deficiency is considered important, then the true analysis begins. Is it a skill deficiency? Mager's most important contribution to the training field was his posing of the question: Could the employee perform the task if his life depended on it? Could your teenager clean her room, if her life depended on it? Could you pass an exam if your life depended on it? Could your employees produce six units per hour if their lives depended on it? If the answer is yes, then the solution is not to teach them something they already know how to do; the solution is to provide the environment that allows or encourages them to do it.

Moving to the right of the flow chart in Figure 3.5, the analyst attempts to determine the cause of poor performance by asking a number of questions. Is the person punished for performing? While this question seems odd, organizational life is full of anecdotes of penalties for performance. The assistant who works twice as hard as another is punished by being given more work. The manager who does make decisions is criticized for the occasional wrong decision.

The next consideration is the determination of rewards for effective performance. Are there positive consequences for performing as desired? Many times, when an employee does something good, the manager says nothing, on the assumption that the employee is being paid to work properly. However, good performance that is not reinforced tends to disappear.

Sometimes, employees assume that their performance does not matter to anyone. When managers sit in their offices and fume over sloppy work but give no feedback to employees, or arrange no consequences for poor performance, the sloppy work will continue. Working with HR developers, managers can set up contingency management programs.

contingency management
the use of rewards and reinforcers to change behaviour

Contingency management is grounded in the belief that every act has a consequence, and if the consequence is perceived as a reward, then the act will be repeated. If there is no consequence or the consequence is negative or

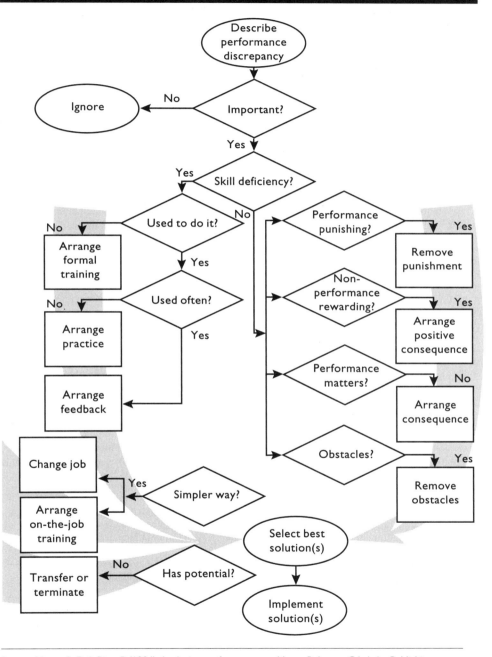

Source: Mager, R. F., & Pipe, P. (1984). Analyzing performance problems. Belmont, CA: Lake Publishing. Reprinted with permission of the publisher. Copyright © 1984 by Lake Publishing Company.

punishing, the action will not be repeated or will be concealed. Imagine the classroom where the instructor never acknowledges students whose hands are raised to ask questions. Soon the students will learn to keep their hands down. Ensuring that no students ask questions can be done even faster by punishing those who ask questions with sarcastic or humiliating replies. Thus, the behaviour of hand raising or asking questions is eliminated, even when the instructor insists he or she values a classroom of debate.

By analyzing rewards and punishments, managers may see that they are asking for safe procedures but castigating those who slow down production. Quality may be the all-important word on the sign in the factory, but employees may be praised for quantity. The determination of what constitutes effective performance, and the management of reinforcement for achieving it, is a far more powerful instrument of change than a training course.

Training is ineffective when the environment is the cause of the poor performance. Obstacles to effective performance may involve lack of authority, inadequate tools or technology, conflicting responsibilities, work overload, and so on.

To restate the critical question asked earlier: Could the employee perform this task if his or her life depended on it? If the answer is yes, say no to training. If the employee couldn't do the work if his or her life depended on it, consider other changes before training.

Following the left side of the flow chart in Figure 3.5, consider if the employee ever performed the task and now needs some practice. Is the employee aware of the standards and receiving feedback on his or her performance against that standard? Students who receive only a grade on an essay will do less well on the next essay than those who receive detailed evaluative comments and feedback. Even supplying a list of the standards expected can improve performance. Dramatic results have been achieved by having employees measure their own performance against the standard.

Instead of training, can the work be rearranged, the employee transferred or terminated, or the job redesigned? For example, one task for a new trainer might be to operate a software package that controls the administration of training courses. If the trainer is a "techno peasant," it might be easier to redesign the job so that a senior clerk operates the system and the trainer does what he or she does best: trains.

Training is one remedy for handling performance problems, but there are others that are more effective and less costly. Training is probably the most expensive solution. The costs of data collection and analysis, program design, salaries of training staff and trainees, travel, audio-visual support, and so on are tremendous. A further problem is that even the best-designed training course doesn't always work because the environment does not support the changed performance. A checklist of the questions to be asked under this model is provided in the Training Today 2 box.

If training seems to be the answer to the problem, then trainers may want to determine the readiness of the employees to be trained. Readiness for training means that employees have the personal characteristics necessary for

TRAINING TODAY 2 The Needs Assessment Checklist

Trainers are often asked to provide training to correct a performance problem. Training is not always the solution, and trainers should ask the following questions before providing training:

1. What are the performance (or operating) problems? Don't ask, "what is the training need?"
2. Describe the current performance and desired performance.
3. Could the employees perform as desired if they had to? Did they ever perform as expected in the past?

4. If employees perform as you want them to, what are the consequences for them?
5. Are there any other reasons why employees may not be performing as desired?
6. If we find a solution to the performance problem, how will we know that the problem has been solved? What behaviours, skills, or results will change?
7. Is training the solution?

---

learning. Some of the factors that determine the ability of the trainee to be trained include the intelligence to learn the required course content and the motivation to want to learn and apply the new learning on the job.

Next we turn to specific methods of collecting information about the performance concern.

DATA-COLLECTION METHODS

The identification of training needs can turn into a comprehensive research study. The cost, the time, and the rigor necessary for doing a perfect needs identification guarantee that most organizations will not do one. This section assumes that conducting some data collection and analysis, rather than having no objective measures, will result in a better training course. For readers interested in a more comprehensive approach to research, the book *Research, Measurement, and Evaluation of Human Resources* will be helpful (Saks, 2000).

The use of multiple methods helps analysts distinguish between perceived needs (what training courses employees feel they need), demand needs (what managers ask for), and normative needs (training needed to meet industry, unit, or job comparative standards) (Lee & Roadman, 1991). The following section describes some of the most common methods of needs identification.

GENERAL METHODS OF DOCUMENTATION (HOW)

Steadham (1980) has developed a useful summary of nine basic assessment techniques, which are reproduced in Table 3.4. The nine methods are:

TABLE 3.4 ADVANTAGES AND DISADVANTAGES OF NINE BASIC NEEDS ASSESSMENT TECHNIQUES

Techniques	Advantages	Disadvantages
Observation • Can be as technical as time-motion studies or as functionally or behaviorally specific as observing a new board or staff member interacting during a meeting. • May be as unstructured as walking through an agency's offices on the lookout for evidence of communication barriers. • Can be used normatively to distinguish between effective and ineffective behaviours, organizational structures, and/or process.	• Minimizes interruption of routine work flow or group activity. • Generates in situ data, highly relevant to the situation where response to identified training needs/interests will impact. • (When combined with a feedback step) provides for important comparison checks between inferences of the observer and the respondent.	• Requires a highly skilled observer with both process and content knowledge (unlike an interviewer who needs, for the most part, only process skills). • Carries limitations that derive from being able to collect data only within the work setting (the other side of the first advantage listed in the preceding column). • Holds potential for respondents to perceive the observation activity as "spying."
Questionnaires • May be in the form of surveys or polls of a random or stratified sample of respondents, or an enumeration of an entire "population." • Can use a variety of question formats: open-ended, projective, forced-choice, priority-ranking. • Can take alternative forms such as Q-sorts, or slipsorts, rating scales, either predesigned or self-generated by respondent(s). • May be self-administered (by mail) under controlled or uncontrolled conditions, or may require the presence of an interpreter or assistant.	• Can reach a large number of people in a short time. • Are relatively inexpensive. • Give opportunity of expression without fear of embarrassment. • Yield data easily summarized and reported.	• Make little provision for free expression of unanticipated responses. • Require substantial time (and technical skills, especially in survey model) for development of effective instruments. • Are of limited utility in getting at causes of problems or possible solutions. • Suffer low return rates (mailed), grudging responses, or unintended and/or inappropriate respondents.
Key Consultation • Secures information from those persons who, by virtue of their formal or informal standing, are in a good position to know what the training needs of a particular group are: a. board chairman b. related service providers c. members of professional associations d. individuals from the service population	• Is relatively simple and inexpensive to conduct. • Permits input and interaction of a number of individuals, each with his or her own perspectives of the needs of the area, discipline, group, etc. • Establishes and strengthens lines of communication between participants in the process.	• Carries a built-in bias, since it is based on views of those who tend to see training needs from their own individual or organizational perspective. • May result in only a partial picture of training needs due to the typically nonrepresentative nature (in a statistical sense) of a key informant group.
Print Media • Can include professional journals, legislative news/notes, industry "rags," trade magazines, in-house publications.	• Is an excellent source of information for uncovering and clarifying normative needs. • Provides information that is current, if not forward-looking. • Is readily available and is apt to have already been reviewed by the client group.	• Can be a problem when it comes to the data analysis and synthesis into a useable form (use of clipping service or key consultants can make this type of data more useable).

continued

Techniques	Advantages	Disadvantages
Interviews • Can be formal or casual, structured or unstructured, or somewhere in between. • May be used with a sample of a particular group (board, staff, committee) or conducted with everyone concerned. • Can be done in person, by phone, at the work site, or away from it.	• Are adept at revealing feelings, causes of, and possible solutions to problems that the client is facing (or anticipates); provide maximum opportunity for the client to represent himself spontaneously on his own terms (especially when conducted in an open-ended, nondirective manner).	• Are usually time-consuming. • Can be difficult to analyze and quantify results (especially from unstructured formats). • Unless the interviewer is skilled, the client(s) can easily be made to feel self-conscious. • Rely for success on a skilful interviewer who can generate data without making client(s) feel self-conscious, suspicious, etc.
Group Discussion • Resembles face-to-face interview technique, e.g., structured or unstructured, formal or informal, or somewhere in between • Can be focused on job (role) analysis, group problem analysis, group goal setting, or any number of group tasks or themes, e.g., "leadership training needs of the board." • Uses one or several of the familiar group facilitating techniques: brainstorming, nominal group process, force-fields, consensus rankings, organizational mirroring, simulation, and sculpting.	• Permits on-the-spot synthesis of different viewpoints. • Builds support for the particular service response that is ultimately decided on. • Decreases client's "dependence response" toward the service provided since data analysis is (or can be) a shared function. • Helps participants to become better problem analysts, better listeners, etc.	• Is time-consuming (therefore initially expensive) both for the consultant and the agency. • Can produce data that are difficult to synthesize and quantify (more a problem with the less structured techniques).
Tests • Are a hybridized form of questionnaire. • Can be very functionally oriented (like observations) to test a board, staff, or committee member's proficiency. • May be used to sample learned ideas and facts. • Can be administered with or without the presence of an assistant.	• Can be especially helpful in determining whether the cause of a recognized problem is a deficiency in knowledge or skill, or by elimination, attitude. • Results are easily quantifiable and comparable.	• The availability of a relatively small number of tests that are validated for a specific situation. • Do not indicate if measured knowledge and skills are actually being used in the on-the-job or "back home group" situation.
Records, Reports • Can consist of organizational charts, planning documents, policy manuals, audits, and budget reports. • Employee records (grievance, turnover, accidents, etc.) • Includes minutes of meetings, weekly, monthly program reports, memoranda, agency service records, program evaluation studies.	• Provide excellent clues to trouble spots. • Provide objective evidence of the results of problems within the agency or group. • Can be collected with a minimum of effort and interruption of work flow since it already exists at the work site.	• Causes of problems or possible solutions often do not show up. • Carries perspective that generally reflects the past situation rather than the current one (or recent changes). • Need a skilled data analyst if clear patterns and trends are to emerge from such technical and diffuse raw data.
Work Samples • Are similar to observation but in written form. • Can be products generated in the course of the organization's work, e.g., ad layouts, program proposals, market analyses, letters, training designs. • Written responses to a hypothetical but relevant case study provided by the consultant.	• Carry most of the advantage of records and reports data. • Are the organization's data (its own output).	• Case study method will take time away from actual work of the organization. • Need specialized content analysts. • Analyst's assessment of strengths/weaknesses disclosed by samples can be challenged as "too subjective."

Source: From Steadham, S.V. (1980). Learning to select a needs assessment strategy. *Training and Development* 30 (January), 56–61. Copyright © 1980 by the American Society for Training and Development, Inc. Reprinted by permission. All rights reserved.

observation, questionnaires, key consultation, print media, interviews, group discussion, tests, records and reports, and work samples. The table gives a complete list of the techniques and their advantages and disadvantages.

Some software firms have developed workforce surveys that can be customized to include questions from broad climate issues to specific job standards. There are many firms that have designed needs assessment software, some of which can be tailored to clients' needs. This technology allows HR personnel to develop customized surveys quickly, and to analyze results by region, unit, and so on. One HR system contained 200 000 pieces of information on 500 employees. This system taped every skill of every employee ranging from forklift and fuel-tank exchange procedures to probing abilities (Rockburn, 1991). This accumulation of data then made it easier to conduct post-tests to determine if learning has occurred.

Comparison of Methods

A study by Preskill (1991) suggests that some methods of analysis are better than others in terms of response rate, quality, usefulness of the data, and cost. Preskill tested three assessment alternatives: closed-ended survey, open-ended survey, and focus groups. A combination of the closed-ended survey and focus-group interviews provided the most practical, useful, and cost-effective information.

There are many other sources of information. Some retail stores assess the competence of their sales staff through the use of professional shoppers, who rate sales performance against established standards (Tritsch, 1991). A bank tests employee knowledge using a computer-based analysis, and then compares the results with supervisory rankings (Tritsch, 1991). A complete list of sources of needs analysis would include

advisory committees	new legislation
appraisals and promotions	new policies
assessment centres	new products
benchmarking	new technology or equipment
checklists	observation
examination of records	performance tests
exit interviews	production records
focus groups	questionnaires
formal interview	regular management reports
formal research	reports from superiors
human resource plans	succession plans
informal interview	survey method
management requests	

The best method depends on the time and money available, the experience of the analyst, and the nature of the responses. Most trainers use surveys. The next section describes some of the issues surrounding sampling.

SOURCES OF INFORMATION (WHO)

Information about organizational and job performance is only as good as the source. One critical question in needs analysis is determining the source of the information. There are several options for the needs analyst.

SAMPLE SIZE

While it may be tempting to survey everyone in the organization, data collection and analysis becomes costly as the sample size increases. Moreover, a small sample of 100 people may generate results identical to a survey of the entire population of 1500; money and respondent time can be saved. The sample size must be robust enough to enable statistical analyses but small enough to provide information in a cost-effective manner.

SAMPLE DEPTH

Surveying only job incumbents about their perceptions of their own abilities may not result in the most objective portrait of performance gaps. Employees may have wish lists for training that do not meet their units needs or that do not address their own weaknesses. Managers, too, should be asked for their performance evaluations. Those who have frequent interaction with job incumbents, such as customers or employees in other departments, should also be surveyed. These different perspectives result in valuable information.

Some organizations use 360 degree appraisals to pinpoint developmental needs. A 360 degree appraisal means that many raters who are familiar with the employee's work assess that performance using some kind of structured form. Raters typically include managers, subordinates, peers, and sometimes customers. Software is available to assist with the administration of this process. The trainer (and the rated employee) can then look for gaps between performance expectations and perceptions of that performance. Some companies even coach people on how to accept this 360 degree feedback and view it constructively so that they can act on the deficiencies.

CONFIDENTIALITY

Surveys must be voluntary and confidential. Employees are naturally wary about the analyses of their jobs or performance. Such performance assessments may be associated with workload or compensation. Front-end support must be created by involving the stakeholders (managers, employee groups, unions, and so on) in the goals and structuring of the survey. Communication from management must reinforce the importance of and rationale for the analysis. Employees should be given written assurance of the voluntary nature of the survey. In addition, questionnaires should be coded so that a specific employee cannot be identified. Feedback to employees should consist of group responses.

DATA-COLLECTION ISSUES

When collecting information from employees, HR analysts should be cautious about relying on self-assessment data and about the use and interpretation of the information. This section outlines some problems with data collection.

SELF-ASSESSMENT

Much of the data collected on performance requires job holders to rate their own performance. This technique has its benefits and its limitations. Employees may be more motivated to be trained if they perceive that their needs are being met by the training program. Employees who are forced to attend training may be reluctant to transfer this training to the job (Noe & Schmitt, 1986). But self-perceptions of need pose many problems for the analyst. Some employees may want training but not need it.

Expressions of need include feelings or desires and may have no relation to performance (Latham, 1988). Several studies have found weak relationships between self-assessment of performance and managerial assessments (Staley & Shockley-Zalaback, 1986; McEnery & McEnery, 1987). More damning is the review of 55 studies that found no strong relationship between self-evaluation of ability and other measures of performance (Mabe & West, 1982). However, a study at IBM demonstrated that employees can be trained in self-assessment by learning to break down a job into its component parts and to analyze skills (Bardsely, 1987). This method has the added benefit of the employees' accepting ownership of their development plans.

EXTENT OF DATA COLLECTION

Sometimes time is a constraint in data collection. The new equipment may be arriving on Monday, and it is easier to train all employees on all procedures instead of determining who needs training on which aspects of the new equipment.

Sometimes, the constraint is the quality of information. Managers may have difficulty answering even the simplest question: What is the expected performance level? In some cases, different managers may perceive different standards as the key measures of performance.

USE OF INFORMATION

Employees responding to questions about effectiveness may fear that the information will be used against them. They may fear a change in compensation, a restructuring or elimination of their jobs, or a negative personnel evaluation with attendant losses of promotion or pay. They may distrust the analyst's ability to keep the data safe from the eyes of their supervisors.

CAUSE AND EFFECT

Many analysts find it difficult to disentangle cause and effect. For example, a poor-quality product may be the result of a lack of knowledge on the part of employees, poorly designed work procedures, or even rumours about a plant shutdown.

COST BENEFIT

One study has determined that a majority of firms do not use formal needs assessment (Saari, Johnson, McLaughlin, & Zimmerle, 1988). People who work in training and development claim that they are not rewarded for taking the time (and money) to conduct needs analysis. Managers seem to feel that they should use training resources to train. They may also feel that they can accurately identify training needs and that more analysis is a waste of time. Managers may even have their own agendas, such as rewarding employees by sending them to exotic locations for training. These managers may resist interference by the "personnel department" in management decisions. See how some training experts handle these situations in the Training Today 3 box.

As HR practitioners become educated and certified in their profession, the importance and application of front-end analysis may increase.

DECIDING IF TRAINING IS THE ANSWER

Training is the best solution under the following conditions:

- the task is performed frequently
- the task is difficult
- correct performance is critical
- the employee does not know how to perform as required (can not do it)
- performance expectations are clear, and employees receive feedback on their performance

TRAINING TODAY 3 I Want the Training Now!

Needs assessment is time consuming and complex, and hard to sell to managers who want just-in-time solutions to urgent problems. When a manager is introducing a new way of working, or an employee can do some critical task, the last thing they want to hear is "wait, we have to do a needs assessment." Does the world of needs assessment exist only in textbooks?

Very few trainers would use the complete needs assessment procedures described here. However, most trainers would use some means of detecting the underlying cause of the performance problem. Here are some ways experienced trainers have used to conduct needs assessments that are more timely and less cumbersome.

- *Ask a series of questions.* When a manager demands a training course for employees, the trainer should start by asking questions related to the nature of the problem and its impact on the business. (The questions of the needs assessment decision tree could be used.) Some trainers even agree to conduct a training course, as per the managers demand, and then renegotiate the assignment as information emerges from interviews with employees before the course. Managers may be

receptive to the emerging data, recognizing the need to design solutions that solve the problem.

- *Use existing information.* Surveys, interviews, and observations are expensive data-collection methods. But most organizations keep customer complaint letters, grievance files, exit interviews, and sales data, which can be re-assessed for needs assessment purposes.
- *Speed up data collection.* Use the Intranet to survey employees. Start discussion groups around the problems.
- *Link assessment and delivery.* Rather than conduct a lengthy needs assessment and then design a training program, some trainers attempt to join the two together, in small steps. For example, if there are star performers, then bring them together in a forum with nonstellar performers to discuss effective techniques. The poorer performers not only are able to compare performance, but to learn how to improve at the same time.

Source: Adapted from Zemke, R. (1998). How to do a needs assessment when you think you don't have time. *Training 35* (3), 38–44.

- there are (or will be) positive consequences for correct work behaviour; there are not negative consequences for performing as required
- other solutions (such as coaching) are ineffective or too expensive (terminating employees and rehiring those with required skills)

If the needs analysis reveals that tasks are not frequently executed, that they are not critical, and that perfection is not required, then performance-improvement solutions such as job aids and coaching are more appropriate. More radical solutions may even be appropriate. Nadler (1990) suggests changing the people through firing and hiring, re-engineering the job, changing the equipment, or changing the organizational structure.

Even if training is determined to be the best solution, the costs and benefits of training must first be estimated. Trainers must ask questions such as "What is the cost of not doing the training?" "What are the monetary benefits to training?" (Chapter 10 on costing training discusses these questions.) Another consideration is the legal requirement to certify knowledge and skill levels for designated workers. A further point is the pressure exerted by top management to conduct the training. It is hoped that this pressure is a result of management objectives and priorities. These three elements are catalysts in the determination of priorities for training.

SUMMARY

This chapter has examined the process of determining training and development needs. The rationale for conducting needs analyses was presented. The diagnostic process was described, with a focus on three areas of concentration: the organization, the job, and the employee. Data collection methods were explained, including issues of sample size and confidentiality. Issues such as the problems with self-assessment methods and the cost benefits of doing needs assessment were delineated.

KEY TERMS

behavioural measures   58
benchmarking   50
competency   53
contingency management   60
culture   50
economic measures   58
employee analysis   56
functional analysis   51

interpretive analysis   51
job   52
job analysis   52
job description   52
needs analysis   44
organizational analysis   48
proficiency tests   58
task   52

EXERCISES

1a. For an example of a needs assessment instrument, access <**www.sales.org**> where you will find a test that measures key sales abilities including communication and negotiation. This test could be used for selecting sales representatives or for identifying competency gaps in the current sales force. Have each member of your working group take the test. Develop a needs assessment report, indicating

current competencies and gaps. Then, using the information from the text, determine if training is the best solution for closing the gaps.

1b. What do you think are the core competencies of a sales job? Take two of these competencies and attempt to describe them in behavioural terms. Brainstorm with your group and construct a BARS-type scale, listing examples of effective and incompetent performance.

2. The manager of training purchased an organizational climate survey that asked employees to rate their competencies in a number of job tasks. However, two items the manager wanted to assess were not part of the vendor's package. These were the coaching abilities of managers and their ability to delegate. Develop a scale for measuring employee performance for these two dimensions. How would you use these to identify performance gaps?

CASE: GENERAL MOTORS

The press operation (blanker area) of the metal fabrication plant at General Motors was undergoing major changes in technology, a new operational philosophy, and new dies. ("Blanker" is a shop term for a press that cuts the shape of a part from a coil of sheet metal, like a cookie cutter. Dies are tools for imparting a shape or finish to an object or material.) Managers were concerned that employees did not have adequate KSAs to deal with these changes and meet production standards. To determine if training was needed, one supervisor and two members of the United Auto Workers formed a needs analysis team.

At the first meeting of the needs analysis team with the client (the blanker area's coordinator), the performance problems were identified as being unable to meet the desired production schedules, efficiency, and cost-per-cut benchmarks. The team determined that the main focus would be on training solutions, but the client would consider any nontraining issues.

The team set out to

1. identify symptoms and causes
2. plan data-gathering techniques
3. collect the data
4. analyze and interpret the data
5. report results and suggest solutions

Step 1. Some of the observable *symptoms* were a decrease in efficiency; an increase in transition time (the time it takes to change a die to run a different part), downtime due to lack of steel, downtime due to repairs on dies. The team felt that some of the *causes* (reasons that could explain what they saw) were frequent scheduling changes; inefficient communication between production, scheduling, and maintenance areas; a storage room so disorganized it was difficult to locate different types of steel rolls or blanks, which in turn caused inventory problems.

Step 2. The team interviewed production and skilled trade workers, their supervisors, scheduling personnel, and the steel expediter to discuss the data-gathering technique. They discovered that the problem snowballed outside of the blanker area and affected other operations.

Step 3. The team collected more data through a survey questionnaire and more interviews. They also held roundtable discussions and assigned subject-matter experts (SME) from each area to examine their departments trouble spots. They also contacted SME from other GM locations to obtain additional information.

Step 4. The team prepared a list of solutions: use a computer program for scheduling; develop and implement an organized floor plan and layout for the storage room; colour code the dies to the presses; provide intermediate training on a software program for ordering steel and on cutting shippers; have the service department give equal priority to the blanker area and other areas.

Step 5. These possible solutions were presented to the various departments, who then came up with a final list of nine solutions: implement a new two-week scheduling program; implement a floor plan and layout for the storage room; institute a preventative maintenance program; provide dedicated service people to the blanker area; divide the blanker area into two separate areas to make it more manageable; implement a skeleton part procedure for dies scheduled for maintenance; colour code the dies to the presses; train production operators in statistical process control; provide a training solution for the steel expediter.

The team prioritized the solutions, costed them, explained the expected results and potential value and benefits, and presented this list to the blanker area coordinator. The solution that would have the most impact was to train production operators in statistical control techniques.

This solution was implemented and the results were:

- 30 percent reduction in scrap rate
- 30 percent increase in efficiency
- 10 percent lower costs
- improved inventory capability and cost
- 35 percent to 80 percent increase in first-time quality
- less downtime for repair
- 7 percent increase in productivity
- worker pride of ownership for these achievements

Source: Adapted from Finison, K., & Szediak, F. (1997). General Motors does a needs analysis. *Training and Development 58* (7), 103–104.

Questions

1. Why would the needs analysis team determine that their main focus would be on training solutions before they did any analysis?

2. Review the symptoms and causes identified in step 1. How many of these appear to have a training solution?

3. The team developed a list of five solutions. Which of these are training solutions?

4. Critique the needs analysis done at General Motors. If you were a consultant to this project, are there any things that you would have done differently? Explain why.

REFERENCES

Bardsely, C.A. (1987). Improving employee awareness of opportunity at IBM. *Personnel* (April).

Bass, B.M., & Vaughn, J.A. (1966). *Training in industry: The management of learning.* Belmont, CA: Wadsworth.

Caravan, T.N. , Costine, P, & Heraty, N. (1995). *Training and development in Ireland: Context, policy, and practice.* Oak Tree Press: Dublin.

Carr, C. (1992). The three Rs of training. *Training 29* (6).

Chevalier, R.D. (1990). Analyzing performance discrepancies with line managers. *Performance and Instruction 29* (10).

Dolan, S.L., & Schuler, R.S. (1994). *Human resource management: The Canadian dynamic.* Scarborough, ON: Nelson Canada.

Estabrooke, M., & Foy, N.F. (1992). Answering the call of tailored training. *Training 29* (10), 84–88.

Froiland, P. (1993). Reproducing star performers. *Training 30* (11).

Geroy G.D. (1986). *Education for work: An integration of vocational education and employer-sponsored training in Minnesota* (Research Report no. 13). St. Paul, MN: University of Minnesota, Training and Research Center.

————. (1990). *Education for work: An integration of vocational education and employer-sponsored training in Minnesota* (Research Report no. 13). St. Paul, MN: University of Minnesota, Training and Research Center.

Geroy, G.D., Wright, P.C. & Caffrey, P.L. (1989). Establishing a multi-craft maintenance operation. *Performance and Instruction 28* (7).

Glaser, E.M., & S.H. Taylor. (1973). Factors influencing the success of applied research. *American Psychologist 28* (2), 579–584.

Goldstein, I.L. (1993). *Training in organizations* (3rd ed.). Pacific Grove, CA: Brooks/Cole.

Hobbs, D.L. (1990). A training-appropriation process. *Training and Development Journal 44* (4).

Kaufman, R. (1991). *Strategic planning plus: An organizational guide.* Glenview, IL: Scott Foreman Professional Books.

Laird, D. (1985). *Approaches to training and development* (rev. ed.). Reading, MA: Addison-Wesley.

Landey, F.J., & Vasey, J. (1991). Job analysis: The composition of SME samples. *Personnel Psychology* 44.

Latham, G.P. (1988). Human resource training and development. *Annual Review of Psychology 39.*

Lee, W.W., & Roadman, K.H. (1991). Linking needs assessment to performance-based evaluation. *Performance and Instruction 30* (7).

Lewis, T., &. Bjorkquist, D.C. (1992). Needs assessment—A critical reappraisal. *Performance Improvement Quarterly 5* (4).

McClelland, S.B. (1995). *Organizational needs assessments.* Westport, CT: Quorum Books.

McEnery, J., & McEnery, J.M. (1987). Self-rating in management training needs assessment: A neglected opportunity. *Journal of Occupational Psychology 60,* 49–60.

Mabe, P.A., & West, S.G. (1982). Validity of self-evaluation of ability: A review and a meta-analysis. *Journal of Applied Psychology 67,* 280–296.

MacNamara, D. (1998, November 16). Learning contracts, competency profiles the new wave in executive development. *Canadian HR Reporter,* pp. G8–G10.

Mager, R.F., & Pipe, P. (1970). *Analyzing performance problems or you really oughta wanna.* Belmont, CA: Lear Siegler, Inc./Fearon.

Mills, G.R., Pace, W., & Peterson, B. (1989). *Analysis in human resource training and organization development.* Reading, MA: Addison-Wesley.

Moore, M.L., & Dutton, P. (1987). Training needs analysis: Preview and critique. *Academy of Management Review 3* (3).

Nadler, L. (1990). *Designing training programs: The critical events model.* Reading, MA: Addison-Wesley.

Noe, R.A., & Schmitt, N. (1986). The influence of trainer attitudes on training effectiveness: Test of a model. *Personnel Psychology 39,* 497–523.

Nowack, K.M. (1991). A true training needs analysis. *Training and Development Journal 43* (4).

Overmeyer-Day, L., & Benson, G. (1996). Training success stories. *Training & Development* (June), 24–29.

Pace, R.W., Smith, P.C., & Mills, G.E. (1991). *Human resource development: The field.* Englewood Cliffs, NJ: Prentice-Hall.

Parry, S.B. (1998). Just what is a competency? *Training 35* (6), 58–64.

Preskill, H. (1991). A comparison of data collection methods for assessing training needs. *Human Resource Development Quarterly* (Summer).

Rockburn, J. (1991, October 15). Streamlining human resources. *The Globe and Mail,* p. B15.

Saari, L.M., Johnson, T.R., McLaughlin, S.D., & Zimmerle, D.M. (1988). A survey of management training and education practices in U.S. companies. *Personnel Psychology 41* (4), 731–744.

Saks, A.M. (2000). *Research, measurement, and evaluation of human resources.* Toronto: Nelson Thomson Learning.

Schuler, R.S. (1992). Linking the people with the strategic needs of the business. *Organizational Dynamics 21* (4).

Sleezer, C.M. (1992). Needs assessment: Perspectives from the literature. *Performance Improvement Quarterly 5* (2).

Staley, C.C., & Shockley-Zalaback, P. (1986). Communication proficiency and future training needs of the female professional: Self-assessment versus supervisors' evaluations. *Human Relations 39*, 891–902.

Steadham, S.V. (1980). Learning to select a needs assessment strategy. *Training and Development Journal 34* (4).

Trainor, N.L. (1998, November 16). Using measurement to predict performance. *Canadian HR Reporter*, pp. 7–8.

Tritsch, C. (1991). Assessing your training. *Human Resource Executive* (May).

Wexley, K.M., & Latham, G. (1991). *Developing and training human resources in organizations* (2nd ed.). New York: Harper Collins.

4

STRATEGIC
GOAL SETTING

CHAPTER GOALS

Training objectives and organizational objectives have a lot in common—they are both results-oriented, performance-based planning tools. The use of objectives tells employees and their managers what is to be learned, and helps them evaluate how performance will be changed as a result of the course. The writing of objectives enables us to answer the critical question, "What should the trainee be able to do at the end of the training program?" This chapter provides a model and techniques for establishing training objectives.

After reading this chapter, you should be able to

* describe how training objectives flow from organizational objectives
* list the advantages of objectives
* specify the five steps to be followed when writing an objective
* prepare a written objective containing the three components of performance, condition, and criterion
* describe the three domains of learning, list the levels within each, and give one example of each level
* discuss the criticisms of writing measurable objectives

FIGURE 4.1 GUIDELINES TO SCREENING AND SELECTION IN EMPLOYMENT

Organizational Strategy

↓

Departmental/functional objectives

↓

Job standards/expectations

↓

Training/Instructional Objectives

↓

Employee performance standards

↓

Departmental records

↓

Concerns, Problems/Gaps

LINKING ORGANIZATIONAL STRATEGY WITH TRAINING

The process of determining what is to be learned can start at the top or from the bottom of the organization. The process, discussed below, is also outlined in Figure 4.1

TOP DOWN

From the top, executives determine organizational strategy. Strategy is both a purpose and a plan. The goals of the organization are established and resources allocated to meet those goals. Typically, private-sector strategies include "to achieve 45 percent market share by 2003" or "to reach 17 percent return on investment." Managers then use the overall corporate strategy to derive departmental or functional goals. Then, individual jobs or job holders are assigned their goals. These individual goals are often negotiated, in some form of management-by-objectives exercise.

For example, Sprint uses the LINK performance management system for linking business objectives, employee development plans, performance evaluation, and training courses (Overmeyer-Day & Benson, 1996). The LINK system operates in a cascading format, starting with executive announcements of business plans at the start of the cycle. Four to six key objectives are identi-

TRAINING TODAY 1   That's the Spirit

The Liquor Control Board of Ontario (LCBO) received two awards in 1998: one for Innovative Retailer of the Year (large store category), which recognizes demonstrated market leadership and innovative approaches to customer and employee relations; and the other award for a staff motivation and development program, called "That's the Spirit." The goal of this program was to increase the customer service skills and knowledge of distilled spirits of the LCBO's 4500 employees.

The original impetus for the program was the threat of privatization. The overall strategy of the government of the day was to privatize, and LCBO knew that it would have to have an educated staff to meet customer demands. The external pressure for change, as described by the Ontario Liquor Board Employees Union, was that the employees better provide the best service, or the public

would endorse the privatization. As it turned out, the government decided against privatization. Another motivator for the program was that consumer drinking habits were changing. Consumers were switching to wine and beer, with the result that spirit sales were cut in half between 1974 and 1994. LCBO believed that a trained workforce would be able to stop the downward trend. Since the training program began, spirit sales have not only stopped declining, but have been increasing.

This case clearly shows that training programs occur as a result of external changes, which may be political and demographic.

Source: Adapted from Kulig, P. (1998, August 19). LCBO has taste for training. *Canadian HR Reporter* 11 (4), 1, 2.

fied for each employee that align with the accomplishment of the business objectives. Then, each employee prepares an individual development plan for the accomplishment of the objectives. Training goals must align with these development plans, and progress is checked by two annual performance reviews.

Sometimes business strategy is determined by environmental threats or changes that require repositioning of the business, and subsequent retraining for employees. See the Training Today 1 box for an example of how this came about at the Liquor Control Board of Ontario.

Bottom Up

Conversely, training objectives can start with someone in the organization having a concern about employee performance or a unit's productivity. A formal needs analysis (described in Chapter 3) results in the identification of specific performance weaknesses or opportunities for improving effectiveness. With these data in hand, the human resource (HR) developer can state specifically the behaviours that are to change. The most effective way to do this is through the preparation of objectives.

Objectives

An **objective** is a statement of what participants are expected to be able to do after a training program. (We are using the term "program," but could use course, session, class, and so on. Generally, a course is a learning experience, usually off the job site, conducted over a specified period. A session might be part of a course or a program. A class might refer to one unit of a course or program. A program might consist of several courses, include on-the-job work experience, and occur over a longer period.) Put another way, an objective is the expected outcome of training. The instructional objective describes the skills or knowledge to be acquired and transferred to the job.

The emphasis in training is on performance, or behaviour on the job. Learning can be described as the process of acquiring new skills, knowledge, and attitudes, while performance is the use of these new skills, knowledge, and attitudes (Nadler, 1990). The establishment of learning objectives focuses on performance on the job. This performance should be observable and measurable.

Advantages of Objectives

As trainers and developers work with programs, they discover that there is a strong case to be made for knowing exactly what a course promises to achieve (its objectives). There are seven reasons for this.

1. Trainees need to have a clear understanding of what is expected of them. Objectives allow them to focus their energies on achieving these goals, rather than to waste energy on irrelevant tasks or trying to figure out what is required of them. Several studies have demonstrated that, if instructors use objectives, students can be more efficient learners (Mager & McCann, 1961; McNeil, 1966; Miles, Kibler, & Pettigrew, 1967). The clarity of the goal and the specific feedback toward its achievement is critical to training. Someone once said that baseball would die if it weren't for its emphasis on performance statistics. Such statistics suggest clear goals for future achievement.

2. Trainees can be assessed prior to instruction to determine if they have mastered any of the objectives. Depending on the results, students can either omit certain sections of a course or undertake other training to master the prerequisites.

3. The selection of content, teaching modes, and evaluation methods is simplified by objectives. Trainers will concentrate on methods that produce results, rather than using favourite or trendy training techniques.

4. Objectives communicate to supervisors, professional groups, assessors, and others what the trainee is expected to have learned by the end of the

training program. Instructors who teach preceding and subsequent units of training also need this information.

5. Management and the training supervisors know exactly what is expected of trainees and can reinforce the new skills learned in the job situation.

6. Accountability for training results may make managers more likely to approve a course that specifies improvements to be achieved. This communicates to employees that training means business and that it is an integral part of the planning of the organization.

7. A precise, objective, and measurable statement of learning objectives enables evaluators to gauge the quantitative benefits of a program. Mager (1975) said it best: "We need to know where we are going before we can get there."

THE WRITING OF OBJECTIVES

The writing of objectives is a skill that can be learned. Skill in writing objectives does not mean that trainers can make lists of behaviour verbs such as "recognize" and "evaluate." The real skill is the ability to rework needs analysis data into performance outcomes.

Five steps should be followed when writing objectives (Cranton, 1989).

1. List the goals of the instruction. An example would be: *The student will be able to describe the domains of learning.*

2. These goals should then be translated into observable or measurable items. The example cited above might then read: *The student will be able to define objectives, discuss five advantages and three limitations of objectives, list the domains of learning, and give an example of an objective within each domain.*

3. The degree of detail must be considered. This will vary with the level of learning within various contexts or institutions and with the learner. We might take one of the above objectives and state: *The student will be able to list the domains of learning with 90 percent accuracy.*

4. The circumstances or conditions of evaluation must be stated. Will the student list the domains alone, or with an open book, within 15 minutes, and so on? The objective should include this information.

5. The next step would be to take the list of objectives and have them reviewed by other instructors and former and current trainees. The goal is to assess whether the objectives are measurable, clear, comprehensive, and achievable, and whether they adequately reflect course content. Adult learners, in particular, should be widely consulted on the learning objectives. This is practical and feasible in a training situation, less so in educational institutions where goals are predetermined.

Objectives should contain the following five elements:

1. *Who is to perform the desired behaviour?* Students and participants are the easiest to identify. In a training situation, where employees are not necessarily students in a classroom, more accurate descriptors might be "all first-level supervisors," "anyone conducting selection interviews," or "all employees with more than one month of experience." The trainer is not the "who," although it is tempting for some trainees to write, for example, that the trainer will present five hours of information on communication. The goal of the instructor is to maximize the efficiency with which all students achieve the specified objectives, not just present the information (Kibler, Barker, & Miles, 1970).

2. *What is the actual behaviour to be employed to demonstrate mastery of the training content or objective?* Words like "type," "run," and "calculate" can be measured easily. Other mental activities such as comprehension and analysis can also be described in measurable ways, as shown at the end of this chapter.

3. and 4. *Where and when is the behaviour to be demonstrated and evaluated (i.e., under what conditions)?* These could include "during a 60-minute typing test," "on the ski hill with icy conditions," "when presented with a diagram," or "when asked to design a training session." The tools, equipment, information, and other source materials for training should be specified. Included in this list may be things the trainee may not use, such as calculators.

5. *What is the standard by which the behaviour will be judged?* Is the trainee expected to type 60 words per minute with less than three errors? Can the student list five out of six categories?

The final written objective will contain three components:

performance the work behaviour of a trainee

1. **performance:** what the trainee will be able to do after the session

condition where, when, how the performance will occur

2. **condition:** the tools, time, and so on under which the trainee is expected to perform

3. **criterion:** the level of acceptable performance

criterion the level of acceptable performance

A well-written objective would read as follows: *The sales representative* (who) *will be able to make 10 calls a day to new customers in the territory assigned* (what, where, when), *and will be able to generate three (30 percent) sales worth at least $500 from these calls* (how, or the criterion).

The first attempt at writing objectives will be difficult. However, after some experience, a generalization of these planning skills will occur. Managers will start thinking in terms of management by objectives and performance appraisals using measurable results. People negotiating assignments and other work will evaluate the contract or objective in terms of its measurability.

Representative workers should be involved in the development of the learning objectives. A team consisting of the trainer, trainees, and their supervisors would be ideal (Laird, 1985). At some point, the objectives should be reviewed with and approved by the executives of the organization and the supervisors of the trainees. Nadler (1990) cites a case in which a sales training program, based on a needs analysis of sales representatives, was rejected by senior management because management were secretly planning fundamental organizational changes.

At this stage, the learning objectives should closely resemble the job analysis (discussed in Chapter 3). For example, one task of the job of a receptionist could be: *The receptionist* (who) *sorts 100 pieces of incoming mail by categories of complaints, requests for information, and invoices* (what) *within 60 minutes, with less than 1 percent processing errors* (how). This could easily become a training objective. A learning objective that reads like an actual job behaviour is more likely to be approved, learned, and used on the job.

In summary, a learning objective contains an observable action, with a measurable criterion outlining conditions of performance.

TYPES OF OBJECTIVES

There is a tool to assist trainers in the development of objectives. Bloom (1956, 1964) compiled a list of specific learning objectives, which he named *Taxonomy of Educational Objectives*. The Taxonomy divides the categories of objectives into three domains: cognitive (knowledge), affective (attitudes), and psychomotor (skills). Each of these domains contains a hierarchical listing of behaviours, on the assumption that each successive behaviour is more difficult than and depends on learning the previous behaviour. This categorization of behaviours is extremely helpful to course designers and will be discussed in some detail.

DOMAINS OF LEARNING

As mentioned, learning is the process of acquiring some new knowledge, attitude, or skill. Performance describes the use of the knowledge, attitude, and skill. Later in the text, we will discuss techniques to ensure transfer of learning to performance on the job. For this chapter, we will concentrate on learning.

In any textbook on learning in psychology or education, the term "domains of learning" accurately portrays a fundamental concept, basically that there are areas and levels of learning. The three basic areas are *cognitive*, *affective*, and *psychomotor*. Most managers and employees would be more comfortable with the comparable terms of knowledge, attitudes, and skills—or simply: the head, the heart, and the hand.

KNOWLEDGE—THE HEAD

This first and largest area of learning, the **cognitive domain**, includes all intellectual processes: recalling facts, understanding concepts, applying these con-

cognitive domain an area of learning that includes all intellectual processes

cepts to practical situations, and analyzing theories (Cranton, 1989). This area is what people generally think of as learning. As a student, you are probably familiar with exam questions that ask you to show that you have mastered learning in this category.

Within this category, Bloom (1956) has identified levels of learning. These levels are arranged hierarchically, and as mentioned the assumption is that the first level must be mastered before the subsequent levels can be learned.

The levels within the cognitive (knowledge) domain are:

1. *Knowledge.* This simplest level of learning includes the recognition and recall of basic facts. Students call it rote learning. Example: *Apprentices will be able to list the six steps in machine assembly, with zero errors, within 10 minutes.* Words that describe this function are: *define, outline, sort, recall, recount, match, record, list, cluster, name, repeat,* and *label.*

2. *Comprehension.* At this level, the student not only knows the information but can demonstrate that he or she understands the material. Example: *Managers will be able to describe in their own words the meaning of sexual harassment.* Key defining words are: *locate, recognize, identify, paraphrase, tell, describe, report, explain, cite, support,* and *summarize.*

3. *Application.* As the label suggests, this step involves the use of knowledge and understanding. After learning rules, principles, or other basic knowledge, the learner attempts to apply this knowledge to problems or new situations. Example: *Building-code inspectors will be able to identify 99 out of 100 building-code infractions during a mock inspection lasting two hours.* Cue words under this category are: *select, use, imitate, demonstrate, apply, frame, illustrate, solve, organize, sequence,* and *manipulate.*

4. *Analysis.* At a higher level, students are able to critically analyze a theory or a concept. By comparing and contrasting information, the student appraises information. (In some cases, the application stage is not a prerequisite for this level.) Example: *While observing a squash match, the trainee will be able to compare and contrast the strategies used by the two players.* This type of learning is more complex and is dependent on understanding the various components of the subject area. This will vary by subject. The descriptive verbs in this category are: *examine, distinguish, differentiate, outline, characterize, compare or contrast, research, interpret, debate or defend, conclude,* and *analyze.*

5. *Synthesis.* At this level, students analyze information from a wide variety of sources and meld the facts and theories into a coherent concept or position. A student paper is the best example of synthesis. At work, the preparation of a proposal or plan is a good illustration of the concept of synthesis. Example: *The student will prepare a paper on a training method, in which the concept is defined, illustrated, analyzed, and a conclusion on its effectiveness is reached.* The critical verbs are: *propose, create, invent, plan, formulate, design, emulate, speculate,* and *construct.*

6. *Evaluation.* The highest level of cognitive learning—evaluation—refers to a student's ability to critique, for example, a performance or a research proposal. This evaluation is not based on an emotional response to the performance or material but is an intellectual process guided by information learned at previous levels. Evaluation implies that a set of criteria for judging has been learned and can be applied. Examples: *Managers will be able to evaluate a new product-development proposal using both internal and external market standards. After observing a hockey game, the learner will be able to rank the players on the basis of technical skill.* Some cue verbs are: *judge, rate, criticize, justify, argue, persuade, value, assess,* and *evaluate.*

The outline of these levels of learning assists the instructor in the design of the training program. Generally, knowledge of concepts precedes understanding. Application is aided by a thorough comprehension of the facts. Synthesis, analysis, and evaluation are dependent on an orderly procession through the levels. As a student, you might recognize that you have moved through these levels of learning in your academic life, with younger students being asked to recall and list, and those students in higher grades or in graduate programs being asked to evaluate.

ATTITUDES—THE HEART

A more precise label for this area of learning is the **affective domain**. Included in this category are attitudes, values, emotions, motivation, beliefs, and interests. These are emotional responses rather than intellectual ones. In most occupations, interest and motivation are critical to performance. In others, such as teaching and nursing, beliefs and values play a critical role in the style of work. In particular, organizations appear more concerned with employee attitudes, such as being a team player, and having concern for the customer. Given this climate, the discussion on the definition and measurement of attitudes is germane.

affective domain an area of learning that includes attitudes, values, emotions, motivation, beliefs, and interests

There are those, such as the behavioural theorists, who argue that attitudes cannot be observed and measured, and therefore cannot be learned (Skinner, 1968). See page 107 in Chapter 5 for a description of the conditioning theory within the behaviourist school. To change a person's behaviour, behaviourists would modify the incentives for desired performance, not the person's attitudes. For example, they would reward managers with praise and financial bonuses if managers promoted women into supervisory positions. Behaviourists would contend that the managerial attitude toward women was irrelevant and that results are the only variable of importance. (Some supervisors and parents embody this position when they state, "I don't care if you like it, just do it.")

Others argue that attitudes are the key components of performance (Rogers, 1969). They insist that attitudes must be modified before behaviour can change. Faced with the challenge of increasing the percentage of women supervisors, these psychologists would attempt to change the attitudes of managers through courses outlining the nature and effects of discrimination, and attempt to increase the sensitivity of managers to equity issues.

Both positions can be understood through the use of examples. We all know of people who were coerced into learning a new skill or attending classes in an area in which they were afraid or resistant, and these people then became converts, learning to like what they had been forced to learn. Examples abound of individuals who have completed courses designed to change their attitudes and who have returned more sensitive and willing to change their behaviour.

However, other examples can be cited of people who attended sensitivity or leadership training and did not modify their practices until management changed the rewards and punishments for inappropriate behaviour. Modifying attitudes is complex, and this controversy is not easily resolved.

Debate on the issue of changing attitudes also focuses on the reluctance of some employees to have their belief systems challenged. They would like to do the job and not be forced into training courses on empowerment and team building. Does the employer have a right to try to change people's beliefs and values?

Some argue that beliefs play a fundamental role in the effective operation of an organization. These people claim that organizations have a right, and even a responsibility, to change the attitudes of managers who believe, for example, that women can never be good supervisors because women are too emotional. But employees argue that they are there to do a job, not to have trainers tamper with their minds. They feel that they have a right to certain beliefs.

Organizations usually resolve this dilemma by arguing that certain attitude-change programs are in compliance with laws, such as employment-equity legislation. People can believe whatever they like, as long as their attitudes result in behaviour and performance that comply with laws such as those concerning human rights.

Obviously, this solution works for practices that are legislated, but it does not resolve the issue for programs that seek to analyze and change attitudes to relationships or openness to change. Critics have argued that managers (and organizations) should be sued for malpractice when they play games with employees, such as those found in the rock-climbing exercises of outdoor training (Zemke, 1978). Any course touching on personal-growth matters could be open to charges ranging from wasting time to harming managerial effectiveness. Indeed, in Atlantic Canada, a group of employees charged their employer with a violation of their rights. In this case, attendance at a course on self-actualization was compulsory. Employees claimed that the beliefs presented about the power of the self interfered with and contradicted their religious beliefs. The employees won and were no longer forced to attend company courses.

To legitimize attitude-change programs, organizations must learn to specify the objectives of these programs. Specifying the agenda will facilitate employees buying in to the programs. In this chapter, we assume that changing attitudes is a legitimate goal in some circumstances, and we provide a framework for the analysis of attitudinal objectives.

LEVELS OF AFFECTIVE LEARNING

1. *Receiving*. At this level, the learner is asked simply to participate in a learning experience. Remember the door-to-door sales representative who primes the customer by pleading, "Just let me demonstrate the product" or your mother imploring you to "Just try the broccoli." Implied in these statements is that after a person listens to information or observes products or demonstrations, he or she might then be more willing to move to the next step. Example: *The employee will listen to the presentation on the need to automate parts of his or her job.* At this level, the trainee is expected to pay attention but is not required to respond.

2. *Responding*. The next level requires a reaction of some kind. These responses could include the expression of an opinion (either positive or negative), or some demonstration of an emotional reaction ("Wow! Uchh!"). Example: *After watching a presentation on the need for robots in the workplace, the trainee will express an opinion about robots.* There is no commitment on the part of participants beyond an affective reaction of interest, enjoyment, and so on.

3. *Valuing*. This stage requires a trainee to express a commitment to the belief or activity. The person is asked to value the material learned and to act upon it. Example: *The employee will be able to identify obstacles and opportunities of automation.*

4. *Organization*. At this stage, the belief or value becomes part of a larger theory or system in the structuring of attitudes. The trainee does not simply believe in isolated values but is on the road to developing a comprehensive philosophy. The result is a complex value system. Example: *The employee will suggest three ways to improve other areas of his or her work through automation.* The key characterization here is the interrelationship of different values.

5. *Characterization*. At this stage, the belief system or philosophy is absorbed into a person's fundamental life beliefs and becomes a principal value for meaning in life. All or most actions will be grounded by the belief. The person is characterized by the value (e.g., she is a feminist; he is a real leader; they are Liberals). Example: *The trainee becomes an advocate for automation in improving work processes.*

The reader should now perceive the development of measurable objectives as a fundamental planning tool, not just in training but in business and personal areas.

This last step represents a philosophy or world view. This is the stage employees might fear and resent, particularly if characterization involves rejecting previously held belief systems. The new belief system, introduced and mandated by the organization, may run counter to values expressed by significant groups or people in the worker's life, such as the church or the family. The controversy surrounding the intrusion and pressure on employees to adopt certain beliefs is not easily resolved.

SKILLS—THE HANDS

psychomotor domain
an area of learning that includes physical skills, such as gross motor skills, dance movements, and nonverbal communication

The third area of learning concerns skills, the **psychomotor domain**. This domain includes physical skills such as the gross motor skills used in operating a saw or the fine motor skills used in drawing. Movements in dance or crafts could be included here. The portraying of emotions through bodily movements, such as the nonverbal communication found in social work or drama, would fall into this category. (Not all skills are in the physical, creative, or technical sectors. Managers need to learn physical skills such as the use of eye contact in negotiation and presentation skills.)

The subcategories in this area are:

1. *Perception.* The learner must first be aware of the tools or objects of learning, or the environment in which the psychomotor response is expected. The senses are alerted, and this forms the basis for the subsequent development of the skill. Example: *The apprentice chef will be able to select the 20 most important kitchen tools of a master chef.* Note that no physical activity is involved but that this level requires the use of the senses and is a prerequisite for the next level.

2. *Set.* A mental or physical set, or preparedness, is required before action is initiated. A mental set may include a visualization of a tennis stroke or a mental listing of the steps involved in preparing a soufflé. Physical preparedness may include standing in the proper position to receive a tennis serve or arriving at the playing field in uniform. Example: *The apprentice chef will be able to assemble the necessary equipment to prepare a cheese soufflé.*

3. *Guided response.* As its name suggests, this level of learning implies a dependency on the instructor to guide the learner through the motions required. The golf student may have the instructor demonstrate how to hold a golf club or the instructor may physically adjust the hands of the trainee on the club. The skill may be broken down into specific movements, which are practised independently while receiving appropriate feedback. Example: *The apprentice chef will model the steps used in making a soufflé, in the correct sequence, as demonstrated by the master chef.*

4. *Mechanism.* With repeated practice of the specific movements, the trainee will perform the task independently and proficiently. Through modelling, guidance, and feedback, the action becomes habitual. Example: *The apprentice chef will create a cheese soufflé.* Usually, this degree of achievement is required: the person will perform the task independently and proficiently.

5. *Complex overt response.* At this stage, the trainee can execute a series of skills, each one composed of specific movements. The result is a sequence or patterns of moves usually associated with the craft or sport. The skill is done without hesitation, and the sequences of skills are done efficiently and effectively. Example: *The apprentice chef plans a menu, buys the ingredients, and prepares and serves a gourmet meal for six.*

6. *Adaptation.* Conditions under which a skill is performed often change. Those players or performers with advanced skills can adapt or adjust their performance immediately. (Once, while this author was watching a play in London, England, the actor's dramatic knifing of an orange miscarried. The actor made up a line to accommodate the blunder, and the show went on.) In sports, movements by opponents make adaptation a valuable level of learning. Example: *The apprentice chef will be able adapt a menu designed for four to serve eight, and will be able to substitute at least three ingredients that are not available.* Varying a response according to changing conditions is the desired characteristic at this level.

7. *Origination.* The most creative skill level compels the trainee to generate new movements or actions. This level would include the writing of a play, the creation of a new style of negotiation, or the development of a new technique for teaching presentation skills. Example: *The apprentice chef will create an original recipe.*

These categories of learning objectives should cover most conditions in training and development, enabling the program developer to more accurately pinpoint the results expected.

CAUTIONS ABOUT LEARNING OBJECTIVES

New trainers might be tempted to write easily measurable objectives such as "the sales representative will be able to recall the six steps to closing a sale." The trainer can quite easily choose both a method and an evaluation system that guarantee that all students obtain 100 percent on a test. But, obviously, this is not what the sales manager wants. She wants the sales representatives to close sales and generate profits. The objective should be stated as a skills objective along the lines of: *In the field, the sales representatives will be able to close sales 30 percent of the time, by the second call. This will represent an improvement of 20 percent over present success rates.* We can then calculate the costs and benefits of the training.

The presentation of objectives in specific steps creates the impression that objectives can be isolated by domain and category. In real life, there is much overlap. For example, a trainer can be expected to learn to present a workshop on negotiation, using a negotiation video and role plays, so that all students participate. In this example, cognitive skills (negotiation principles), attitudinal skills (encouraging participation), and motor skills (operating a VCR) are all required. From a practical viewpoint, it is not necessary to isolate the categories in every instance.

OBJECTIONS TO THE USE OF OBJECTIVES

TIME

The development of measurable objectives takes time. This time could be spent convincing managers to buy into the training or in actually doing the training. Obviously, there is the hope that the use of objectives will save time. By stating clearly what we are hoping to accomplish, we will not waste time on other activities.

The amount of time involved in developing objectives is highly dependent on the level of detail required. Little time is required to think about and write: "list the three domains of learning." But a considerable amount of time is required to write objectives for a training session for a person with a mental disability learning to clean stores, for example. The activities of cleaning would have to be broken down into small and specific steps to accommodate the ability of the trainee. At the other end of the continuum, the difficulty of writing objectives for leadership training occurs because leadership effectiveness has never been usefully defined and measured. The trainer must spend a considerable amount of time defining leadership effectiveness at his or her company.

RIGIDITY

Critics of objectives argue that once goals are written, they are written in stone. This allows for no flexibility in the program to include unexpected learner interests or relevant current issues. In the program design, however, time can be built in for discussion of student interests and current issues. Trainers should also be alert to unexpected outcomes. Students may learn statistics and learn to hate statistics. If this is seen as an undesirable outcome, what aspects of the program can be changed?

STIFLING THE LEARNER

Students are told what to learn, and they memorize it and regurgitate it is the thrust of this argument. But as we have seen, the higher levels within the domains of learning encourage creativity and independent thinking on the part of the learner. Surely the evaluation of a research proposal or the creation of a new method to teach tennis represent highly creative and individual acts.

Some critics have obviously misunderstood the nature of objectives. It is true that you can give students easily accomplished objectives, such as to define role play and to name three circumstances for which role play is effective. But you can also solicit three novel ways to use role plays, or ask for the preparation of a role play using information from a recent work experience; this is not spoon-feeding students information.

SOME JOBS DON'T HAVE STANDARDS

If some jobs don't have standards of performance, then how are performance appraisals conducted? How do managers know if an employee is doing well? Does it matter if an employee's performance is good? Does it matter if the job exists? The first step is to define the job; from this, deficiencies in performance can be more accurately determined.

For example, in real life, professors mark original essays and managers rate performance without written standards. These standards exist in their minds; behavioural objectives simply make them explicit. We would argue that all jobs do indeed have standards.

TRIVIAL LEARNER BEHAVIOURS

This criticism is related to the objection cited above. Critics contend that minor and insignificant objectives are easiest to operationalize, with the result that really meaningful outcomes of education may be under emphasized (Popham, 1968).

However, the truth is that explicit objectives (with significant educational learner behaviours) make it far easier for educators and trainers to attend to important instructional outcomes. A trainer of managers might say that his or her goal is to make people better communicators, but in fact what he or she is asking them to do is to memorize key words like "active listening," without being active listeners.

DEHUMANIZING

Behaviour can be objectively, mechanistically measured; hence, there must be something dehumanizing about the measurement approach. Adults resist being measured and associate this with exams and tests. But there are sophisticated ways of measuring quality as well as quantity of learning. The process need not be dehumanizing, like true–false tests, but can be liberating and creative, such as making a presentation to colleagues.

UNDEMOCRATIC

Specifying in advance what we expect the learner to learn runs counter to a tradition of freedom of expression and democracy. In reply to this concern, we suggest that the trainer negotiate the objectives with the students, after a process of consultation. A needs analysis is an important part of this consultation.

Related to this democracy argument is the one that individual trainees should not have to conform to a group standard. Critics argue that adults are capable of self-diagnosis and are capable of assessing their own needs. Miller (1983) counters that trainees should negotiate with the program developers to ensure that the objectives do meet their needs. Involving the trainees at the needs analysis stage is important. Furthermore, the success of a training event increases when everyone agrees upon, or contracts for, the intended outcomes.

More important, however, is that education and training are not entirely, or even largely, open to negotiation. Neither governments nor corporations would want university students or new supervisors to define their goals entirely independent of the "authorities." Trainers and managers will always define what they want the learner to learn, more or less efficiently.

A related argument contends that rigid adherence to objectives eliminates the possibility of learning opportunities in the classroom. There is nothing preventing spontaneous discussions from contributing to student learning; objectives merely inform the instructor about whether these opportunities are diversions or irrelevant entertainment for the class (Popham, 1968).

THIS AIN'T LIFE

Trainers rarely specify their goals in terms of measurable learner behaviours, so let's be realistic. But there is a distinction between recognizing the status quo and applauding it.

Performance-based objectives may not be relevant to all types of training. Programs that develop leaders or creative thinkers may require broad objectives that are individualized and flexible. These objectives differ from performance-based objectives in that they can be customized to the individual, they may take a long time to show results, and the process is emphasized over the results (Stonehall, 1992).

ACCOUNTABILITY

With measurable objectives, trainers might be judged on their ability to produce results in learners rather than on the many other bases of competence. Objectives (and therefore trainers) can be measured, and trainers will be judged on their ability to attain these objectives. They should be.

Trainers should be judged on ends, not means. Some current indices of trainer effectiveness include: emotional reaction of audiences (jokes and stories help); the comfort level of the room; and the amount of free time during training. Trainers may even be judged on method; some trainees favour case studies or games and may dislike a trainer who uses computer-assisted instruction. Results should be the principal criterion of evaluation.

In summary, we believe that learning objectives play a fundamental role in the effective management of performance. The Training Today 2 box offers some summary suggestions about the preparation of these objectives.

SUMMARY

After reading this chapter, we hope that you will be able to list the levels of learning, be motivated to use them, and have the skills to do so. The preparation of learning objectives was discussed in detail using the framework of the cognitive domain, the affective domain, and the psychomotor domain. Concerns about the use of objectives were described.

KEY TERMS

affective domain   85
cognitive domain   83
condition   82
criterion   82

objective   80
performance   82
psychomotor domain   88

EXERCISES

1. Identify a skill that your roommate, partner, or parent would like to acquire. Some examples might be to use a particular software package for the computer, to use the cleaning cycle on the oven, or to gain a better understanding of existentialism. Study the task and develop learning objectives in each of the three categories—knowledge, skills, and attitude. Exchange

these with a student partner, who will assess them in terms of the criteria outlined within this chapter (measurable performance, using who, when, where, and how criteria).

2. Read the following objectives and re-write them so that they conform to the standards of performance, condition, and criterion outlined in this chapter:

- The trainer will spend 30 minutes discussing time-management tips.

- The trainees will be able to manage their time more effectively.

- The purpose of the seminar is to teach time-management techniques.

- After attending the course, employees will be able to make lists and put let-ters beside the items on the list, enabling them to manage time more effectively.

3. Phone, write, or e-mail any training company that is distributing brochures or pamphlets that describe the courses they are offering. You might even check the continuing education department of your own campus. Using the checklist of suggestions found in the Training Today 2 box, evaluate the goals of the training programs. Make a list of examples of poorly written objectives (the don't side), and then prepare examples of well-written objectives.

CASE: CHANGING EMPLOYEE MINDS

For many employees, the chance to attend a training course is a wonderful opportunity. Sask Tel employees were excited about a six-week training course to prepare them to be part of a team learning about process re-engineering to redesign business processes and improve company performance. Instead of re-engineering training, these employees were part of a social engineering experiment after which half of the 24 participants required psychological counselling or stress leave. The employees claimed they were brainwashed. The union claims that this training program was one more reason why Sask Tel had its first general provincewide strike in 88 years.

What went wrong? The company included this training as part of a two-million-dollar corporate makeover to make it more competitive. At the outset, the managers believed that they were simply implementing courses that would tap the potential of employees and enable them to become more productive. Sask Tel was not the only company trying to capitalize on the human potential movement, which meant designing ways to tap the values and beliefs of employees to increase performance effectiveness. But the techniques of changing belief systems are not well established, and it is more an art than a science. Other Canadian firms found themselves unknowingly buying training programs from religious cults. Trans Alta paid a consulting company $24 million to train 1500 employees. These employees were subjected to daily sayings that ended with employees saying "amen," and to supervisors conducting daily mood checks so that inappropriate emotions could be monitored and changed. Public criticisms of employees were encouraged in an effort to improve performance, but these public humiliations left employees in tears, and some quit the company. After employees leaked news of this abusive treatment to CBC-TV, the CEO placed ads in newspapers, and sent letters to all workers apologizing for their distress.

The re-engineering program at Sask Tel proved more damaging than that at Trans Alta. Windows were papered over to prevent people seeing in or out. Employees were discouraged from communicating with each other. There was a lot of jargon (terms such as "blue-skying," "thinking outside the box"), and employees felt that they were trapped in a 1984 Orwellian nightmare. The original program, scheduled to last six weeks, was continually extended. The consultants were highly aggressive, and employees were told to play the game or get out. Fearing for the jobs, the employees played the game, at great personal costs.

Source: Kay, E. (1996, November). Trauma in real life. *The Globe and Mail: Report on Business Magazine*, pp. 82–92.

Questions

1. Training managers often listen to sales pitches of consultants and training companies. They may find themselves buying questionable training programs. Describe how the preparation of objectives could have prevented these disasters. What other measures can companies undertake to protect themselves from these situations?
2. These training sessions were designed to change employee's attitudes. Does management have the right to do this? Under what circumstances? What are the legal and ethical issues? Should employees give informed consent? Do these types of training programs violate individual rights?

REFERENCES

Bloom, B. (Ed.). (1956). *Taxonomy of educational objectives: The cognitive domain.* New York: David McKay.

———. (1964). *Taxonomy of education objectives: The affective domain.* New York: David McKay.

Cranton, P. (1989). *Planning instruction for adult learners.* Toronto: Wall and Thompson.

Kibler, R.J., Barker, L.L. & Miles, D.T. (1970). *Behavioral objectives and instruction.* Boston: Allyn and Bacon, Inc.

Laird, D. (1985). *Approaches to training and development* (2nd ed.). Reading, MA: Addison-Wesley.

McNeil, J.D. (1966). Concomitant of using behavioural objectives in assessment of teacher effectiveness. Paper presented at the American Educational Research Association Convention, Chicago, IL.

Mager, R.F. (1975). *Preparing instructional objectives* (2nd ed.). Belmont, CA: Fearon.

Mager, R.F., & J. McCann. (1961). *Learner controlled instruction.* Palo Alto, CA: Varian and Associates.

Miles, D.T., Kibler, R.J., & L.E. Pettigrew. (1967). The effects of study questions on college students' test performance. *Psychology in the Schools 4*, 25–26.

Miller, G.V. (1983). Individualizing learning objectives. In Baird, L.S., Schneider, C.E., & Laird, D.E. (Eds.), *The Training and Development Sourcebook.* Amherst, MA: Human Resource Development Press.

Nadler, L. (1990). *Designing training programs: The critical events model.* Reading, MA: Addison-Wesley.

Overmeyer-Day & G. Benson. (1996). Training success stories. *Training and Development* (June), p. 24–29.

Popham, W.J. (1968). Probing the validity of arguments against behavioural goals. Paper presented at the annual American Educational Research Association Conference, Chicago, IL.

Rogers, C.R. (1969). *Freedom to learn.* Columbus, OH: Charles E. Merrill.

Skinner, B.F. (1968). *The technology of teaching.* New York: Appleton Century-Crofts.

———. (1974). *About behaviorism.* New York: Alfred A. Knopf.

Stonehall, L. (1992). The case for more flexible objectives. *Training and Development* (August).

Zemke, R. (1978). Personal growth training. *Training Magazine* 15 (5).

5

....

PROGRAM
DESIGN

CHAPTER GOALS

In the previous two chapters, we outlined the process of identifying training needs and the development of training objectives. The next step in the training and development process is the actual design of training programs. This chapter incorporates data from the needs analysis and training objectives to produce a blueprint for the design of a training program or course. Proper program design is important for four reasons. First, a competently prepared training plan will make the task of competing for funding easier. Second, a good plan will enable training activity to be directed toward real training problems, not symptoms of problems. Third, the planning document will ensure that the problems under consideration can be solved by training and not some other intervention or method. Fourth, good planning leads to enhanced credibility with line managers. All of these factors combined will help the training department implement and deliver sound training programs.

After reading this chapter, you should be able to

*   describe the 10 steps of program design

....

- discuss the factors to consider when deciding to purchase or design a training program
- understand the process of deciding on the content for a training program
- identify the skills and characteristics of effective trainers
- explain conditioning theory, expectancy theory, goal setting theory, and social learning theory and their implications for the design of training programs
- describe the learning principles and how they can influence learning, retention, and transfer of training
- describe the factors to consider when deciding who should attend a training program
- summarize the difference between on-the-job and off-the-job training methods
- describe the types of materials, supplies, and equipment required for a training program
- identify the factors to consider when choosing a training site
- summarize the information that should be included in a lesson plan
- discuss the events of instruction and the problems and solutions of training delivery

INTRODUCTION TO TRAINING PROGRAM DESIGN

The design of a training program involves several phases. These phases are sequential, with the output of one phase becoming the input to the next. The first two of these phases—needs analysis and setting objectives—have been carefully outlined already. At this point in the training and development process, a number of critical activities and decisions need to be made that revolve around transforming training objectives into an actual training program.

In particular, the following issues and activities need to be addressed during the program design stage:

1. Decide whether to purchase or design a training program.
2. Determine the training content.
3. Decide on a trainer for the program.
4. Select the trainees to attend the program.
5. Decide on the training methods.
6. Identify the required training materials and equipment.
7. Choose a training site.

8. Schedule the training program.

9. Prepare a lesson plan.

10. Deliver the training program.

In the remainder of this chapter, each of the 10 steps outlined here will be discussed. To create some realism in the presentation of each of these issues, we will use an example of an organization called Vandalais Department Stores that wants to train all of its human resources staff on how to conduct structured employment interviews. The company is a large retail chain with 50 stores across Canada. As a result of a serious performance problem of the sales associates in many of the stores, the company conducted a needs assessment, which indicated that unstructured employment interviews were being used to make hiring decisions and were the root of the problem. As a result, many unqualified employees were being hired and then fired. Because it is well known that structured employment interviews have high validity (Pulakos & Schmitt, 1995; Campion, Palmer, & Campion, 1997), the company decided that it must start using structured interviews to hire future sales associates, and that the current staff in human resources will need to be trained on how to conduct structured employment interviews. Based on the needs assessment, the following training objective was written: *Employees in human resources will be able to conduct structured employment interviews during the selection process. Ninety percent of new hires will receive above-average performance ratings after six and twelve months on the job, and less than 1 percent will be terminated due to poor performance after one year.*

One of the first issues that must be addressed is whether or not the training program should be purchased or designed. We look at that next.

THE DECISION TO PURCHASE OR DESIGN A TRAINING PROGRAM

Once it has been determined that a training program is an appropriate course of action to manage a performance problem, the human resource professional faces a make or buy decision. Many private training companies and consultants in Canada offer an extensive array of courses on general topics such as computer training and customer service. In many cases, it is more economical for an organization to purchase these materials, packaged in professional formats, than to develop the materials themselves, which in many cases will be used only once or twice. For example, most HR managers do not design training courses in basic skills; they form alliances with educational institutions, community colleges, or private organizations that specialize in developing and delivering basic skills training programs (Hays, 1999). Organizations also prefer to use outside consultants for sexual harassment training (Ganzel, 1998).

The advantages of packaged programs are high quality, immediate delivery, ancillary services (tests, videos), the potential to customize the package to the organization, benefits from others' implementation experience, extensive testing, and often less expense than internally developed programs (Nadler & Nadler, 1990).

Training programs developed internally by an organization also have some advantages including security and confidentiality, use of the organization's language, incorporation of the organization's values, use of internal content expertise, understanding of the specific target audience and organization, and the pride and credibility of having a customized program (Nadler and Nadler, 1990).

Given the pros and cons of both alternatives, how does a training manager decide to purchase or design a training program? Obviously, one of the most important factors to consider is the cost of each alternative. A cost–benefit analysis would be necessary to determine the best option. Some types of training programs will be much more costly to design than to purchase. However, there are other factors that should also be considered in addition to cost.

For example, does the human resource department have the time and expertise to design a training program? Designing a training program from scratch requires expertise in many areas such as training methods and principles and theories of learning. If the human resource department does not have this expertise in-house then they will need to purchase all or part of a training program. As well, developing a training program is a time-consuming endeavour. Unless a human resource department has a training function and training personnel or is otherwise well staffed, it may not have the time to design or deliver training programs.

Time is also a factor in terms of how soon the organization wants to begin training. Given the amount of time required to design a new training program, if there is a need or desire to begin training as soon as possible then the organization will need to purchase a training program. In effect, the sooner that the organization wants to begin training, the less likely there will be sufficient time to design a new training program.

Another important consideration is the number of employees who will need to be trained and the extent to which future employees will also receive training. If a relatively small number of employees require training, then it is probably not worthwhile to design an entire training program. However, if a large number of current employees need to receive training as well as future employees, then designing a new training program from scratch makes more sense. In other words, to the extent that the training program will be used for many employees in both the short- and long-term, a decision to design the program is more favourable.

Although we have been referring to the purchase of an entire training program, it is important to realize that purchasing can involve buying particular training materials such as a video package or buying an entire training program that is specially designed for the organization. As well, a consultant could be hired to design and deliver a training program or it can be delivered by persons within the organization once it has been designed by a consultant. Organizations can also purchase off-the-shelf training programs that are already designed and contain all the materials required to deliver a training program.

Finally, returning to the opening case, because the organization plans to train all current and future human resources staff in all regions of the country, they have decided to design a training program with the help of two human resource professors. There are currently 15 regional offices with three to five staff in the HR department in each office, all of whom will need to receive the training.

THE TRAINING CONTENT

Once a decision has been made to design a training program, decisions must be made about the training content. This is a crucial stage as one wants to be sure that the training content matches the training needs and objectives. The importance of this has been noted by Campbell (1988) who states, "by far the highest-priority question for designers, users, and investigators of training is, What is to be learned? That is, what (specifically) should a training program try to accomplish, and what should the training content be?" (p. 188).

To understand the importance of this issue, consider an organization that sells dental equipment and supplies. Although the company regularly offers new products, they do not sell very well. The reason appears to be because the sales force concentrates on repeat sales of more common supplies and materials. There are a number of reasons why this might be the case. For example, the sales force might not be sufficiently informed about the new products or they might not have the skills required to sell them. Other reasons could be a lack of motivation or an attitude problem. The point is that the content of a training program can be directed toward any one or more of these areas. Obviously, designing a training program to inform the sales force about the new products will not be very effective if what they are lacking are sales skills. Getting the content right is one of the most important stages in training design.

You should have a good idea of the nature of the training content from the needs assessment and the training objectives. This is another reason why it is so important to conduct a thorough needs assessment prior to designing a training program. As well, employees' current levels of knowledge and skills can be compared to the organization's desired levels as indicated by the performance goals or objectives. The gap between the two represents the organization's training needs and determines the precise content of the training course. According to Donald Kirkpatrick (1994), trainers should ask themselves, "What topics should be presented to meet the needs and accomplish the objectives?" (p. 11). The answers to this question should help in identifying the content to include in a training program.

However, even if one knows, for example, that employees have insufficient knowledge of how to conduct structured employment interviews, it still remains to be determined what content will be used in the training program. That is, we still need to translate training objectives into training content and to also determine the sequence in which the content will be learned (Campbell, 1988). It is not sufficient to simply say that the training content should focus on structured interviewing.

Being more precise about training content can occur in a number of ways. One of the most common and effective ways to identify training content is to consult with subject-matter experts who are knowledgable in a particular area and know the topic well enough that they can specify the training content (Campbell, 1988). For example, to determine the content of a training program to fulfil the training objective regarding structured employment interviews, one can consult with human resource professionals, consultants, or professors. It is also possible that some members of the organization's human resource department will have some knowledge about structured employment interviews. On the basis of the subject-matter experts' judgments one can identify the content required to achieve the training objective.

A second source of training content is the research and theory that can be found in the academic and practitioner literature. In the case of structured employment interviews, there are dozens of articles and research papers on how to design and conduct structured interviews.

A third possibility would be to purchase an off-the-shelf training program on structured employment interviews. This would likely include a lesson plan, an instructor's guide, training materials and exercises, and perhaps a videotape. Whichever of these sources are used, it is important to realize that ultimately a judgment will have to be made about what content will best fulfil the training needs and objectives. This decision will not always be easy. For example, in the case of employment interviews, there are many different ways to conduct a structured interview.

Returning to the training program on structured employment interviews, a good place to start would be the substantial literature on interviewing. For example, in a review of structured interviews, Campion, Palmer, and Campion (1997) identified the following 15 ways that employment interviews can be structured to enhance the content and evaluation process of the interview:

1. Base questions on a job analysis.
2. Ask exactly the same questions of each candidate.
3. Limit prompting, follow-up questioning, and elaboration on questions.
4. Use better types of questions.
5. Use longer interviews or more questions.
6. Control ancillary information.

7. Do not allow questions from candidates until after the interview.

8. Rate each answer or use multiple scales.

9. Use detailed anchored rating scales.

10. Take detailed notes.

11. Use multiple interviewers.

12. Use same interviewer(s) across all candidates.

13. Do not discuss candidates or answers with other interviewers.

14. Provide extensive interviewing training.

15. Use statistical rather than clinical prediction.

This information can be used in part as the content for our training program. However, even with this much detail, we still need to decide on the type of structured interview or interview questions. There are a number of different types of structured interviews. Two of the best known types are the experience-based and the situational interview. The main difference between them is the nature of the questions. Experience-based interviews ask questions about past job and life experiences that are job-relevant. For example, applicants are typically asked how they handled situations in the past that are similar to those they will face on the job. In contrast, the situational interview asks applicants to respond to questions about how they would handle or manage hypothetical job-related situations or "what if" types of questions. Although research has found both types of structured interviews to have higher validity than unstructured interviews, a recent study comparing the two types of interviews found that the validity of the experience-based interview for predicting job performance was higher (Pulakos & Schmitt, 1995).

Based on this information, the company decided that they will use experience-based structured interviews. They hired two professors of human resources to conduct a job analysis and to design an experience-based interview to hire sales associates. They also decided that the content of the training program will consist of information on structured interviews based on a number of the points identified by Campion et al. (1997). In particular, trainees will be trained to conduct structured employment interviews according to the following learning behaviours:

1. Ask exactly the same questions of each candidate.

2. Limit prompting, follow-up questioning, and elaboration on questions.

3. Use experience-based interview questions.

4. Do not allow questions from candidates until after the interview.

5. Rate each interview answer using the scales for each question.

6. Take detailed notes.

7. Use statistical rather than clinical prediction.

Now that the content of the training program has been determined, a *lesson* objective can be written, keeping in mind that the *training* objective is the overall objective of the training program. A more specific lesson objective is as follows: *Employees in human resources will be able to conduct the experience-based structured employment interview for the sales associate position and correctly perform the seven key behaviours.*

Now the trainer for the training program must be chosen.

THE TRAINER

Who should be the trainer? At first, this might seem like a trivial question. After all, isn't this the job of the human resource department or the training director? In some cases the answer is yes, but in many training situations the answer to this question depends on a number of important factors.

First, it is important to realize the importance of a good trainer. Regardless of how well a training program is designed, the success of a program rests in large part on the trainer. In other words, no matter how good the training program is, if the trainer is ineffective the program will suffer.

What then are the qualities of a good trainer? This question should be easy for students to answer if they consider the courses they have enjoyed and those that they found less memorable. One of the first things that comes to mind is probably the extent to which the instructor was knowledgable about the course material. This is usually referred to as subject-matter expertise. A trainer should be well versed if not an expert on the topic or content area being taught. Not only will trainees learn more, but the trainer will be perceived as more credible. Very often those persons who conduct training in an organization do so because they have expertise in a particular area.

Students also know, perhaps all too well, that no matter how well informed or knowledgable the instructor, a course can still be inadequate to the extent that the instructor is not very good at delivering the material. In addition to subject matter expertise, good trainers must also have good verbal or communication skills, interpersonal skills, organizing and planning skills, and so on. In other words, the trainer must have the skills necessary to be able to deliver the training material and content so that it is understandable to trainees.

A third category of trainer characteristics is the ability to make the material interesting rather than dull and boring. Students probably have had instructors who knew the material and were able to deliver it, but all the same, they did not make it very interesting. A good trainer should also be enthusiastic and excited about the training material and capable of arousing the interest and motivation of trainees.

One of the difficulties in choosing a trainer is that, on the one hand, very often those individuals who have the subject-matter expertise required to deliver a training program do not have the other skills and characteristics of a good trainer. On the other hand, those who are skilled trainers such as members of human resource departments often do not have the subject-matter expertise to conduct many training programs in their organizations.

One solution to this problem has been to teach subject-matter experts how to become effective trainers. These programs are known as *train the trainer* and focus on the skills that are required to be an effective trainer. As described in the Training Today 1 box, with the increasing use of technology in the workplace, more subject-matter experts are being asked to become trainers. In addition to learning how to communicate and to develop interest and enthusiasm, trainers also need to know how people learn. In this regard, a number of learning theories and learning principles have important implications for the design and delivery of training programs. However, before discussing learning, let's just note that the two human resource professors who designed the experience-based employment interview have been chosen to be the trainers for the structured employment interview training program. This is because they have subject-matter expertise, they are obviously experienced instructors, and they are enthusiastic about their work. They also are knowledgable about our next topic, learning and learning theories.

TRAINING TODAY 1   Training Subject-Matter Experts to be Trainers

Because of their technical expertise, an increasing number of employees are being drafted into the role of trainer. Organizations, especially smaller ones without training departments, have long relied on their resident experts to teach others to program their voice mail, send faxes, and log on to their computers. But as technology has transformed office equipment into souped-up vehicles on multilane electronic autobahns, it's not always possible to navigate just by reading the manual and relying on intuition.

Just because a person has crafted countless PowerPoint presentations or designed award-winning Web pages doesn't mean he or she will be able to teach others to do the same. Often, organizations assume that teaching should come naturally to employees who know their stuff and have spent countless hours sitting in classes themselves. "Unfortunately, many companies have said all one needs to be a good technical instructor is subject matter expertise," says Michael Nolan, president of Friesen, Kaye and Associates, an Ottawa firm that works with nontrainers or subject matter experts (SMEs) who find themselves having to teach what they know to others. "It goes much farther than that. They have to have other skills that they haven't developed in the environment in which they've worked." They have to understand, for example, how adults learn, what to do when participants behave like mules, and how not to feel as though they've been caught in a klieg light when someone asks them a question they can't answer.

Nolan predicts SMEs won't replace professional trainers—even in the IT field. But when these experts are called on to share their knowledge, they need support. That's where the training department comes in. "Instructors in the training department can provide a fabulous experience by coaching and mentoring," he says.

Excerpted from Kiser, K. (1999, April). When those who "do," teach. *Training*, 36(4), 42–48.

WHAT IS LEARNING?

learning the process of acquiring knowledge and skills and a change in individual behaviour as a result of some experience

While training is the focus of this book, it is important to keep in mind that what we are really trying to accomplish through the process of training is learning. So what is learning? **Learning** is the process of acquiring knowledge and skills. It can also be thought of as a process in which an individual's behaviour is changed through experience (Hinrichs, 1976). For our purposes, that experience is training and development. Learning occurs then "when one experiences a new way of acting, thinking, or feeling, finds the new pattern gratifying or useful, and incorporates it into the repertoire of behaviours" (Hinrichs, 1976, p. 833). When a behaviour has been learned, it can be thought of as a skill.

What exactly do people learn? Recall from Chapter 4 that there are three domains of learning: cognitive (knowledge), affective (attitudes), and psychomotor (skills). Within each domain, there are levels that can be arranged hierarchically—the first level must be mastered before subsequent levels can be learned. Another important classification of learning outcomes that is often referred to in the training literature was developed by Gagne (1984). According to Gagne (1984), skills or learning outcomes can be classified in five general categories: (1) *verbal information* (facts, knowledge, principles, and information or what is known as declarative knowledge), (2) *intellectual skills* (concepts, rules, and procedures), (3) *cognitive strategies* (the application of information and techniques), (4) *motor skills* (coordination and execution of physical movements that involve the use of muscles), and (5) *attitudes* (preferences and internal states associated with one's beliefs and feelings), which are considered to be the most difficult domain to influence through training (Zemke, 1999).

Now that we have described what people learn, let's look at how people learn.

HOW DO PEOPLE LEARN?

Researchers have studied learning and have developed a body of knowledge and theories about the learning process. Theories are very important because they allow practitioners to understand how something works or why it happens. Theories represent an attempt to organize knowledge so that we can use it in a variety of situations. For years, researchers have deplored the lack of integration of learning theories into training design (Goldstein, 1991; This & Lippet, 1983). Clearly, trainers should have at least some understanding of learning theories.

Intuitively, most trainers use some guidelines derived from learning theories. For example, those charged with influencing behaviour or performance recognize the value of rewarding good performance. This intuition is substantiated by numerous experiments conducted under the auspices of the behaviourist school of learning. To validate many of the recommendations contained here, short descriptions of the most important learning theories are presented.

THE CONDITIONING PERSPECTIVE

Researchers such as Pavlov, Thorndike, Skinner, and Hull all approached learning as a process of association. Behaviourist B.F. Skinner (1953) defined learning as a relatively permanent change in behaviour in response to a particular stimulus or set of stimuli. The behaviourist school believes that learning is a result of rewards or punishments, which follow a response to a stimulus. In this trial-and-error approach, a stimulus or cue would be followed by a response, which is then reinforced and strengthens the likelihood that the response will occur again. For example, behaviourists argue that similar principles are at work when an adult submits an innovative proposal and is praised, and when a pigeon pecks a red dot and is given a pellet of food. When a response is reinforced through food, money, attention, or anything pleasurable, then the response is more likely to be repeated. If there is no reinforcement, then, over time, the response will cease. If the response is punished, then it will not be repeated. The conditioning framework is illustrated in the following diagram.

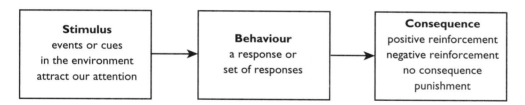

Negative reinforcement is the removal of a negative outcome after an act. To illustrate this concept, think of an alarm clock ringing. When you turn it off, the noise stops (the negative consequence is removed). Similarly, think of your course instructor chewing out the class for not participating and threatening to start picking students at random to answer questions. When students begin to participate more, the instructor stops chewing them out and threatening to choose students at random (the negative consequence is removed). It is important to realize that this is not the same as punishment in which one receives a negative consequence for doing something undesirable. In the example above, a desirable behaviour is being learned and increased (i.e., class participation) by a negative reinforcer that is removed when the desirable behaviour occurs.

Managers and trainers use conditioning principles when they attempt to influence employee behaviour. Linking desired complex behaviour to pleasurable consequences is based on three connected concepts: *shaping, chaining,* and *generalization.*

Shaping is extremely important for learning complex behaviour. Imagine trying to train a dog to fetch the newspaper from the front gate every morning.

shaping the reinforcement of each step in a process until it is mastered

You could wait forever for this response to occur naturally so that you could then reinforce it with a dog biscuit. A more efficient method for teaching this behaviour is to reward the dog in small steps (give food as the dog moves toward the gate, then as he approaches the exact spot, then sniffs the paper, and so on). Shaping refers to the reinforcement of each step in the process until it is mastered, and then withdrawing the reinforcer until the next step is mastered. Role plays and behaviour modelling make extensive use of this concept, rewarding trainees for the acquisition of separate skills performed sequentially.

chaining the reinforcement of entire sequences of a task

Chaining is the second important concept. Ultimately, what we want the dog to do is to get the newspaper from the front gate every morning. During shaping, the dog learns each separate step of this task and is reinforced for each successive step. The goal, however, is for the dog to learn to combine each step and perform the entire response. This combination is what chaining involves, and it is accomplished by reinforcing entire sequences of the task and eventually reinforcing only the complete task after each of the steps have been learned.

generalization the conditioned response occurs in circumstances different from those during acquisition

The third important concept is **generalization**: the conditioned response occurs in circumstances different from those during acquisition (Pearce, 1987). The learning process in a classroom is kept deliberately simple. All extraneous factors are removed so the trainee can concentrate on learning a skill such as negotiation. The trainer then changes the learning environment to better reflect reality. For example, the trainer can change a role play script from negotiating with one's supervisor on the deadline for a project to negotiating to buy a car. The trainee learns to generalize the skill from a simple, controlled environment to a different, more difficult one. This is the goal of trainers—that learning acquired during training will be imported into and used in the work environment.

When applied to training, the conditioning perspective suggests that trainees should be encouraged and reinforced throughout the training process. In other words, they should be reinforced for attending training, learning the training material, and applying it on their job. Based on the conditioning perspective, we would expect training to be more effective to the extent that trainees are reinforced for these behaviours.

COGNITIVE THEORIES OF LEARNING

The cognitive perspective has some similarities to the conditioning perspective. The principles of both build upon precepts of stimuli and consequences. However, cognitive theorists believe that cognitive processes (thoughts, feelings, observations) play an important role in learning. They argue that learning would be a slow and error-prone if everyone had to attend to cues, act, and then be reinforced. Learning to drive a car or deal with a violent client might be activities too dangerous to even begin. Instead, much learning occurs through cognitive processes such as imitation and modelling. We observe the actions of others, paying attention to the reinforcing or punishing outcomes of their behaviour. We are conscious of copying the modelled behaviour and the consequences that we can expect to receive. Considerable research has demonstrated that people observe and reproduce the actions and attitudes of models (Luthans & Davis, 1983).

Three of the most important cognitive theories of learning with implications for the design of training programs are expectancy theory, goal setting theory, and social learning theory.

EXPECTANCY THEORY

Expectancy theory (Vroom, 1964) has its basis in studies of motivation and is a more cognitive approach to conditioning. According to expectancy theory, the energy that a person directs toward an activity is a direct result of the following three components:

1. The individual's *expectancy* (subjective probability) that effort will lead to the achievement of the training goal or activity.

2. The *instrumentality* (subjective likelihood) that attainment of the activity will result in consequences or reinforcers.

3. The *valence* (subjective attractiveness) of the consequences to the individual.

The expectancy theory linkages can be written as the following equation:

$$\text{Effort} = \text{Expectancy} \times (\text{Instrumentality} \times \text{Valence})$$

In other words, effort or motivation is a function of people's beliefs that they can achieve a particular level of performance, and this will lead to consequences that are attractive to them.

The implications of expectancy theory for training are straightforward: trainees must believe that they are capable of learning the training material and achieving the training objective(s) (expectancy); learning the training material and accomplishing the training objectives will result in consequences (instrumentality) that are desirable (valence) to trainees. Simply put, you are more likely to learn something if you believe you can learn it and that you will be rewarded with something you value once it has been learned.

GOAL SETTING THEORY

Goal setting theory is based on the idea that people's intentions are a good predictor of their behaviour. According to the theory, goals are motivational because they direct people's efforts and energies and lead to the development of strategies to help them reach their goal. For goals to be motivational, however, they must have a number of characteristics.

First, goals must be specific in terms of their level and time frame. General goals that lack this type of specificity tend not to be motivational. Second, goals must be challenging to be motivational. Goals should not be so easy that they require little effort to achieve, and they should not be so difficult that they are impossible to reach. Third, goals must be accompanied by feedback so that it is possible to know how well one is doing and how close one is to reaching a goal. Finally, for goals to be motivational, people must be committed to them (Locke & Latham, 1990).

Goal setting theory has important implications for the design of training programs. Prior to training, trainees should have specific and challenging goals for learning the training material, and they should be provided with feedback during and after the training program so that they know if they have accomplished their learning goals. Setting specific and challenging goals should improve trainees' motivation to learn as well as their performance on the learned task.

SOCIAL LEARNING THEORY

According to social learning theory, people learn by observing the behaviour of others, making choices about different courses of action to pursue, and by managing their own behaviour in the process of learning (Bandura, 1986). In other words, social learning theory involves observation, self-efficacy, and self-management.

People learn by **observation**. They observe the actions of others and the consequences of those actions. If the person being observed (the role model) is credible and knowledgable, their behaviour is more likely to be imitated. The imitation will occur particularly if the role model is reinforced for the behaviour. Junior trainees watch the intense work hours of the senior staff. They then work the same long hours, in the expectation that they too will be rewarded with promotions. As you can see, this combines some elements of expectancy theory with behaviourist theory. But there are four additional elements that are critical for observational learning to take place: attention, retention, reproduction, and reinforcement.

Learners must first attend to the behaviour (i.e., must be aware of the skills that are observable). They must remember what they observed, somehow coding it in their own repertoire so that they can recall the skills. They must then try out the skill (i.e., try to reproduce it). As you have probably experienced, watching someone conduct a job interview does not mean that you can do the interview exactly the same way. If the reproduction results in positive outcomes (i.e., reinforcement), then the learner is likely to retain the new skills. Many training videos use social learning theory concepts to model the desired behaviour.

While observation may provide the observer with information necessary to imitate the modelled behaviour, we know that people do not always attempt to do the things that they observe other people doing. For example, a novice skier might watch his friends skillfully make their way down a steep hill but refuse to follow suit. This is because he might not have the confidence or the belief that he will be able to do it. Such beliefs are known as **self-efficacy** and refer to judgments that people have about their ability to successfully perform a specific task. Self-efficacy is a cognitive belief that is task specific, as in the

observation learning by observing the actions of others and the consequences

self-efficacy judgments that people have about their ability to successfully perform a specific task

example of the skier's confidence that he can ski down a steep hill. The novice skier might have low self-efficacy to ski down the hill but very high self-efficacy that he can get an "A" in his training course!

So what factors influence a person's self-efficacy? Self-efficacy is influenced by four sources of information. In order of importance they are: task performance, observation, verbal persuasion and social influence, and one's physiological or emotional state (Bandura, 1997). The self-efficacy of the skier can be strengthened not only by observing his friends' behaviour, but also by their encouragement that he can make it down the hill, his feelings of comfort and relaxation rather than fear and anxiety, and most important, his own successful attempts at skiing down the hill.

Self-efficacy has been shown to have a strong effect on people's attitudes, emotions, and behaviour in many areas of human functioning. Self-efficacy influences the activities people choose to perform, the amount of effort and persistence they devote to a task, affective and stress reactions, and performance outcomes (Bandura, 1997). Self-efficacy is also a key factor in training. Research has shown that the effectiveness of many training programs is partly due to the strengthening of trainees' self-efficacy to perform the training task (Saks, 1997; Haccoun & Saks, 1998).

The third component of social learning theory is called **self-management**. The previous theories we have discussed take the position that an individual's behaviour is regulated by external rewards and punishments. However, it is also possible for people to control and manage their own behaviour through a series of internal processes that enables them to structure and motivate their behaviour. These internal processes involve observing one's own behaviour as well as the behaviour of others, setting performance goals, practising new and desired behaviours, keeping track of one's progress, and rewarding oneself for goal achievement (Bandura, 1986).

self-management
managing one's own behaviour through a series of internal processes

Self-management has been found to be related to cognitive, affective, and behavioural outcomes (Bandura, 1986) and to be an important method of training. For example, Frayne and Latham (1987) conducted a study in which employees received self-management training to increase their job attendance. The results indicated that, compared to a group that did not receive the training, employees who received self-management training had higher self-efficacy for attending work and increased job attendance. In a follow-up study, Latham and Frayne (1989) found that these benefits continued up to nine months after the training. Several other studies have also demonstrated that self-management training leads to improvements in skill acquisition and maintenance (Gist, Stevens, & Bavetta, 1991).

Social learning theory has important implications for the design of training programs. In particular, trainee learning can be improved by providing trainees with models who demonstrate how to perform a training task; by strengthening trainee self-efficacy for successfully learning and performing the training task; and by teaching trainees to regulate and manage their performance of the training task.

LEARNING PRINCIPLES

Other important considerations in the design of training programs are principles of learning. These principles are important because they have been shown to affect trainees' learning and retention of training material (Baldwin & Ford, 1988). As well, because practice is necessary in the acquisition of new skills (Hinrichs, 1976), it is important for the trainer to understand how to incorporate practice into the design of training programs. The conditions of practice include: active practice, massed or distributed training, whole or part training, overlearning, task sequencing, and knowledge of results.

active practice
providing trainees with opportunities to practise performing a training task

One of the most important conditions of practice is known as **active practice**. A student who practices answering possible exam questions learns more than someone who just reads the text book. A manager would learn more about interviewing by actually conducting a mock interview than by listening to a lecture on interviewing. In general, both adults and children learn by doing. Training programs should include opportunities for active practice.

massed versus distributed training
how the segments of a training program are divided and whether the training is conducted in a single session (massed) or is divided into several sessions with breaks or rest periods between them (distributed)

Practice is more effective when practice periods are spread over time, rather than massed together (Baldwin and Ford, 1988). **Massed versus distributed training** has to do with how the segments of a training program are divided. Massed practice, or cramming, is practice with virtually no rest periods, such as when the training is conducted in one single session instead of being divided into several sessions with breaks or rest periods between them. Students might argue that they can succeed on an exam for which they have crammed, but research shows that memory loss after cramming is greater than if a student had studied over several weeks (Goldstein, 1993). Furthermore, organizations would prefer that trainees retain material over many months, rather than just knowing it for the course test or simulation. Research has shown that material that was learned under distributed practice is retained longer (Baldwin & Ford, 1988). Trainers teaching a new skill, such as negotiations, could increase learning by spacing the training and practices over a week of two-hour sessions, rather than cramming it into an eight-hour day. Distributed practice is most effective for trainees with little or no experience and when the rest periods are shorter early on but longer later in training (Bass & Vaughn, 1969).

whole versus part training whether the training material is learned and practised at one time (whole) or one part at a time (part)

Whole versus part training has to do with whether all of the training material is learned and practised at one time or one part at a time (Baldwin & Ford, 1988). For example, piano students often learn complex pieces one hand at a time. Research has found that the best strategy depends on the trainee and the nature of the task. Whole training is more effective when the trainee has high intelligence, practice is distributed, the task organization of the training material is high, and task complexity is low (Baldwin & Ford, 1988). Generally speaking, when the task itself is composed of relatively clear and different parts or subtasks, it is best for trainees to learn and practise each part at a time and then perform all parts in one whole sequence. However, if the task itself is relatively simple and consists of a number of closely interrelated tasks, then a strategy of whole learning makes more sense.

Overlearning is another condition of practice that refers to learning something until the behaviour becomes automatic. In other words, trainees are provided with continued opportunities for practice even after they have mastered the task (Baldwin & Ford, 1988). It is an effective way to train people for emergency responses or for complex skills in which there is little time to think in a job situation. It is also important for skills that employees might not need to use very often on the job and might quickly lose. Overlearning will help to ensure that performance of the task will be habitual or automatic. Automaticity refers to the performance of a skill to the point at which little attention from the brain is required to respond correctly (Yelon & Berge, 1992). Typing is the most common example of automaticity. Overlearning is an effective method in both cognitive and physical tasks. The greater the degree of overlearning, the longer the resulting retention of the training material (Driskell, Willis, & Copper, 1992).

Task sequencing has to do with the manner in which the learning tasks are organized and arranged. The basic idea is that learning can be improved by dividing the training material into an organized sequence of subtasks. The idea behind task sequencing was first proposed by Gagne (1962) who argued that practice is not enough for learning to occur. What is most important is that the distinct subtasks be identified and arranged in a logical sequence. In this manner, a trainee will learn each successive subtask before the total task is performed. The trainee learns to perform each step or task in the proper order or sequence. According to Gagne (1962), what is most important in the design of training is the identification of the component tasks or subtasks and the arrangement of them into a meaningful and suitable sequence.

Knowledge of results refers to information or feedback about trainees' performance on the training task. Research indicates that knowledge of results and feedback is critical for learning (Baldwin & Ford, 1988). First, it allows trainees to correct mistakes and improve their performance. Second, positive feedback can help build confidence and strengthen trainees' self-efficacy. And third, positive feedback can be reinforcing and stimulate continued efforts and learning. However, for feedback to be effective, it should be accurate, credible, timely, and positive (Campbell, 1988).

In addition to these conditions of practice that can influence trainee learning and retention, there are also a number of other learning principles that can improve the chances that trainees will be able to apply what they learn in training on-the-job. For example, building on similarities encourages transfer. Trainers should ensure that the training situation reflects the work environment to some degree. **Identical elements** involves providing trainees with training experiences and conditions that closely resemble those in the actual work environment. Identical elements theory states that transfer will occur only if identical elements are present in both the old (training course) and new situations (Bass & Vaughn, 1969). This raises the question of what exactly is to

overlearning continued practice, even after trainees have mastered a task, so that the behaviour becomes automatic

task sequencing dividing training material into an organized and logical sequence of subtasks

knowledge of results providing trainees with information and feedback about their performance on a training task

identical elements providing trainees with training experiences and conditions that closely resemble those in the actual work environment

be made identical? According to Baldwin and Ford (1988), there are at least two answers to this question.

First, one can design a training program with high physical fidelity by making the conditions of the training program such as the surroundings, tasks, and equipment similar to the work environment. Second, one can achieve psychological fidelity to the extent that trainees attach similar meanings to the training and job context. Identical elements have been shown to increase trainees' retention of motor and verbal behaviours (Baldwin & Ford, 1988).

Another training design principle is known as **general principles**. General principles involves teaching trainees the general rules and theoretical principles that underlie the use and application of particular skills. It is a good idea to include in the training program an explanation of the theory or general principles, provide a demonstration of these, and have employees participate in a task simulation. On-the-job application is more likely when trainees are taught the general rules and theoretical principles that underlie training content in addition to the application of skills (Baldwin & Ford, 1988).

Finally, **stimulus variability** involves the provision of a variety of training stimuli and experiences such as multiple examples of a concept or practice experiences in a variety of situations (Baldwin & Ford, 1988). The idea behind this concept is that trainees' understanding of training material can be strengthened by providing numerous examples of a concept because they will see how the concept can be applied in a variety of situations, allowing greater generalization of the new skills. This prevents the potential problem that trainees' learning will be limited to a narrow range of situations.

Stimulus variability can be incorporated into a training program in a number of ways, such as by using different models that vary in terms of their characteristics (e.g., gender or age), modelling different situations (e.g., different types of negotiation scenarios for a training program on negotiation skills), and by using models with different levels of competence in performing the training task (successful and unsuccessful). As well, trainers can increase stimulus variability simply by describing a variety of examples and experiences related to the training content, and by asking trainees to discuss their own work experiences in relation to the training material. Using several examples during the course of a training program has been found to be more effective than simply repeating the same example (Baldwin & Ford, 1988).

How can all of these design issues be incorporated into the training program on structured employment interviews? Table 5.1 provides an outline of how each of these principles of learning can be incorporated into the structured interview training program.

SELECTING THE TRAINEES

Who should attend a training program? This is an important question as money and time can be wasted if the wrong people attend and, of course, prob-

---

general principles teaching trainees the general rules and theoretical principles that underlie the use and application of particular skills

stimulus variability the provision of a variety of training stimuli and experiences, such as multiple examples of a concept, or practice experiences in a variety of situations

TABLE 5.1 STRUCTURED INTERVIEW TRAINING PROGRAM

APPLICATION OF LEARNING PRINCIPLES

Active Practice: Trainees should be given opportunities to practise conducting a structured experience-based interview and the seven learning behaviours.

Massed or Distributed Training: Factors such as the nature of the training material in terms of the amount and the complexity of the task should be considered when deciding on massed versus distributed training, as well as time and resource considerations. For the structured interview training program, because the steps are all closely related and integrated, a massed strategy is appropriate.

Whole or Part Training: Because the seven learning behaviours are closely interrelated it makes more sense to use a whole strategy in which trainees learn and practise the entire task of conducting a structured experience-based employment interview.

Overlearning: Overlearning can involve a review of the seven learning behaviours at several times during the course of the training program as well as several practice sessions.

Task sequencing: We would first identify the main tasks involved in conducting a structured employment interview and then arrange them into a meaningful order or sequence.

Knowledge of results: Trainees can practise conducting a structured employment interview and receive feedback on their performance.

Identical Elements: Focus on the selection of sales associates for the organization and replicate the actual interview setting and process conducted by the organization, including office surroundings and distractions. Create training materials that require the same cognitive and behavioural processes that the trainees would use in an actual hiring situation.

General Principles: Trainees can be taught about the theory behind the use of structured interviews and experience-based interview questions rather than just being told how to conduct the interview (e.g., the importance of past behaviour for predicting future behaviour).

Stimulus Variability: Modelled demonstrations of interviews can be shown that vary the characteristics of the job applicants. For example, it would be useful to vary the qualifications of job applicants (i.e., qualified versus unqualified for the sales associate position). It would also be a good idea to vary the competence of the model conducting the interview with respect to the main learning behaviours. That is, models can be shown conducting an unstructured and a structured interview.

lems are likely to continue if those who really need the training do not attend. As a starting point, one must carefully select trainees based on their abilities, aptitudes, and motivation. The employees must be assessed or tested to determine current knowledge and skill levels. Performance tests or interviews could be conducted to develop a base line of competencies. These tests can also act as motivators in the sense that they indicate the need for change and can also indicate if some employees already know some of the material. These knowledgable employees can either bypass certain learning modules or can act as coaches during the training process.

According to Kirkpatrick (1994), the following four decisions need to be made when selecting participants for a training program:

1. Who can benefit from the training?
2. What programs are required by law or by government edict?
3. Should the training be voluntary or compulsory?
4. Should the participants be segregated by level in the organization, or should two or more levels be included in the same class?

The information on employees' competencies should help to answer the first question. The answer to the second question can be obtained by contacting government agencies or labour boards. With respect to the third question, Kirkpatrick (1994) argues that some programs be compulsory. If a program is voluntary then there will be some employees who need the training but will not attend. When the training material is required for a group of employees, the program should be compulsory. The answer to the last question depends on the climate in an organization and the rapport that exists between different levels in the organization. The main issue is whether subordinates will feel comfortable enough to speak and participate if their supervisors are present. If this is the case then it is often a good idea for different levels to attend a training program together.

training plan indicates who in an organization needs training, the type of training that is needed, and how the training will be delivered

Information on who requires training can be incorporated into a training plan. A **training plan** indicates who in an organization needs training (e.g., human resource staff), the type of training needed (e.g., structured employment interviewing), and how the training will be delivered (in a formal classroom) (Ford, Major, Seaton, & Felber, 1993).

In the case of the training program on structured employment interviews, the training program will be compulsory for all HR staff in the organization so that they can implement structured and experience-based interviews throughout the organization for the hiring of sales associates.

TRAINING METHODS

Once the training content and trainees have been identified, the next step is to determine what training methods will be used (Campbell, 1988). The topic of training methods is extensive and as a result the next two chapters are devoted to it. For now we will present a brief introduction to this important part of training design.

Training methods can be arranged into a number of different categories such as active versus passive methods or one-way versus two-way communication. For our purposes, we will distinguish training methods in terms of where they take place since this is a fairly tangible distinction. That is, some training methods occur on the job, such as coaching and performance aids, while others take place off the job and usually in a classroom, such as lectures or games and simulations.

A variety of off-the-job and on-the-job training methods are described in Chapters 6 and 7. These methods differ in terms of their effectiveness for teaching different types of training material and for various learning outcomes. The fact is that there is an enormous number of training methods from which to choose. The choice of method will be constrained by time, money, or tradition.

Research shows that learning and retention are best achieved through the use of training methods that promote productive responses from trainees (Campbell, 1988). Productive responses are those in which the trainee actively uses the training content rather than passively watches, listens, or imitates the trainer. In addition, it is also believed that training methods that encourage the active participation of trainees during training also enhances learning (Thoms & Klein, 1994).

Ultimately, the objectives of a training program and the training content should help to determine the most appropriate training methods to use. In the case of the training program on structured employment interviews, three training methods are used. First, a lecture and discussion method is used to impart knowledge about structured interviews and experience-based interview questions. Second, an audio-visual method with behaviour modelling is used to demonstrate or model to trainees how to conduct a structured employment interview. And third, a role play method is used so trainees have some practice and experience in learning how to actually conduct a structured experience-based employment interview.

TRAINING MATERIALS AND EQUIPMENT

All training programs require the use of training materials, supplies, and equipment. Once we have a good idea of the content of a training program and the methods we'll use, we can determine the materials, supplies, and equipment that will be required.

With the determination of the supplies necessary for training, such as manuals or equipment such as VCRs, the training budget is more easily developed, the program more accurately costed, and the actual training session more likely to run smoothly. Commonly ordered supplies include overhead projectors, material such as transparencies or acetates, VCRs and tapes, and workbooks or manuals.

Neophyte trainers will often purchase or rent videos or films to make the course more entertaining. While it is important that trainee attention be maintained, videos should have an instructional objective directly related to course content. Videos must be introduced by asking participants to identify information and elements related to that part of the course. Trainees will then be prepared to discuss these at the conclusion of the video. Handouts such as course outlines that indicate the course objectives, the material to be covered, and a schedule of training activities, as well as articles and copies of the trainers' transparencies, are often required and will have to be prepared.

For the purposes of the training program on structured employment interviews, the following materials for trainees will be required: course booklet that includes a course outline, an article on structured interviewing and one on experience-based interviews, copies of the instructor's transparencies, the role play exercise, the experience-based interview questions and guide for the sales associate position, and a pen and pad of paper. Materials required for the trainer include: a flipchart and markers as well as a purchased videotape showing an unstructured and structured employment interview. The equipment required will be an overhead projector, a TV monitor, and a VCR.

THE TRAINING SITE

The training site is the actual location or room where the training will take place. Off-the-job training can take place in rooms located within an organization's offices, a learning or training centre owned by the organization, or at a rented facility such as a hotel. Many organizations such as the Bank of Montreal and CIBC have their own training centres. However, for organizations that do not have training facilities, space must be found and rented. In this case, an important concern will be the amount of travel time required for trainees to get to the training site and ensuring that trainees have transportation.

Whether the training takes place in an organization's facilities or one that needs to be rented, a number of factors need to be considered to ensure that the training program runs smoothly.

First, the training site should be conducive to learning. This means that the training environment should be comfortable in terms of things like space, lighting, and temperature. This might seem like a trivial point, but have you ever attended a class and the room temperature was a bit on the cold side? Or how about one that was too crowded and you had to stand or sit on the floor because there was not enough space? Chances are it caused you some discomfort and interfered with your learning.

Second, the training site should be free of any noise or distractions that might interfere with or disrupt trainee learning. How often have you been in class where you had to strain to hear the instructor over the chatter coming from outside the classroom? Obviously, noise can interfere with learning. Distractions can also be a problem. This is one reason why it is sometimes preferable to conduct a training program away from the organization. Otherwise, trainees might be tempted to step out of the training session to take care of business. This, of course, is not likely if they are far from their desk and the workplace.

Third, the training site should be set up in a manner that is appropriate for a particular training course. For example, if trainees will be viewing a video, will they be able to see the screen and hear the video? If trainees will be required to work in groups, will there be sufficient room for them to move around the room and interact with their group members? Are the seats arranged in a way that will allow trainees to interact and see each other, and will the trainer be able to interact with the trainees? Are the chairs movable or fixed? Again, these may be trivial issues but have you ever been in a classroom where you could not see the chalkboard or the screen at the front of the room? These types of problems can interfere with learning and negatively affect the effectiveness of the training program. An important part of training design is making sure that the training site is comfortable, free of distractions, and suitable for the training program.

In the case of the structured employment interview training program, it will be conducted at Vandalais Department Stores Learning Centre, located in Vancouver.

SCHEDULING THE TRAINING PROGRAM

The scheduling of a training program must take into consideration a number of important factors. In effect, one has to arrange the training schedule so that it can accommodate all of the participants. For example, when is the best time for employees to attend a training program in terms of the day of the week, the time of day, and time of year? When will they be available to attend training? This will probably depend on the organization and the business it is in. Most businesses have periods or seasons when they are especially busy and scheduling a training program during these times is likely to result in some resistance and perhaps low attendance. One should also be sensitive to the needs and desires of employees and their supervisors. Would it be preferable to hold the training during office hours or after hours, such as in the evenings or on the weekend? Employees and their supervisors should be consulted to determine the best time and schedule for them to attend a training program (Kirkpatrick, 1994).

A second consideration is the availability of the trainer. Whether the trainers are from the human resource department or elsewhere in the organization, they will likely have many other responsibilities that will restrict their availability. Trainers from within the organization will have to receive release time from their other duties to prepare and deliver the training program. If the trainers are from outside of the organization, then they will also have some restrictions regarding their availability and will have to be contracted for a particular date.

A third consideration in scheduling the training program is the availability of the training site, equipment, materials, and so on. To the extent that the training site and equipment are regularly used, one will have to schedule them in advance. In addition, if materials need to be designed or purchased, they will need to be available in time for the training program.

Finally, when scheduling a training program, one also has to consider whether it would be best to offer it all at once, such as one day versus four two-hour sessions in the case of an eight-hour program, or all in one week versus one day each week for five weeks (or once a month for five months) in the case of a five-day program. As indicated earlier when we discussed massed versus distributed training, this depends in part on the complexity of the training material and the experience level of the trainees. There are also issues of resources and logistics. Sometimes it is just not feasible to conduct a training program over a longer period of time. Whenever possible, however, Kirkpatrick (1994) recommends that it is best to spread the training out as an ongoing program, such as a three-hour session once a month.

Returning to the training program at Vandalais Department Stores, the scheduling of the training program would have to consider when the HR staff from the various regions would be able to attend the training. This is especially important given that most of them will have to travel to the company's learning centre in Vancouver. At the same time, the availability of the trainers for particular dates will also have to be identified given that they too will have to travel to the training site and may not be available on certain dates. And because the learning centre is frequently used for various training activities and management development, its availability must also be determined. In addition, the purchase of the video and the design of the training materials must be prepared in advance of the training program. Finally, because the trainees and trainers must travel to the company's learning centre, the training will have to be scheduled for one day rather than as an ongoing program.

THE LESSON PLAN

The **lesson plan** is the blueprint that outlines the training program in terms of the sequence of activities and events that will take place. As such, it is a guide for the trainer that provides a step-by-step breakdown for conducting the training program. A good lesson plan should be prepared in advance of a training program and should be detailed enough that any trainer could use it to guide him or her through the training program. Much of what has been determined in the previous phases will be indicated in the lesson plan. Some of the things that should be listed on the first page or cover of a lesson plan are the training objectives, classroom requirements, training aids and equipment, and trainee supplies and handouts (Donaldson & Scannell, 1986).

Table 5.2 presents the cover page of the lesson for the structured employment interview training program at Vandalais Department Stores. Table 5.3 presents the detailed lesson plan for the training program.

TABLE 5.2   LESSON PLAN COVER PAGE

Organization: Vandalais Department Stores
Department: Human Resources
Program Title: Structured Employment Interviews
Instructor(s):   Professors A. Saks and M. Belcourt, York University
Time Allocation: 1 Day
Trainees: All employees in the Human Resource Department
Where: Vandalais Learning Centre, Vancouver, B.C.

Training Objectives

Employees will be able to conduct an experience-based structured employment interview for the sales associate position and correctly perform the seven key behaviours.

Classroom Requirements

Horseshoe seating arrangement with seating for 50 people and areas for trainees to break out into groups.

Training Aids and Equipment

VCR and TV monitor; videotape: "How to Conduct a Structured Employment Interview"; overhead projector with screen; markers and transparencies; flipchart, paper, and markers.

Trainee Supplies

Pen and paper.

Trainee Handouts

1. Course objectives and outline.
2. Article on structured employment interviews.
3. Article on experience-based employment interviews.
4. List of the seven key behaviours for conducting a structured employment interview.
5. Copy of the experience-based employment interview for the sales associate position with interview questions and scoring guide and instructions.
6. Role play exercise.

Once the lesson plan has been completed, there are a number of important activities regarding how to effectively administer the training program. **Training administration** involves the coordination of all of the people and materials involved in the training program. For example, employees and their supervisors have to be informed of the program in terms of its purpose and content, as well as where and when it will take place. In addition, those who are planning to attend need to be enrolled in the program. Trainers must also be informed of this information as they will need to know how many trainees will be attending and the scheduling of the program. If trainees are to receive training materials or information prior to attending the program, then this will have to be prepared and sent to them.

training administration
the coordination of all the people and materials involved in the training program

TABLE 5.3　STRUCTURED EMPLOYMENT INTERVIEW LESSON PLAN

Objective

Employees will be able to conduct an experience-based structured employment interview for the sales associate position and correctly perform the seven key behaviours.

Trainees:　　　　　　Members of the Human Resource Department.

Time:　　　　　　　9 a.m.– 5 p.m.

Course Outline

9:00 – 10:00	Introduction lecture on the problem of poor employee performance of sales associates and the use of structured and unstructured employment interviews for selection.
10:00 – 10:30	Show video of an unstructured employment interview followed by a discussion.
10:30 – 10:45	Break
10:45 – 11:15	Show video of a structured employment interview followed by a discussion.
11:15 – 12:00	Review the seven key behaviours of conducting a structured employment interview.
12:00 – 1:00	Lunch
1:00 – 2:00	Lecture on experience-based interview questions and review of the interview questions and guide developed for sales associates.
2:00 – 2:30	Review of the seven key behaviours in conducting a structured employment interview.
2:30 – 2:45	Break
2:45 – 3:30	Role play practice exercise: In groups of three, assign participants the roles of interviewer, interviewee, and observer. Review script for roles and instruct trainees to demonstrate the seven key behaviours of a structured interview using the sales associate experience-based interview questions. Have observer provide feedback using feedback guidelines contained in the role play exercise booklet and evaluate the interviewer's performance on the seven key behaviours using the evaluation form provided. Switch roles until each group member plays the role of the interviewer.
3:30 – 4:30	Regroup for discussion of role play exercise. Discuss how it felt to be the interviewer and the interviewee and the observer's perspective.
4:30 – 4:45	Review the seven key behaviours of the structured employment interview and the importance of using structured interviews and the experience-based interview for hiring sales associates.
4:45 – 5:00	Closing. Review objectives and give pep talk about conducting structured employment interviews and using the experience-based interview. Thank participants and hand out training certificates.

In addition, all of the materials and equipment must be ordered and prepared in time for the training program. The training site must be booked and any equipment required must be made available. In some cases, this might involve renting equipment. As well, supplies such as pens, paper, transparencies, and so on must be ordered. Finally, the training administrator or coordinator will need to prepare a budget that includes the costs of all of the expenses incurred in the design and implementation of the training program. The calculation of the costs of training programs is discussed in Chapter 10.

Returning to the structured employment interview training program, it should be apparent that the HR staff in all regions of the country will need to be informed of the training program, as will the trainers. In addition, a room that can accommodate 50 people at the company's learning centre will have to be booked along with the required equipment. All of the training materials and supplies will have to be ordered. As well, because most of the trainees and the trainers will be travelling to the training site, their travel arrangements and accommodations will have to be coordinated. For example, the company might want to book hotel rooms for everyone at a hotel near the company learning centre. And finally, arrangements will also have to be made for refreshments and food for the duration of the training program.

The development of a lesson plan is a critical phase in the design of a training program. It allows for both the approval and the smooth operation of training activities. It also enables expenditures to be budgeted for and monitored. The development of a lesson plan sets the stage for the administration of the training program and is a signal to other members of the organization that training is to be conducted in a professional manner.

DELIVERY OF THE TRAINING PROGRAM

Once the lesson plan has been prepared and the administrative activities have been completed, the program is ready to be implemented and delivered. For many trainers and especially novices, this is actually the most difficult part of the training design process. There are, however, a number of fairly basic steps to follow when delivering a training program, including beginning with an ice breaker such as a humorous story to help trainees relax, getting trainees' attention and interest, informing trainees of the learning objectives, presenting the training material, providing guidance, allowing time for trainees to practise the training task, providing trainees with performance feedback, and providing guidance on performance and transfer (Gagne, 1987).

As discussed by Zemke (1999), Gagne describes the following nine events of instruction that a trainer should follow for trainees to learn the training material:

1. *Gain attention.* Draw trainees into the learning by presenting a thought-provoking problem.

2. *Describe the goal.* Inform trainees of what they will learn and what they will be able to accomplish.

3. *Stimulate recall of prior knowledge.* Discuss what trainees already know and how it is relevant and connected to the training material.

4. *Present the material to be learned.* Present the material in a logical sequence one subtask at a time (i.e., task sequencing).

5. *Provide guidance for learning.* In addition to presenting the training content, provide trainees with guidance and tips on how best to learn the material.

6. *Elicit performance practice.* Give trainees an opportunity to practise and apply the training knowledge and skills.

7. *Provide informative feedback.* Let trainees know if their responses and behaviours are correct, and why they are correct or incorrect.

8. *Assess performance.* Test trainees on their learning of the training material and mastery of the task.

9. *Enhance retention and transfer.* Discuss with trainees how the training material can be applied to their job and actual work situations they have encountered.

While these activities are fairly straightforward, there are many potential problems that trainers must deal with during the course of delivering a training program. To learn more about these problems and to identify some solutions, Richard Swanson and Sandra Falkman (1997) conducted a study in which they asked novice trainers about the problems they have had when delivering a training program. After content analyzing the responses, the authors identified the following 12 common training delivery problems:

1. *Fear.* Fear that is due to a lack of confidence and feeling anxious while delivering the training program.

2. *Credibility.* The perception that they lack credibility in the eyes of the trainees as subject-matter experts.

3. *Personal experiences.* A lack of stories about personal experiences that can be used to relate to the training content.

4. *Difficult learners.* Don't know how to handle problem trainees who may be angry, passive, or dominating.

5. *Participation.* Difficulty getting trainees to participate.

6. *Timing.* Trouble with timing and pacing of the training material and worries about having too much or too little material.

7. *Adjusting instruction.* Difficulty adjusting the training material to the needs of trainees or being able to redesign the presentation of material during delivery.

8. *Questions.* Difficulty using questions effectively and responding to difficult questions.

9. *Feedback.* Unable to read trainees and to use feedback and evaluations effectively.

10. *Media, materials, facilities.* Concerns about how to use media and training materials.

11. *Opening, closing techniques.* The need for techniques to use as icebreakers, introductions, and effective summaries and closings.

12. *Dependence on notes.* Feeling too dependent on notes and trouble presenting the material without them.

These 12 common delivery problems of novice trainers have three basic themes: (1) problems pertaining to the trainer, (2) problems pertaining to how the trainer relates to the trainees, and (3) problems pertaining to presentation techniques. Fortunately, the authors of this study also asked expert trainers for strategies and solutions for dealing with each of the 12 delivery problems. For example, to deal with the problem of fear, a trainer should be well prepared, use icebreakers and begin with an activity that relaxes trainees and gets them talking and involved, and acknowledge one's fear and understand that it is normal (Swanson & Falkman, 1997). Table 5.4 lists the experts' solutions to each of the delivery problems, which should prove helpful to trainers who have some of the problems described.

TABLE 5.4   EXPERT SOLUTIONS TO THE 12 MOST COMMON TRAINING DELIVERY PROBLEMS OF NOVICE TRAINERS

1. Fear.
   A. Be well prepared and have a detailed lesson plan.
   B. Use icebreakers and begin with an activity that relaxes trainees.
   C. Acknowledge the fear and use self-talk and relaxation exercises prior to the training.

2. Credibility.
   A. Don't apologize. Be honest about your knowledge of the subject.
   B. Have the attitude of an expert and be well prepared and organized.
   C. Share personal background and talk about your area of expertise and experiences.

3. Personal experiences.
   A. Relate personal experiences.
   B. Report experiences of others and have trainees share their experiences.
   C. Use analogies, refer to movies or famous people who relate to the subject.

4. Difficult learners.
   A. Confront the problem learner and talk to them to determine the problem.
   B. Circumvent dominating behaviour by using nonverbal behaviour such as breaking eye contact or standing with your back to the person.
   C. Use small groups to overcome timid behaviour and structure exercises where a wide range of participation is encouraged.

5. Participation.
   A. Ask open-ended questions and provide positive feedback when trainees participate.
   B. Plan small group activities such as dyads, case studies, and role plays to increase participation.
   C. Invite participation by structuring activities to allow trainees to share early in the program.

TABLE 5.4 (continued)

6. Timing.

   A. Plan for too much material and prioritize activities so that some can be omitted if necessary.

   B. Practise presenting the material many times so that you know where you should be at 15-minute intervals.

7. Adjusting instruction.

   A. Determine the needs of the group early in the training and structure activities based on them.

   B. Request feedback by asking trainees how they feel about the training during breaks or periodically during the training.

   C. Redesign the program during breaks and have a contingency plan in place.

8. Questions.

Answering questions

   A. Anticipate questions by writing out key questions that trainees might have.

   B. Paraphrase and repeat a question so everyone hears the question and understands it.

   C. Redirect questions you can't answer back to the trainees' and try to find answers during the break.

Asking questions

   A. Ask concise and simple questions and provide enough time for trainees to answer.

9. Feedback.

   A. Solicit informal feedback during training or breaks on whether the training is meeting their needs and expectations and watch for nonverbal cues.

   B. Do summative evaluations at the conclusion of the training to determine if the objectives and needs of trainees have been met.

10. Media, materials, facilities.

Media

   A. Know how to operate every piece of equipment you will use.

   B. Have backups such as extra bulbs, extension cords, markers, tape, and so on, as well as bringing the material in another medium in case one has problems.

   C. Enlist assistance from trainees if you have a problem and need help.

Materials

   A. Be prepared and have all the material placed at trainees' workplace or ready for distribution.

Facilities

   A. Visit facility beforehand to see the layout of the room and where things are located and how to set up.

   B. Arrive at least one hour early to set up and handle any problems.

11. Opening, closing techniques.

Openings

   A. Develop a file of ideas based on experimentation and observation.

   B. Develop and memorize a great opening.

   C. Relax trainees by greeting them when they enter, taking time for introductions and creating a relaxed atmosphere.

Closings

   A. Provide a simple and concise summary of the course contents using objectives or the initial model.

   B. Thank participants for their time and contribution to the course.

TABLE 5.4 (continued)

12. Dependence on notes.

    A. Notes are necessary.

    B. Use cards with an outline or key words as prompts.

    C. Use visuals such as notes on the frames of transparencies or your copy of the handouts.

    D. Practise and learn the script so you can deliver it from the key words on your note cards.

Source: Swanson, R.A., & Falkman, S.K. (1997). Training delivery problems and solutions: Identification of novice trainer problems and expert trainer solutions. *Human Resource Development Quarterly 8*, 305–314. © 1997 by Jossey-Bass Inc. Reprinted with permission.

SUMMARY

This chapter outlined the main steps in the preparation and design of a training program. Through the careful development of objectives (resulting from the needs analysis), the trainer can identify the current gaps in knowledge and skills, the precise program objectives, and the most appropriate training content. Once the training content has been determined, it is possible to begin to make decisions that will form the basis of the lesson plan, including the trainer, trainees, training methods, training materials and equipment, the training site, and the training schedule. Once the lesson plan is complete, the trainer must make the necessary arrangements for the program followed by its delivery. One of the most important steps in this process is deciding on the use of training methods. As we will see in the next two chapters, there are many possible off- and on-the-job methods of training.

KEY TERMS

active practice   112

chaining   107

general principles   114

generalization   108

identical elements   113

knowledge of results   113

learning   106

lesson plan   120

massed versus distributed
   training   112

observation   110

overlearning   113

self-efficacy   110

self-management   111

shaping   107

stimulus variability   114

task sequencing   113

training administration   121

training plan   116

whole versus part training   112

EXERCISES

1. Think of the best and worst training experience that you have ever had. For each one, indicate the purpose of the training, the objectives, and the content. Then make a list of all the reasons why you feel that it was the best and worst training experience you have ever had. Based on your lists, what are some of the things that make a training program effective?

2. If you have a drivers licence, then you probably remember what it was like to learn how to drive. Chances are you stepped into a car with a friend or family member who told you what to do. And if you have ever taught someone how to drive, you probably did the same thing. Did you remember to tell them everything they needed to know? What are the things you told them to do first? Could you have done a better job teaching them to drive? Probably. Refer to the section of this chapter on task sequencing. Recall that task sequencing involves dividing a task up into its component parts or subtasks, and then ordering them into a meaningful or logical sequence. Now try to design a driver training program based on task sequencing. In other words, make a list of all of the subtasks involved in driving a car and then organize them into a logical sequence for the purpose of teaching somebody how to drive.

3. Contact the human resource department of an organization and request a meeting with somebody in the department whom you can interview about the organization's training programs. Develop a series of questions so that you can learn about each of the following design issues in terms of a particular training program that the organization has implemented:

   - Was the training program designed by the organization or purchased? What were the reasons for designing or purchasing the program?

   - What is the content of the training program and how was it developed?

   - Who is the trainer of the program and how was he or she chosen?

   - Who were the trainees and how and why were they chosen to attend the program?

   - What training methods were used and why?

   - What training materials and equipment were used?

   - Was a lesson plan prepared for the program? If not, why? If so, what things were included on it?

   - Describe the training facility and why it was chosen.

   - Describe the schedule of the training program and how it was determined.

   - Who administered and coordinated the training program and what did this involve?

   - How was the delivery of the training program conducted? What are some problems that have occurred in the delivery of the training program and what strategies are used to deal with them?

   Based on the information you have acquired, conduct an evaluation with respect to how effectively you think each of the stages were performed, and list some recommendations to improve each phase.

4. Have you ever wondered what your instructor does to prepare for a class? To find out, choose one of your classes and try to describe each of the following:

- the objectives of the class
- the content of the class
- the trainer (experience, job title, etc.)
- who the trainees (students) are (e.g., major, work experience, etc.)
- the training methods used

- the training materials and equipment
- the training site
- the class schedule
- the lesson plan
- the administration of the class (what was involved?)
- the delivery of the material (events of instruction) and any delivery problems and strategies used to deal with them

Based on your description, how effective was the class? How can it be improved?

RUNNING CASE PART 1: VANDALAIS DEPARTMENT STORES

Refer to the case of Vandalais Department Stores described in this chapter. Discuss the implications of each of the following learning theories for the design of the structured employment interview training program. In other words, how would you design the training program to make it more effective based on each of the following theories:

- conditioning theory
- expectancy theory
- goal setting theory
- social learning theory

REFERENCES

Baldwin, T.T., & Ford, J.K. (1988). Transfer of training: A review and directions for future research. *Personnel Psychology 41*, 63–105.

Bandura, A. (1986). *Social foundations of thought and action: A social cognitive theory*. Englewood Cliffs, NJ: Prentice-Hall.

———. (1997). *Self-efficacy: The exercise of control*. New York: W.H. Freeman & Co.

Bass, B.M., & Vaughn, J.A. (1969). *Training in industry: The management of learning.* Belmont, CA: Wadsworth.

Campbell, J.P. (1988). Training design for performance improvement. In Campbell, J.P. & Campbell, R.J. (Eds.), *Productivity in organizations: Frontiers of industrial and organizational psychology* (pp.177–216). San Francisco, CA: Jossey-Bass.

Campion, M.A., Palmer, D.K., & Campion, J.E. (1997). A review of structure in the selection interview. *Personnel Psychology 50,* 655–702.

Donaldson, L., & Scannell, E.E. (1986). *Human resource development: The new trainer's guide* (2nd ed.). Reading, MA: Addison-Wesley.

Driskell, J.E., Willis, R.P., & Copper, C. (1992). Effects of overlearning on retention. *Journal of Applied Psychology 77,* 615–622.

Ford, J.K., Major, D.A., Seaton, F.W., & Felber, H.K. (1993). Effects of organizational, training system, and individual characteristics on training director scanning practices. *Human Resource Development Quarterly 4,* 333–351.

Frayne, C.A., & Latham, G.P. (1987). Application of social learning theory to employee self-management of attendance. *Journal of Applied Psychology 72,* 387–392.

Gagne, R.M. (1962). Military training and principles of learning. *American Psychologist 17,* 83–91.

———. (1984). Learning outcomes and their effects: Useful categories of human performance. *American Psychologist 39,* 377–385.

———. (1987). Introduction. In Gagne, R. M. (Ed.), *Instructional technology: Foundations* (pp. 1–9). Hillsdale, NJ: Erlbaum.

Ganzel, R. (1998, October). What sexual harassment training really prevents. *Training 35* (10), 86–94.

Gist, M.E., Stevens, C.K., & Bavetta, A.G. (1991). Effects of self-efficacy and post-training intervention on the acquisition and maintenance of complex interpersonal skills. *Personnel Psychology 44,* 837–861.

Goldstein, I.L. (1991). Training in work organizations. In Dunnette, M.D. & Hough, L. (Eds.), *Handbook of Industrial and Organizational Psychology* (2nd ed.), Vol. 2. Palo Alto, CA: Consulting Psychologists Press.

———. (1993). *Training in organizations* (3rd ed.). Pacific Grove, CA: Brooks/Cole.

Haccoun, R.R., & Saks, A.M. (1998). Training in the twenty-first century: Some lessons from the last one. *Canadian Psychology 39,* 33–51.

Hays, S. (1999, April). Basic skills training 101. *Workforce 78* (4), 76–78.

Hinrichs, J.R. (1976). Personnel training. In Dunnette, M.D. (Ed.), *Handbook of industrial and organizational psychology* (pp. 829–860). Skokie, IL: Rand McNally.

Kirkpatrick, D.L. (1994). *Evaluating training programs: The four levels.* San Francisco, CA: Berrett-Koehler Publishers.

Latham, G.P., & Frayne, C.A. (1989). Self-management training for increasing job attendance: A follow-up and a replication. *Journal of Applied Psychology 74,* 411–416.

Locke, E.A., & Latham, G.P. (1990). *A theory of goal setting and task performance.* Englewood Cliffs, NJ: Prentice-Hall.

Luthans, F., & Davis, T. (1983). Beyond modelling: Managing social learning processes in human resource training and development. In Baird, C.,

Schneier, E., & Laird, D (Eds.), *The training and development sourcebook*. Amherst, MA: Human Resource Development Press.

Nadler, L., & Nadler, Z. (1990). *The handbook of human resource development* (2nd ed.). New York: John Wiley and Sons.

Pearce, J.M. (1987). A model of stimulus generalization in Pavlovian conditioning. *Psychological Review 94*, 61–73.

Pulakos, E.D., & Schmitt, N. (1995). Experience-based and situational interview questions: Studies of validity. *Personnel Psychology 48*, 289–308.

Saks, A.M. (1997). Transfer of training and self-efficacy: What is the dilemma? *Applied Psychology: An International Journal 46*, 365–370.

Skinner, B.F. (1953). *Science and human behaviour*. New York: McMillan.

Swanson, R.A., & Falkman, S.K. (1997). Training delivery problems and solutions: Identification of novice trainer problems and expert trainer solutions. *Human Resource Development Quarterly 8*, 305–314.

This, L., & Lippet, G. (1983). Learning theories and training. In Baird, L. S., Schneier, C. E., & Laird, D. (Eds.), *The training and development sourcebook*. Amherst, MA: Human Resource Development Press.

Thoms, P., & Klein, H.J. (1994). Participation and evaluative outcomes in management training. *Human Resource Development Quarterly 5*, 27–39.

Vroom, V. (1964). *Work and motivation*. New York: Wiley and Sons.

Yelon, S., & Z. Berge. (1992, September). Practice-centred training. *Performance and instruction*, 8–12.

Zemke, R. (1999). Toward a science of training. *Training 36* (7), 32–36.

6

··

OFF-THE-JOB TRAINING METHODS

CHAPTER GOALS

In this chapter, we will discuss training methods used mostly in the classroom or away from the job site. This chapter discusses the most common of these training methods. After reading this chapter, you should be able to

- describe the following training methods: the lecture, behavioural modelling, technology-based training, cases, games, simulations, role plays, group discussions, and action learning
- list the advantages and disadvantages of each training method
- outline how to effectively use each technique
- choose an effective method to attain your learning objectives

The chapter presents training methods in order of degree of trainee involvement, from passive to active. We start with lectures, because there is relatively little trainee input possible or encouraged, and end with action learning where trainees manage the learning process.

··

LECTURING

lecture a training
method in which the
trainer organizes the
content to be learned and
presents it orally

There are few people who have not experienced a lecture. A **lecture** transmits information orally, with little listener involvement.

The advantages of a lecture are significant. Large amounts of information can be transferred to large groups of trainees in a relatively short period of time, at a minimal expense. Key points can be emphasized and repeated. Trainers can be assured that the listeners are all hearing the same message, which is useful when the message is extremely important, such as instructions or changes in procedures. The lecture is especially valuable as a method to explain to trainees what is to follow in the rest of the learning session. For example, a lecture could be used to highlight the key learning points of a subsequent video or role play. Many employees are comfortable with the lecture as a familiar teaching method that requires little participation.

The lecture, as some of us have experienced, does have drawbacks as a training method. While useful for knowledge transfer, it is not effective for the development of skills or the modification of attitudes. The lecture does not accommodate any differences in student ability, and all listeners are forced to absorb information at the same rate. Trainees are also forced to be passive learners, with little opportunity to connect the content to their own work environment, or to receive feedback on their understanding of the material. To overcome these disadvantages, most lecturers build in time for discussion, questions and answers, and other opportunities for trainee involvement. Despite all the disadvantages of lectures compared to other forms of training, 70 percent of organizations use them. The trainer can use the lecture method effectively by following these guidelines.

TIPS FOR TRAINERS "Where do I begin?" is a question asked by most first-time lecturers. The answer is: "First you have to know what you want to do (the objective) and how much information you need to impart." Objective-setting has been covered elsewhere in this text, but on a pragmatic level the lecturer should be able to write a concise statement describing what the trainees will be able to do or accomplish by attending any given lecture.

Either through previously gained knowledge or the ability to research a topic, the lecturer or teacher will gather and arrange information in a logical manner. Logic could dictate a progression from the general to the specific, or from the specific to the general, depending upon the subject matter.

This information can be transcribed onto cards or sheets of paper. An effective technique is to rule off a wide (5 cm to 8 cm) margin down the right-hand side of each page. Then detailed information can be placed in the body of the page, while headings are written in the margins. Renner (1989) has suggested that no more than six major points be illustrated during each half hour of a lecture. It takes practice to get the timing of a lecture right. Only through experience can one judge the amount of material needed for any given amount of time. Break the lecture into 10 to 15 minute segments with a short stretch time in between. Summarize the material at both the beginning and the end, and stop occasionally to allow students to catch up and to write their own summaries. Finally, time should be scheduled for questions and answers.

A lecturer who drones on for an entire hour is rarely effective. Depending on audience needs and motivation level, the delivery should be punctuated with a variety of supplementary material or exercises. Stories, case incidents, graphics, humour, trainee presentations, videos, and question and answer sessions are but a few of the techniques lecturers use to maintain interest and, perhaps even more important, to instill in the trainee the love of, or at the least respect for, the subject matter. Lecturers not only represent themselves but also function as ambassadors for their institution or firm *and* their discipline. A poor lecture, then, not only shows the trainer in a bad light but forms trainee attitudes toward entire sections of curriculum.

To ensure that listeners are listening, Bata Limited requires those attending conferences, which are largely lecture based, to return to work prepared to give a session to their peers on what they have learned, and what is applicable to their company (Kulig, 1998).

BEHAVIOUR MODELLING

People learn by observing the behaviour of others. Children watch action figures such as the Teenage Mutant Ninja Turtles and, with no formal training, will leap into kung fu positions at the cry of "kowabunga!" Teenagers surreptitiously observe the posturing of the cool kids. Administrative trainees watch very carefully how the senior team leader makes a presentation to her boss.

Behaviour modelling is a teaching method in which a model demonstrates key behaviours, which the trainees observe and then attempt to replicate. Behaviour modelling is based on social learning theory and observation learning principles discussed in Chapter 5, and is an extremely effective method for learning skills and behaviours, but not so effective for absorbing factual information. Behaviour modelling is used mainly to teach interpersonal skills such as supervision, negotiation, communication, sales, and so on.

The behaviour modelled can be both positive and negative, and can range from interviewing skills to murder. Experts debate whether television is responsible for copy-cat murders such as those that occurred in Alberta modelled after the black trench coat murders in Colorado.

Trainers have to plan the process very carefully, so that trainees are able to practise the behaviour, view feedback as positive and helpful, and are motivated to use the new behaviour on the job. Trainees will resist behaviour modelling if the behaviours are incongruent with common work practices. They are highly sensitive to trainers and managers walking the talk (i.e., using the behaviours they are endorsing).

behaviour modelling
a training method in which a model demonstrates key behaviours, which trainees observe and attempt to replicate

TIPS FOR TRAINERS   Behaviour modelling instruction is founded on four principles of learning: imitation (modelling), behavioural rehearsal (practice), reinforcement (reward), and transfer (Robinson, 1982). The process is straightforward. A learner observes a model in a particular scenario, such as a selection interview or handling a customer complaint. This situation can be filmed or conducted live. Models can be anyone—parents, peers, celebrities—although people with authority or charisma are the models most likely to be copied. Sabido in Mexico City ran a popular soap opera showing celebrities enrolling in, studying in, and graduating from literacy courses. After watching this popular show, the number of Mexicans enrolled in literacy courses increased from 90 000 to 840 000 in one year (Sabido, 1981). The model should be someone with whom the trainee can identify and should have desirable qualities, such as power or status. Under these conditions, the trainee is more likely to want to imitate the model's behaviour.

In addition, the trainees must have sufficient trust in the facilitator to experiment (i.e., to try new behaviour in front of a group). Sometimes, a traditional and ineffective scenario is enacted to increase motivation to try the new positive model. (John Cleese of Monty Python fame used this technique very effectively in his humorous video series on interviewing.)

The trainee observes the behaviour then attempts to re-enact the scenario. The trainer should have broken down the skills to be learned into a series of critical steps, which can be modelled independently. After viewing the model, the participants practise the behaviour, one step at a time. When one step is mastered and reinforced, the trainer moves to the next critical skill. Specific feedback is given immediately. This step-by-step process results in the solid development of skills and the confidence needed to use them (Georges, 1988).

Transfer of the new skill to the workplace is always the weak spot in the training cycle. Old patterns are comfortable and familiar. By overpractising or overlearning the skill, however, its use may become automatic. Reinforcement of newly acquired skills ensures their repetition. When these reinforcers are in place, behaviour modelling training can have long-lasting and positive outcomes (Buller & McEvoy, 1990).

TECHNOLOGY-BASED TRAINING

training technology any technology that delivers or supports the training process

Training technology will be broadly defined in this section. Any technology that delivers education or training, or supports the delivery of these subjects, would be included in the definition. The field of training technology is changing rapidly. This change is sustained by the increase in storage capacity of personal computers, the growth of expert and authoring systems, and the development of generic courses. The trend for organizations to computerize office procedures facilitates the introduction of computer-based training (CBT). Industries with a high investment in technology infrastructure use CBT more extensively than others (Stahmer, 1991). Combine this technology with the desire of students to control the pace and place of learning and the growth potential of distance learning is obvious.

Distance learning and distance education are general terms referring to learning methods in which information is communicated from a central source to individuals or groups at locations separate from the source, usually through the use of technology. The most common methods of distance learning include correspondence courses, which can include audio- and videocassettes, supplemented by workbooks and even supervised off-site exams.

Technology-based training is considered valuable for students or employees who live in remote areas; when there is an insufficient number of students enrolled in a course to justify hiring an instructor; for trainees who are less mobile than others because of parenting or work responsibilities; and for trainees who have disabilities.

Motivation seems to be a big problem in learning. Students report feeling isolated and missing the collegial nature of classroom learning (Robinson, 1982). Another problem is the high cost of course development, particularly when advanced technology is used. However, the advantage of nearly universal access overrides concerns about motivation and cost.

The following sections examine common technologies in training, beginning with a description of the technology and an assessment of strengths and weaknesses.

Audio-visual Techniques

Videos, slides, and overheads are often used by trainers to supplement lectures and other training methods. A video is never used alone but is used to illustrate a way to behave in a certain situation in behaviour modelling, or to demonstrate effective and ineffective methods for a discussion group. Many managers have learned correct interviewing techniques through videos. Slides and overheads highlight the important parts of a lecture or discussion, allowing students to remember key items. Effective slides also structure note taking for students.

One advantage of these audio visual techniques is the ability to control the pace of the training. A slide or a video clip can be seen again to clarify a concept. Trainees receive consistent information from these tools, no matter where or how often the training is given. Most important, a video or slide can show a situation that is difficult for a trainer to describe, such as a hostile customer or a dangerous malfunction in equipment. Using a video playback to show trainees how they handled a situation provides the kind of objective feedback not easily obtained from other observers.

The principle drawback of videos in particular is that the humour and dramatic effects can turn a training session into entertainment. The students are laughing, but are they learning?

TIPS FOR TRAINERS   Before a video is shown, the trainer should discuss the learning objectives, the key points, and ask the audience to pay particular attention to certain parts, because the discussion question, which is then given to the participants, should focus on these points.

Videos and slides should be screened for dated language, sexism, and racism, all of which diminish the educational impact.

VIDEO CONFERENCING

video conferencing
consists of linking an expert to employees via two-way television

Video conferencing consists of linking a subject-matter expert to employees by means of two-way television (video). This allows people at two or more locations to see, hear, and speak with one another and permits simultaneous meetings in different locations. Video conferencing is used to bring in an expert from another location, to hold meetings with staff working in various locations, and to communicate corporate information that needs to be rapidly disseminated and accepted.

Unsettled political conditions and incidents like the Gulf War (which made some executives wary of travel terrorism) and decreases in the costs of technology have made video conferencing more acceptable and affordable. In addition, employees in remote locations and those with limited flexibility (e.g., with child-care arrangements), stand to benefit from this technology, which allows them to be trained at their own workplace.

Companies like Stentor claim that training by live TV reduces the travel and labour costs of training, gets consistent or uniform training quickly to a large number of people, brings the subject-matter expert to all trainers, enhances company revenues by implementing training faster (down from three months to two weeks), and distributes complex information over periods of time. BCTel uses simulations and video conferencing to teach financial skills to employees in a deregulated environment (Filipczak, 1994).

The disadvantage of this method is that there is less personal attention given to trainees. This problem can be remedied by having a facilitator on-site or by allowing for interactive questioning while training takes place.

COMPUTER-BASED TRAINING

Multimedia can mean almost anything. Chalk and talk are multimedia, so is a slide show with two projectors. A virtual-reality simulator for teaching pilots is also multimedia. However, the term multimedia is evolving to mean any instructional delivery system that includes a computer. The Association of Multi-Image International defines multimedia as "presentations of a visual or audio-visual nature that are created using integrated computer technology." This method combines audio, video, computer graphics, and text and is presented via computer disc and associated technologies.

Experts predict that within 10 years, only 5 percent of training will take place in classrooms. Imagine a world in which a wide variety of databases, computer networks, and bulletin boards free individuals to create unique learning packages and experiences, allowing them to solve business problems as they arise (Geber, 1994, Salopek, 1998b).

This vision is being realized. A smart card has been developed for distance education in which an employee or student uses the card to register and request training materials, to link with tutors and other participants, and to study at home (*The Training Technology Monitor,* 1993). Ernst and Young have implemented an interactive multimedia program to train thousands of new accountants each year just in time and at their own pace.

The advantages of multimedia training are significant. Computers can simulate situations where skills, knowledge, or behaviours can be practised and tested. Training can look and feel like work. Reports from industrial users of multimedia training suggest that training time is reduced, test scores remain the same, but on-the-job performance is better than that given by conventional training methods (Greengard, 1993). The traditional classroom model is collapsing as companies are speeding up the time-to-market process, with even stable institutions like banks introducing new products every two to three months. Organizing groups of trainees to attend classes is too slow; technology moves the information faster.

The main reason that the Hudson's Bay Company uses CBT is that it can standardize training for its 65 000 employees (Allan, 1993). This method can provide immediate feedback to users. The feedback ranges from a simple prompt indicating that the answer is right or wrong to the execution of another program segment in which trainees are routed through a complex maze of reviews and reinforcements based on their input. Courses can be custom designed for use by pretesting trainees and, where proficiency is indicated, bypassing some modules.

All the learning senses, not just the eyes, are activated with the use of multimedia. Research has shown that the wider the range of media used, the greater the proportion of trainees who succeed in learning effectively (Smith, 1986). Mastery of skills is about 25 percent higher using CBT than other methods. Learning time is reduced by 30 to 50 percent (Stahmer, 1991). Use of multimedia increases retention, motivation, and interaction (Salopek, 1998a). Trainees can learn at their own pace, with reinforcement and feedback from an endlessly patient tutor. The courseware is available 24 hours a day. This method reduces the need to wait until a group of trainees is ready to take a course, such as a company orientation program. CBT allows trainees to track their own progress and test themselves. The technology easily generates tests that can provide legal documentation for proof of competency levels. When an accident or safety incident results in a lawsuit, the employer can prove that the training program was undertaken and that a desired level of competence was reached. These training statistics could reduce corporate liability. As well, the use of computers virtually eliminates cheating. Questions are randomly administered to students with photo identification and secret passwords. After a lapse of time, retesting is done with a different set of questions.

Geographic flexibility is a major advantage to a computer-based technology. Trainees can learn at their home or workplace. High overhead costs of traditional training (travel, accommodation, training facilities) make technology-based training advantageous to companies with national or international employees. Savings occur at around the 2000-employee level and will reduce costs by 40 percent over other methods (Stahmer, 1991).

Not everything about training technology is positive. Multimedia instructional technology demands more trainee involvement and interaction but, paradoxically, offers less interpersonal contact. However, instructors and students of Internet courses at York University claim that they have more interaction via e-mail and online discussion groups than they would have in a classroom.

Individuals have learning preferences or styles. If a trainee prefers to be taught by a human, then this technology would disadvantage that employee. However, the technology does reduce some of the weaknesses of human-based training. Students who are too embarrassed to ask a question in class can do so electronically, directly to the instructors, or repeat some basic material without other students knowing. No student is aware of how slowly another student is progressing through the material and how often that student is seeking remedial work. Trainers are aware of workers who are reluctant to attend training classes because their limited knowledge of the subject would be exposed. This instructional format reduces these group pressures.

The major disadvantage to the immediate implementation of multimedia training is the cost. Estimates are that it takes 200 to 300 hours of design and development to produce one hour of instruction (Miles & Griffith, 1993). A full-motion colour-and-sound courseware would likely cost $200 000 for 30 hours of instruction. However, for a company training thousands of employees, there are definite cost savings with this method.

THE CASE STUDY METHOD*

case study method
a teaching technique in which students discuss, analyze, and solve problems based on a real situation

The primary use of the **case study method** is to encourage open discussion and criticism of situations. The method allows students to think for themselves and develop problem-solving skills while the teacher functions as a catalyst to learning. Students apply business-management concepts to relevant real-life situations as a case study should "focus on a contemporary phenomenon within some real-life context" (Yin, 1985, p. 13). Case studies help develop analytical ability, sharpen problem-solving skills, encourage creativity, and

*Although the work has been rewritten extensively, recognition should be given to Daniele Bastarche, who completed the original research for this section while an MBA candidate in the Faculty of Administration at the University of New Brunswick.

improve the organization of thoughts and ideas (Pearce, Robinson, & Zahra Shaker, 1989). The objectives of a case are (1) to introduce realism into the student's learning, (2) to deal with a variety of problems, goals, facts, conditions, and conflicts that often occur in the real world, (3) to teach students how to make decisions, therefore, most cases present situations in which problems are correctable, and (4) to teach students to be creative and think independently (Yin, 1985).

More than 70 percent of business schools use case-simulation methods. Several studies have found that using cases improves communication skills, offers a reward of solving problems, and enables students to better understand management situations (Wright, 1992). For the case method to be successful, however, certain requirements must be met. For example, the qualifications of both the students and the teacher (human and social factors) affect the ability to analyze cases and to draw conclusions. As well, space and time dimensions are relevant; students need time to analyze cases properly. Finally, case studies and discussions work best in an open and informal atmosphere (Craig, 1987).

Cases may be written in various styles, presenting either single problems or a number of complex interdependent situations. They may be concerned with corporate strategy, organizational change, departmentalization, or any problem relating to a company's financial situation, marketing, human resources, or a combination of these activities. Some case reports describe the organization's difficulties in vague terms, while others may state the major problems explicitly.

In addition to the various styles of case writing, methods of presentation also differ. Cases do not always have to be in written form. Sometimes it is more effective to present cases using audio-visual techniques. This approach has advantages for both the students and the teachers in that teachers do not have to do as much research and writing, while students are able to identify better with the characters (Craig, 1987). A second alternative to a written case presentation is the live case method. Businesses may contact schools to report certain undesirable symptoms of problems; students then analyze the situation and report back to the company. This approach has been called operational consulting (Schnelle, 1967).

TIPS FOR TRAINERS   Certain requirements should be met when writing a traditional case. The case should be a product of a real organizational situation. A fictitious case could be regarded with boredom and distrust, as the setting may be unrealistic (Craig, 1987). Ideally, cases should be written by more than one person. Collaboration on the presentation of facts ensures a more realistic situation and helps to reduce biases. Although it is difficult, the case writer must not make assumptions; only facts should be included. "The case writer must report to the best of his/her ability the relevant facts of the situation at the time the decisions needed to be made or the problem existed" (Leenders & Erskine, 1973, p. 11). The author of a case, then, must relate core issues to the reader, not personal bias.

Case studies often concentrate on the corporate strategy of a company within an industry setting. Businesses do not usually follow predetermined behaviour. "It may well be frustrating when companies do not seem to act like textbook models" (Kenny, Lea, & Luffman, 1992, p. 451). The complexity of business situations makes decisions and analyses challenging. In addition, despite their length, most cases do not contain complete information on the organization or all the relevant inputs. This incompleteness is part of the benefit of using the case method, as students must learn to deal with incomplete data (Kenny et al., 1992).

As a case study is a description of a typical management situation, it is often difficult to know what to include and what to omit. Most cases give an overall description of the company and the industry situation. The length of a case report varies. A typical case, however, will be up to 20 typewritten pages. The key issues and the relevant details should be included to give the reader enough information to make a qualified decision. Some case studies disclose what management decisions were made when attempting to solve the organization's problems. Cases vary depending on the intended purpose of the writer and according to the issue being examined.

A teaching note provides communication between the case writer and those who teach the case. In its strictest sense, a teaching note would include information on approaches to teaching a specific case. Some teaching notes, however, are more detailed, containing samples of analyses and computations. In addition, teaching notes may state the objectives of the case and contain additional company information not available to the student (Leenders & Erskine, 1973).

As most of these cases are excessively long and extremely complex, they have not generally found favour with trainers in business, particularly those training front-line supervisors. There is an offshoot of this technique, however, the case incident concept, that can be used to great advantage with a wide variety of learners at many levels.

THE CASE INCIDENT CONCEPT*

case incident a teaching method in which one part of an organization problem is presented for analysis

Unlike the typical case study, the **case incident**—usually no more than one page in length—is designed to illustrate or to probe one specific concept or theory (Wright, 1988). Most management textbooks, for example, include a case incident at the end of each chapter. (There is a case incident at the end of this chapter). The case incident, then, has become one of the most accessible ways of injecting an experiential or real-world component into the traditional classroom and lecture setting.

*This section is adapted from Wright, P. C. (1988). *The trainer's case compendium*. Bradford: MCB University Press; and Simulating reality: The case incident as a commonly available yet underutilized resource. (1992). *Association of Management Proceedings: Education 10* (1), 46–50.

Case incidents are useful when one topic or concept needs to be stressed. Since they are short, valuable time is not taken up by differences in trainee reading speeds. When larger, more traditional cases are used, advance preparation is necessary as some trainees may become bored, since they will be finished reading before the others. Also, slow readers may become embarrassed. The incident's brevity reduces the differences in reading times so that all trainees can participate without a lot of advance preparation.

The use of incidents leads to improved group discussion and presentation skills; indeed, the team-building aspects of this technique are a valuable precursor to participation in major group projects or longer, more traditional cases, and are a good way of getting shy individuals to speak out; otherwise, first exposure to the case-study format can prove frustrating. In addition, sophisticated technology is not required. Incidents are also useful as changes of pace if one dominant training technology or method is in use.

The final (and perhaps the most important) advantage of the incident concept is that trainees are able to use their own experiences. If the material is written well, the problem presented in each incident will encourage the application of current knowledge, leading to increased confidence and classroom participation.

The use of incidents has two main disadvantages. Some individuals are bothered by the lack of background material. Indeed, at times it is necessary for trainees to make assumptions and instructors may be asked by some groups to sketch in the background. Similarly, attempts to use incidents in cross-cultural settings, such as training managers in China, met with mixed results: the trainees could not fill in the background, since they had limited knowledge of Western society *and* cultural relationships can differ widely across countries.

Incidents have been used successfully in both high-tech and in more traditional organizations. Supervisors seem to like the hands-on aspects of solving a specific management problem. Similarly, fourth-year university students have found the incident technique to be a welcome relief from the traditional lecture format. Incidents have been found valuable in class sizes of up to 70, although the logistics of handing out paper to a group of that size must be considered. For younger students, lack of work or life experiences tends to elicit shallow answers based on speculation and ill-informed opinion.

TIPS FOR TRAINERS   Case incidents work well in two ways. First, the trainees can be divided into groups of between three and seven. One trainee can be assigned the chore of making notes on the discussion, while another can be designated group spokesperson. After the group work has been completed, the trainer can ask each spokesperson to summarize results. This process can lead easily into a general group discussion.

The second approach is to have the trainees read the case and discuss it as one group. This method is especially useful when an example is needed to illustrate a specific point. The technique here would be to stop the training, ask the trainees to read the incident, and then to lead the full group in a short discussion. As soon as the point has been made, the instructor should continue quickly, so as not to lose the trainees' interest.

Should time be a factor, or if reading skills are poor, the incident can be given out in advance. Advance reading seems to allay the fear of learning by this method, especially when dealing with trainees of varied cultural and social backgrounds.

GAMES AND SIMULATIONS

Games and simulations attempt to recreate reality by simplifying situations to a manageable size and structure. These models or active representations of situations are designed to increase trainee motivation, involvement, and learning. They are also used when training in the real world might involve danger or extreme costs. The first management-training game may have been the use of chess to teach military strategy.

There are differences between games and simulations. **Games** represent reality but tend to be more simplistic, more manual, and less amenable to computer analysis (Clark, 1985). Games tend to have rules, generate scores, and the participants are seen as players. An employment law game, Winning through Prevention, teaches HR managers about lawful termination, discrimination, and workplace safety. Players who answer correctly get promoted; those who answer incorrectly are faced with a lawsuit (Atkins, 1999). Nike, a company with worldwide sales of US$9 billion in 1997, uses a game, Gold of the Desert Kings, to teach teamwork, developed by Eagles Flight of Guelph, Ontario.

Simulations tend to be operating models of physical or social events, designed to replicate environments (i.e., they attempt to represent reality). An example of a physical representation used in training is the flight simulator designed to teach pilots to fly. These flight simulators mimic flight exactly but pose no risk to humans or equipment. A social-model simulation example would be the exercise commonly used in business schools. Students are asked to run a company operating in a free-market system and to manipulate factors such as price and production. This simulation is designed to teach students about laws of supply and demand. Simulations can be used to teach not only technical skills but soft skills. Royal Bank Financial Group of Canada trained all 58 000 employees in coaching skills using a five hour CD-ROM simulation (Salopek, 1998b).

Games and simulations incorporate many sound principles of learning: learning from experience, active participation, direct application to real problems, and incorporation of knowledge, skills, and values in learning (Saunders, 1988). They are used to enhance the learning process by injecting fun, stimulating competition, generating energy, and providing opportunities for people to work together.

The risks in the use of games and simulations are the possibility of learning the wrong things; the possibly weak relation to training objectives; the

games activities characterized by structured competition that allow employees to learn specific skills

simulations operating models of physical or social events designed to represent reality

emphasis on winning; and the resultant overconfidence in one's ability to manipulate the environment (Greenlaw, Herron, & Ramdon, 1962).

TIPS FOR TRAINERS   The design of the game or simulation begins with a critical question: What is the key task to be learned? At the beginning of the exercise, the trainer should state the learning objective, as participants will compete to win, not to learn. Then the roles of the players must be defined. Models of effective performance are built into the program. Simulations and games allow more flexibility than most other exercises, as complicating factors or unexpected events can be built into the program. For example, in a pilot-training simulation, a blizzard may be introduced.

With technology as the base for many simulations, it is tempting to use the same technology found in the workplace as the training technology. This may not be such a great idea. One trader, working on software simulating financial transactions, pressed the wrong key during training and posted an offering of futures contracts worth US$16 million, which his employers were obliged to honour ("Trader's goof," 1998).

ROLE PLAY

Role play is a method in which employees are given the opportunity to try on or practise new behaviours in a safe situation. The emphasis is on doing and experiencing. This training method is most useful for acquiring skills in human relations or for changing attitudes. By playing the role of another, participants develop empathy for others. For example, a customer-service representative could be given instructions to play the part of a disgruntled client with a major problem. The representative can experience the frustrations of responses like "That's not my department," and "Just fill in that form over there; no, not that one."

While playing roles is a natural activity for children ("I'm the dragon, you're the monster"), acting in front of others is openly resisted by most adults. The role of the trainer is crucial. Trust has to be established. Participants should be warmed up by involving them in minor role situations, such as suggesting that a person ask one pre-set interview question. The trainer can reinforce risk taking and use mistakes as learning opportunities. Trainers could ask people to show all the wrong ways to handle an angry customer. When a critical mistake is made, the trainer can start again or rewind the case. In one role play, a police officer was testing methods of talking to a potential suicide victim on a bridge. The officer made the fatal mistake of saying, "Go ahead, I dare you," and the role-play partner jumped. The trainer immediately stated, "Well, that approach didn't work, would you like to try another?" He rewound the case and demonstrated the true value of role playing: the opportunity to practise behaviours in a safe environment (Sink, 1993). The goal of the debriefing is to teach, not to humiliate, as discussed in the Training Today 1 box.

role play   a training technique in which trainees practise newly learned skills in a safe environment

TIPS FOR TRAINERS Role play consists of three phases: development, enactment, and debriefing. A role play must be carefully designed to achieve its objectives. The scenario includes information on the time, place, character relationships, and instructions to the participants. Participants are then assigned roles and given some time to become familiar with the material. The most important stage is the debriefing, which should last two to three times longer than the enactment. In this phase, participants discuss the outcomes, correct learning is reinforced, and connections with previous learning and the real world are made. This is done by establishing the facts (what happened, what was experienced), analyzing the causes and effects of behaviours, and planning for skill or attitude changes. Some of the risks of role playing are addressed in the Training Today 1 box.

TRAINING TODAY 1 Training as Torture

Imagine standing in front of the entire class and being asked a question you are unable to answer. This feeling of humiliation and losing face does not lead to enhanced learning or better performance on the job. Yet, for many trainees, this is what happens in experiential training. Experiential training methods, including role playing, behaviour modelling, and games encourage trainee participation. Learning theory teaches us that by increasing trainee participation and active involvement, trainees learn more. But not always.

Many training methods put trainees on the spot—literally in the spotlight, forced to act in situations in which they feel very uncomfortable. One executive was encouraged to describe a time at work when he had faced a difficult situation in order to illustrate how corrective counselling worked. The person playing the role of counsellor criticized him extensively, with no intervention from the trainer. This was not training, this was torture. The outcome can be worse than losing face and not learning. Trainees may not want to return to any training course; they may actively sabotage the next sessions.

Here are some tips for trainers to take the torture out of training. Don't use games and role plays just to play

and have fun. There must be a purpose, a learning outcome, that you should share with the trainees. Try the exercise you have designed or chosen. If you are uncomfortable doing it, don't use it. Don't think that unlearning previous habits means going through extremely difficult events, like boot camp. People don't learn to swim by being thrown into the deep end of the swimming pool. Not everyone has to participate in a participative workshop. Some people can play different roles (such as observing or note taking) rather than the high profile "let us show them how they are doing it wrong" simulations. Warm-up exercises and limiting the size of the group may also create a supportive environment in which to risk behaviour by role playing or asking questions.

And if an individual does lose face? Trainers can make favourable comments by focusing on the correct actions, inviting observers to empathize with the person facing the difficulties of the task in the exercise, and asking the others to appreciate the risks taken by those who did play the game.

Source: Becker, R. (1998). Taking the misery out of experiential training. *Training 35* (2), 79–88.

GROUP DISCUSSION

Group discussion is one of the primary ways to increase trainee involvement in the learning process. It has been known for some time that group discussion serves at least five purposes:

1. It helps members recognize what they do not know but should know.
2. It is an opportunity for members to get answers to questions.
3. It allows members to get advice on matters that are of concern to them.
4. It allows persons to share ideas and derive a common wisdom.
5. It is a way for members to learn about one another as people (Zander, 1982, p. 31).

group discussion a training technique in which a leader facilitates the analysis of a problem or case

Group discussions facilitate the exchange of ideas and are a good way to develop critical thinking skills. Social and interpersonal skills are also enhanced. However, group discussions are not effective with large numbers of participants because many remain silent or unable to participate. Some group members will dominate; others' contributions will not be useful; and still others may become dogmatic in their positions on issues. Group discussions take a lot of training time, and must be carefully facilitated to manage the outcomes.

TIPS FOR TRAINERS   The group discussion is most effective when the leader can convince group members that a collective approach has some advantage over individual approaches to a problem (Gabris, 1989). Thus, the trainer should create a participative culture at the beginning of the learning process. The trainer's task, then, is to get the group to buy into the process as an activity that is both interesting and useful.

The major difficulty with expert-led groups is that comments tend to be addressed to the trainer. When faced with this situation, the best technique is to reflect the questions or comments back to other group members. Not surprisingly, positive reinforcement is critical. Reluctant members are drawn out, while the trainer utilizes the energy of more assertive individuals. When the group strays off topic, the trainer gently refocuses the discussion, supporting the participation while changing the substance (Renner, 1988; Conlin, 1989; Whyte, 1989; Wein, 1990).

As all groups quickly generate a power structure, the key to forming successful peer groups is to ensure that one individual does not dominate the discussion. The trainer does not have to be obvious (e.g., putting all the dominant personalities together). More subtle techniques can be used. For example, group members can be given roles that change with each discussion—scribe, presenter, discussion leader. If groups are kept small—four to six seems to work best (Renner, 1989)—then most members have something to do, increasing participation and decreasing chances for some individuals to dominate the process. It is harder to be aggressive when taking notes or trying to summarize the thoughts of others.

This issue is important. As Weisband (1992) suggests, the first person to speak out and to advocate a position might, in many circumstances, influence the entire discussion. The final outcome can be predicted with some certainty, especially if groups were exposed to preliminary discussions before a group member put forth a first position.

A warning to trainers dealing with groups of mixed educational backgrounds: be aware of reading speed and literacy problems. Often group work requires the participants to read a passage, case incident, or problem. Reluctance or hostility to do so may point to illiteracy. Be gentle, work the informal group process by finding a place in a hallway for someone to quietly read the material, or if this process is too obvious, summarize the main points before you assign the work. People who don't read well often have excellent memories; with care, they'll get by (Keller & Chuvala, 1992).

Of note, too, is that groups should be assigned a well-defined, easily understood task, one that is doable within the allotted time frame. Learning groups should be given every opportunity to look good in front of their peers, especially if they have to report back to a class or seminar. Since many training facilities are less than ideal, seating arrangements will vary. Any configuration that puts trainees in close proximity to one another will do, but a circle arrangement with no obvious leader's position or place is probably best. Size of group is important, too; certainly, more than 10 would be hard to handle if everyone is to participate.

Advanced communication technology is changing the way in which individuals can interact and make group decisions; many social, psychological, and physical barriers are breached. In contrast to face-to-face work, for example, Kiesler and Sproull (1992) suggest that computer-aided group work generates more aggressive and outspoken interaction, more equal participation, and more risk taking and innovation when making decisions. Trainers involved with interactive distance-learning technologies, then, should be prepared to cope with these more assertive behaviours. Also, it has been noted that the process can take longer.

ACTION LEARNING

action learning a training method in which trainees accept the challenge of studying and solving real-world problems, and accept responsibility for the solution

One of the principles outlined in the section on learning in Chapter 5 was that the most effective way of learning is by doing. **Action learning** provides the trainee with opportunities to test theories in the real world. Reginald Revans, the originator of action-learning principles, emphasizes that the learner develops skills through responsible involvement in some real, complex, and stressful problem (Revans, 1982). The action-learning method compels trainees to identify problems; develop possible solutions; test these solutions in a real-world, real-time situation; and evaluate the consequences. The aim is to solve a business problem.

The goals of action learning are to involve and to challenge the trainee. The cognitive objectives to be achieved are of the highest order: analysis, synthesis. The attitudinal objectives move the trainee from passive observation to identification with the people and the vision of the organization. This method moves students from information receivers to problem solvers. Action learning incorporates more of the adult learning principles than any other method of training: motivation, active participation, reinforcement, association, and task significance.

The majority of the time spent in action learning is dedicated to diagnosis of the problems in the field. The problems and the inherent value systems supporting the problems are assessed and challenged. This work is always done in groups, and learning by-products include group and interpersonal skills, risk taking, responsibility, and accountability (Revans, 1984). Professions use action learning to train and socialize their students. For example, students in social work are often sent to work with the homeless or welfare recipients. These students are encouraged to apply their theoretical knowledge in the field. Industry is using the precepts of action learning when employees take responsibility for quality-improvement projects. Ontario Hydro uses action-learning techniques in strategic planning, quality improvements, and a labour management project. The Faculty of Environment Studies at York University uses it as a change technique (under a different name) to solve problems such as pollution or the homeless.

Action learning projects require a commitment of energy and time from participants and their managers. Solving real organizational problems can be stressful for trainees. The difficulties of working in teams on real problems may lead to conflict and increased anxiety.

TIPS FOR TRAINERS   The action learning projects must be challenging and allow the development of alternatives. The problem must be real, and trainees should buy into the importance of the organizational problem. Trainees should receive some release time to work on the project and some training in group work skills to enable collaboration. The group working on the project should be small (four to seven members) enough to develop trust, but contain a diverse set of skills to enable creative solutions. The learning process should be monitored and the trainees held accountable for their proposed solutions.

WHICH TRAINING METHOD IS BEST?

Although we discussed training methods one by one, trainers mix or combine training methods (e.g., case studies with lecturing). This combination of methods allows participants to learn in ways that work for them, allow multiple learning outcomes to be achieved, and increases the possibility that the training will be applied on the job. Trainers need to become skilled in a variety of approaches to learning.

Trainers use a variety of methods to achieve the various objectives of the training program. Their preferences may be influenced by developmental costs or difficulties in implementation. Although there is very little information about the relative effectiveness of these methods available, Table 6.1 summarizes the results of one study in which employers were asked to report the use of instructional methods (Industry Report, 1999).

Few studies have been conducted comparing the relative effectiveness of training methods. The Belcourt and Saks (1998) survey, completed by 150 experienced professional trainers (members of the OSTD), revealed a hierarchy of effectiveness in training methods. As a general principle, the more highly involved the trainee is in the learning process and the more the training situation resembles the job, the more likely it is that transfer will occur. These methods include on-the-job and one-on-one training, simulations, role plays, behaviour modelling, self-study, case studies, and multimedia. A combination of these methods results in even greater transfer. Other methods, such as lectures, discussions, video conferencing, and lunch and learn programs, were not related to transfer, perhaps because these techniques allow (and indeed require) that trainees be passive absorbers of information.

Two other large surveys of training directors found that each of nine training techniques were effective in achieving different types of training goals (Carrol, Paine, & Ivancevich, 1972; Newstrom, 1980). For example, the case study was rated as most effective for problem-solving skills and computer-based instruction best for knowledge retention. Role play was evaluated as the best for changing attitudes and developing interpersonal skills. However, these are only individual perceptions and do not provide information on actual trainee achievements. The effectiveness of a training method depends entirely upon its efficacy in the achievement of learning objectives, which, as you may remember, can be grouped into head, hand, and heart (knowledge, skills, and attitudes). However, a method can be extremely effective for teaching a skill, but be so expensive to design and administer that trainers always consider cost as well as benefits. Trainers will choose one method over another if a trainee is more likely to apply the newly acquired skills on the job. Table 6.2 summarizes these three decision factors and rates the methods against them:

- determine the learning objective, and match the training methods to that objective
- consider the costs of the method and its potential benefits
- determine suitability for transfer to the organization

Use the lecture method when you want to impart large amounts of information quickly and cheaply to large groups of people. To teach skills such as

TABLE 6.1 REPORTED USE OF INSTRUCTIONAL METHODS

METHOD	PERCENTAGE USING METHOD
Classroom—live	90
Workbooks/manuals	74
Videotapes	70
Public seminars	56
Computer-based training	54
Self study—no computers	39
Role plays	37
Internet	36
Audiocassettes	36
Case studies	33
Games or simulations	23
Video conferencing	23

TABLE 6.2 CHOOSING A TRAINING METHOD

Method	METHOD IS EFFECTIVE FOR THE LEARNING OF ...			COSTS		USE ON THE JOB
	knowledge	skills	attitudes	Dev $	Admin$	Transfer
Lecture	yes	no	no	low	low	low
Video	yes	no	yes	high	low	med
Discussion	no	no	yes	low	low	low
Behaviour modelling	no	yes	no	high	high	high
Role play	no	yes	yes	mod	mod	high
Case study	yes	med	yes	mod	low	med
Case incident	med	med	med	med	med	med
Games	no	med	no	med	med	low
Simulations	yes	yes	no	high	high	high
Tech-based training	yes	yes	no	high	low	high

interviewing to all managers, the most effective method is behaviour modelling.

The table does not list other factors that are important to a trainer. How skilled is the trainer in a particular training technique? If a trainer does not understand technology, then that option may be eliminated. Another critical factor not explored in the summary table is the profile of the trainees. Are they motivated enough for action learning? Do they have the literacy skills necessary to understand a lengthy case? Equally important is the support from management, both in time and resources. Would an employee be allowed the time necessary to participate in action learning, or be given just enough time off work to attend a lecture? Is there equipment support to run a simulation or a technology-based method?

Each method has its place; the choice varies according to the learning objectives, the cost of development and administration, its potential for transfer, trainee characteristics, trainer skill or preference, trainee characteristics, and resource support. Mixing, adapting, and blending methods will result in more learning.

SUMMARY

The most frequently used off-the-job training techniques were discussed. These included lecturing, behaviour modelling, technology-based learning, cases and case incidents, games and simulations, role play, and action learning. The advantages and disadvantages of each method were outlined. Suggestions on the use of these methods were given. The final section presented a way to determine which method is best, given the objectives and resources available.

KEY TERMS

EXERCISES

1. Working in small groups, prepare a 30-minute lecture (on a topic of your choice), following the guidelines for trainers outlined in the text.

2. Technology-based training has so many advantages over other training that an increasing percentage of training budgets are being used for this method. Go to these sites: <**www. sdla.org**> (US Distance Learning Association), <**www.trainingsupersite. com**> (Lakewood Publications online, including articles from training magazine and related newsletters). Find articles on technology-based training and, in conjunction with your text book, develop a list of the advantages and disadvantages of technology-based training.

3. For information on thousands of courses, go to the human resources development site, the interactive training inventory <**www.trainingiti.com**>. Identify the methods used to teach various topics. Choose three courses that you would like to take, and identify the training method used. Discuss the advantages and disadvantages of each of the methods.

4. You have been asked to develop a course to teach senior executives how to use e-mail. Which training method would you use and why?

RUNNING CASE PART 2: VANDALAIS DEPARTMENT STORES

Refer to the Vandalais Department Stores case described in Chapter 5. What are the training methods that are being used in the structured employment interview training program, and what are the advantages and disadvantages of using each of them in a training program? If you were designing this training program, would you choose to use the same training methods? Explain your reasoning.

Consider each of the training methods described in this chapter. For each one, answer the following questions:

1. Describe how each training method might be used for the structured employment interview training program.

2. What are the advantages and disadvantages of using each training method for the structured employment interview training program?

3. How effective do you think each training method would be for the structured employment interview training program?

4. If you were designing the structured employment interview training program, which training methods would you include in your program and why?

TRAINING METHODS

- lecturing
- behaviour modelling
- technology-based training
- the case method
- the case incident method
- games and simulations
- role play
- action learning

REFERENCES

Allan, K. (1993). Computer courses ensure uniform training. *Personnel Journal* (June), 65–71.

Atkins, E. (1999, March) Winning through prevention. *Workplace News*, p 9.

Belcourt, M., & Saks, A.M. (1998). Training methods and the transfer of training. *Canadian Learning Journal* (February), 3.

Buller, M., & McEvoy, G. (1990). Exploring the long-term effects of behaviour modelling training. *Journal of Organizational Change Management 3* (1).

Carrol, S.J., Paine, F.T., & Ivancevich, J.J. (1972). The relative effectiveness of training methods—expert opinion and research. *Personnel Psychology 25*, 495–510.

Clark, B. (1985). *Optimizing learning: The integrative education model in the classroom.* New York: New York Press.

Conlin, J. (1989). Conflict at meetings: Come out fighting. *Successful Meetings 38* (6), 30–36.

Craig, R.L. (1987). *Training and development handbook: A guide to human resource development* (pp. 414–429). New York: McGraw-Hill Inc.

Filipczak, B. (1994). Distance teamwork. *Training 31* (4), 71.

Gabris, G. 1989. Educating elected officials in strategic goal setting. *Public Productivity and Management Review 13* (2), 161–175.

Geber, B. (1994). The wonderful world of cyber Sally. *Training 31* (5), 8.

Georges, J.C. (1988). Why soft-skills training doesn't take. *Training 25* (4), 44–45.

Greengard, S. (1993). How technology is advancing. *HR Professional Journal 72* (9), 28–31.

Greenlaw, B., Herron, M., & Ramdon, L. (1962). *Business simulation in industrial and university education.* Englewood Cliffs, NJ: Prentice-Hall.

Industry report. (1999). *Training 36* (10), p. 54.

Keller, S., & Chuvala, J. (1992). Training: Tricks of the trade. *Security Management 36* (7).

Kenny, B., Lea, E., & Luffman, G. (1992). *Cases in business policy* (2nd ed.). Oxford: Blackwell Publishers.

Kiesler, S., & Sproull, L. (1992). Group decision making and communication technology. *Organizational Behaviour and Human Decision Processes 52* (1), 96–123.

Kulig, P. (1998, November 2). Conferences: personnel development or personal perk. *Canadian HR Reporter*, p. 20.

Leenders, M.R., & Erskine, J.A. (1973). *Case research: The case writing process.* London: University of Western Ontario Press.

Miles, K.W., & Griffith, E.R. (1993). Developing an hour of CBT: The quick and dirty method. *CBT Directions* (April–May), 28–33.

Newstrom, J.W. (1980). Evaluating the effectiveness of training methods. *Personnel Administrator 25* (1), 55–60.

Pearce, J.A., Robinson, R.B., Jr., & Zahra Shaker, A. (1989). *An industry approach to cases in strategic management.* Boston: Irwin Publishing.

Renner, P. (1988). *The quick instructional planner.* Vancouver: Training Associates Ltd.

———. (1989). *The instructor's survival kit* (2nd ed.). Vancouver: Training Associates Ltd.

Revans, R.W. (1982). *The origins and growth of action learning.* Gock, Sweden: Bratt-Institute for Neues Lernen.

———. (1984). Action learning: Are we getting there? *Management Decision Journal 22* (1), pp. 45–52.

Robinson, J.C. (1982). *Developing managers through behaviour modelling.* Austin: Texas.

Sabido, M. (1981). *Towards the social use of soap operas.* Mexico City, Mexico: Institute for Communications Research.

Salopek, J. (1998a) Quotient. *Training and Development 52* (11), 21–34.

———. (1998b) Workstation meets Playstation. *Training and Development 52* (8), 26–35.

Saunders, D. (1988). *Learning from experience through games and simulations.* London: SAGSET Publications.

Schnelle, K. (1967). *Case analysis and business problem solving.* New York: McGraw Hill.

Smith, R. (1986). *The scope and growth of distance education.* Regional seminar on distance education. Bangkok: Asian Development Bank.

Stahmer, A. (1991). Use of technologies for training in Canadian companies (Report 651). Ottawa: Employment and Immigration.

Traders goof cost $16 million. (1998, November 20). *The Globe and Mail*, p. B3.

Wein, G. (1990). Experts as trainers. *Training and Development Journal 44* (7), 29–30.

Weisband, S. (1992). Group discussion and first advocacy effects in computer-mediated and face-to-face decision-making groups. *Organizational Behaviour and Human Decision Processes 53* (3), 352–380.

Whyte, G. (1989). Group think reconsidered. *Academy of Management Review 14* (1), 40–56.

Wright, P. (1988). The incident as a technique for teaching undergraduates in hospitality management and food administration. *Hospitality Education and Research Journal 12* (1), 16–28.

————. (1992). The CEO and the business school: Is there potential for increased cooperation? *Association of Management Proceedings: Education 10* (1), 41–45.

Yin, R.K. (1985). *Case study research: Design and methods.* Beverly Hills: Sage Publications.

Zander, A. (1982). *Making groups effective.* San Francisco: Jossey-Bass Publishers.

7

ON-THE-JOB
TRAINING METHODS

CHAPTER GOALS

This chapter looks at methods used by managers and performance experts
to train employees on the job. In contrast to the previous chapter, which
examined training that typically occurs away from the job, here we examine
on-the-job techniques to teach skills, as well as more general developmental
methods including mentoring and coaching.

After reading this chapter you should be able to

- design a learning experience to teach a new skill on the job
- describe how performance aids and electronic performance support
  systems can improve performance on the job
- discuss the advantages and disadvantages of coaching and mentoring
- outline the role of the government, labour, and industry in operating an
  effective apprenticeship program
- evaluate the effectiveness of self-learning as a training method
- describe the steps in organizational development

We start with the most basic form of training that has been used since the beginning when one person had to teach someone how to do something.

SHOW AND TELL

on-the-job training (OJT) a training technique in which inexperienced employees learn through observing and being instructed by more experienced employees

The most common practice for teaching employees new skills is to assign them to a manager or an experienced operator. Most of us remember the time when someone was assigned the task of teaching us how to perform some company task, such as operating a cash register, or learning how to make a request for supplies. **On-the-job training (OJT)** consists of two steps: preparation and instruction (Rothwell & Kazanas, 1990). During the preparation phase, the instructor breaks down the job into small tasks, prepares all the equipment and supplies necessary to do the task, and allocates a time frame in which to learn each task. The instruction phase consists of tell, show, explain, and demonstrate. The instructor tells the trainee the goal of the instruction, demonstrates how to do the task, and then explains the key components. Another demonstration should follow. At this point, the trainee should try the task, under guidance, and with feedback and reinforcement. Each task is learned in a similar way, until the whole job can be completed without error. Refer to the Appendix for a step-by-step description of this useful technique.

From an employer's viewpoint, there is ample evidence to indicate that OJT affects both organizational and individual performance. Among factory employees, for example, those who have had OJT and longer experience tend to receive better performance ratings than those without training and with less experience (Nollen & Gaertner, 1991). Younger employees who have experienced some formal OJT appear to be less likely to switch jobs (Lynch, 1991), show improved morale, and are easier to cross-train (Rothwell & Kazanas, 1990). On-the-job training should be less expensive, because there is no need to develop training materials. The only cost will be the loss of labour time for the teacher and the student, but even during this time some production occurs. There is little need for off-site classrooms or transportation expenses. In an ideal OJT environment, trainees are learning skills they can use immediately, and receive feedback and reinforcement when they do.

The small-business sector—where most new employment is being created—rarely offers courses and workshops for employees. OJT is ideal for small companies because of the limited investment needed to conduct the training. Furthermore, in small companies it may be possible to pair employees with similar languages.

The risks are that an inept employee will transfer less than desirable work habits to a new employee. OJT means that the traditional ways of doing things will be passed on to all newcomers. It is unlikely that managers or other employees have any skills or knowledge about teaching, and will not realize the importance of learning principles such as feedback, reinforcement, and practice. Another problem occurs when those doing the training are worried that the newly trained employees will one day take over their jobs. The instructors must have some incentive for passing on their knowledge and skills. Some of these trainers abuse their position by making the trainee do all the dirty work. The trainee may not learn more advanced skills. OJT can be time consuming, and some employees feel penalized when they can't make as much money or meet their goals because of the time they wasted training. Most of these problems can be overcome by providing training and incentives to the OJT instructors. The Training Today 1 box describes the characteristics of an effective OJT instructor.

PERFORMANCE AIDS

A **performance aid** is *any* device that helps an employee do the job. Aids can be signs or prompts ("Have you turned off the computer?"); trouble-shooting aids ("If the red light goes on, the machine needs oil"); instructions in sequence ("To empty the machine, follow the next five steps"); a special tool or gauge (a long stick to measure how much gas is in an inaccessible tank); flash cards to help counsel clients; or pictures (of a perfectly set table, for example) (Meyers, 1991; Ukens, 1993).

performance aid a device that helps an employee perform on the job

The motivation behind the use of performance aids is that requiring the memorization of sequences and tasks sometimes takes too much training time, especially if the task is not repeated daily. As well, new employees can be on the job more quickly if armed with a series of temporary performance aids. Finally, routine (and not so routine) trouble-shooting and repair responses can be performed much more quickly and with less frustration.

Employees who are placed in positions where they must react very quickly may not be able to rely on memory. A panel operator in a nuclear power plant, for example, may have 15 seconds (or less) to perform a series of safety sequences. In the less hectic world of insurance sales, one manager found that a potentially sound sales trainee constantly neglected to complete the entire sales sequence and paperwork. Both these employees, despite their vastly different work environments, were helped by performance aids.

In the first instance, an indexed manual containing various operating sequences was developed and placed on a wheeled trolley within easy reach of all the operators' positions. The sales problem was solved by creating a checklist containing all the steps or tasks to be completed each time the salesperson visited a prospective client. Each step completed was checked off by the employee and the sheet was signed and dated. The manager then reviewed each call with the trainee. In this case, the checklist was discarded after about three weeks as the sales trainee was performing to the standards set by management (Arajis, 1991).

When designing visual performance aids that help employees remember key information, all the skills of the graphic artist's craft should be utilized. Ease in reading, space between letters, colour, boldness, symbols, and graphic language ("Pull Here!") are all used to communicate (Arajis, 1991; Cowen, 1992; King, 1994). Audio aids also must clearly communicate intent. A taped warning ("Connect your safety harness!") may be useless, but a buzzer alarm is hard to ignore.

The designers of every training program, then, should consider how performance aids might save money and time. With ingenuity, the trainee's work-life not only can be made easier but significant improvements in both performance, downtime, and safety records can result. Performance aids work much better when they are based on technology, as are electronic performance-support systems.

ELECTRONIC PERFORMANCE-SUPPORT SYSTEMS

electronic performance-support system (EPSS)
a computer-based system that provides information, advice, teaching on the job to improve performance

An **electronic performance-support system (EPSS)** is a computer-based system that improves employee productivity by providing on-the-job access to integrated information, advice, and learning experiences (Raybould, 1990). More simply, they are computer programs that help solve work-related problems. These systems provide several types of support including assisting, warning, advising, teaching, and evaluating. They are job aids.

All of us who have pressed the HELP icon on a computer and received instructions on how to design a pie chart have experienced EPSS. The goal of an EPSS is to provide whatever is necessary to generate performance and learning at the time it is needed. This brings training back full cycle to its origins. Workers first learned on the job site with master craftsmen, using observation, explanation, questions, and coaching. With large numbers of employees to train, training moved out of the workplace and into formal classrooms. This resulted in moving training out of the job context. Subject-matter experts, not job experts, taught. With computers, we can return to the advantages of having someone constantly on the job to assist with questions and problems. When KPMG, one of the six big accounting firms, needed to train all its employees on a new tax-planning service, it chose EPSS over classroom training. The EPSS saved in delivery time (consultants did not need to spend three weeks in classrooms) and reduced costs in updates (Smith, 1996).

Alberta Pacific Forest Industries and Bayer Inc., at their Sarnia plant extol the advantages of EPSS for their safety, maintenance, and laboratory training: learning occurs when workers need it most, on site; it allows for continual upgrading; it allows for individual differences in the pace of learning; and it allows links to suppliers' training and tracks learning accomplishments (Kulig, 1998).

EPSS offers even more advantages than computer-based training. With EPSS, information is accessed only when it is needed. Only the information that is needed is given; there is no information overload. It is ridiculous to expect that enough information can be crammed into everyone's memory during training, then banked for access later. EPSS is particularly useful for training in high-turnover jobs, like hotel staff (Gebber, 1991), and tasks that are difficult, are performed infrequently, and must be performed perfectly (Ruyle, 1991). As increasing number of employees use personal computers, EPSS will become the norm in training employees such as cashiers, bank tellers, insurance agents, and so on.

Resistance to computer-based training stems from a hesitation on the part of the organization to commit to rapidly changing hardware. Currently, companies are investing in only a limited number of learning stations, where trainees go to work on courseware. The high cost and rapid obsolescence of the hardware necessary to run the courseware make managers reluctant to invest. Until every employee is provided with a personal computer that can handle multimedia applications, the many advantages of training technology are reduced.

A second inhibiting factor is the instructors themselves. Some traditional trainers are not computer literate, and rightly fear the change to computer-based training. They recognize that they can be replaced by the technology. A low-threat opportunity to allow trainers to test the multimedia approach is to place the learning stations in the classroom (O'Keefe, 1991). Most industry analysts perceive these two barriers as temporary problems. Computer-based training will become a standard way of supplying information, particularly for current generations who are not computer phobic.

APPRENTICESHIP

An **apprenticeship** can be described as an integrated human resource development (HRD) technique that combines on-the-job training with classroom

apprenticeship a learning experience that combines on-the-job training with classroom instruction

instruction. Apprenticeship training involves teaching skills and the supporting theory. The job-instruction component is used to teach the requisite skills of a particular trade or occupation. Classroom instruction, which comprises a relatively minor portion of the program (usually about 10 percent), teaches related theory and design concepts. For example, the four-year plumber program includes only three eight-week in-school sessions. In the classroom, plumber apprentices learn about such things as the physical properties of piping and other plumbing materials, industry codes, safety rules and operating procedures, trade tools and equipment, soldering techniques, and the characteristics of various fittings and piping systems. On the job, the trainees become familiar with relevant codes, regulations, and specifications, and learn to install, service, and test systems and equipment.

In Canada, the present apprenticeship system covers more than 65 regulated occupations in four occupational sectors: construction (e.g., stone mason, electrician, carpenter, plumber), motive power (motor-vehicle mechanic, machinist), industrial (industrial mechanic, millwright), and service (baker, cook, hairstylist). In some of these regulated occupations, apprentices must earn a certificate of qualification by passing a provincial government examination. Apprentices who pass an interprovincial examination with a minimum grade of 70 percent are awarded a red seal, indicating their qualifications are acceptable across Canada. Despite the fact that there is a labour shortage in trades and those trained in the trades are guaranteed employment, Canadians do not actively pursue vocational training, as discussed in the Training Today 2 box.

PARTNERS IN APPRENTICESHIP

Apprenticeship training differs from other job-instruction techniques in that it is regulated through a partnership among government, labour, and industry. In Canada, the federal government pays for in-school training and income support; provincial governments administer the programs and pay for classroom facilities and instructors; employers absorb the costs of workplace training; and apprentices initiate the process by finding employers willing to sponsor them.

This partnership can provide an effective and powerful mechanism to match human resources with opportunities in industry, given social and economic constraints. The conflicting goals of each partner, however, can have an impact on the effectiveness of apprenticeship as a training method and a possible solution to shortages of skilled labour. Consensus among the partners and cooperation among program participants are critical elements in the smooth and efficient operation of the system (McKenna, 1993).

Unlike corporate-sponsored training programs that address the specific needs of an organization, apprenticeships are focused on the collective training needs of specific occupations within broad industrial categories (Moskal, 1991). Consequently, the skills learned through apprenticeship training are

TRAINING TODAY 2 University or Vocational Education for Canadians?

Training must fit into a national culture or this activity will not be effective, used, or accepted. Consider the following scenario: Newly married Mr. and Mrs. Jones, a middle-class couple, are watching their baby daughter crawl around on the rug. He turns to her (or vice versa) and says: "Isn't she a bright little one, darling? I'll bet she grows up to be a fine journeyman electrician!"

An unlikely statement, indeed, for apprenticeships have never captured the imagination of the Canadian public, politicians, or educators. Except in the construction industry (there are a few other exceptions), apprenticeships have never fit into the Canadian culture. Mr. or Mrs. Jones is much more likely to say: "I'll bet she grows up to be a fine electrical *engineer*," librarian, teacher, or any other occupation traditionally viewed as acceptable in middle-class society. Even parents who earn a lot of money and respect as tradespeople want their children to go to university.

Industry, too, generally has been unwilling to invest in apprenticeships because, in the past, skilled-labour shortages could be made up through immigration. As our standard of living fell relative to other countries throughout the 1980s and 1990s, however, fewer trained individuals immigrated to this country. The result is that Canada now faces a critical shortage of skilled labour. Only 30 percent of our high-school graduates are expected to earn college diplomas or university degrees. To remain competitive, politicians and educators must refocus their attention toward the 70 percent who will most likely constitute the much needed pool from which future skilled employees and technicians are drawn.

To make apprenticeships more acceptable as an alternative to college or university, the prestige of technical studies has to be raised and hands-on (cooperative) components made more meaningful (Reynolds, 1993). Students and parents must become convinced that the apprentice concept leads to an acceptable living standard and that the training does not lead to dead-end, uninteresting careers (Del Valle, 1993).

If apprenticeship training could be adapted to suit the large number of emerging white-collar and technical occupations (Graham, 1989), the public's image of apprenticeship would be improved and the resulting programs would fit more securely into the Canadian culture. In addition, these programs would be more attractive as vehicles of upward mobility, especially if there were a closer link to the higher-education system. The oft-touted German example is of particular importance here, as 65 percent of graduating engineers have previous apprenticeship training (Hrynyshyn, 1993). In the United States, a machinist trained to program and operate computer-controlled machines in the shop can earn US$50 000 to US$80 000.

Given the skills shortage crises faced by many industrial sectors, it is likely that increased emphasis will be placed on apprenticeships, as this method is one of the most effective and practical ways of teaching skills occupations.

---

transferable within an occupation, across a province, and across Canada. For example, in the construction industry, carpenters, electricians, plumbers, and masons are trained to meet standards recognized throughout the trade. This flexibility provides advantages to the worker and the industry when regional fluctuations occur in the supply and demand of skilled labour. The system also is highly dependent on employers, however, for they must accept the responsibility for establishing and maintaining adequate standards of job performance.

In determining acceptable qualifications and performance standards for the future, industry and government must address the special needs of new labour groups like women and minorities, eliminating standards or test criteria that might unjustly limit opportunities. For example, criteria pertaining to physical strength might be relaxed or eliminated by making simple changes in job design. Employers that intend to utilize apprenticeships also will need to become more sensitive to the special needs of working mothers and to the various religious or cultural backgrounds of employees as more flexible work schedules may be required to better accommodate those with family or other commitments (Still, 1992).

THE ROLE OF GOVERNMENT   The role of government is to administer apprenticeship programs and to ensure that the demands and needs of both industry and labour are fairly addressed. Without government intervention and commitment, the system can rapidly deteriorate, providing industry with the opportunity to exploit apprentices. Government also provides funding (provincially) through the various ministries of education or colleges and universities that supply classroom facilities and instructors, and (federally) through Human Resources Development Canada, which offers training allowances to apprentices during in-class periods.

Governments also strive to ensure that programs are compatible with general economic and social policies that impact on the business environment and the labour market. For example, adjustments to tax and trade policy, such as the Goods and Services Tax (GST) and the Free Trade Agreement, can cause industry to pursue new business and marketing strategies that can have an effect on economic growth and labour markets. Similarly, changes in immigration policy, human rights legislation, human resource legislation, and subsidization can alter the labour-pool mix and the types of jobs available. Legislation prohibiting discrimination based on sex and other characteristics, for example, has created potential opportunities for women in nontraditional occupations (Brodsky, 1989). Conversely, the redistribution of government funding from public education to public health care creates budget constraints that place a greater economic burden on industry to absorb the costs of training.

A high-priority concern voiced by apprentices is their potential for career advancement. Modifications to the education system could enhance the mobility of apprentices interested in professional careers by eliminating barriers between academic and training programs. Upgrading apprenticeship programs to include general knowledge in language, math, and science, might enable apprentices to apply credits toward higher education or other programs.

THE ROLE OF LABOUR   The interests of labour are represented by advisory committees made up of union and selected industry representatives. Some trade unions tend to focus on restricting the numbers of certified tradespeople to maintain wage levels and job security for their members. Conversely, a number of unions have established supplementary classroom training programs independent of the formal apprenticeship system to train apprentices to meet their own specified criteria. This practice may attest to the perceived ineffectiveness of the present system and its inability to respond quickly enough to changes demanded by industry; however, this activity may also serve as a screening process to restrict the hiring of externally trained workers (who would not meet the criteria) and to help retain members trained in-house.

The cooperation of unions in the system is important, given their power and highly organized structures (Riccucci, 1991). Unions can help ensure that the interests of apprentices are protected in the workplace and that their training meets established standards. Unions can also play a key role in helping to select and train industry trainers to ensure their teaching abilities are as effective as their trade skills.

THE ROLE OF INDUSTRY Employers provide on-the-job training without subsidy, pay the apprentices and certified workers who teach them, absorb lost productivity as the apprentices learn their skills, and accommodate apprentice's absences during classroom training. The reasons for the reluctance of employers in apprenticeship programs have focused on cost. Employers bear 90 percent of the cost of apprenticeship training. Until recently, it was cheaper for companies to hire skilled immigrants from Europe than to train apprentices. Current trends in our labour market, however, are creating new demand. All sectors of Canadian industry will need to focus attention on training skilled workers; apprenticeship training is one of the most viable options. Increasing participation rates might provide the impetus needed to revive and to improve apprenticeship training in Canada.

Industry commitment and initiative are the driving forces behind the success of apprenticeship programs elsewhere because opportunities for trainees must be created, and employers are solely responsible for hiring apprentices and for providing them with adequate training, experience, and wages. Employers can improve the training further by establishing standard qualifications for workplace trainers.

Unfortunately, many managers do not realize the cost benefits of apprenticeship, as it is always difficult to relate training directly to increased productivity and profitability. As a result, some employers have attempted to take advantage of the system by not providing adequate training or resources, preferring instead to keep apprentices in the same jobs long enough to increase their output and contribution to revenues. Employers also have no guarantee that the apprentices they train will remain with them once they have completed their programs. If apprentices choose to leave, their employers will have borne their training costs without receiving the expected benefits.

Industry also responds more rapidly than government to changes in the economy. During past recessionary periods, many employers have quickly reduced their apprenticeship programs to save costs, resulting in an immediate and long-term impact on the labour market (Donnelly, 1994).

Regardless of the support that government agencies and educational institutions may provide, it is still more efficient for businesses to be predominantly responsible for training their own skilled workers. In addition to cost and the many practical considerations (employers already have the tools, equipment, materials, and experts needed for training purposes), industry also is better able to keep pace with changes in technology and product innovation.

THE EFFECTIVENESS OF APPRENTICESHIP AS A TRAINING METHOD

The effectiveness of a training intervention can be measured in two ways: its ability to achieve the specified learning objectives, and the contribution of these objectives to an industry's overall goals. If the benefits of apprenticeship training cannot be related to a company's profitability, employers will not be willing to participate. This factor is particularly relevant in apprenticeship schemes that are based on voluntary cooperation among industry, labour, and government. Because industry must take the initiative to make a program work and must also bear most of the cost, employers must be convinced of the cost benefits before a program will be accepted.

The cost-effectiveness of apprenticeship training, however, is difficult to determine with any accuracy. Some early studies indicated that employers are able to recover their investment between the second and third years of an apprentice's term. Obviously, the "break-even" point will vary widely depending on the industry and the depth and quality of training provided. In cases where the expected payback period exceeds the training period, employers may be even more reluctant to invest in a program. In addition, because apprentices' skills are transferable once they are certified, graduates may choose not to continue working with their sponsoring firms. Unfortunately, the high cost of apprenticeship sometimes leads to an exploitation of apprentices by employers who seek to offset their expenses by using them as a source of cheap labour.

Despite the recent infusion of government funding, much of Canada's apprenticeship system remains antiquated. Outmoded legislation, outdated curricula, poor pay for teachers, archaic entry and completion regulations, and low-prestige entry modes still combine to discourage many young people from considering careers in the skilled trades. Program expansion and enhancement would be key elements in creating apprenticeships that meet the needs of current and future industries, while developing attractive and challenging career alternatives for a greater segment of our labour force.

COACHING

A **coach** is a seasoned employee (most often a manager) who works closely with another employee to motivate, to teach, and to provide support through feedback and reinforcement. The coach also guides the employee in learning by helping to find experts or resources. Although coaching has evolved into a motivational technique that is seen as a prelude to progressive discipline, and as a method for dealing with performance problems, it will be discussed here as a vehicle for self-development in the more positive sense. Closely related to self-development, the coaching function can be defined as the planned use of opportunities in the work environment to improve or to enhance employee strengths or potential. Weaknesses are considered only if they prevent the employee from functioning, or if they are below the manager's tolerance level (Lovin and Casstevens, 1971; Frankel & Otazo, 1992).

coach an experienced employee who motivates, teaches, and supports another employee

The key elements in this definition of coaching are: "planned," "opportunities in the work environment," and "strengths." First, the process revolves around an agreed-upon plan or set of objectives developed mutually by employee and manager. Development does not occur haphazardly or by chance; the process proceeds in a logical agreed-upon fashion. Second, the work environment is the training laboratory (sometimes expanded to include the community) as transfers, special assignments, assigned responsibility, vacation replacements, conference speaking engagements are coaching opportunities. The necessary formal infrastructure, perhaps attached to the firm's appraisal or evaluation system, must be in place for the system to work (Blakesley, 1992).

Most managers want to influence their employees' performance. How (or if) they go about this task determines in large part the characteristics of the superior/subordinate relationship and whether the organization is effective. Employees react to these attempts to influence them according to their desire for variety or challenge, their ability to cope with pressure or stress, and the rate at which they can deal with change. A manager must realize that each individual is unique and must value this uniqueness; only then will he or she take the time to help the employee develop through coaching strategies (Hopkins & Kleiner, 1993; Jacobs, 1989).

As well, much of the literature deals with employee *weaknesses*. The manager must fight this tendency, concentrating instead on improving strengths. If, for example, an employee is shy, with poor public-speaking skills, it makes little sense to "coach" that employee by allowing him or her to attend departmental-level meetings as the manager's representative. Not only will his or her performance likely be poor (a reflection on the coach), but the employee's inadequacies will be accentuated and made known to a larger group. Conversely, an employee who excels at public speaking might be asked, as part of a planned developmental strategy, to help present the unit's annual report to senior management, further improving upon a considerable strength (Beh, 1993).

To make coaching work, the employee and the coach must trust each other; otherwise development will be seen by the employee as extra work. Indeed, perhaps the most important aspect of the coaching process is ongoing dialogue and feedback. It is only under these conditions that employees participate willingly in a two-way process that often requires extra effort and risk taking (Kruse, 1993).

The coaching process begins with a dialogue between coach and employee, during which a set of objectives is defined. Then, coaching opportunities are identified by a mutual examination of the environment. A long-term plan is struck, along with an evaluation or measurement procedure. As well, the process is fitted into the employee's career-development goals and usually made part of the organization's long-term strategies. The term "usually" is used to cover the situation in which an employee is leaving an organization by mutual consent, perhaps because he or she has outgrown a job and wishes to move on. Here, the employer can help the individual leave on amiable terms by continuing the coaching activity.

The employee performs the agreed-upon task (see below) and then reports to the supervisor both informally and formally during the annual or semi-annual evaluation. They discuss and agree, or maybe disagree, on the results of the current program and then plan the next round of activity, as coaching is an ongoing process (Kroeger, 1991). With practice, this approach develops into a continual transfer of skills (Whittaker, 1993; Azar, 1993).

Several devices can be used as coaching tools. For example, a special-project assignment that will enhance a specific skill is a useful approach, as there is no need to reorganize other work or to hire additional staff. Conversely, job rotation often requires extensive preparation, in that employees exchange entire jobs on a long-term basis.

Although vacation replacement has long been used as an upgrading technique, its usefulness has been questioned. The replacement position rarely carries real authority. Most employees play only a caretaker role, then return to their original jobs without having accomplished or learned much.

A more useful coaching technique is to design a method or schedule of representation, either at meetings or as committee members. Depending upon the skill or knowledge to be developed, the benefits can be significant, as this long-term exposure to more senior colleagues benefits the employee, while freeing the coach for other tasks. In large retail organizations, for example, a management trainee may be rotated through several departments before choosing one in which to specialize.

Where assignments outside the regular work area are impractical, job redesign or restructuring may be used. Here, some portion of the job is changed so that new skills must be used. The restructuring of one job may, of course, affect the work of others. Job redesign should be part of an overall work strategy that embraces an entire work unit.

There may be situations in which even job restructuring is impossible. The coach may then have no choice but to suggest job enlargement—the employee taking on more work. Although often not a popular alternative, it may be necessary that an employee perform certain new tasks to grow professionally. A larger job may be the only answer. This approach will work best with individuals who have been on the job for some time and are mature to the task. A less-experienced person might panic when faced with more work.

As the last three coaching activities to be mentioned here—conference attendance, professional memberships, and teaching/publishing—take place outside the firm, the coach must be concerned with control over the process. Conferences, in particular, can be treated as social events rather than as serious opportunities to learn. Although there may be spinoff benefits (e.g., exposure to leading experts or networking), conferences must be chosen where attendance will meet a clearly defined purpose.

Similarly, professional societies can be used for a number of reasons—networking, publicity, leadership development, training, updating, and group-participation enhancement. Again, these functions need to serve a planned purpose. If, for example, an employee's job provides little opportunity to manage others, the coach might suggest a term as chairperson of the annual conference committee. Likewise, an employee who shows promise as a speaker might be coaxed into volunteering as master of ceremonies for a fundraiser, thus gaining more experience in public speaking.

Undoubtedly, many more ideas for coaching could be found. For example, some senior executives hire professional coaches to improve their skills, as discussed in the Training Today 3 box. The key is to constantly remind oneself that coaching is the *planned* acquisition of skills and knowledge through the use of existing, or carefully modified, opportunities in the work or professional environments. This focus will prevent both the squandering of developmental opportunities on those who won't benefit and the loss of many potential training activities.

MENTORING

A process similar to coaching, mentoring places junior employees in contact with senior people who take a personal interest in their career advancement. A **mentor** is a senior, experienced, competent manager who provides coaching and counselling, and opens doors for a more junior employee, the protégé. Mentors play two major roles: career support and psychosocial support. Career support activities include coaching, sponsorship, exposure, visibility, protection, and the provision of challenging assignments. Psychosocial support roles include that of being a friend who listens and counsels, who accepts and provides feedback, and a role model for success (Noe, 1999). For example, the story is told of a young MBA who, during a presentation by a vice president,

mentor a senior manager who coaches, counsels, and supports a junior employee to enhance career opportunities

TRAINING TODAY 3 Coach or Couch?

Executives already have the club memberships and the luxury cars. They may even have a personal fitness trainer. Now the best perk is the executive coach. Despite being at the top of the organization, surrounded by employees, customers, and competitors, executives often feel lonely, isolated, and unable to discuss their work problems with trustworthy advisors. Enter the personal coach, mentor, adviser, or friend.

Executive coaching is one of the fastest growing segments of the consulting business. Numbers are hard to determine, as most companies keep these relationships confidential. It is estimated that each executive coach mentors about six senior people. Coaches are usually found by word of mouth, and charge $150 to $500 dollars per month for weekly half-hour telephone sessions.

What does the executive coach do? Well, it varies by client. Discussions centre around leadership and how to move the organization from one stage to another. Just talking freely is one benefit cited because most executives are careful when talking to employees as there is always a political context. Executives are very cautious about revealing their fears and doubts in the office. The coach, however, is not a therapist, but an adviser who helps with the thinking process. Coaches tend to be specialists in areas such as strategic management or human resources,

and limit their advice to these types of issues. For example, one coach persuaded the CEO of a medium-sized company to search further than the two candidates he had identified for a job reporting to him, and the extra effort resulted in an excellent candidate, not just an acceptable one.

Sometimes companies call in coaches when there is a problem. Coaches often help executives with interpersonal skills where, for example, an executive's abrasive style is alienating employees and colleagues. Some senior managers may be explosive or even dysfunctional, and the executive coach has to be tough enough to give advice, while running the risk of being fired. One way to show the need to change is for the coach to shadow the executive, following him to meetings and then referring to specific incidences to support the counsel.

If the executive is seriously dysfunctional, then the executive coach makes a referral to a licensed psychologist or psychiatrist. The coach is not there to do psychotherapy, but to help a manager function more effectively in the workplace.

Sources: Hamilton, K. (1996, February 5). Need a life? Get a coach. *Newsweek*, p 48; Grossman, R. J. (1996). Advisors for hire. *HR News*, p. 2; Filipczak, B. (1998). The executive coach: Helper or healer? *Training* 35 (3), 30–36.

---

spotted an error in some figures. She pointed out the mistake during the seminar in very forthright terms. The vice president didn't mind, but the resulting backlash from the middle manager responsible for preparing the data caused her to leave the job. A mentor would have coached this young person in the art of seminar participation (particularly in those conducted by vice presidents) or protected her from the wrath of an ego-bruised senior colleague. With a mentor, the protégé could have learned the political skills necessary for survival within the firm.

Both professional and academic research consistently have suggested that intensively mentored professionals have greater career prospects and higher incomes than other similar groups. For example, Chao, Walz, and Gardner (1992) found "clear differences" between what were termed "mentored individuals" and "non-mentored" individuals, while Scandura (1992) suggested that protégés' promotion records and wage levels were related directly to career and social-support systems provided through mentoring. These findings are supported by previous work. Dreher and Ash (1990), for example, found a positive relationship between mentoring, promotion, and income, as well as enhanced satisfaction with wages and benefits.

The mentor–protégé relationship used to be informal, with a senior person recognizing the talent of a junior employee and wishing to help. However, organizations now recognize mentoring as a valuable employee development tool and have moved to formalize the relationships. Jackson (1993) and Noe (1999) highlighted several areas of concern to managers wishing to implement formal mentoring programs:

- *Choice of mentors.* Mentors must be motivated to participate in the program and to make sufficient time available to their protégé. They also need to be knowledgable about how the organization really works. Participation should be voluntary. Inevitably, some assigned relationships will not work out. A procedure needs to be in place to allow either party to cancel the arrangement without too much loss of face, and employees should feel free to end the relationship without fear of retaliation.

- *Matching mentors and protégé(s).* Matching is an important process that needs to be handled with care. Should males be matched with males; females with females? There may not be enough senior women to mentor all the junior women. Hostility from men when women network with one another make some women reluctant to take on the mentoring role (Gallege, 1993). Those mentors close to retirement perform better in both the vocational and psychosocial functions (Mullen, 1998). It is important that the relationship remain confidential and for the protégé to know that it will be confidential. The right mentor must be chosen. The protégé is unlikely to feel comfortable, for example, if the mentor is his or her boss.

- *Training.* Mentors and protégés both need training. This process should entail more than giving mentors a book to read about mentoring. It should, for example, involve the opportunity to share experiences about mentoring. The training of protégés, usually as part of the induction process, is partly concerned with demonstrating the organization's commitment to mentoring, but also involves setting appropriate expectations for the mentoring relationship. Mentors could be chosen for this training, based on their previous track record in developing employees.

- *Structuring the mentoring relationship.* Some programs set out time limits on the relationship and specify minimum levels of contact. Goals, projects, activities, and resources are spelled out. The program is evaluated and those areas in which either mentors or protégés report dissatisfaction are redesigned. While commitment must be made at all levels, it is at the individual level that the process can most easily break down. Signals sent by derailed mentoring schemes include delay between assignment and first meeting with protégé, poor meeting locations (e.g., the cafeteria), and infrequent contacts.

The mentoring function can be a major factor in long-term career development. Every individual needs to learn about career options—both internal and external. Often, such information is known only to insiders (e.g., mentors). As well, strengths, weaknesses, skills, and even interests often are best assessed by an objective outsider (e.g., the mentor). Finally, career-development action plans are best assessed in concert with a more seasoned individual, one able to spot pitfalls and omissions. As an HRD intervention, then, mentoring can be one of the most useful tools to help meet what Jackson (1993) calls the "career development challenge."

SELF-DIRECTED LEARNING

self-directed learning (SDL) a process in which the individual identifies the resources necessary to learn KSA, and then manages the learning experience

Self-directed learning (SDL) is a process that occurs when individuals (sometimes groups) seek out the necessary resources to engage in learning that enhances their careers and personal growth. In the SDL model, employees assess their own needs, use a variety of organizational resources to meet those needs, and are helped with evaluating the effectiveness of meeting their needs. SDL can be as simple as a booklet that describes a new procedure or a multimedia program that teaches project management skills.

People have always learned by themselves. The Ontario Institute for Studies in Education found that about three-quarters of all adults had at least one self-directed learning project each year (OISE, 1998). Adults spend about 15 hours a week in informal learning activities. Think of your own life. You teach yourself to surf on the Net, to grow vegetables, to manage your money, and learn about the history, culture, and currency of a country you plan to visit. Many adults prefer to be self-directed learners, but years of waiting passively for training courses may have suppressed this natural curiosity to know more. However, it appears that those that manage their own learning climb higher on the corporate ladder (Zemke, 1998).

The concept has become increasingly popular because traditional training methods lack the flexibility to respond quickly to dramatic and constant organizational change. Indeed, many organizations hire people as much for their current skills as their ability to learn. Learning to learn may be the most important attribute an employee brings to the job. See the Training Today 4 box for a list of the advantages and disadvantages of self-directed learning.

Motorola implemented a SDL approach to its training program. Forty percent of their employees undertook self-study courses. The research showed that the average cost for the SDL was $7.76 per hour, compared to $13.34 hourly for classroom instruction. The results demonstrated that SDL was as effective or better than the traditional training approach. There is a strong connection between SDL and the learning organization, as discussed in Chapter 14.

Closely related to self-managed learning is self-development. Remember that SDL provides knowledge and skills for the immediate job, while the focus of self-development is to develop skills for the long term, for careers. Although employers are increasingly moving toward developing their human resources (HR) through self-managed learning, their people need a process by which to increase capabilities and skills.

Despite the rhetoric, there appears to be one issue constantly overlooked: employees need help with self-development. Indeed, it is suggested that German and Heath's (1994) work in the career-development field also holds true for the self-development process.

Employee-initiated career development does involve *self-responsibility*, although the irony is that most of us need help with it. There are elements of *partnership* not only between the individual and the organization as first thought, but also with fellow employees through peer mentoring. There is *integration* at the individual level in addition to the individual–organization interface (German & Heath, 1994, p. 14).

Self-development, therefore, is a function that must be carefully planned, monitored, and nurtured, otherwise, self-responsibility can become a synonym for neglect.

ORGANIZATIONAL DEVELOPMENT

The final performance management method often leads to workplace redesign. Hence, its application may result in training, retraining, or the use of any alternative or supplement to training.

Organizational development (OD) is a process that uses our knowledge of the social sciences to plan, design, and implement changes in the work

organizational development (OD) a planned organization-wide change effort using the knowledge from the social sciences to increase organizational effectiveness and health culture and procedures, to make the work setting more palatable, and to increase organizational effectiveness and/or profitability. The steps include: information gathering, problem identification, action or intervention planning, intervention or implementation, and evaluation (White & Bednor, 1991).

The OD approach to changing the way an organization operates works best when:

- an outside, trained change agent is hired;
- senior managers recognize that there are problems and want real change;
- senior managers strongly support the change initiative and are willing to seek out and listen to opinion leaders at all organizational levels;
- there are early successes that encourage further interest and participation from all levels;
- there is respect for the management talents of those in whose unit or function the change is occurring;
- both line and staff personnel cooperate in the change effort;
- there is effective coordination, communication, and control of the change process;
- there is an evaluation procedure that measures the results, and these results (both successes and failures) are communicated widely (Vecchio, 1988);
- change is viewed by all employees as a long-term necessity to remain competitive;
- reward systems reinforce change (Cherrington, 1994).

Proponents of OD try to mobilize the organization's entire HR pool toward achieving the employer's mission, while simultaneously creating a viable, growing organization of people whose personal needs for self-worth, growth, and satisfaction are significantly met at work (Hersey & Blanchard, 1988).

Remembering that culture, systems, and (ultimately) behaviour must be changed, there are numerous techniques the OD specialist can use. Cherrington (1994), for example, divides interventions into five categories: interpersonal, group, intergroup, organizational, and cultural. Under interpersonal, he places coaching or counselling, sensitivity training, and process consultation (problem diagnosis and alternative solution evaluation).

Group interventions consist of group problem-solving meetings, team-building meetings, analysis of roles (to reduce role confusion), and responsibility charting—an intervention that clarifies responsibilities concerning decision-making and taking action.

Interventions that focus on intergroup relationships include

- identifying the common foe: for example, focusing attention on an enemy that threatens both groups
- working together: groups are forced to interact, communicate, and solve common problems or reach common goals

- interchanging members by rotating group members among or between groups
- confronting conflict sessions in which groups are brought together to air differences, while solving common problems

Organizational interventions are comprehensive, affecting an entire work group or firm. Structural change, for example, can have significant and lasting impact on both the individual and the way an organization operates. Similarly, sociotechnical system design, involving the creation of work teams and the systems that allow them to function effectively, is typically concerned with developing the skills and attitudes necessary for employees to work autonomously.

Total quality management (TQM) (see Chapter 11) is also part of OD, but better research is needed on the implementation process. Finally, the most difficult area in which to work, cultural intervention, refers to the systematic change or clarification of collective corporate or organizational identity (e.g., what it is really like to work here).

As these techniques are concerned with the effectiveness of the entire organization, they are often combined into "a consideration in general of how work is done, what the people who carry out the work believe and feel about their efficiency and effectiveness, rather than a specific, concrete, step-by-step linear procedure for accomplishing something" (Burke, 1994).

The entire OD movement has its critics. Hersey and Blanchard (1988), for example, suggest there are more OD intervention failures than successes. A different focus was taken by McKendall (1993), who argued that OD intervention, in the drive to encourage cooperation, increases the power of management. Further, she accuses OD practitioners of "self-deception" in the creation of a discipline (OD) that has (wrongly) been given the label "scientific," when the major aim is the qualitative institution of social and environmental reforms (Van Eynde, Church, Hurley, & Burke, 1992).

Despite these criticisms, however, OD remains a major method for increasing employee effectiveness. The technique cannot be discounted as long as the movement continues toward democratic, participative management.

SUMMARY

As the theme of this text is to manage performance, not performers, this chapter has outlined some on-the-job training methods. Performance aids and electronic support systems help an employee to perform sequences without memorization or prompt proper behaviour in some way. Apprenticeships, while not highly valued, are a good solution to labour market shortages. The idea that self-directed learning and self-development as methods of coping with continual change fits well with our view that formal learning can be too inflexible to meet individual needs. Similarly, we stress that coaching must not be seen as a method for dealing with performance problems but for self-development in a more positive sense. OD is a complex intervention technique that uses social science principles to improve work environments. Planned utilization of learning opportunities in the workplace, therefore, can be used to help employees to achieve their long-term career goals.

KEY TERMS

apprenticeship   161
coach   167
electronic performance-
   support systems (EPSS)   160
mentor   169

on-the-job training (OJT)   158
organizational development
   (OD)   173
performance aid   159
self-directed learning (SDL)   172

EXERCISES

1. Describe the similarities and differences between coaching and mentoring.

2. Most adults engage in many learning projects independently of work and school. Learn how they do this by accessing <**www.snow.utoronto.ca**>, the web site of the Adaptive Technology Resource Centre. Read also Tim Seiferts's book *Human Learning and Motivation: Readings*, published by Memorial University Press, St. John's, Newfoundland, 1995. Make a list of everything you have learned independently over the past few years.

3. Ask your friends if they would accept a paid training experience that consisted of the following benefits:

- they would be given structured classroom training and on-the-job assignments
- they would be coached and supervised throughout the learning experience
- they would be paid to learn
- they would be certified at the end of learning the job
- they would be guaranteed employment at high wages

If they answer "yes!" then tell them about becoming an apprentice electrician or carpenter. What is their reaction? Do students resist the certification programs in the traditional vocations and embrace certification in human resources or technology? Why?

CASE: WHY CARL LEFT—A WORKPLACE DILEMMA

John Webster was head of the tool-and-die section at Keswick and Sons Ltd. A hard taskmaster who had learned his trade in Great Britain, he had trained almost 100 apprentices, only to watch as a large portion left for other companies as soon as they obtained their journeyman's papers. The company had invested hundreds of thousands of dollars in the apprenticeship program over the last dozen years and John sensed that management was reluctant to support the plan much further. John was watching this year's crop of four apprentices, therefore, with a particularly anxious eye.

Carl Vox was one of the best apprentices Keswick and Sons had attracted in a long time. Not only was he brighter than most and quick to learn, but he was a hard worker who disliked making mistakes. John felt Carl had the ability to become a master tradesman. He hoped that Carl would continue his studies, as the company desperately needed skilled people of Carl's calibre.

John's hopes, however, were not to be realized. On the day Carl graduated, after accepting congratulations, receiving a gift, and being taken out to a sumptuous dinner, Carl confided to John that he had been offered a job as a sales representative by a large German specialized machinery firm. Nothing John said could make Carl change his mind. Carl talked of the freedom sales would offer him and how he felt that his future did not lie in a "dingy old factory."

Feeling more depressed than he had felt in a long time, John returned to the plant to find a note from Mr. Keswick: "See me when you return." John went immediately to the president's office to be told that unless retention rates for the apprenticeship program showed marked improvements next year, Keswick and Sons would be abandoning that type of training in favour of direct recruitment of skilled tradesmen from overseas.

John's next stop was the personnel department. "Maybe," he thought, "I can get help in developing some sort of program to keep these young people here once they graduate."

QUESTION

1. As a group, brainstorm some solutions to this problem.

RUNNING CASE PART 3: VANDALAIS DEPARTMENT STORES

Refer to the Vandalais Department Stores case described in Chapter 5. Do you think that off-the-job training methods are sufficient to make the structured employment interview training program effective? Explain your reasoning. Should on-the-job training methods be used as well? What would be the benefit of including on-the-job training methods in the structured employment interview training program?

Consider each of the following on-the-job training methods described in this chapter.

- show and tell
- performance aids
- coaching
- self-directed learning

For each one, answer the following questions.

1. Describe how each training method might be used for the structured employment interview training program.

2. What are the advantages and disadvantages of using each training method for the structured employment interview training program?

3. How effective do you think each training method would be for the structured employment interview training program?

4. If you were designing the structured employment interview training program, which training methods would you include in your program and why?

5. Finally, review the material in the Appendix and describe how you could use on-the-job training as a training method for the structured employment interview training program. Be sure to describe how you would proceed in each of the phases. Will this training method make the training program more effective?

REFERENCES

Arajis, B. (1991). Getting your sales staff in shape. *Graphic Arts Monthly 63* (5), 125–127.

Azar, B. (1993). Striking a balance. *Sales and Marketing Management 145* (2), 34–35.

Beh, H. (1993). Mentoring the young manager. *Asian Business 29* (7), 63.

Blakesley, S. (1992). Your agency … leave it better than you found it. *Managers Magazine 67* (4), pp. 20–22.

Broadwell, M. (1969). *The supervisor and on-the-job training.* Reading, MA: Addison-Wesley.

Brodsky, M. (1989). International developments in apprenticeship. *Monthly Labour Review 112* (7), 40–41.

Burke, W. (1994). *Organization development* (2nd ed.). Reading, MA: Addison-Wesley.

Chao, G., Walz, P., & Gardner, P. (1992). Formal and informal mentorships. *Personnel Psychology 45* (3), 619–636.

Cherrington, D. (1994). *Organizational behaviour.* Boston: Allyn and Bacon.

Cowen, W. (1992). Visual control boards are a key management tool. *Office Systems 9* (10), 70–72.

Del Valle, C. (1993, April 26). From high school to high skills. *Business Week 3316*, pp. 110–112.

Dreher, G., & Ash, R. (1990). A comparative study of mentoring among men and women in managerial, professional, and technical positions. *Journal of Applied Psychology 75* (5), 539–546.

Frankel, L., & Otazo, K. (1992). Employee coaching: The way to gain commitment. *Employment Relations Today 19* (3), 311–320.

Gallege, L. (1993). Do women make poor mentors? *Across the Board 30* (6), 23–26.

Gebber, B. (1991). Help! The rise of performance support systems. *Training Magazine 28* (12), 23–29.

German, C., & Heath, C. (1994). Career development 2000. *Training and Development 12* (5),12–14.

Gold, L. (1981). Job instruction: Four steps to success. *Training and Development Journal 35* (9), 28–32.

Hersey, P., & Blanchard, K. (1988). *Management of organizational behaviour* (5th ed.). Englewood Cliffs, NJ: Prentice Hall.

Hopkins, R., & Kleiner, B. (1993). How to be an effective coach in business. *Agency Sales Magazine 23* (6), pp. 57–61.

Hrynyshyn, T. (1993). Siemens chief critical of skilled labour shortage. *Computing Canada 19* (11), p. 1.

Jackson, C. (1993). Mentoring: Choices for individuals and organizations. *The International Journal of Career Management 5* (1), 10–16.

Jacobs, D. (1989). Coaching employees to perform better. *Management World 18* (4), 6–9.

King, W. (1994). Training by design. *Training and Development 48* (1), 52–54.

Koehler, K.G. (1992). Orientation: Key to employee performance and morale. *CMA Magazine 66* (6), p. 6.

Kroeger, L. (1991). Your team can't win the game without solid coaching. *Corporate Controller 3* (5), 62–64.

Kruse, A. (1993). Getting top value for your payroll dollar. *Low Practice Management 19* (3), 52–57.

Kulig, P. (1998, March 23). When training meets performance support. *Canadian HR Reporter 11* (6), 17–18.

Laird, D. (1985). *Approaches to training and development* (2nd ed.). Reading, MA: Addison-Wesley.

Lovin, B., & Casstevens, E. (1971). *Coaching, learning, and action.* New York: American Management Association.

McKendall, M. (1993). The tyranny of change: Organizational development revisited. *Journal of Business Ethics 12* (2), 93–104.

Meyers, D. (1991). Restaurant service: Making memorable presentations. *Cornell Hotel and Restaurant Administration Quarterly 32* (1), 69–73.

Moskal, B. (1991). Apprenticeship: Old cure for new labor shortage? *Industry Week 240* (9), 30–35.

Mullen, E.J. (1998). Vocational and psychosocial mentoring functions: Identifying mentors who serve both. *Human Resource Development Quarterly 9* (4), 319–331.

Nadler, L. (1982). *Designing training programs.* Reading, MA: Addison-Wesley.

Noe, R. A. (1999). *Employee training and development.* Boston: Irwin McGraw Hill.

Nollen, S.D., & Gaertner, K.N. (1991). Effects of skill and attitudes on employee performance and earnings. *Industrial Relations 30* (3), 435–455.

Odiorne, G.S. (1970). *Training by objectives.* London: Collier-Macmillan.

O'Keefe, B. (1991). Adopting multimedia on a global scale. *Instruction Delivery Systems* (September/October), 6–11.

Ontario Institute for Studies in Education (OISE). (1998). *National research network on new approaches to life long learning.* Toronto: University of Toronto Press.

Raybould, B. (1990). Solving human performance problems with computers—A case study: Building an electronic performance support system. *Performance and Instruction* (November–December), 4–14.

Renner, P.F. (1989). *The instructor's survival kit.* Vancouver: Training Associates Ltd.

Riccucci, N. (1991). Apprenticeship training in the public sector. *Public Personnel Management 20* (2), 181–183.

Rothwell, W.J., & Kazanas, H.C. (1990). Planned OJT is productive OJT. *Training and Development Journal 44* (10), 53–56.

Ruyle, K. (1991). Developing intelligent job aids. *Technical and Skills Training* (February/March), 9–14.

Scandura, T. (1992). Mentorship and career mobility: An empirical investi-

gation. *Journal of Organizational Behaviour 13* (2), 169–174.

Sloman, M. (1989). On-the-job training: A costly poor relation. *Personnel Management 21* (2), 38–42.

Smith, K. (1996). EPSS helps accounting firm reduce training time, improve productivity during transition to new service emphasis. *Lakewood Report on Technology for Learning* (April), p 8.

Stern, S., & Muta, H. (1990). The Japanese difference. *Training and Development Journal 44* (3), 74–82.

Tench, A. (1992). Following Joe around: Should this be our approach to on-the-job training? *Plant Engineering 46* (17), 88–92.

Ukens, C. (1993). Cards help pharmacists counsel patients in a flash. *Drug Topics 137* (1), 24–27.

Van Eynde, D., Church, A., Hurley, R., & Burke, W. (1992). What OD practitioners believe. *Training and Development 46* (4), 41–46.

Vecchio, R. (1988). *Organizational behaviour.* Chicago: Dryden Press.

White, D., & Bednor, D. (1991). *Organizational behaviour.* Needham Heights, MA: Allyn and Bacon.

Whittaker, B. (1993). Shaping the competitive organization. *CMA Magazine 67* (3), p. 5.

Zemke, R. (1998). In search of self-directed learners. *Training 35* (5), 61–68.

APPENDIX

The Craft and the Art of Workplace Training

Thus far, training has been viewed in a relatively abstract way, and we have avoided detailed how-to prescriptions for getting the job done. Setting the more practical element in an appendix allows for the introduction of step-by-step systems without altering the general flow of the book. The focus here is on face-to-face encounters with trainees, emphasizing on-the-job training (OJT).

WHAT IS OJT?

Although OJT has been practised since at least the Middle Ages, the concept was formalized by the U.S. army during World War II. OJT is the design and application of a series of steps that enable the trainee to perform a job while either working on the job or preparing to work on the job in the immediate future. For the new employee, OJT is part of the orientation process, while for the experienced person, OJT updates present job behaviours or provides cross-training for flexibility (Koehler, 1992; Tench, 1992).

Sloman (1989) studied three British National Training Award winners that paid particular attention to the OJT delivery. From their programs he developed a set of rules governing good on-the-job training.

1. In terms of planning and preparation, OJT should not be managed differently from other types of training.
2. OJT should be integrated with other methods.
3. Ownership must be maintained, even when consultants are used.
4. OJT trainers must be chosen with care and trained properly.

WHO TRAINS?

A large percentage of OJT is performed either by experienced employees or by (immediate) supervisors. Regardless of the approach, the prime prerequisite is that the trainer like people. Just as Disney Corp. finds it easier to teach friendly people the art of customer service, great training begins with a fundamental attitude of helpfulness and caring. As well, employees or supervisors who are required to train must want to be trainers, be good communicators, and be expert in their skill area. Patience and respect for differences in the ability to learn also are important as the trainer sets the initial mood or climate of the learning experience (Renner, 1989; Tench, 1992). Once suitable individuals are found, they need train-the-trainer training and rewards for OJT activities. It is of little use to give training responsibilities to an already busy employee, for example, without restructuring his or her job to include a training element. Nor is increased pay always the most sought after reward (although it doesn't hurt). Recognition, the chance to add variety to the workday, respect from new employees, training certificates, and the prospect of either promotion or cross-training all help to make OJT worthwhile for the individual.

How To Do OJT

Given that OJT has been a longstanding weak spot in North American training practice (Stern & Muta, 1990), it is not surprising that little seems to have been written specifically about how to do OJT. Even some of the classic examples of training literature have remarkably little to say on the subject (Odiorne, 1970; Nadler, 1982; Laird, 1985).

There are two notable exceptions: Martin Broadwell's fine book *The Supervisor and On-the-Job Training*, written in 1969, along with Rothwell and Kazanas's 1990 article, "Planned OJT is Productive OJT." (See the list of references at the end of this chapter.) The latter updates the technique, but Broadwell's work is unique in its emphasis on the trainer and on employee preparation.

Bearing in mind that OJT will be but one element in the training plan, job analysis and determination of objectives will have been completed. As well, the essential psychology about how and why people learn will have been taught as part of a train-the-trainer course.

I. The Preparation Phase

The OJT process consists of a preparation phase and an activity, or doing, phase. As nothing can destroy learning effectiveness faster than an unprepared instructor, Broadwell begins with self-preparation.

Any face-to-face encounter in business needs to be planned, but when training, preparation becomes especially important. Aside from routine precautions about using the most up-to-date job analysis, manuals, and other information—knowing what you're talking about—the key activity during this preparation phase is to develop a communications strategy that fits the trainee (don't forget to find out what the trainee already knows) or the situation. A lecture, for example, would not be an appropriate method for training groups in the art of lift-truck maintenance. Even when a lecture might be the right approach, support materials like overhead projection and handouts have to be carefully constructed to fit the audience.

As Renner's (1989) *Instructor's Survival Kit* and other publications contain detailed information on this phase, no attempt will be made to reproduce these data here. Instead, an abbreviated techniques chart is included here to illustrate some of the many ways in which OJT can be accomplished.

On-the-spot lecture	Gather trainees into groups and tell them how to do the job.
Viewed performance/ feedback	Watch the person at work and give constructive feedback, such as when the sales manager makes a call with a new salesperson.
Following Nellie	The supervisor trains a senior employee, who in turn trains new employees (showing the ropes).
Job-aid approach	A job aid (step-by-step instructions or video) is followed while the trainer monitors performance.
The training step	The trainer systematically introduces the task.
Sequence	Following a planned sequence. On-the-spot lecture: Gather trainees into groups and tell them how to do the job.

Each one of these communication techniques requires a different type and level of preparation. The instructor needs to understand the background, capabilities, and attitudes of his or her trainees as well as the nature of the tasks to be performed before choosing a technique or combination of techniques.

Note that trial and error has *not* been included here. Very few circumstances justify throwing an employee into a new position without proper training. Learning from one's mistakes is not only inefficient, but can be humiliating, dangerous, or lead to poor customer relations.

The second part of the preparation phase concerns the trainee. There are three stages: putting the individual at ease, guaranteeing the learning, and building interest and showing personal advantage (Broadwell, 1969).

1. The trainer must remember that the trainee may be apprehensive; it is unwise to begin too abruptly. Some small talk may be appropriate to relax the trainee and to set the tone for the training sessions. Most individuals learn more readily when relaxed. A short conversation concerning any matter of interest—the weather, sports, a work-related item—should be effective. Obviously, the topic chosen must be suitable for the situation.

2. When the conversation does turn to the training session, the trainer needs to guarantee to the employee that learning is possible. Again, use a simple statement, "Don't worry about this machine, Sally; in about three hours you'll be operating it almost as well as everyone else. I've trained at least 10 people in this procedure." The trainee now knows that it is possible to

learn (i.e., learning will take place) and that the instructor has the ability to teach the process, adding to her confidence.

3. Although the instructor may be interested, the trainee might be apprehensive or may not understand the effect OJT will have on the quality of his or her worklife. Developing trainee enthusiasm sometimes is difficult, but pointing out some personal gain helps to create interest. The idea that the training activity will lead to something positive creates the opportunity to design rewards: more self-esteem, easier work, higher-level work, less routine, more control over work, greater opportunity or security. Once the appropriate reward is found (provided it can be obtained), most employees will respond to OJT.

Some people will resist, however, as training is change and individuals accept change at different rates. This trainee preparation phase will identify those who are not responding. As the trainer is responsible for meeting measurable objectives, it is important to evaluate the likelihood of cooperation among trainees so that individual remedial action can be taken.

One way to defuse resistance is to train employees in order of their perceived enthusiasm. When the resisters see others reaping the rewards of training, they usually agree to be trained, albeit grudgingly. As the instructor does not own the trainees' attitude, only their behaviour, training objectives can be met even though the work situation is not ideal.

II. The Steps in OJT

If the trainee is to perform a task or an operation, he or she should be positioned slightly behind or beside the instructor so that the job is viewed from a realistic angle. The step approach to the OJT process then can be utilized (Gold, 1981; Broadwell, 1986; Rothwell and Kazanas, 1990), as follows:

1. Show the trainee how to perform the job.
   - Be sure to break the job into manageable tasks; present only as much as can be absorbed at one time. Remember, too, that individuals learn at different speeds, so some trainees, for example, may be able to learn six or seven sequences at once, while others can absorb only four or five.
   - Repeat Step 1 as necessary; be patient.
   - Don't forget to tell *why* as well as how.
   - Point out possible difficulties as well as safety procedures.
   - Encourage questions.
2. Repeat and explain key points in more detail.
   - Safety is especially important.
   - Take the time to show how the job fits into any larger systems.
   - Show why the job is important.

- Show why key points are more important than others.
- Repeat Step 2 as necessary; be patient.
- Encourage questions.

3. Allow the trainee to see the whole job again.
   - Ask questions to determine level of comprehension.
   - Repeat Step 3 as necessary; be patient.
   - Encourage questions.

4. Ask the trainee to perform less difficult parts of the job.
   - Try to ensure initial success.
   - Don't tell how. If possible, ask questions, but try to keep trainee's frustration level low.
   - Repeat Step 4 as necessary; be patient.

5. Allow the trainee to perform the entire job.
   - Gently suggest improvements where necessary (i.e., keep feedback positive).
   - If needed, repeat Step 4 until the trainee feels comfortable.
   - Repeat Step 5 as necessary; be patient.

6. Leave the trainee to work alone.
   - Tell when and where to find help if necessary.
   - Supervise closely, then taper off as the employee gains in confidence and skill.

While these steps may seem elaborate, they must be applied with the complexity and possible safety hazards of the job in mind. Very simple tasks may require only one demonstration. As well, employees bring different skills and backgrounds to the workplace. Competent preparation will eliminate overtraining and the resultant boredom and inattention.

Case: TPK Appliances

When TPK, a manufacturer of small appliances—electric kettles, toasters, and irons—automated its warehouse, the warehouse crew was reduced from 14 to 4. Every one of the displaced stockmen was assigned to another department, as TPK had a history of providing stable employment.

Jacob Peters, a stockman with more than 15 years of service, was transferred to the toaster assembly line to be retrained as a small-parts assembler. When he arrived to begin his new job, the foreman said, "This may be only temporary, Jacob. I have a full staff right now, so I have nothing for you to do, but come on, I'll find you a locker." As there really was no job for him, Jacob did nothing for the first week except odd jobs such as filling bins. At the beginning of week two, Jacob was informed that a vacancy would be occurring the next day, so he reported for work eager to learn his new job.

The operation was depressingly simple. All Jacob had to do was pick up two pieces of metal, one in each hand, place them into a jig so that they were held together in a cross position, and press a button. The riveting machine then put a rivet through both pieces and an air jet automatically ejected the joined pieces into a bin.

"This job is so simple a monkey could do it," the foreman told Jacob. "Let me show you how it's done," and he quickly demonstrated the three steps involved. "Now you do it," the foreman said. Of course, Jacob did it right the first time. After watching him rivet two or three, the foreman left Jacob to his work.

About three hours later, the riveter started to put the rivets in a little crooked, but Jacob kept on working. Finally, a fellow worker stopped by and said, "You're new here, aren't you?" Jacob nodded. "Listen, I'll give you a word of advice. If the foreman sees you letting the rivets go in crooked like that, he'll give you hell. So hide these in the scrap over there." His new friend then showed Jacob how to adjust his machine.

Jacob's next problem began when the air ejection system started jamming. Four times he managed to clear it, but on the fifth try, he slipped and his elbow hit the rivet button. The machine put a rivet through the fleshy part of the hand, just below the thumb.

It was in the first aid station that the foreman finally had the opportunity to see Jacob once again.

QUESTIONS

1. Comment on the strengths and weaknesses of Jacob's orientation and on-the-job training.
2. Outline how the process should have been conducted.

NOTE: This story is a fictional version of a real-life situation that existed at Canadian General Electric many years ago.

8

....

TRANSFER OF
TRAINING

CHAPTER GOALS

If employees are seen as resources, money spent on training then must be viewed as investment in human capital development. If employees do not learn, or do not use what they have learned on the job, then this investment is wasted. This chapter outlines methods for optimizing this training investment.

In particular, this chapter examines training and management practices that can facilitate the transfer of training. The transfer factors are grouped by time: before, during, and after training. After reading this chapter, you should be able to

- define transfer of training
- list the methods that can be used to increase transfer before a training program
- discuss what a trainer can do during training to increase the transfer of training to the job
- describe a learning culture
- discuss what trainers and managers can do to ensure that the knowledge, skills, and abilities learned during training are applied on the job

MAXIMIZING RETURN ON INVESTMENT

Organizations concerned about their training investment are interested in knowing how much of what is learned during a training program actually translates into changes on the job. The course itself is just the acquisition phase; trainers can easily prove that trainees leave the programs with new skills. But if trainees do not apply these newly acquired skills on the job, then most of the resources spent on designing and conducting training courses are wasted.

transfer the application in the work environment of the skills acquired during the training program and the maintenance of these acquired skills over time

Employers are increasingly focusing their attention on implementation and maintenance; they are concerned with the *transfer* of training. **Transfer** is the application in the work environment of the skills acquired during the training program, and the maintenance of these acquired skills over time (Baldwin & Ford, 1988). Estimates vary from one penny to one dime about how much of every dollar spent on training is actually implemented on the job. But no one had recently measured the return on the training dollar, and that return had never been measured in Canada. In our research, we found that trainees implement around 60 percent of their new knowledge and skills right after the training course, but this amount drops to around 30 percent six months later. Less than half of training dollars invested result in actual change on the job (Saks & Belcourt, 1998).

However, we do know how to increase the amount of transfer and the duration of transfer. We have assembled the best transfer practices and grouped them into categories of before training, during training, and after training. Reading this chapter will be made easier by consulting the analytical framework presented in Table 8.1.

Transfer matters. Our study finds that organizations that pay attention to transfer and are effective at it report that they are better able to attract and retain essential employees, that the quality of their products and services is higher than competitors, and that their sales growth, market share, and profits are higher than those organizations that do not do transfer well (Saks & Belcourt, 1997).

BEFORE TRAINING STARTS

This section focuses on the pre-work necessary to select candidates for training and prepare the work environment for the return of the trainee with new knowledge, skills, and abilities. (The authors recognize that implementing all the ideas presented in these three phases is not possible in every organization. However, the implementation of some is imperative to ensure transfer.)

TABLE 8.1 TRANSFER FRAMEWORK

Before Training

A: Selection of trainees	• ability
	• aptitude
	• personality

B: Preparing the work environment	
Trainees	• involvement
	• pre-tests
	• choice
Management	• active support
	• needs assessment
	• career counselling
	• grouping trainees
	• mentoring

During Training	• feedback
	• practice
	• contingencies

After Training	
Trainee strategies	• self-management
	• relapse prevention
Management strategies	• opportunity
	• reinforcement

SELECTION OF TRAINEES

TRAINABILITY   The first question that must be answered before an employee undertakes a change program is: Can this individual be trained? An examination of three characteristics (ability, aptitude, and personality) of potential participants may provide answers to this question.

Ability refers to the knowledge and skills the individual already possesses, and may include cognitive skills and psychomotor skills. Examples of cognitive skills include basic numeracy and literacy, the intelligence to learn complex rules and procedures, and so on. Cognitive ability (verbal comprehension, quantitative ability, and reasoning ability) is related to the ability to learn and to succeed on the job. Psychomotor abilities include the eye–hand coordination necessary to operate machines and the visual acuity needed to detect defects. The potential trainee must have certain basic skills to undertake training that leads to more advanced skills.

ability the knowledge and skills (mental and physical capacity) to perform a task

aptitude the potential
ability to perform a task

Aptitude refers to the potential of the employee. For example, an employee may not know how to program software, but given her superior intelligence and capacity for logical problem-solving, you could conclude that she would succeed in a programming course.

Both abilities and aptitudes can be measured by cognitive tests and by work-sample tests. Cognitive tests, such as intelligence tests, will include subtests of specific abilities such as numerical reasoning, spatial aptitude, deductive reasoning, and verbal ability. The subtests provide important information about the ability of a potential trainee to learn the material.

Work-sample tests consist of a sample of the skills or abilities needed for job performance. Thus, a person who is interested in becoming an assembler of electrical components might be given the chance to observe a skilled assembler perform a series of simple tasks. The candidate would then be asked to perform the task and would be rated against a standardized checklist. Research on the effectiveness of job-sample tests has proven that they predict not only later training performance, but also attendance and dropout rates (Robertson & Downs, 1989). See the Training Today 1 box for the kinds of performance tests used by the British Columbia Ministry of Forests to select forest fire fighters.

Although most work-sample tests involve the demonstration of psychomotor skills, they are equally effective with knowledge-based tests (Reilly & Israelski, 1988). Trainers can use a sample of the course material to test the degree to which trainees can learn information in a fixed time. A candidate for a programming course could be given a written test that requires solving a logic problem. If the trainee does well against a standardized appraisal form, then the trainer could be reasonably certain that the candidate would do well in training.

The use of these tests may provide significant savings for employers. Some courses in electronics cost an employer $30 000 per trainee and last six months. An hour-long test that could predict training performance is obviously a prudent investment.

Researchers have isolated several personality traits that help to predict success in training courses. Indeed, these traits seem to predict success in other endeavours as well. The most commonly cited success traits are need for achievement (Baumgartel, Reynolds, & Pathan, 1984) and internal locus of control (Noe, 1999). A person with a high need for achievement likes to accomplish something difficult as rapidly and as independently as possible. A person with an internal locus of control believes that he can manipulate the environment and control his fate. These two traits can be measured by personality tests, but these tests usually are not available to trainers who are not psychologists. However, trainers can measure other traits using simple questionnaires.

motivation the effort
and persistence necessary
to complete a task

Motivation is one of these traits. **Motivation** refers to the trainee's effort, persistence, and choices. How much effort will the trainee expend to learn the material and to attempt to use it? Motivation can be influenced by internal factors, such as an innate need for achievement, and by external factors, to be discussed later in this chapter. For example, those students who take a course in

TRAINING TODAY 1 Work-Sample Tests for Fire Fighters

Applicants for the job of fire fighter at British Columbia Ministry of Forests are required to pass work-sample tests before they can be selected for the job and commence their training. The competition for openings is fierce, with about 25 applicants for every job. Scientists designed the tests after studying the job of a fire fighter. The tests required candidates to lift a 23 kilogram bar upright in a rowing motion 18 times, lug pumps and hoses weighing 50 kilograms over timed distances, and perform a shuttle run—darting back and forth at an increasingly faster pace between cones set 20 metres apart. However, a challenge by a female fire fighter who, after three successful years on the job, failed a running test that required her to run 2.5 kilometres in 11 minutes, resulted in a court ruling that the running test was not a bona fide occupational requirement, and that the test did discriminate against women, who failed the test in greater numbers than men.

To become a fire fighter in Toronto, applicants must also pass work-sample tests: carry a 9 kilogram cylinder on their backs, lift a 25 kilogram ladder, climb a 12 metre ladder, crawl in a small space with their eyes covered until they find a dummy body (to test for claustrophobia), and carry a dummy through an obstacle course, all while wearing 20 kilograms of fire fighter clothing. The deputy fire chief in Toronto claims that the tests are job specific and demonstrably necessary. He says the fact that 90 percent of men who try these tests pass and that 50 percent of women who try pass is an unavoidable consequence.

Source: Brooks, J.R. (1999, September 14). Must a fire fighter be fleet footed? *The Globe and Mail*, p. D14. Wente, M. "Fifth Column", *The Globe and Mail*, September 14, 1999, A22.

training because the time slot is good or because the course is compulsory are less motivated to learn the content that those students who want careers as trainers.

One motivational component that is gaining attention is self-efficacy. As discussed in Chapter 5, self-efficacy is the belief in one's capability to perform a specific task (Bandura, 1997); it refers not to the actual skills you have, but to your judgments about what you can do with those skills (Mager, 1992). In training, self-efficacy refers to the trainee's belief that she can actually learn the material and be able to use it successfully. CEOs who think that a word processing program is too complicated to learn and use would be examples of trainees with low self-efficacy. Studies of managers learning to use software programs show that those with high self-efficacy do better and have a higher motivation to learn than those with low self-efficacy (Gist, 1989; Gist, Schwoerer, & Rosen, 1989). If you believe you can learn, you do learn.

This belief is a critical factor in understanding learning because it is possible that trainees can actually learn the required knowledge and skills but believe that they cannot do the job. Motivation to learn is in turn related to learning achievement (Tannenbaum, Mathieu, Salas, & Cannon-Bowers, 1991). Trainees with low self-motivation and low self-efficacy can benefit from training enhancement procedures (TEP) (Saks & Haccoun, 1997). To increase motivation and self-efficacy, for example, the trainer could solicit trainee input into the content and arrange a meeting with the supervisor, showing support for the training outcomes and negotiating learning goals.

Trainers can maximize the acquisition and ultimate transfer of new skills and knowledge by assessing applicants' readiness (abilities, aptitudes, and motivation to learn). But the organization has little control over these mostly intrinsic characteristics. If everyone in a group needs to be trained, regardless of personal traits, human resource developers can use several methods to prepare the trainees and their work environments to maximize transfer.

PREPARING THE WORK ENVIRONMENT

Before the course begins, trainers should work actively with both trainees and their managers to facilitate the ultimate transfer of newly acquired behaviour to the job situation.

Consider the learning environment most people experience: as students in school, we were told what, when, and how to learn. Learning is supposed to pay off in some unknown way in the distant future.

As adults, employees need to know why they are learning material. They are concerned with its immediate and practical application, and with its relevance to their problems or needs. Adults tend to be problem-centred in their approach to learning. Using this basic insight, McMaster University in Hamilton, Ontario, redesigned its medical degree program. Instead of teaching medicine by subject matter (chemistry, physiology), they created a problem-centred curriculum. After identifying about 200 of the most common medical problems faced by physicians, McMaster developed learning modules containing everything a doctor needed to know about anatomy, pharmacology, and so on to solve the problem. (For a thorough discussion on the needs of adult learners, consult *The Adult Learner: A Neglected Species* by Malcolm Knowles [Houston, Texas: Gulf Publishing Co., 1990].)

Other contrasts between the school experiences of children and the training experiences of adults are highlighted in Table 8.2. The factors listed in this table have powerful implications for trainers at every stage of the transfer cycle. Before training starts, trainees must be involved in needs assessment, identification of real job problems, career planning, precourse assignments, and goal setting.

INVOLVEMENT OF THE TRAINEE   Trainees must be involved in the development of their change experiences. Involvement in the design and planning of the learning experience is one way to get trainees to jump aboard. The person in the boat with you seldom bores a hole in it (Broad & Newstrom, 1992). Precourse work or assignments may also serve to involve participants.

TABLE 8.2 TEACHING CHILDREN AND ADULTS

FACTOR	CHILDREN	ADULTS
Personality	Dependent	Independent
Motivation	Extrinsic	Intrinsic
Roles	Student	Employee
	Child	Parent, volunteer, spouse, citizen
Openness to change	Keen	Ingrained habits and attitudes
Barriers to change	Few	Negative self-concept
		Limited opportunities
		Time
		Inappropriate teaching methods
Experience	Limited	Vast
Orientation to learning	Subject-centred	Problem-centred

IMPLICATIONS FOR TRAINERS
- Adults need to know why they are learning.
- Adults can learn independently, and may prefer to do so.
- Adults are motivated by both intrinsic and extrinsic rewards.
- Adults' previous experiences should be used in training.
- Adults should be given safe practice opportunities.

PRE-TESTS   Pre-tests are useful for determining the entry-level skills of employees so that courses can be designed appropriate to the trainees' skill levels. Chapter 9 on evaluation will explain how these pre-tests serve as data that are useful for measuring change in performance because of the training course. But pre-tests are equally important for designing courses that motivate trainees. Pre-tests allow trainers to design individual and tailor-made paths of learning for adults.

These pre-tests are particularly useful if the results are fed back to the employee. People are generally unaware when their behaviour is ineffective or inappropriate, and so have little incentive to change. Most change programs are built on the concept that "unfreezing" must precede change (Lewin, 1958). *Unfreezing* means that trainees must recognize or be aware of the disadvantages of their current way of doing things, and must unlearn this style. To facilitate unfreezing, trainers could provide proof that current knowledge or skills

TRAINING TODAY 2 Establishing a Need to Learn

When Swissair 111 crashed off the coast of Peggy's Cove, Nova Scotia, in 1998, experts speculated that the pilots erred, prolonging the flight by dumping fuel instead of attempting to land with a full fuel tank. The senior pilot may have made the wrong choice, but no junior pilot would challenge the senior pilot's decision. Those who have studied other airplane crashes find that junior staff were often afraid to challenge the senior staff. In an effort to avoid airline accidents caused by pilot error, the United States Air Force set out to train its pilots in assertiveness techniques. First, they had to demonstrate that the pilots

did indeed need this training. They asked the training candidates to describe incidents in which they had flown with a pilot who had used unsafe procedures, had experienced a potentially life-threatening incident in which crew coordination was a factor, or had been pressured to fly when they felt that safety was compromised because of weather or mechanical problems. Trainees who had experienced these situations (and therefore had a perceived need for training) learned more than those who had not (Smith-Jentsch, Jentsch, Payne, & Salas, 1996).

are inadequate. Tests provide this kind of objective feedback. After present deficiencies are revealed, new information is more likely to be absorbed, integrated (re-frozen), and transferred. When training is presented without unfreezing, trainees may distort information or only perceive information that is consistent with their current beliefs (Hastie & Kumar, 1979). Tests or work samples are important, therefore, not only for predictions of performance, but also for receptiveness and transfer of training.

The information from pre-tests allows trainers to demonstrate in an objective manner that training is needed. This information can also serve as course material from the real world of the trainee. The motivation of adult learners is increased by the demonstration of the need to learn new skills, and by relating the new skills to their problems or work situations. See the Training Today 2 box for an example of how one company prepared its trainees to accept the need to learn new ways of doing things.

Research has documented that trainees who believed in the results of the needs assessment achieve more in training and find the training more useful than those who do not (Noe, 1986; Noe & Schmitt, 1986).

CHOICE   Another variable that must be considered when dealing with adults is choice. Children have no choice about attending school. Adults may have some choice in company programs, but here opinion is divided. Some argue that by making attendance mandatory, managers communicate the importance of training and ensure that all employees are using the same skills, thus providing powerful reinforcements (Broad & Newstrom, 1992). In one study, researchers found that a mandatory course resulted in higher intentions to transfer training to the workplace (Baldwin & Magjuka, 1991). A study by Hicks and Klimoski (1987), however, found that managers who could choose whether to attend a performance-appraisal workshop achieved more from attending the workshop than those who were forced to attend. Providing detailed information about the workshop, which was designed to facilitate the managers' attendance decision, rather than just providing the typical positive overview, also resulted in greater achievement (Hicks & Klimoski, 1987). But as indicated in Chapter 5, sometimes compulsory attendance is required.

INVOLVEMENT OF MANAGEMENT

The need for management support is a recurrent theme throughout this text. In this section, we present concrete suggestions that move beyond verbal pleas for "support, please."

ACTIVE SUPPORT   Before an employee is sent to a training program, managers should have to complete a questionnaire and respond to interview questions ascertaining the need for, and potential application of, the course material. CIBC requires managers who have requested training to answer questions such as: What is the training need? What are the employees doing now and what should they be doing? Why do you feel that training will solve the problem? What would you want employees to be able to do after the training?

Needs Assessment. Managers should be part of the needs-assessment phase, for both microcourses (individual) and macrotraining (group development programs). If there is a match between the content of the program and departmental or trainee needs, then the manager must move beyond support to involvement and commitment.

Broad and Newstrom (1992) suggest having managers complete a form that commits them to support. Such a form is presented in Figure 8.1.

FIGURE 8.1 TRAINING SUPPORT CONTRACT— SUPERVISOR

I, _____, agree to

- provide time for the employee to complete precourse assignments.
- provide release time for attendance, and ensure that the employee's workload is undertaken by others to eliminate interruptions.
- review the course outline with the employee, and discuss situations in which the newly acquired knowledge and skills can be used.
- provide timely opportunities to implement the skills, and reinforce new behaviours upon the return of the trainee.

Signature _____

Title   _____

CAREER COUNSELLING   Another useful role for managers to play before a training course is that of career counsellor. Trainees who have had discussions regarding their careers and who have established career goals or plans are more likely to benefit from training than others (William, Thayer, & Pond, 1991). Where possible, trainees should be told of the benefits of learning the new skills. These benefits could range from fewer client problems and increased speed in processing orders to more personal incentives such as promotion or increases in pay.

Groups of Trainees. Sending several or all members of a department to the training course also facilitates training transfer. Peers not only provide technical support for the transfer of training, but also provide moral encouragement through the development of a transfer culture, and by using catch phrases and anecdotes jointly encountered in training.

COURSE MENTOR   Another useful precourse suggestion is to pair the trainee with an graduate of the program who can identify the benefits and barriers to implementation. This mentor might also serve to alleviate the anxiety of the adult learner, who may lack self-confidence in his ability to master new material.

Implementing these suggestions before training begins will result in a heightened attention to learning and a focus by the trainee on the importance of learning how to transfer. A critical part of ensuring that training sticks is the culture of the organization and, in particular, the organization's beliefs and values about the importance of learning.

THE LEARNING CULTURE

learning culture a work environment that encourages, promotes, and supports the continual acquisition, application, and sharing of knowledge, behaviour, and skills from many sources

The work environment has a direct impact on employees' motivation to learn and their desire to apply what they have learned. The work environment (i.e., the culture of the organization) can send messages to employees that learning is important and highly valued. But what is a learning culture? A **learning culture** is one that encourages, promotes, and supports the continual acquisition, application, and sharing of knowledge, behaviour, and skills from many sources. This can be seen as a system of social support for learning. Review the Training Today 3 box to determine if you work for an organization that has a learning culture. A strong learning culture is a good predictor of transfer of training (Belcourt & Saks, 1997).

Effective training begins years (not months) before the kick-off speech for the training course. Many pre-training activities are relatively easy to include as part of the training process, and they can help facilitate transfer. We summarize these in the Training Today 4 box.

TRAINING TODAY 3 The Learning Culture

We know that a learning culture within an organization makes employees want to learn and apply that learning on the job.

Here are some ways that you can determine whether you work for an organization that has a learning culture:

- You feel that acquiring knowledge and skills is an essential part of your job.
- Your assignments are challenging and are designed to help you develop new skills.
- Your co-workers help you learn by sharing their job knowledge and by helping you understand how your jobs are interconnected.

- You are rewarded for learning new things.
- You are given opportunities on your job to apply what you have learned.
- You feel that you work in a place where innovation is encouraged.
- You feel that your organization wants to be the best in its sector, and you, too, want to put forward your best effort.

Adapted from: Tracey, J.B, Scott, I.T., & Kavanagh, M.J. (1995). Applying training on the job: The importance of the work environment. *Journal of Applied Psychology 80* (2), 239–252.

TRAINING TODAY 4 Optimizing the Transfer of Training Before the Course Begins

- Identify trainee needs.
- Obtain trainee input about content and methods.
- Give pre-reading, assignments, and the release time to prepare.
- Require discussions with supervisors that include the content and benefits of the training program and the

setting of performance goals for improvement in specific skills.
- Encourage supervisors to attend advance orientation programs or the training program itself.

DURING THE TRAINING

This section examines the acquisition of skills during a training course, using principles derived from adult learning. As discussed in Chapter 5, when designing a training program, the trainer should include feedback, practice, and contingencies that will optimize employee learning and transfer.

FEEDBACK

The most fundamental step in improving performance is to provide knowledge about present performance. Providing this knowledge was seen in the previous section as a first step in unfreezing present behaviour. Unless adults

TRAINING TODAY 5 How to Give Feedback

Feedback can be very effective in changing behaviour, if the person giving the feedback is seen as being constructive, not critical. Here are some tips on how to do it right.

- *Timing:* Try to provide the feedback immediately after the behaviour or performance is observed.
- *Be specific:* Feedback works when it is specific. Don't say, "You moved the arm wrong," but, "You have the arm tilted at 30 degrees."

- *Guide:* After discussing what was poorly done, provide guidance on the correct performance. ("You had the arm titled at a 30 degree angle; you will find it easier or quicker to tilt it 90 degrees.")
- *Reward correct performance:* "Good, you have the right 90-degree angle," not just "good."

have evidence that their present performance is not as effective as it could be, they have little motivation to change.

If the trainee has not received this feedback before the course begins, then the first stage in the design process is to develop an exercise, role play, or questionnaire that provides relatively objective feedback on present knowledge, skills, or attitudes. Many commercial training establishments supply assessment inventories that measure conflict styles, leadership styles, knowledge about sexual harassment, attitudes toward conflict, and more. These tests allow adults, whose attitudes and habits may be ingrained and difficult to change, to realize the nature of their present behaviours, and provide impetus to change. These tests build on Lewin's (1958) theory that trainers must unfreeze behaviour, teach new skills, and re-freeze the new behaviour before any change will occur.

During training, feedback can be provided to guide trainees as they attempt new behaviours. This feedback should be designed to correct performance. When incorrect responses are given, the feedback should include the correct response. Negative feedback ("you failed to acknowledge the client's problem") will not be perceived as punishing if the source is knowledgable, friendly, trustworthy, and powerful enough to affect outcomes like promotions (Ilgen, Fisher, & Taylor, 1979). Training Today 5 summarizes the key elements in effective feedback.

Feedback in some learning situations consists of test results. Tests are usually graded by some combination of measurements against an objective standard (criterion) and a group standard (normative). Criterion-reference measures compare an individual with a given performance requirement or standard, regardless of how others perform (Nadler & Nadler, 1990). This approach is used for knowledge tests, such as theories of electricity.

The normative approach compares learners with one another for ranking (as is done in schools). Adults should be evaluated against the attainment of specific criteria, not compared publicly to their peers. In other words, evaluations such as final tests and exams should be criterion related, not normative. Adults should not be graded on a curve (Bass & Vaughn, 1969).

In a study of the effect of feedback on the performance of hourly workers, Miller (1965) concluded that the relevance, specificity, timing, and accuracy of the feedback are the critical factors in mastery of learning. Trainees receiving this type of feedback are more likely to adjust their responses toward the correct behaviour, more likely to be motivated to change, and more likely to set goals for improving or maintaining performance (Locke & Latham, 1990). Training methods such as computer-assisted instruction and structured behaviour modelling have feedback as an integral and imbedded benefit.

PRACTICE

Learning is often defined as a relatively permanent change in behaviour resulting from reinforced practice or experience (Wexley & Latham, 1991). **Practice** is defined as repetition or rehearsal so that responses or behaviour can be improved. Practice can be a physical activity (learning to type) or a mental activity (memorizing the categories of learning objectives). Obviously, feedback is an essential prelude to practice.

learning a relatively permanent change in behaviour resulting from reinforced practice or experience

A demonstration of the correct response or behaviour is a good start for practising a response. After a demonstration, trainees should begin with practice that is coached and guided by the trainer, moving through critical tasks (Yelon & Berge, 1992). The next step is practice with coaching from peers. The final stage is independent practice. At this point, the trainer could vary conditions so that the skill is executed in different situations. In this way, the trainee is more likely to use the skill on the job.

practice repetition or rehearsal so that responses can be improved

Practice does not suggest that there can be no theory in training. There is evidence that trainees learn better when a theoretical framework, general principles, or key elements of the content to be learned are given (Goldstein, 1993).

In practising mental skills, the strategies trainees use to aid memory include the use of mnemonics or organizers. Mnemonics is a learning tool that helps us memorize, for example, the names of the Great Lakes by using a simple word, such as HOMES (Huron, Ontario, Michigan, Erie, and Superior). Organizers are cues that may be verbal, quantitative, or graphic, already understood by trainees, and used to incorporate new knowledge. For example, the icons or symbols of a file cabinet or wastebasket used in software programs aid the new user in identifying ways to save or trash information. Trainees can use these mental models to improve learning by focusing on important components and relationships, organizing new material, and linking these to current knowledge (Mayer, 1989).

Finally, as we discussed in Chapter 5, there are several ways to design training programs to improve and facilitate the transfer of training. In particular, training programs should be designed with identical elements so that the training situation reflects the job or work environment. Another design issue is general principles. Training might occur as follows: start with an explanation of the theory or general principles, then provide a demonstration of these, have employees participate in a simulation, have them practise on the job with feedback and coaching, and then guide the employee with a mentor (Anthony, Perrewe, & Kacmar, 1993). Stimulus variability requires that the training program include different examples and provide trainees with various opportunities to practise the training material (Baldwin & Ford, 1988).

CONTINGENCIES

As you may recall from Chapter 5, contingency theory states that behaviour that is reinforced by desirable consequences strengthens and occurs more frequently in response to similar stimuli. Reinforcers or rewards can be psychological, such as praise, recognition, or attention. They can also be more tangible, such as gold stars, marks, bonuses, or promotions.

Contingencies, or consequences, may be the only possible motivation tool in some training situations. A clerk who has to memorize hundreds of regulations with little meaningfulness to her personal life may respond only to extrinsic rewards or even to punishments.

Is punishment effective? Overall, the answer has to be "no." Punishment, while appearing to produce instant results by stopping dysfunctional behaviour, has serious consequences. Punishment tells the individual to stop, but does not tell the individual what the correct thing to do is, creating anxiety. Punishment works only when the enforcer is present. The teenager still smokes when no authority figures are present; the worker arrives late when the boss is away. Punishment produces anger and retaliatory behaviour against the one administering the punishment. In summary, punishment is not a good idea.

Rewards have none of these side effects. Rewards tell the employee what is being done correctly and encourage repetition. Rewards feel good—workers will continue the good behaviour and provide proof of this even when the reward-giver is absent if workers feel positively about people who reward them.

Managing the strength and timing of the reinforcer can increase the effectiveness of reinforcers. Success can be seen as a reward, while failure feels like a punishment. Therefore, trainers should construct the learning experience in manageable chunks in which the trainee experiences success. (However, if the task is too easy, trainees will not perceive it as success.)

The timing of reinforcers can shape behaviour. For example, instead of waiting until a manager conducted a perfect appraisal interview (and waiting forever!), trainers praised the specific isolated behaviours of good interviewing as they occurred. Over time, the accumulation of isolated behaviours results in good appraisal behaviour. In this way, response patterns are shaped.

When learning new tasks, continual reinforcement is ideal. However, after some learning is achieved, partial reinforcements are as effective and much more similar to the real world. Back on the job, it is unlikely that the trainee will be praised every time he or she does something correctly.

Although in a training situation the trainer can easily use reinforcers such as praise, an external agent is giving these rewards. The ideal situation is to create an atmosphere in which the reinforcers become intrinsic or internal. Workers may do things the right way because the right way gives them pleasure, or saves time, or solves their problems.

The trainer can increase the trainee's intrinsic motivation to learn. Some approaches emphasize the future value of the skill and relate the content to interesting, meaningful materials outside the training program (Bass & Vaughn, 1969). Trainees learn and remember meaningful material more easily than material unrelated to their lives (McGehee & Thayer, 1961). Trainers can use information, problems, and anecdotes collected from the needs analysis to provide the link between classroom material and work situations. New material should be introduced using terms and examples familiar to employees. Providing an overview of the course, presenting the material logically, and moving from the least to the most complex material aid memory. The inclusion of managers as leaders of program components also increases the meaningfulness of the material (Nadler, 1982).

Another reason for moving toward intrinsic reinforcement is that reinforcements are highly personal: some people may be encouraged by public praise but others may find this embarrassing.

In summary, during a training program, trainers should incorporate active feedback, practice, and contingencies into the program. The Training Today 6 box provides some suggestions for how to increase the possibility that trainees will apply what they have learned once they are back on the job.

AFTER THE TRAINING PROGRAM

After a training course, most participants are motivated to try to use their new skills, but only some are able to do so. Some quit trying because they receive no support for their attempts. Others give up after initial attempts because they encounter problems in the application and the old technique seems to work better and faster. The trainer who is aware of these universal problems of transfer can devise strategies to manage the transfer and to prevent a relapse to precourse behaviours. There are two components to these post-course strategies: the trainees and their managers.

TRAINEE STRATEGIES

SELF-MANAGEMENT

In Chapter 5 we discussed self-management as one of the components of social learning theory. We also noted that employees can be trained to manage their own post-course behaviour (Latham & Frayne, 1989). By self-management we mean that trainees set goals, formulate written behavioural contracts, and administer their own contingencies.

We also noted the relevance of goal setting theory for the design of training programs. Numerous research studies have demonstrated that people who set specific, difficult goals achieve the best performance (Locke & Latham, 1990). At Canada Life, 1900 employees and managers have been trained to regularly set goals (Commanducci, 1998). Trainers should incorporate goal setting as an essential part of the training program. One method of goal setting is to prepare a performance contract.

performance contract an agreement outlining how the newly learned skills will be applied to the job

A **performance contract** is a statement, mutually drafted by the trainee and the trainer near the end of the course, that outlines which of the newly acquired skills are seen as beneficial and how they will be applied to the job. A copy can then be given to the trainer, a peer, or the supervisor, who will monitor progress toward these goals. The more specific the goals, the more likely they are to be attained. An example of a specific goal might read: "Identify five new customers within 30 days." Trainees could submit progress reports to both the human resources developer and the employees' managers. A variation on the timing (i.e., signing the contract jointly before the course) alerts the trainee to the critical elements of the program and commits the supervisor to monitoring progress (Leifer & Newstrom, 1980).

The importance of goal setting must be emphasized. Considerable research demonstrates that setting goals results in superior performance (Goldstein, 1993). From these studies, we know that trainees should willingly agree to the goals; that the goals must be specific, not vague; that the goals should be challenging but matched to the ability of the trainee; and that there must be a feedback mechanism to allow for the measurement of progress.

Besides goals, another simple technique can assure effective transfer. Job aids can increase the transfer of material learned to the job (Thiagarajan, 1990). Job aids include checklists, posters, instructions embedded into software, and easily referenced instructions. For example, employees learning about hazardous-waste management could be provided with a checklist that summarizes the major steps for handling radioactive material. This checklist, if prepared as a colourful poster, will increase the chances of employee application. Job aids are useful when performance is difficult, is executed infrequently, can be done slowly, and when the consequences of poor performance are serious (Ruyle, 1990). A summary of these self-management techniques is found in Training Today 7.

RELAPSE PREVENTION

Relapse prevention utilizes behavioural principles to sensitize trainees to the possibilities of skills erosion and "immunizes" them against factors in the environment that cause the erosion (Tziner & Haccoun, 1991). Relapse prevention training sensitizes trainees to barriers in the workplace that might inhibit or prevent them from successfully applying what they have learned (Saks & Haccoun, 1997). The technique was adapted from programs for treating addictive behaviours such as smoking and drinking (Wexley & Latham, 1991). Relapse in the work context means reverting to using the old skills or pre-training behaviour on the job.

relapse prevention a process of sensitizing trainees to the possibilities of skills erosion, and immunization against these occurrences

Relapse prevention consists of making trainees aware that relapse will occur and that temporary slips are normal. They are asked to identify those barriers to implementation and those situations in which relapse is likely to occur. People trying to quit smoking, for example, know that relapse is most likely to occur after meals, with coffee. For each of the new skill areas, trainees are asked to develop a coping strategy. For example, if workers think they will abandon the new ways when there is too much work, time-management techniques could be discussed.

Relapse-prevention programs work. Trainees who receive training in relapse prevention show higher levels of course knowledge and use the knowledge more (as rated by their supervisors) than those who do not receive this training (Tziner & Haccoun, 1991).

Behavioural checklists are another method used to prevent relapses (Wexley & Nemeroff, 1975). In one study, a group of participants was given checklists derived from the behaviours learned on the course and received training in monitoring and recording their behaviour. This group was better at applying the new skills than the group that did not receive the checklists.

Learners should expect a follow-up report to training from the training department (Nadler & Nadler, 1990). They should know what will be expected and that these results will be shared with their supervisors. Trainers could even consider a follow-up assignment.

Scheduling alumni days can reinforce the training (Parry, 1990). About five weeks after the course, participants reunite to discuss successes and barriers to implementation. This time should be considered the real graduation day. Having a group of graduates who meet monthly can further strengthen an alumni network. For macro development (or organization-wide) projects, this alumni association could create newsletters and arrange for guest speakers. Indeed, Buller and Cragun (1991) argue that networking is the most important outcome of training. Their study, conducted with managers who had attended a training course, demonstrated that the training broadened the managers' network of relationships within the company and that this, in turn, enabled them to get work done more effectively across organization lines.

With goal setting and relapse-prevention programs, trainees are more likely to apply what they have learned. If these strategies are coupled with support from the organizational environment, the likelihood of transfer of new skills to the job is increased.

MANAGEMENT MAINTENANCE STRATEGIES

Training alone is rarely successful in achieving long-term performance improvement. Indeed, perhaps as few as 20 percent of performance problems are caused by lack of knowledge or skills (Spitzer, 1990). The work environment must be managed to provide opportunities for optimum performance and to reinforce this performance when it occurs.

OPPORTUNITY

Training transfer can be inhibited by the "bubble" syndrome, in which the trainee is expected to use the new skills without support from the environment (Hatcher & Schriver, 1991). Management can burst the bubble by ensuring that time between training and on-the-job application is minimal. Assignments or opportunities to try the new skills should be given as soon as the trainee returns from the course.

Managers can also help by allowing the trainee time to try out or even experiment with new behaviours without adverse consequences. An organizational climate characterized by high appreciation for performance and innovation has a positive impact on the transfer of skills (Baumgartel et al., 1984). Organizations that place a high value on learning develop a cultural norm in which the acquisition and application of new knowledge and skills is institutionalized (Zucker, 1987).

REINFORCEMENT

The problem with reinforcement during a training course is that it may be too frequent. The problem after the course is that reinforcement may be infrequent or nonexistent. Behaviour that is not reinforced is not repeated. If the sales representative dutifully submits the reports as taught but no one even notices they are filed, then the representative will waste no further energy doing this task. A Xerox study showed that only 13 percent of trainees were using their new skills six months after training when management did not coach and support their use (Zucker, 1987). Supervisors of trainees should be themselves trained to observe and reinforce the new skills, while being patient and tolerant of errors.

A second problem with reinforcement of skills or behaviours in the work environment is the possibility of reinforcing behaviour that conflicts with the newly acquired skill (Baird, Schneier, & Laird, 1983). For example, managers may be praising the practice of safety, while the organization's incentive system rewards faster production of units. Sometimes the problem is not this obvious. For example, shop floor supervisors were taught active listening skills to resolve grievances at the first stage of resolution. However, they quickly learned that they could save time and trouble with aggrieved employees by passing the grievance to the next level of management. Therefore, before the trainee returns from training, an appraisal of the real and hidden contingencies in the job setting should be done. (If this is done early enough, at the needs-analysis stage, there may be no need for training. Employees may already know what to do; the environment just may not support it. See Chapter 3 on needs analysis.)

Sometimes, trainees may not perform in the new way because they do not see any benefit for doing so. Outcome expectancies influence behaviour. If a trainee believes that a pay increase or a promotion will result from the application of certain skills, then she is more likely to apply them (Bandura, 1977). If the new skills are incorporated into merit-pay plans, then the probability increases that employees will use them (Wexley & Latham, 1991). Conversely, employees who apply the new skills and receive no rewards are very disappointed and are more likely to withdraw (emotionally or physically) from the job (Caplow, 1983). The employee who returned to school to get a degree and then received no recognition or promotion for all that hard work understands this phenomenon.

Reinforcement should be used because it works. A Motorola Inc. study found that in plants where management reinforced quality-improvement training, an additional $33 return on every training dollar invested was received (Clemmer, 1992).

Supervisors are more likely to reinforce newly learned skills if they also have been trained or have participated as trainers in the course (Wexley & Latham, 1991). In this way, managers can both model the behaviour and observe its occurrence. Senior executives at Vancouver-based Finning Ltd., the world's largest Caterpillar dealer, are the first to attend training and help deliver the training (Clemmer, 1992). This cascading effect tells employees that management is serious about the learning and application of new skills. In addition, when managers are required to teach the new skills, they learn them very well. They are also aware that their employees are watching them to see if they practise what they preach.

There are dozens of other easy-to-do methods managers can use to help returning trainees. These methods include discussing transfer, reducing job pressures initially, arranging for co-workers to be briefed by the trainee, arranging practice sessions, publicizing successes, and giving promotional preference to those trained employees (Broad & Newstrom, 1992). Western Gas Marketing, Ltd. of Calgary rates their managers on the application of new skills on their performance-appraisal form (Clemmer, 1992).

For a summary of the research validated post-course training tips for optimizing the transfer of training, consult the Training Today 8 box.

As you have seen, the context in which training takes place has a powerful effect on employees' abilities and motivation to learn and use new knowledge, skills, and abilities. The conclusion to be drawn from all this research is that training cannot be seen as an isolated event. The course, or development program, should be one activity among dozens in a carefully designed effort to improve performance. The target should be performance.

SUMMARY

This chapter examined the factors that facilitate the transfer of learning to the job. These methods include preparatory steps before the training course and reinforcement procedures after the course. The role of the trainer in maximizing the learning during the course and its ultimate transfer to the work environment was discussed. The role of the trainee in self-management was presented, coupled with the things that a manager can do to increase the likelihood that the new KSAs will be applied on the job.

KEY TERMS

ability   189

aptitude   190

learning   199

learning culture   196

motivation   190

performance contract   202

practice   199

relapse prevention   203

transfer   188

EXERCISES

1. After the final exam, do students forget 90 percent of what they learn in their school courses? How could you design an educational experience for students so that they would remember and use 90 percent of the material learned in the classroom?

2. Psychologists can use personality and interest tests to determine whether employees have the interests and traits to benefit from training. These tests have to be validated for the training courses in your organizations, and in most cases, must be administered by a psychologist. However, you can see what tests look like and complete some online by going to <**www.2h.com/Tests/personality.html**>. Scan the list of inventories, tests, and surveys and identify those that might be useful for predicting success on a training course.

CASE: THE SCHOOL BOARD

Carlos daSilva was sitting at his desk in the training office, thinking about his meeting scheduled for 2 p.m. He was looking forward to the meeting with the superintendent of the school board, knowing that he would be praised for the multimedia interactive communications program he had designed. For years, parents, students, and teachers had been complaining that nobody listened, that decisions were made without participation, and that good ideas went unacknowledged. A needs analysis (using a survey of teachers and students) had confirmed that these problems were widespread.

As a recently appointed trainer with a strong background in teaching, Carlos tackled the communications problem as his first assignment. He designed what he immodestly considered the finest three-day communications program in any school board. He had spent months on the design: finding videos, CD-ROMS, exercises, and games that taught active listening, upward communication, brainstorming, and other areas identified in the survey.

However, the meeting with the superintendent went poorly. Although some teachers loved playing with the latest teaching technology in the communications course, most did not change their behaviour at work. A second analysis showed that the old problems persisted.

As an experienced trainer, you realize that Carlos has made a classic training mistake. He had spent most of his time and energy on developing the program and had failed to consider the transfer of the newly acquired knowledge and skills of the work environment. Describe in detail what Carlos could have done (before, during, and after the course) to ensure that the problems identified in the survey would not have persisted.

RUNNING CASE PART 4:
VANDALAIS DEPARTMENT STORES

Refer to the Vandalais Department Stores case described in Chapter 5. Discuss some of the factors that might inhibit the transfer of the structured employment interview training program. What are some of the things that can be done so that these factors do not prevent the transfer of training?

Design a transfer-of-training program by describing what you would do before, during, and after training to optimize training effectiveness and facilitate the transfer of the structured employment interview training program. In addition, describe how you would apply each of the following strategies to the structured employment interview training program:

- self-management
- relapse prevention
- goal setting

If you only had time to use one of these strategies for the structured employment interview training program, which one would you choose and why?

REFERENCES

Anthony, W.P., Perrewe, P.L. & Kacmar, K.M. (1993). *Strategic human resource management*. Fort Worth, TX: Dryden Press.

Baird, L., Schneier, C.E. & Laird, D. (1983). *The training and development sourcebook*. Amherst, MA: Human Resource Development Press.

Baldwin, T.T., & Ford, J.K. (1988). Transfer of training: A review and directions for future research. *Personnel Psychology 41*, 63–105.

Baldwin, T.T., & Magjuka, R.J. (1991). Organizational training and signals of importance: Linking pretraining perceptions to intentions to transfer. *Human Resource Development Quarterly* (Spring), 25–36.

Bandura, A. (1977). *Social learning theory*. Englewood-Cliffs, NJ: Prentice-Hall.

———. (1982). Self-efficacy mechanism in human agency. *American Psychologist 37*, 122–147.

———. (1997). *Self-efficacy: The exercise of control*. New York: W.H. Freeman and Company.

Bass, B.M., & Vaughn, J.A. (1969). *Training in industry: The management of learning*. Belmont, CA: Wadsworth.

Baumgartel, H., Reynolds, M., & Pathan, R. (1984). How personality and organizational climate variables moderate the effectiveness of management development programs: A review and some recent research findings. *Management and Labour Studies 9*, 1–16.

Belcourt, M., & Saks, A.M. (1998). After delivery. *Canadian Learning Journal* (May), 9–10.

———. (1998). Training methods and the transfer of training. *Canadian Learning Journal* (February), 3.

———. (1997). Effects of pre-training activities and a learning culture on the transfer of training. *Canadian Learning Journal*, 10–11.

———. (1997–98). Benchmarking best training practices. *Human Resources Professional* (Dec/Jan), 33–35.

Broad, M.L., & Newstrom, J.W. (1992). *Transfer of training*. Reading, MA: Addison-Wesley.

Buller, P.F., & Cragun, J.R. (1991). Networking: The overlooked benefit of training. *Training and Development 45*, (7), 41–44.

Caplow, T. (1983). *Managing an organization*. New York: Holt.

Clemmer, J. (1992, September 15). Why most training fails. *The Globe and Mail*, p. B26.

Commanducci, M. (1998). Training employees to be high performers. *Canadian HR Reporter* (September), 6.

Gist, M.E. (1989). The influence of training method on self-efficacy and idea generation among managers. *Personnel Psychology 42*, 787–805.

———. (1990). Transfer training method: Its influence on skill generalization, skill repetition, and performance level. *Personnel Psychology 43* (Autumn), 501–523.

Gist, N., Schwoerer, E., & Rosen, B. (1989). Effects of alternative training methods on self-efficacy and performance in computer software training. *Journal of Applied Psychology 74*, 884–891.

Goldstein, I.L. (1991). Training in work organizations. In Dunnette, M.D., & Hough, L. (Eds.), *Handbook of Industrial and Organizational Psychology* (2nd ed.), Vol. 2. Palo Alto, CA: Consulting Psychologists Press.

————. (1993). *Training in organizations: Needs assessment, development, and evaluation* (3rd ed.). Pacific Grove, CA: Brooks/Cole.

Hastie, R., & Kumar, P.A. (1979). Person memory: Personality traits as organizing principles in memory for behaviour. *Journal of Personality and Social Psychology 37*, 25–38.

Hatcher, T., & Schriver, R. (1991). Bursting the bubble that blocks training transfer. *Technical and Skills Training* (November–December), 12–15.

Hicks, W.D., & Klimoski, R.J. (1987). Entry into training programs and its effects on training outcomes: A field experiment. *Academy of Management Journal 30*, 542–552.

Ilgen, D.R., Fisher, C.D., & Taylor, M.S. (1979). Consequences of individual feedback on behaviour in organizations. *Journal of Applied Psychology 64*, 349–371.

Knowles, M. (1990). *The adult learner: A neglected species*. Houston, TX: Gulf Publishing Company.

Latham, G.P., & Frayne, C.A. (1989). Self-management training for increasing job attendance: A followup and a replication. *Journal of Applied Psychology 74*, 411–416.

Leifer, M.S., & Newstrom, J.W. (1980). Solving the transfer of training problems. *Training and Development Journal* (August), 34–46.

Lewin, K. (1958). Group decision and social change. In Maccoby, E.E., Newcomb, T.M., & Hartley, E.L. (Eds.), *Readings in social psychology*. New York: Holt.

Locke, E.A., & Latham, G.P. (1990). *A theory of goal setting and task performance*. Englewood Cliffs, NJ: Prentice-Hall.

McGehee, W., & Thayer, P.W. (1961). *Training in business and industry*. New York: Wiley.

Mager, R.F. (1992). No self-efficacy, no performance. *Training 29*, (4), 32–36.

Mayer, R.E. (1989). Models for understanding. *Review of Educational Research 59*, 43–64.

Miller, L. (1965). *The use of knowledge of results in improving the performance of hourly operators*. General Electric Company, Behavioral Research Service: Detroit.

Nadler, L. (1982). *Designing training programs: The critical events model*. Reading, MA: Addison-Wesley.

Nadler, L., & Nadler, Z. (1990). *The handbook of human resource development* (2nd ed.). New York: John Wiley & Sons.

Noe, R.A. (1986). Trainee attributes and attitudes: Neglected influences on training effectiveness." *Academy of Management Review 4*, 736–749.

Noe, R.A., & Schmitt, N. (1986). The influence of trainer attitudes on training effectiveness: Test of a model. *Personnel Psychology 39*, 497–523.

Parry, S. (1990). But will they use it? *Training and Development Journal* (December), 15–17.

Reilly, R.R., & Israelski, E.W. (1988). Development and validation of mini-courses in the telecommunications industry. *Journal of Applied Psychology 73*, 721–726.

Robertson, I., & Downs, S. (1989). Work sample tests of trainability: A meta-analysis. *Journal of Applied Psychology 74*, 402–410.

Ruyle, K.E. (1990). Developing great job aids. *Technical and Skills Training* (July), 27–31.

Saks, A.M., & Belcourt, M. (1997). Transfer of training in Canadian organizations. *Update* (September), 9–10.

Saks, A.M., & Haccoun, R.R. (1997). The psychology of transfer of training. Update. *Ontario Society for Training and Development* (May/June), 11–12.

Smith-Jentsch, K.A., Jentsch, F.G., Payne, C., & Salas, E. (1996). Can pre-training experiences explain individual differences in performance?" *Journal of Applied Psychology 81* (1), 110–116.

Spitzer, D. (1990). Confessions of a performance technologist. *Educational Technology* (May), 12–15.

Tannenbaum, S.I., Mathieu, J.E., Salas, E., & Cannon-Bowers, J.A. (1991). Meeting trainee's expectations: The influence of training fulfilment on the development of commitment, self-efficacy, and motivation. *Journal of Applied Psychology 76*, 750–769.

Thiagarajan, S. (1990). ID Basics: 1, 2, 3 7. *Performance and Instruction* (November/December), 1579.

Tziner, A., & Haccoun, R.R. (1991). Personal and situational characteristics influencing the effectiveness of transfer of training improvement strategies. *Journal of Occupational Psychology 64* (2), 167–177.

Wexley, K.N., & Latham, G.P. (1991). *Developing and training human resources in organizations* (2nd ed.). New York: Harper Collins Publishers.

Wexley, K.N., & Nemeroff, W.F. (1975). Effectiveness of positive reinforcement and goal setting as methods of management development. *Journal of Applied Psychology 60*, 446–450.

William, T.C., Thayer, P.W., & Pond, S.B. (1991). Test of a model of motivational influences on reactions to training and learning. Paper presented at the meeting of the Society for Industrial and Organizational Psychology, St. Louis, MI.

Yelon, S., & Berge, Z. (1992). Practice-centred training. *Performance and Instruction* (September), 8–12.

Zucker, L. (1987). Institutional theories of organization. *Annual Review of Sociology 13*, 443–464.

9

....

EVALUATION

CHAPTER GOALS

Evaluation is the link that closes the training process chain, which began with needs assessment. The processes of needs identification and evaluation share common measurement methods. Needs assessment identifies the problem to be solved; evaluation is the process that determines if the problem has been solved. Stated more broadly, **evaluation** is the procedure that determines the effectiveness of a training program. This chapter examines why evaluations should be conducted and the reasons why they are sometimes not conducted. Four types of evaluations—reaction, learning, behaviour, and results—are described in detail. Methods for assessing the effectiveness of training interventions are presented.

evaluation the process of data collection used to determine whether training is effective

After reading this chapter you should be able to

- explain why evaluation is a very important component of the training cycle
- describe the reasons why trainers might not conduct evaluations
- list the four types of evaluations, and give an example of how each could be measured

- describe issues in evaluation
- describe a model platform for assessing the impact of a training program on organizational effectiveness

RATIONALE FOR EVALUATION

Evaluation of activities is done for many reasons. Often, human resource developers want to determine the value or effectiveness of a workshop or program to assist them in making a purchase decision. This form of evaluation, called *summative* evaluation, can be used to assess any aspect of the full program including the instructors, the methods, or the facilities (Smith & Brandenburg, 1991).

More commonly, trainers evaluate programs for *formative* reasons: how can the processes and outcomes be improved? A question like this can be answered by assessing participant reactions and changes in outcomes.

In addition to these two reasons, there are several other grounds for assessing the development activity. Managers who make decisions about attendance at programs rely on evaluation information. Trainers can use the objectively measured results of a successful program to increase credibility and funding for other programs. Participants can even benefit from a measurement of learning. As seen in Chapters 5 and 8, feedback and reinforcement of learning are powerful tools in motivating employees to continue using the skills. Evaluation methods that use time-series analysis and control groups help determine whether the training program was responsible for observed changes, or whether other factors caused the change.

Senior executives have a right to expect a cost–benefit analysis of any program, including development programs. The training department benefits as well. For example, the TD Bank increased its training budget by 50 percent in 1998 after the department was able to prove that training led directly to increased profits (Larin, 1998). The next chapter describes methods of conducting a cost–benefit analysis of a change program. This chapter discusses evaluations of training programs.

BARRIERS TO EVALUATION

Very few HRD programs are subjected to evaluations. One study reported that the average organization allocates only 4 percent of its development budget to evaluation (Stone & Meltz, 1993). Most of the feedback about a course examines only trainee reactions, not the hard data of impact on organizational outcomes (Dixon, 1990).

Trainers cite many reasons for not conducting evaluations. A study of training professionals revealed that most did not do evaluations because they were too time-consuming or expensive, top management did not care, and the effect of the course was too difficult to isolate among many variables (Grider, 1990).

Some developers fear that negative results will jeopardize their careers. But results are seldom negative in a simplistic fashion. More often, the program sets into motion diverse situations, where trainees and their managers change many behaviours. Viewing evaluation data in a formative light—designed to improve, not punish developers—mitigates the negative effect.

Trainers report that evaluation is the most difficult aspect of their jobs (Gallagan, 1983). We hope that, after reading this chapter, you will be able to see that evaluation can be done for a reasonable cost and effort. But first, a summary of the reasons evaluations are important:

- to determine if the program has met the objectives, or solved the problem
- to identify the strengths and weaknesses of a program
- to determine the cost–benefits of the program; related to this, evaluation helps ascertain which change technique is the most cost-effective
- to assist managers in the determination of which employees would most likely benefit from the program
- to reinforce the expected results among the participants
- to use the evaluation data to reinforce the value and credibility of HRD programs

The evaluation of training and development programs and activities must be planned at the beginning of the training process. The evaluator should use the data and methods from the needs-assessment procedure and the learning objectives to determine if the desired changes have occurred.

TYPES OF EVALUATION

The evaluation of HRD programs usually focuses on the impact of the training activity on the trainee. However, other areas that may be evaluated include the value of the training materials, the effectiveness of the trainer, and the influence of the environment to which the development activity is transferred (Pace, Smith, & Mills, 1991).

Training materials are evaluated for their ability to produce the desired outcomes. This process of evaluation starts early in the developmental stage and continues to the transfer-of-skills stage. Trainers are assessed for their knowledge, their ability to communicate this information (presentation skills), and their ability to adapt to learner requirements. However, the principal focus of most evaluations is the impact of training on the trainee.

A good place to start measuring outcomes is by reviewing the taxonomy of learning objectives that were described in Chapter 3. If these objectives are well written, then the measurement of them is easy. If the goal is to increase knowledge or skills, or change attitudes, trainers can measure results against the clearly articulated goals.

Some have suggested that the taxonomy of objectives is too simple, and does not capture real learning or change. They argue for the measurement of learning outcomes that are more comprehensive and interrelated. The model proposed by Kraiger, Ford, and Salas (1993) uses as its base the concept of changes in the same three functional areas—cognition, skills, and attitudes—outlined in Chapter 3. However, these researchers have probed further. For example, the cognitive category includes not only the acquisition of knowledge, but also the ability to organize that knowledge, and strategies to acquire and apply that knowledge. Nevertheless, the most widely used model remains that of Donald Kirkpatrick.

Kirkpatrick (1983) developed a model of evaluation that researchers and writers still find useful. Kirkpatrick's framework considers the impact of training and development on the trainee in three areas: reaction, knowledge of learning, and behaviour. His fourth sphere is the impact on the organization (results). To simplify, the four key questions to be answered are:

- *Reaction*—Did they like it?
- *Learning*—Did they learn it?
- *Behaviour*—Did they use it on the job?
- *Results*—Did this change organizational effectiveness?

In a survey of 150 experienced, professional trainers in Canada, Belcourt and Saks (1998) report that most (75 percent) evaluated reaction, 40 percent evaluated learning, 20 percent evaluated behaviour, and 20 percent examined end results, or the actual return on investment, always or most of the time.

The next section examines these four levels of evaluation.

REACTION

reaction trainees' perceptions of the training program

The measurement of trainee **reaction** or satisfaction is the most common evaluation method. This method is used most frequently because it is easy to administer, collect, and analyze the data.

Usually, trainees complete a questionnaire at the end of a training program asking them to indicate their satisfaction with the content, the facilities, the trainer, the methods, and so on. Critics of this measure of satisfaction call these questionnaires smile sheets. They claim that all these forms are measuring is the entertainment value of the trainer or the video. This happiness index, they argue, has little to do with a participant doing a better job after training.

PROBLEMS   The problems associated with self-reporting were thoroughly discussed in Chapter 3. The self-report form is fraught with problems of reliability and validity. A study by Dixon (1990b) of 1400 trainees concluded that there was no significant relationship between how much participants said they enjoyed the course, how the instructors were rated and how much they felt they learned, and how well they actually did on the performance measure. This is not as surprising as it first appears. Many of us have had the experience of listening to someone tell us how to, for example, change a tire, have felt satisfied that we really understood the task, but were then unable to do it.

Also, trainers are rewarded for their personality and energy in the room rather than for the amount learned. Review the material in Chapter 5 for the characteristics of an effective trainer.

Another explanation for the lack of correlation between enjoyment and learning is that while having learned something feels good, the process of learning is often arduous. All these reasons make the use of happiness sheets suspect. However, management seems to want them; they are more economical and easier than any other form of evaluation. Their usefulness can be increased by careful design.

OPTIMIZING REACTION FORMS   Linking the reaction sheet to the objectives of the programs allows the trainer to measure critical factors, such as the effectiveness of the case method for learning a management skill. Recently, there have also been several advances in reaction measures. For example, Warr and Bunce (1995) developed a tripartite model of training reactions that includes three types of reaction measures: (1) enjoyment of training, (2) usefulness of training, and (3) difficulty of training. The measure of training usefulness has been found to be particularly important. In a study by Alliger, Tannenbaum, Bennett, Traver, and Shotland (1997), reaction measures of training usefulness—or what they called "utility" reactions (i.e., the extent to which trainees believe the training will be useful to them when performing their jobs)—were found to be more strongly related to trainee learning and on-the-job performance than more traditional affective reaction measures (i.e., how trainees feel about a training program). An example of a well-designed reaction rating form is presented in Figure 9.1.

Evaluators should allow lots of time at the end of a program for questionnaire completion so that trainees will respond thoughtfully. Responses should be anonymous. If comparisons of reactions between groups are needed (such as new employees versus skilled employees), a code could be developed. Note too that space should be allowed for more open-ended feedback.

BENEFITS   Reactions obtained at the completion of a program give the trainers immediate feedback and allow them to make quick adjustments to the next course, but these reaction forms serve many other purposes.

The most obvious contribution of reaction forms to the HRD function is the positive feedback that can be given to management as a sign that the program is effective (at least in the participants' eyes). Data from many participants balance the effect of the one participant who may complain to top management that he or she thought that the course was useless.

FIGURE 9.1   COURSE RATING FORM

Course or Session: _____   Instructor: _____

Content:

Please answer the following questions using the scale of

1. disagree strongly   2. agree   3. agree strongly

_____ The material presented will be useful to me on the job.

_____ The level of information was too advanced for my work.

_____ The level of information presented was too elementary for me.

_____ The information was presented in manageable chunks.

_____ Theories and concepts were linked to work activities.

_____ The course material was up to date and reliable.

Instructor:

Please rate the instructor's performance along the following dimensions:

_____ Needs improvement

_____ Just right, or competent, effective

_____ Superior or very effective performance

The instructor

_____ Described the objectives of the session.

_____ Had a plan for the session.

_____ Followed the plan.

_____ Determined trainees' current knowledge.

_____ Explained new terms.

_____ Used work and applied examples.

_____ Provided opportunities for questions.

_____ Was enthusiastic about the topic.

_____ Presented material clearly.

_____ Effectively summarized the material.

_____ Varied the learning activities.

_____ Showed a personal interest in class progress.

_____ Demonstrated a desire for trainees to learn.

Perceived Impact:

_____ I gained significant new knowledge.

_____ I developed skills in the area.

_____ I was given tools for attacking problems.

_____ My on-the-job performance will improve.

Please indicate what you will do differently on the job as a result of this course.

Overall Rating:

Taking into account all aspects of the course, how would you rate it?

_____ Excellent _____ Very Good _____ Good _____ Fair _____ Poor

Would you take another course from this instructor?   _____ Yes _____ No

Would you recommend this course to your colleagues?   _____ Yes _____ No

Another benefit of reaction questionnaires is a psychological one. Trainees who have had a chance to comment on the program, make suggestions for improvements, and indicate how much they have learned might be more motivated to transfer that learning to the job than others who leave a program without providing input.

To summarize, care in the design of the reaction form will result in useful information for the developers and management. The next factor that can be measured is the amount of learning that has occurred.

LEARNING

The measurement of the amount of **learning** that has resulted from a training program is the second-easiest method of evaluation. About 40 percent of trainers use this type of evaluation. Learning refers to all those cognitive, attitudinal, and skill components that were thoroughly defined and discussed in the chapter on learning objectives. *The taxonomy of learning* is a classification system of objectives that provides useful information about the types of learning that can be measured. As indicated earlier, Kraiger et al. (1993) developed a comprehensive classification scheme for learning outcomes that includes cognitive outcomes (i.e., verbal knowledge, knowledge organization, and cognitive strategies), skill-based outcomes (i.e., knowledge compilation and automaticity), and affective outcomes (i.e., attitudinal and motivational). Alliger et al. (1997) have divided learning measures into three subcategories: (1) immediate post-training knowledge, which measures trainee learning immediately after a training program, (2) knowledge retention, which measures trainee learning sometime after a training program, and (3) behaviour or skill demonstration, which measures trainees' ability to perform the training task during the training program.

learning a relatively permanent change in behaviour

The best way to measure learning is to administer a test at the beginning of the program (pre-test) and then administer the same test at the end of the program. Any gains might be attributed to the course or program. (Improvements on this research design are covered in a later section.) The test can be a paper-and-pencil test of knowledge, such as those found in schools and referred to as quizzes, exams, or tests. These types of tests, familiar to everyone who has attended school, use formats like true or false, multiple-choice, short-answer, and essay questions. Figure 9.2 presents an array of these options. The test items listed in Part A of Figure 9.2 are termed objectively scored tests because there is only one correct answer possible.

Part B gives some examples of subjectively scored test items. Test items that are considered subjective are essay questions, oral interviews, journals, and diaries. Here, several answers might be acceptable, and markers have some latitude in their interpretation of the correctness of the answer.

Tests can also be simulations conducted in realistic situations. For example, a pilot could be tested in a virtual-reality airplane. The skills of a drug counsellor could be tested using actors as drug addicts. A test could be con-

FIGURE 9.2 TESTING FORMATS

Part A: Objectively Scored Tests

True or False

1. A test is valid if a person receives approximately the same result or score at two different testing times.   True _____   False _____

Multiple Choice

2. The affective domain of learning refers to

_____ skills

_____ attitudes

_____ knowledge

_____ all of the above

_____ 2 and 3

Matching

3. For each of the governments listed on the left, select the appropriate responsibility for training and place the letter next to the term.

_____ 1. federal   a. displaced workers

_____ 2. provincial   b. language training

_____ 3. municipal   c. student summer work

Short Answer

4. Kirkpatrick identified four types of evaluation. These are:

_____

_____

_____

Part B: Subjectively Scored Tests

Essay

5. Describe how and why the process of needs assessment is a critical step in the measurement of the effectiveness of an HRD intervention.

Oral

6. The measurement of training has many potential benefits. Identify these benefits. Discuss the reasons why, given these advantages of measurement, most trainers do not evaluate training.

Observation Checklist

7. The customer service representative

greeted the customer   _____

approached the customer   _____

offered to help   _____

FIGURE 9.2   TESTING FORMATS (continued)

Rating Scale

8. Indicate the degree to which you agree or disagree with the statements below:

    Scale: 1 = strongly disagree   2 = disagree   3 = agree   4 = strongly agree

    During a selection interview, the interviewer
used behavioural-based questions	1	2	3	4
looked for contrary evidence	1	2	3	4
used probing questions	1	2	3	4

Diaries, Anecdotal Records, Journals

9. In your journal, write about your experiences working with someone from a different culture. Record the date, time, and reason for the interaction. Describe how you felt and what you learned.

---

ducted as a role play (for negotiation skills) or a practice session (for tennis certification). These tests are normally called performance tests.

The development of tests that are standardized, reliable, and valid usually requires the services of a psychologist or an educational measurement specialist. Practically speaking, most trainers can do a good enough job by following a few procedures. First, the test items should reflect the learning objectives, which have been specified in measurable terms (see Chapter 4). Second, the tests should be given to a pilot group to look for errors, inconsistencies, and so on. Third, a group of new employees and a group of very experienced or skilled employees should take the test. The results should demonstrate significant differences between the two groups. Only at this point should trainees be given the test.

Tests are useful for reasons other than evaluating changes in learning. A testing hurdle at the end of a course increases trainee motivation to learn the material (Smith & Merchant, 1990). Trainees at General Dynamics took this hurdle seriously. Employees were not allowed access to the manufacturing resource planning software until they had passed a competency test (Smith & Merchant, 1990).

The information that tests provide to trainers is invaluable. In cases of accidents and litigation, the employer can prove that the employee was trained to the necessary levels. Furthermore, if trainees consistently score low on some aspect of the course, the trainer is alerted to the fact that this component needs to be revised. More information may be required or exercises may have to be added to ensure that learning does occur. At General Dynamics, trainers became extremely motivated because the trainees had to learn and could not be brushed off by hinting that they could "always learn misunderstood material back on the job." Furthermore, the trainer cannot assume that because the participants score well on tests, they do well on the job. It is on the job where the real measurement of the payoff of training begins.

Behaviour

behaviour observed
performance

A trainee can enjoy a training course and pass a test *and* still perform poorly on the job. Organizations that fund training are most interested in seeing that the training is transferred to the job. **Behaviour** is a conventional term for performance. The evaluation of behaviour is really an evaluation of the application of the learning.

Assessing whether skills learned off the job are transferred to the job can be done in several ways. Observers, such as subject-matter experts and managers, can rate job performance before and after training. An example of such a rating form is shown in Figure 9.3.

FIGURE 9.3   OBSERVATION RATING FORM

Rate the customer-service representative who reports to you on the following dimensions. Check where you would position the representative's performance on each dimension, indicating your rating before (B) and after (A) the "Quality in Customer Service" course:

The scale to be used in rating performance is as follows:

    5—outstanding

    4—superior

    3—satisfactory

    2—minimum standard

    I—needs substantial improvement

Observation Checklist:

Before		After
_____	Greets customers in friendly manner	_____
_____	Serves customers promptly	_____
_____	Uses open-ended questions	_____
_____	Identifies barriers to sales	_____
_____	Other	_____

Other people who interact with the participant can be asked for their views. Customers can be surveyed by phone or by questionnaire about the effectiveness of the behaviour of the newly trained employee. Videotaping on-the-job behaviour is a novel way for subject-matter experts to judge performance. Subordinates can be asked in interviews or focus groups to rate a manager's new competence in performance appraisal. Xerox uses many methods to ascertain behaviour changes, including post-course observations of trainees in their regular jobs, interviews with their managers, and a review of performance appraisal forms (Olian & Durham, 1998). TD Bank uses a very simple approach. Participants in training programs are asked to describe three or four examples of when they used the new knowledge or skill on the job (Larin, 1998).

These surveys are usually done some time after the course. There must be time for trainees to become comfortable with newly acquired skills and to be given opportunities to demonstrate them. (The chapter on transfer of training offers suggestions for methods to increase the likelihood of the newly acquired skills being used on the job.) The time lag for assessment of behaviour ranges from a few weeks to as much as two years, in the case of managerial skills. In these cases, performance-appraisal information should highlight the changes.

RESULTS

The most difficult step in evaluating a training program is the measurement of its impact on organizational indices. **Results,** in organizational terms, are quantifiable changes in areas like turnover, productivity, quality, time, profitability, customer complaints, and so on. In most instances, the objective is to cost the program and determine the net benefit. The next chapter is devoted to procedures for doing this costing analysis. Basically, managers should be looking at **hard data** results like time, outputs, inputs, and frequencies; in other words, anything that can be measured objectively. ACCO World Corp., a manufacturer of school supplies ranging from paper clips to binders, tracked the effect of training on new production hires. After training, new hires were able to produce vinyl binders at a 5 to 10 percent higher rate than tenured operators. The trainer then leveraged this result to continue the training and expand it to tenured operators (Flynn, 1998).

Companies can calculate the productivity effect of training. For example, Anderson Consulting trained tax consultants in tax law, and compared the amount of work completed and the amount of revenue generated before and after the course. Those consultants who had taken the course had more billable hours than those who had not (Olian & Durham, 1998). But sometimes these hard data are difficult to obtain, and rather than measure return on equity, some trainers are turning to soft data measures, such as return on expectations.

RETURN ON EXPECTATIONS

Sometimes, because of the difficulty of measuring quantifiable results (hard data), evaluators turn to soft data as a substitute. See Table 9.1 for a list of hard data and soft data measures.

Soft data include measures of work climate, feelings and attitudes, and difficult-to-measure skills like decision making. The reasoning is that if employees can demonstrate a skill such as initiative, this will ultimately have an impact on the organization's bottom line; but it is difficult to assign a dollar value to this, or to prove that changes in attitude do make a difference. Consider this approach as moving from calculating return on investment to calculating **return on expectations** (Flynn, 1998). Those who are involved in training decide exactly what they expect from the training. These expectations form the goals for training, and some time after the course, managers decide if

results outcomes used to evaluate the effectiveness of a training program

hard data those factors that can be measured objectively

soft data measures of perceptions of employees' attitudes toward organizational processes

return on expectations the measurement of a training program's ability to meet managerial aspiration

TABLE 9.1 EXAMPLES OF HARD DATA AND SOFT DATA

HARD DATA		SOFT DATA	
Output	units produced units sold jobs completed calls answered	**Work habits**	absenteeism lateness safety infractions turnover
Quality	scrap and waste product defects customer complaints	**Work climate**	grievances, complaints job satisfaction culture

Time	downtime
	overtime
	time to completion
		Management	quality of decisions
			conflict resolution
			successful
			    completion of
			    projects

Cost	overhead variable costs accident costs sales expenses benchmarks		implementation of new ideas using new skills

Source: Adapted from Phillips, J. (1996). How much is the training worth. *Training & Development* (April), 20–24.

the performance results are in line with their expectations. One organization that was restructured into product-performance teams was unable to place a dollar value on the cross-functional training employees had received, but managers were able to articulate improvements they noticed after the training. The numbers are not absolute, but managers are not only saying that time is being managed better, but that 95 percent of deadlines are being met. They feel that this anecdotal evidence does have an impact on the bottom line, and that profits improvements are noticeable.

Anderson Worldwide was the winner of a best practices award in 1995 for its creation of a tool to measure training outcomes by managing these expectations (Overmeyer-Day & Benson, 1996). They contacted multiple stakeholders to obtain a clear picture of training expectations and priorities. They have developed a sophisticated system called concept mapping, which enables the integration of input from different people on competencies of employees about to attend training. They then used statistics to compare expectations to outcomes, thus measuring return on expectations.

Training value, measured in dollars, can be determined from these soft measures. Fitz-Enz (1994) provides a concrete example, using the concept of informed judgment. He asked managers to identify the core competencies of managers. Coaching was one of these. He then asked managers to identify the costs or tangible consequences of poor coaching. Assignments that had to be reworked were one such consequence. The frequency of this happening, the cost associated with the hourly rate of poorly coached employees, for example, were calculated until managers were able to give a plausible figure to the difference between good and poor coaching. In this way, even soft skills or work processes can be assigned value.

Some companies establish a relationship between training, a soft measure, and a hard measure. Sears Roebuck & Co. found a direct correlation between employee satisfaction, customer satisfaction, and profitability. Sears found that if employee satisfaction scores on factors such as treatment by bosses increased by 5 percent, then customer satisfaction increased by 1.3 percent, which then led to a 0.5 percent jump in revenue (Laabs, 1999). This employee-customer-profit model has become a world-class performance benchmark. Employees are trained through distance learning courses (to accommodate employees in 800 stores) on selling techniques. The employees demonstrate their mastery through a voice-response testing system, which also measures employee attitudes. Sears's cash registers randomly spew out receipts that ask customers to call an automated toll-free number and respond to questions. These employee satisfaction and customer satisfaction scores are then benchmarked against competitors. Since 1995, Sears's employee satisfaction scores have been rising, and customer satisfaction scores have increased more than twice as much as any other retailer, with an increase of 200 million dollars (US) in additional revenues.

Several problems are associated with measuring results. Not only does it take more time to collect this data, but also the actual effect of the training program is most difficult to assess. In one example, all the senior managers of a firm attended a three-week leadership course. The company had always kept records of productivity and so on, and so could compare operating results before the course and after the course. There were no significant changes in these numbers. The conclusion was that the course was a failure. There are some difficulties with this conclusion, however. At the same time that the managers were being trained, a new competitor with an excellent track record in the United States entered the Canadian market. Customers and market share were being lost. No one will ever be able to determine if more customers would have been lost if managers had not used their new skills.

Furthermore, the effects of changing managerial behaviour and organizational culture are not felt for years. During that time, factors such as interest rates and competitor actions may have an impact on operating results.

Tightly controlled experimental designs can solve some of these problems, but they are unlikely to be used in a business environment. The next section discusses ways in which evaluators can appropriate the principles of research and apply them to the real world. This is called action research.

ACTION RESEARCH DESIGN

The design of the method to determine if a training and development program has caused a change in behaviour is important. The design allows managers and developers to state, "Yes, the training program, and not some other factor, resulted in these changes." This section presents an array of designs, from the most commonly used to the best. The differences between these designs can be followed more easily by consulting Table 9.2.

TABLE 9.2 RESEARCH DESIGN

DESIGN TYPE	PRE-TEST	PROGRAM	POST-TEST		
A. Post Only	No	Program	Yes		
B. Pre and Post	Yes	Program	Yes		
C. Post only with Control Group					
Trainees	No	Program	Yes		
Control	No	No Program	Yes		
D. Pre and Post with Control Group					
Trainees	Yes	Program	Yes		
Control	Yes	No Program	Yes		
E. Time Series					
Trainees	Yes	Program	Test 1	Test 2	Test n
F. Time Series with Control Group					
Trainees	Yes	Program	Test 1	Test 2	Test n
Control	Yes	No Program	Test 1	Test 2	Test n

Although the evaluation process uses many of the same criteria and methods as research, the focus in evaluation is the effect on the organization (Baird, Schneier, & Laird, 1983). The focus in pure research, with its controlled conditions in the laboratory, is on the testing of hypotheses.

Design A (in Table 9.2), which consists of assessing trainees only after the program, is the most common form of evaluation in organizations. Unfortunately, it tells us almost nothing about the effectiveness of the course. (Sometimes, knowing how much trainees know after the course is important for certification purposes.) We cannot say that trainees have learned or improved because we do not know what they knew or did before they started training. There is no baseline of information. Baseline data are usually collected from the three areas of knowledge or skill, on-the-job performance, and organization results. These correspond to learning, behaviour, and results in Kirkpatrick's model. The establishment of baselines is probably the evaluator's most important task. There has to be a picture, a record of what is happening, before anything changes. This picture should be as normal a picture as possible (i.e., the records should not be contaminated by strikes or measurements taken around holidays, and so on). As is demonstrated in Chapters 5 and 8, sometimes feedback of actual performance results in improved performance. So, if you do no other form of measurement, collect baseline data.

Design B is better, because it does collect this information in some form of pre-test. (The word test is used in its broadest form. As noted above, it could be simulations, records, interviews, as well as exams and questionnaires.) By pre-testing participants, information about their knowledge and skills gives us baseline data. A change can be measured. The principal problem with this design is that it cannot be said that training caused the change. For example, at the same time that the sales representatives are taking a sales training course, management may decide to change their compensation package. (Multiple solutions are often implemented when management perceives a performance problem.)

However, Design B cannot help the evaluator determine if the training program or the new compensation package changed sales performance. Furthermore, the training course is not the only source for acquiring new skills. One study found that supervisors learned management skills not only from the leadership course, but also from co-worker's advice, through trial and error, and from courses outside of work (Mitchell, 1994).

Design C would provide additional information. Design C uses a control group, a group of employees that does not participate in the sales training. This control group should be composed of sales representatives who are similar in characteristics, such as experience and education, to those receiving the training. (Candidates selected for future training but not attending the first courses would be ideal.) Both the control group and the trainees (the experimental group) would be measured. If there were differences in performance, it would be tempting to conclude that the sales training was effective. However, unless the two groups were identical on key characteristics, we could also hypothesize that the training group was more motivated to sell (because the members wanted the course first). The training may have been irrelevant, except for the possibility that it identified the most eager employees.

Design D could solve this problem. The evaluator would assess all sales representatives before the training program. Then, participants for the first course could be chosen on a random basis. (Those not chosen would be assigned to a later course.) The participants would undergo training. Both the control group and the training group would be tested after training. If the trained group improved on the measures, an organizational analyst could reasonably conclude that the training was effective. In addition, the performance of the two groups could be compared and, in some cases, a dollar value could be assigned to the improvement.

However, because some changes in skills are subject to time lags, as was shown earlier, the best design would include a series of measures of time. This design also silences the criticism that some employees improve simply because of maturation or experience.

Design E portrays a plan in which participants are tested following the course, and perhaps every six months afterward for a period of two years. This retesting helps trainers discern whether the training simply boosts skills for a while and then tapers off.

Design F represents the ultimate in training evaluation. The use of pre-tests and post-tests, using a time series, with both the trainees and a control group, allows evaluators to determine cause and effect. This type of design is rarely implemented. It is simply too expensive and time-consuming for most human resource departments. However, in the long run, developmental programs that are ineffective probably waste more time and money.

Using the Results

The clients of the action-research results include the human resource developers, management who approved and funded the intervention, and potential participants and their managers. Their two questions are: Did it work? Was it worth it? Trainers may be reluctant to evaluate their efforts objectively; the task is made less difficult by presenting the results in context. Context means that the users of the information must understand the rationale for the evaluation and the limitations of the research design. In addition, users should be given some understanding of the meaning of the information collected.

Raw data are of little use to management, unless they are able to compare them and assign value to them. Comparative information helps determine value. For example, the data that reveal that an instructor is perceived to be competent by 70 percent of the students become more meaningful when other information reveals that other instructors consistently receive a 90 percent competency rating. Also, knowing that a training program resulted in a $50 000 increase in sales only becomes relevant when compared to the costs of other interventions. If, for example, supervisory attention and support for sales representatives result in a net benefit of $10 000, then the effectiveness of a training intervention can be accurately evaluated.

Value also implies significance. In practical terms, is it significant (i.e., does it really make any difference) if health and safety offices scored 72 percent on a safety test, while the control group scored 58 percent? Significance has many meanings. Statisticians use it as a measure meaning that the difference was real and important. (Organizations can use experts or software to tabulate data for significant differences.) This is the numerical meaning, a first step in determining significance.

A second meaning may be a legislative one. The 20-percent improvement in safety knowledge may be irrelevant if safety officers are required by law to know 100 percent of the course content. But managers may find even 100 percent insignificant if accidents and claims do not decrease as a result of the course. Conversely, some managers want to hear positive comments about the course and weigh these comments as much as changes in job behaviour. The conclusion is not that you can't win; the conclusion is that multiple measures with control groups must be used.

PRINCIPLES OF EVALUATION

- Evaluation should be planned at the same time that a needs identification is done and an intervention (training course, developmental activity) is designed.
- The design should use at least a pre- and one post-measure, with the control group consisting of units or participants scheduled for later interventions.
- Multiple measures should be taken. Evaluations should consider measuring not just reactions but learning, behaviour, and results. The measurement of these should look not only at operation figures but should include surveys of observers.

Table 9.3 outlines the levels of evaluation, the data to be collected, and the method of collecting data.

ISSUES IN EVALUATION

The presentation of the various research designs may have only convinced you that training is difficult, costly, and risky. The reaction to these problems is that, in reality, most managers do not conduct evaluations. This short-term cop-out works when profits are high and when the participants are clapping loudly. However, when organizational performance deteriorates and employees become anxious, the training department should have some evaluative data available to prevent the elimination of their function.

The key words in conducting an evaluation in an organization are feasibility and flexibility. Trainers and developers must have some elementary training in the setting of measurable objectives, the measurement of their attainment, and reasonable research designs. With this understanding, trainers

TABLE 9.3 EVALUATION METHODS

LEVEL	DATA	METHOD
Reaction	Opinions	Forms
	Attitudes	Questionnaires
Learning	Knowledge	Objectively scored tests (true or false, multiple choice, short answer, etc.)
		Subjectively scored tests (essays, papers, interviews)
	Skills	Simulations, role plays,
	Attitudes	Role plays, surveys
Behaviour	Performance	Supervisors, subordinates, customers, etc. complete rating forms or participate in interviews
Results	Hard Data	Records from production, finance, human resources
	Soft Data	Surveys and interviews

should be able to manage a crude evaluation that will answer the critical question: Did the program make a difference?

Coupled with feasible evaluation is the concept of a flexible evaluation. Trainers should look at multiple ways to gather information. Given that there are organizational constraints, trainers should be flexible in their approaches. For example, if the company does not want to divide potential trainees into control and trained groups, then the trainer should train in stages. The control group simply becomes the next group to be trained (if the program is successful).

Given all these prescriptions for a healthy measurement program, let us use the principles of feasibility and flexibility to design a model, but practical, program.

A MODEL EVALUATION

The General Hospital is required by provincial law to train all its employees in WHMIS (Workplace Hazards Materials Information Systems). To comply with this legislation, and to establish proof that everyone has knowledge of WHMIS (in case of an accident, and subsequent legislation), the General Hospital has devised the following plan for training.

PHASE I: CONDUCT A NEEDS ASSESSMENT

The General Hospital needs to know not only whether all employees have the required level of knowledge about hazardous materials, but also whether they can apply them on the job. The needs assessment is therefore composed of two parts: a knowledge test and an observation of workplace practices.

The knowledge test consists of 100 items, mainly multiple choice and short answer. An example would be:

Carbon monoxide is a

1. gas
2. liquid
3. solid

The short-answer items ask questions such as "When sulphuric acid is spilled on the skin, what first aid procedures are appropriate?"

Then safety officers were trained to observe safety behaviour of employees on the job, using a standardized checklist.

In these ways, a baseline of knowledge and behaviour was established.

PHASE II: CONDUCT A TRAINING COURSE

The training course was conducted (using a combination of presentations, videos, and multimedia interactive computer training).

PHASE III: CONDUCT AN EVALUATION

Before leaving the training room, all trainees were required to complete the same knowledge test as previously completed.

A reaction form was designed to measure satisfaction with the content, the instructor, and the learning media. Participants were also asked to identify barriers to the implementation of safe practices and to develop, with the help of the instructor, a program to ensure the transfer of the newly acquired skills and knowledge.

Both the knowledge tests and the reaction forms were analyzed to determine the weaknesses and strengths of the program.

PHASE IV: CONDUCT A FOLLOW-UP

One month and then six months after the course, safety officers observed the workplace practices of all employees. Statistical analysis of the differences before the training course and after the training course established that the course was effective in increasing knowledge about WHMIS and in improving safe workplace behaviour.

PHASE V: CONDUCT A COMPARISON

Records had always been kept on the number of accidents, workers' compensation claims, sick days due to accidents, and so on at the company. These records were analyzed, comparing the data before the course and after the course. In this way, the trainers were able to show that the WHMIS training course had the following bottom-line impact:

	Before	**After**
Accidents	1129	351
Sick days	1345	121
Claims	274	107

Students who wish to develop their own model evaluation systems are encouraged to complete the exercises at the end of the chapter.

SUMMARY

This chapter examined the reasons why trainers do not conduct four levels of evaluation, and why they should. The evaluation levels of reaction, learning, behaviour, and results were described. Problems in each of the measurement steps were identified, and practical solutions proposed. A model research design was presented.

KEY TERMS

behaviour 222

evaluation 213

hard data 223

learning 219

reaction 216

results 223

return on expectations 223

soft data 223

EXERCISES

1. Since you are reading this text, you are probably part of a course in training and development. Within teams, develop a reaction form that rates the effectiveness of the course, the instructor, the methods, the instructional technology, and so on. Design a method to measure the amount of learning that has occurred in one session or module.

2. Return to the exercise described in Chapter 3, "Needs Analysis." Assume that a training intervention occurred and that the reaction to the program has already been assessed. Devise ways of measuring any changes in learning, behaviour, or results. Try to use the same instruments or techniques that established the baseline or gap. Design the best or model evalua-

tion program that will ensure you can state to management, "These changes are attributable to the training intervention."

3. If you are a consultant trying to sell your training services and programs to organizations, you will be asked for information about the effectiveness of your programs. How would you provide this information? The Web site managed by Services Industries and Capital Projects Branch of Industry Canada will help you make a business case for your training project: <**www.strategis.ic.gc.ca/cgi-bin/ basic/e**>.

CASE: SIX SIGMA

Six sigma is a management tool used to improve quality by identifying and reducing the number of defects or errors. Sigma is a statistical term measuring the degree to which a process varies from perfection. Six sigma is a rigorous system that uses data collection and statistical analyses to identify sources of errors and correct them. For example, a company operating at four sigma (which is the operating range for most companies) has about 6210 defects per million units processed. A six-sigma company has only 3.4 defects per million units processed. Imagine being 99.9997 percent perfect!

General Electric is working toward becoming a six-sigma company. The GE empire consists of many companies, including those in broadcasting, power, appliances, aircraft engines, and finances. Each sigma improvement at GE represents $7 to $10 billion annually in savings, which is the cost of scrap, reworking parts, and fixing mistakes. Overall GE executives predict that six-sigma training will result in $10 to $15 billion annually in revenue increases. Companies that have implemented six sigma report that they now have faster product development, greater customer satisfaction, lower capital spending as capacity is released, and more productive research and development. Analysts report GE will attain 5 percent earnings per share growth annually, attributed to six sigma.

Most companies apply this process improvement tool to manufacturing operations, but GE Capital is using it as well for commercial transactions. GE Capital is analyzing its operations to reduce defects in mortgage applications, credit card transactions, and customer service centres. For example, customers told GE Capital that a critical quality issue for them was how often a salesperson could answer a question without having to look into it and get back to them. Each sales person kept a detailed diary for a week, logging the number of questions they were able to answer immediately. The result? Only 50 percent of questions asked could be answered right away. The data was then analyzed to determine which types of questions sales people were unable to answer. This information was used to design training to reduce the gap to a six-sigma level of quality.

GE will spend US$400 million on training the entire workforce to think like engineers. While the tool is statistical in nature, the training sounds more like a martial arts course. Black belts are employees trained to work full-time on projects to eliminate errors. Black belt, borrowed from martial arts, refers to the mental discipline and extensive training that employees master. Black belts undergo four months of training in statistical tools and software programs, spend two years to become experts in their use, and then attain certification after managing 20 six-sigma projects that achieve the intended savings. Green belts work part-time on quality projects. Training is expensive, with consultants charging US$1 million to license the method and train a core group of black belts. Training each additional class of black belts costs $150 000. GE Canada, a wholly owned subsidiary of GE, will train 617 green belts, black belts, and master black belts among its workforce of 9500. Employees like six sigma better than other process improvement programs like total quality management because it is quantitative, not anecdotal.

To indicate how seriously the company takes the training, Jack Welch, CEO of GE, announced in 1998 that no employees would be considered for promotion to any management job unless they have completed green belt or black belt training. Moreover, 40 percent of executive bonuses will be based on their ability to achieve six-sigma goals.

Source: Walmsley, A. (1997). Six sigma. *Report on Business Magazine* (October), 56–68.

QUESTION

1. Using Kirkpatrick's model of evaluation, identify which levels of evaluation GE is using to measure the impact of training. Within each level, specify the measures used. Could the results be attributed to anything else besides the training program?

RUNNING CASE PART 5:
VANDALAIS DEPARTMENT STORES

Several days before the structured employment interview training program for Vandalais Department Stores (refer to Chapter 5 for details on the training program), the director of human resources contacted the two professors who were going to deliver the training program. She was concerned about being able to demonstrate the value of the training program to management. Following a lengthy discussion, the two professors agreed to conduct an evaluation of the training program. Unfortunately, they had not planned on conducting an evaluation, and now must decide how to proceed. Using the material in this chapter, develop a plan to evaluate the structured employment interview training program. In particular, you should provide specific details regarding each of the following issues:

1. What will you measure as part of the evaluation and why?

2. For each of the measures you indicated above, describe exactly how you will measure them.

3. How will you design your evaluation study? Consider each of the designs in Table 9.2. For each design, describe how you would use it to evaluate the structured employment interview training program and its advantages and disadvantages. Finally, which design will you choose to evaluate the training program and why?

4. What evaluation methods will you use? Consider each of the methods in Table 9.3.

REFERENCES

Alliger, G.M., Tannenbaum, S.I., Bennett, W., Traver, H., & Shotland, A. (1997). A meta-analysis of the relations among training criteria. *Personnel Psychology 50,* 341–358.

Baird, L.S., Schneier, C.E., & Laird, D. (1983). *The training and development sourcebook.* Amherst, MA: Human Resource Development Press.

Belcourt, M., & Saks, A.M. (1998). After delivery. *Canadian Learning Journal* (May), 9–10.

Dixon, N.M. (1990a). *Evaluation: A tool for improving HRD quality.* Belmont, CA: University Associates.

———. (1990b). The relationship between trainee responses on participant reaction forms and post-test scores. *Human Resource Development Quarterly 1* (2), 129–137.

Fitz-Enz, J. (1994). "Yes—you can weigh training's value. *Training 31* (7), 54–58.

Flynn, G. (1998). The nuts and bolts of valuing training. *Workforce 17* (11), 80–85.

Gallagan, P. (1983). The numbers game: Putting value on HRD. *Training and Development Journal 37* (8), 48–51.

Grider, D.T. (1990). Training evaluation. *Business Magazine 17* (1), 2024.

Kirkpatrick, D.L. (1983). Four steps to measuring training effectiveness. *Personnel Administrator 28* (11), 19–25.

Kraiger, K, Ford, J.K., & Salas, E. (1993). Application of cognitive, skill-based and affective theories of learning outcomes to new methods of training evaluation. *Journal of Applied Psychology 78* (2), 311–328.

Laabs, J. (1999). The HR side of Sears' comeback. *Workforce 78* (3), 24–29.

Larin, N. (1998). Who understands return on investment better than a bank? *Canadian HR Reporter,* p. 2–8.

Mitchell, K.D. (1994). Putting evaluation to work for human resources development. *Public Productivity and Management Review 18* (2), 199–214.

Olian, J.D., & Durham, C.C. (1998). Designing management training and development for competitive advantage: Lessons from the best. *Human Resource Planning 21* (1), 20–31.

Overmeyer-Day, L., & Benson, G. (1996). Training success stories. *Training and Development*, 24–29.

Pace, R.W., Smith, C.P., & Mills, G.E. (1991). *Human resource development: The field*. Englewood Cliffs, NJ: Prentice-Hall.

Smith, J.E., & Merchant, S. (1990). Using competency exams for evaluating training. *Training and Development Journal 44* (8), 65–71.

Smith, M.E., & Brandenburg, D.C. (1991). Summative evaluation. *Performance Improvement Quarterly 4* (2), 35–38.

Stone, T., & Meltz, N. (1993). *Human resource management in Canada* (3rd ed.). Toronto: Holt, Rinehart & Winston.

Warr, P., & Bunce, D. (1995). Trainee characteristics and the outcomes of open learning. *Personnel Psychology 48*, 347–375.

10

....

COSTING TRAINING PROGRAMS

CHAPTER GOALS

Evaluation determines whether the training goals were achieved; costing determines how much the training cost and provides information to support calculations of cost–benefits. Costing is a complex and time-consuming process that many training specialists traditionally have avoided. The reasons are many: some managers are skeptical about the theoretical underpinnings of costing, while others suggest, rightly, that in business not everything is quantifiable. Indeed, many managers suggest that some quality issues and processes—employee motivation, communication techniques—make people feel good about themselves and the company they work for, and you just cannot put a dollar value on them. Still others are afraid that costing (when tied to benefit analysis) might expose some training programs as noncontributors, thus putting their careers at risk (Phillips, 1992).

After reading this chapter, you should be able to

- understand the relationships between investments in training and the payback from training

- understand the need to sell training costs–benefits to senior management

- conduct a cost–benefit analysis of a moderately complex training program
- understand how utility analysis can be used to calculate the financial benefits of a training program
- describe the activities for supporting the costing function and the issues associated with reporting and selling cost–benefit analysis

The Importance of Costing

costing   the process of identifying all the expenditures used in training

Costing is the process used to identify all the expenditures used in training. The amount spent on training in North America averages 0.9 percent of organizations' budgets. Similarly, a survey of 150 leading Canadian corporations reveals those companies spent an annual average of $1800 per employee—4.2 percent of payroll—on training and other types of human resource development (Commanducci, 1998; Flynn, 1998). Managers want an account of how well that money was spent (Flynn, 1998). Trainers need to learn to speak the language of senior management, and that language is financial.

Trainers who have lost their jobs because of budget reductions, or whose departments have been eliminated or drastically reduced, tend to be strongly supportive of costing and evaluation, or benefit analysis. The reasons are obvious; managers "want to hear trainers talking about return, profits, and assessment," because too often funding has been wasted on training designs that were too introspective and that disregarded the need for more results-oriented development activity (Blanden et al., 1991).

As well, the credibility issue discussed previously must be kept in mind. An educational software-development company on the East coast, for example, was in desperate need of curriculum-development specialists who would work with clients to create learning packages that could later be made into interactive video training modules. Because no trained people were available locally, this company obtained government assistance, developed a training program, and advertised widely for former teachers and others with appropriate computer skills and with training in psychology. The number of applicants was so large that the screening and interview processes took two months, consuming a considerable amount of valuable management time.

Unfortunately, two weeks before the course was to begin, the company realized that someone had forgotten to add the cost of equipment rental into the budget. Suddenly, the entire project was not financially viable and the course was cancelled.

Consider the embarrassment: the government grant had to be returned; the 15 trainees, some of whom had refused other opportunities, had to be contacted; the company's entire product-development strategy had to be reworked. As the personnel manager said when she sheepishly contacted one of the trainees: "This is one of the worst days in my professional life!" You can imagine, too, that senior management had a few choice words for the person responsible for costing the program.

Costing training activity, then, is important. Professionals who perform this function well turn this traditionally soft area of management into something very real. Without costs, benefits can't be measured. Without measurable results or benefits, the entire training function is not credible and is more subject to the last hired, first fired syndrome.

Training activity directed toward measurable objectives must become part of an organization's culture, or way of doing things. To this philosophical stance must be added the determination that training will be considered the same way as any other investment.

With the advent of activity-based management systems, managers are demanding a more rigorous tracking of all business processes (Holder, 1997; Trussel & Bitner, 1998). Some training units are even providing training for suppliers and customers, both domestic and foreign (Williams, 1999). As training now may be conducted for other corporate entities outside the organization, a training measurement system accepted and understood by senior executives is an essential management tool (Bassi & Van Buren, 1999; Watson, 1998).

Training becomes an expenditure of capital now, with anticipation that future benefits will occur over and above the initial investment. Training ideas should compete for investment funds with other options, all of which provide some return at some risk. Rate of return on investment in a training activity is compared with many other possible alternatives (Bedinham, 1998).

When decisions about training have to win approval from other managers outside the training function, arguments about the "goodness" or the value of training are unlikely to prevail (Vander Linde, Harney, & Koonce, 1997); developing cost (and benefit) calculation techniques that are convincing, thorough, and cost-effective in themselves is a necessity. The philosophy of exposing training to competitive pressures puts an end to the idea that "training is just something we do." It cancels the fuzzy "how to manage your boss" course and focuses training strategies on the design of competencies and performance-effectiveness criteria (Spencer & Spencer, 1993).

COMPLEX INTERACTING FORCES

The philosophy and the culture that force training into a category of needs-based investment cannot separate inputs (cost) from outputs (benefits or evaluation). The costs an organization is willing to absorb are directly proportional to the forecasted benefits and the perception of risk (i.e., the perceived probability of actually reaping those forecasted benefits).

Too often, however, the *direct* results of training are impossible to measure, and costing aimed at the wrong level will meet with skepticism. A training initiative may pass the budget-review process and meet all the professional criteria but still have no obvious direct results (Baird & Meshoulam, 1992). For example, how much does supervisory training contribute to profitability? Costing this type of learning activity can be both extremely difficult to figure out and to sell to management. There are too many complex variables that might interact to nullify the training. The management style of the supervisor's superior, the physical working conditions, the investment in equipment, the way the employer introduces change, and the state of the organization (e.g., growing, stable, or downsizing) are but a very few of the variables that affect the ability to manage.

The trainer is likely to be working as part of a team geared toward improving employee effectiveness for which other nontraining factors are likely to be more important. Many authors insist that training achieves but one small part (usually about 20 percent) of overall effectiveness improvement; the rest is found in changing the environment—support systems, equipment, work methods, and physical conditions (Gordon, 1992; Willyerd, 1997; Wright & Geroy, 1999).

In this situation, the cost of training tends to be part of a larger budget. The total improvement program is sold to senior management. Training results are hidden and not measured directly; only the key performance factor counts. Simplifying complex situations by using substitute or second-level measures may be a compromise, but the alternative can be what Agresta (1992) called "paralyzed-in-place," a feeling that the situation is completely intangible (or impossible), therefore, no cost data are presented at all.

Once again, one can use the example of supervisory training. Let's suppose that the goal is to reduce the firm's average order-cycle time by some clearly measurable amount. Depending on the work situation, any number of variables might affect performance. The storage or warehousing system, the telecommunications system, the paperwork or order-form flow, the job design, the responsibility or authority given to individuals at various levels, the production-scheduling techniques, and a host of other factors may need to be studied. To these tangible environmental concerns must be added the manner in which people are managed and supervised.

No matter how sophisticated the systems and the technology, full productivity will not be achieved without attention to human issues and concerns. For example, supervisory training is often a necessary ingredient in the total productivity- or competitiveness-improvement scenario. But some measurement of productivity is the key performance factor. To attempt a cost–benefit analysis isolating the contribution of training to the whole would be futile. The cost of training becomes part of an investment aimed at improving one or more key performance factors that may include changes to many other variables, thereby gaining competitive advantage through creativity and innovation (Cook, 1998).

Since there may be a temptation in these complex situations to trust technology and to avoid investing in human resources development (HRD), the story of a West Coast sawmill and lumber kiln-drying operation must be told. In attempting to increase productivity, management invested $5 million in state-of-the-art equipment from Germany. Then they put people accustomed to running chain saws in the bush in charge of the operation, expecting immediate improvements. Predictably, the results were disastrous. The company went bankrupt.

When analyzing the failure, the consultant hired by the firm's creditors contacted the German manufacturer. The manufacturer appeared to have recommended that two or three individuals be trained to the technologist level. This process would have involved an orientation at a similar facility in North America and at least two weeks training in the manufacturer's German plant. Then, an experienced engineer would have been sent to the West Coast facility to help the newly trained technologists with start up, providing another two weeks of on-the-job training. The manufacturer guaranteed a certain productivity level. Total training cost would have been $50 000, but managers who would finance $5 million in equipment balked at spending an additional 1 percent on the training! The machines were supposed to improve productivity and, indeed, if operated properly would do so. The cost of training could not be *directly* linked to improvements and, therefore, was seen as an expendable frill. Besides, who sends sawmill operators to Europe, a perk normally reserved for managers?

Depending on the situation, costing may be the first step in measuring the direct result of a training program, or costing can be one variable in a budget designed to enhance a key performance factor. The costing process is similar in both situations, although the task of selling the program to senior management can be different—a topic explored in more detail at the end of this chapter.

MEASURING DIRECT INPUTS (COSTS)

Direct costs refer to those expenditures applied directly to the training program, such as the trainer's time, equipment costs, material, and consulting fees. The most important issue to remember when costing a training program is not to leave out some item critical to the investment-decision process—like equipment rental for a curriculum-development specialist course. Fortunately, several authors have developed checklists to help practitioners prepare cost estimates. Head's (1987) award-winning book consists almost entirely of costing sheets, far too detailed to reproduce in this chapter. His costing analysis covers more than 100 pages, including basic cost factors (overhead), data gathering, student, instructor, course development, facility, and maintenance costs. Although published more than a decade ago, this unabashedly how-to publication is recommended highly for those readers who want to create comprehensive, functional cost worksheets.

direct costs the expenditures directly related to the training program

A more manageable example has been adapted from Warren (1979), who included a cost worksheet that summarized *direct* costs in sufficient detail for most purposes (see Figure 10.1).

FIGURE 10.1 COSTING SHEET

1. Fixed-cost factors
    i.   Overhead—AC/heat/light; space; rental/lease; communications; per input hour   _____
    ii. Supervisory allocation per input hour   _____
    iii. Equipment cost per input hour   _____
    iv. Administrative support cost per input hour   _____
    v.   Training unit fringe benefits cost per input hour _____
         Total fixed costs per input hour   _____

2. Needs Analysis
    i.   Professional hours ____ @ $____/hour = cost   _____
    ii. Support hours ____ @ $____/hour = cost   _____
    iii. Transportation expenses   _____
    iv. Material   _____
    v.   Consulting fees   _____
    vi. Other costs   _____
         Total direct needs-analysis costs   _____

3. Program Development
    i.   Professional hours ____ @ $____/hour = cost   _____
    ii. Support hours ____ @ $____/hour = cost   _____
    iii. Material   _____
    iv. Consulting fees   _____
    v.   Subject-matter expert/management and staff input
         ____ hours @ ____/hour = cost   _____
    vi. Other costs   _____
         Total direct program-development costs   _____

4. Program Delivery
    i.   Administration hours   _____
         @ $_____/hour = costs   _____
    ii. Administrative support hours   _____
         @ $_____/hour = costs   _____
    iii. Presentation/delivery hours   _____
         @ $_____/hour = cost   _____
    iv. Technical support hours   _____
         @ $_____/hour = cost   _____
    v.   Trainee materials costs   _____

FIGURE 10.1 COSTING SHEET (continued)

vi.   Transportation/accommodations/meals

     a. staff   _____

     b. trainees   _____

vii. Facilities rental   _____

viii. Equipment   _____

     Total direct program-delivery costs   _____

5. Evaluation/Cost–benefit Analysis

   i.   Professional hours   _____

       @ $_____/hour = cost   _____

   ii.   Support hours   _____

       @ $_____/hour = cost   _____

   iii. Management input hours   _____

       @ $_____/hour = cost   _____

   iv.   Trainee input hours   _____

       @ $_____/hour = cost   _____

   v.   Transportation costs   _____

   vi.   Material costs   _____

   vii. Consulting fees   _____

     Total evaluation cost   _____

6. Revision Costs

   i.   Professional hours ___ @ $____/hour = cost   _____

   ii.   Support hours ____ @ $____/hour = cost   _____

   iii. Management/staff collaboration hours ____ @

       $____/hour = cost   _____

     Total evaluation cost   _____

7. Total Direct Program Cost

   1 + 2 + 3 + 4 + 5 + 6 = Total Direct Cost   _____

INDIRECT COSTS

In many organizations, a measurement of direct costs is acceptable; the indirect costs are absorbed in total organizational overhead. **Indirect costs,** those expenditures that are not part of the training course per se, include things such as the cost of paying an employee when that employee is not working and the expenses associated with sub-standard work while a trainee is learning. Any training activity, however, has both opportunity costs (i.e., the trainees could be doing something else) and a measurable labour cost. The *costing sheet*, then, might be expanded to include

indirect costs expenditures not related directly to the design, development, or delivery of a training program

- total trainee salaries cost   _____
- lost production cost   _____
- replacement cost   _____
- overtime cost   _____
- increased supervision cost for iii and iv   _____
- reduced quality cost   _____
- new skills on-the-job training costs   _____
- increased scrap/spoilage costs   _____
- other indirect costs   _____

    Total indirect costs   _____

Obviously, by combining direct and indirect costs, a more complete analysis of the real cost of a training program to the organization can be obtained. What constitutes acceptable cost inputs depends on the type of training to be conducted and the organization's culture. The trainer will do whatever it takes to create a cost–benefit analysis that can compete for scarce investment funds.

The costing sheet presented here is only one example; it may need to be modified to suit an organization's unique circumstances. One common change would be to recategorize trainee salaries from indirect to direct costs. The idea is not to worry about labels but to design a format that has credibility.

MEASURING ALTERNATIVES

Again, depending upon the type of training and the alternative sources available, the person responsible for HRD may need to compare options. One of the foremost North American authorities on costing, Dr. Gary Geroy from the Colorado State University, uses the following simplified comparison worksheet:

Program _____	Analyst _____	Date _____
Option 1. _____		2. _____
Performance Value	$ _____	$ _____
Minus Cost	_____	_____
Net Benefit	$ _____	$ _____

To complete the analysis, Geroy then combines the cost inputs with an estimate of the value of the HRD program (performance value) to the organization to obtain a net benefit—a topic to be discussed later in this chapter.

The case study that follows illustrates how this cost-comparison technique works and how different organizations may require cost data at various levels of complexity and detail.

FIGURE 10.2 SIMPLIFIED COMPARISON WORKSHEET

Program* _____   Analyst _____   Date _____
                    Option name   1. _____   2. _____

	(Option 1)	(Option 2)
Analysis:		
Needs assessment	_____	_____
Work analysis	_____	_____
Proposal to management	_____	_____
Other _____	_____	_____
Other _____	_____	_____
Design:		
General HRD program design	_____	_____
Specific HRD program design	_____	_____
Other _____	_____	_____
Other _____	_____	_____
Development:		
Draft and prototype	_____	_____
Pilot test and revise	_____	_____
Production and duplication	_____	_____
Other _____	_____	_____
Other _____	_____	_____
Implementation:		
Program management	_____	_____
Program delivery	_____	_____
Participant costs	_____	_____
Other _____	_____	_____
Other _____	_____	_____
Evaluation:		
Program evaluation and report	_____	_____
Performance followup	_____	_____
Other _____	_____	_____
Other _____	_____	_____
Total HRD program costs	$ _____	$ _____
	(Option 1)	(Option 2)

*Reproduced with the author's permission.

A COST-COMPARISON ANALYSIS[1]

Situation: You are part of an organization that designs electronic systems. A recent reorganization has created a project-management division that places all lead engineers on projects in one group rather than being spread across several

[1]Prepared by Dr. Gary D. Geroy, Colorado State University at Fort Collins. Reproduced with permission from his client organization.

operations. The purpose of the reorganization was to allow the engineers to have less hands-on technical activity and focus more on theory development, design, and management of others on projects. A manager from your firm with an outstanding record in project management now heads the management group. The group consists of 10 lead engineers. You have been experiencing an alarming rate of turnover in electronic engineers since this group was established. A needs assessment reveals that the engineer types who make up this management group are very unskilled in communicating directions, delegating, and handling people-crisis issues. Data from the exit interviews reveal that the inability of project managers to manage crises and the inability to transmit clear guidelines and directions have been the primary frustrations. Your needs assessment also confirms that the members of the organization and the management group itself feel that this reorganization was a good decision.

The crisis in the organization resulting from the high turnover rate is a financial one. Finding, hiring, and relocating an engineer with the appropriate credentials and experience costs the organization approximately $75 000. In the past nine months, your organization has replaced five engineers. At this rate you anticipate you will replace a total of six engineers before the year is complete. You have been asked to recommend a training activity to address the management skills deficiencies in this group. The goal is to reduce the turnover rate to two engineers per year.

Your options are to send each project manager in the group to a management development institute identified by the president of the corporation, arrange for a vendor-delivered training program in house, or develop a coaching program to help these managers acquire the necessary skills. Your director has suggested that the last option might take 9 to 12 months to achieve the desired results. The probabilities are low to none that the managers will develop the skills needed on their own on the job. Your organization will not consider salaries or other normal employee maintenance costs as training expenses. A budget of $7000 will be provided for materials and $17 000 for consulting fees to support a coaching approach to solving the problem.

The following information is provided to help you make your decision.

Vendor-supplied program:
   15 four-hour sessions delivered on site over a six-month period—
   $15 000 per trainee

Management Development Institute:
   80-hour program delivered off site over a two-week period—
   $10 000 per trainee (this includes airfare, lodging, food, and materials)

Materials Budget to Support Coaching Option: $7000

Needs Analysis	10%
Work Analysis	5%
Design	5%

FIGURE 10.3 COST ANALYSIS WORKSHEET

	M.D. Institute	Outside Vendor	Coaching
Analysis:			
Needs Assessment	$_____	$_____	$ 10,700
Work Analysis	$_____	$_____	$ 4,350
Design:			
Program	$_____	$_____	$ 350
Instructional Aids	$_____	$_____	$ 0
Development:			
Pilot Testing	$_____	$_____	$ 0
Formative Evaluation			
(during the HRD activity)	$_____	$_____	$ 0
Instructional Aids	$_____	$_____	$ 1,050
Implementation:			
Delivery	$ 100,000	$ 150,000	$ 3,500
Management	$_____	$_____	$ 0
Evaluation:			
Summative Evaluation	$_____	$_____	$ 3,000
Training Revision	$_____	$_____	$ 0
Maintenance of Trainee Behaviour	$_____	$_____	$ 1,050
(A) Total	$ 100,000	$ 150,000	$ 24,000
(B) Trainees	10	10	10
Cost Per Trainee (A)/(B) =	$ 10,000	$ 15,000	$ 2,400

Development	15%
Implementation	50%
Evaluation	15%
	100% allocation

Figure 10.3 shows the actual cost analysis worksheet used by Geroy's client. This case study is important for four reasons.

1. It shows how the original costing sheet (Figure 10.1) can be modified to meet the client's needs. The substitution of a "maintenance of behaviour" category for the nebulous term "Performance follow-up," for example, makes this cost easier to sell. Also, there was no need to make a "proposal to management." The problem was well understood and immediate.

2. Management was not interested in a cost breakdown for either the Institute or the in-house vendor program, hence the single cost entered in the

"Delivery" column. In contrast, had this client been a government agency, a detailed breakdown of both bids might have been required.

3. As discussed previously, costs of salaries and benefits, overhead, and cost-productivity measures are not included. In this case, the problem had to be solved. Management was not interested in fine-tuning the costs.

4. A nontraining option is being considered. Coaching, an on-the-job learning technique (discussed in Chapter 7), is by far the cheapest option. Whether coaching will be the method chosen would require a benefit analysis. The important issue, however, is that traditional training may not be the best investment. All appropriate HRD methods should be considered.

A choice among the alternatives, then, should not be made without an estimate of the benefits likely to be received under each system.

ESTIMATING NET BENEFITS

net benefits   the estimated value of the performance improvement over the cost of improving that performance

Estimating **net benefits**, or return on investment, is one of the most difficult tasks for HRD practitioners. How benefits are calculated depends on the training situation, management needs, and the data available. Because of these difficulties, three examples will be presented here. First, Geroy's case study will be completed. Costs have been calculated suggesting that the coaching option would be the most effective. When the "Net Benefit Value Calculation Worksheet" is completed, however, a different picture emerges.

Using Geroy's benefit-estimation method, the Management Development Institute becomes the most attractive option, in quantitative terms. Few managers, however, would make the final decision based on these criteria alone. As previously suggested, there are qualitative concerns that become part of the analysis—reputation of the training institute, past experience, trainee perceptions of the options, the degree to which the training can be customized, and the time factor—all will be considered before a final decision is made. The key issue is that management has been given a credible tool with which to make a **return-on-investment (ROI)** decision.

return on investment (ROI)   a comparison of a training program's financial benefits and costs

The second ROI model has been adapted from Gordon (1991, pp. 22–23) and concerns the analysis of a two-week, 12-module learning program for courier van drivers. This example is significant because no needs analysis could be done—the course had been in place since 1982. If a cost analyst has input into training design, sometimes the objectives chosen for measurement can be written so that benefit calculation is made easier (Long, 1990). Here, the analyst had to work with a mature program using any data he could collect. In the Training Today 1 box on page 250, Gordon (1991) describes the ROI study, costing about $10 000, carried out by the Memphis-based air-freight company, FedEx.

The FedEx example shows quite clearly that it is possible to compute ROI, or net benefit, from traditional training activities. The process only works, however, if managers are prepared to accept the inevitable assumptions that

FIGURE 10.4 NET BENEFIT VALUE CALCULATION
WORKSHEET

	Institute Option 1	Option 2	Coaching Option 3
A. Data Required for Calculations			
(a) What is the desired performance as a result of worker training?	4 reductions per group	4 reductions per group	4 reductions per group
(b) What unit(s) of measure will be used to describe the performance?			
(c) What is the dollar value that will be assigned to each unit of measure?	$75 000	$75 000	$75 000
(d) What is the estimated training time to reach the goal?	.04 year	.5 year	1.0 year
(e) What is the current level of worker performance?	0 reduction	0 reduction	0 reduction
(f) How many workers will participate in the training?	10	10	10
B. Calculations to Determine Net Performance Value			
(g) What is the estimated performance level during training? Will trainee produce during training? _____ No = 0 _____ Yes = a + e / 2	0	2	2
(h) What is the length of the period being evaluated (at a minimum this will be the longest "d" of all options under consideration)?	1.0 year	1.0 year	1.0 year
(i) What is the estimate of the total number of units (b) that will be achieved during training? [d × g]	0	1	2
(j) What is the estimate of the total individual performance (or the evaluation period [(h − d) × a] + 1)?	3.84 reduction	3.0 reduction	2.0 reduction
(k) What is the value for the total performance for the evaluation period? [c × j]	$288 000	$225 000	$150 000
(l) What is the net performance value gain? [k + (e × c × h)]	$288 000	$225 000	$150 000
(m) Do you want to calculate the total net performance value of all trainees? _____ Yes = l × f __X__ No = net performance value of 1 trainee which is of (l)	$288 000	$225 000	$150 000
Net Benefit	$288 000	$225 000	$150 000
Cost (from Cost-Analysis Worksheet)	$100 000	$150 000	$ 24 000
Final Net Benefit	*$188 000*	*$75 000*	*$126 000*

TRAINING TODAY 1 FedEx Measures the Cost of Training

The course in question was the company's two-week, 12-module basic training program for new couriers—the people who drive vans (usually) to the front of your office building, take the elevator up to the receptionist's desk or the mail room or wherever, and pick up or deliver your Federal Express packages. The program had been running since the early 1980s.

The study tracked three groups of 20 employees each. In the first group were recent graduates of the basic training course—new employees who had completed the course (and been on the job) no more than 90 days before the study began.

In the second group were new couriers sent to their job assignments without going through the course. "This meant we were accepting the risk of sending out 20 untrained people," Addicott noted. (Addicott was the manager in charge of training.) Well, almost untrained. Their managers were told to do no more (and no less) on-the-job training than normal to prepare them for their new jobs. Managers typically ride with new couriers to familiarize them with their routes, teach them how to fill out an air bill, and generally show them the ropes. Also, the "untrained" group received defensive driving and dangerous-goods training, as required by the Department of Transportation. What they didn't get was the two-week course.

In the third group were veteran couriers who had been with the company for five or more years. FedEx wanted to examine the possible need for reoccurrence training in matters such as filling out an international waybill and converting pounds to kilos.

Nobody in any group was told about the study. The performance of these 60 people was monitored daily, for 90 days, by their managers. The managers used checklists to track 18 performance indicators, determined by a task force of experts—namely, FedEx managers who oversee couriers. Some of those performance indicators were: accidents, injuries, time-card errors, domestic air bill errors, international air waybill errors, pickup manifest errors, courier-caused wrong-day deliveries, customer complaints, and so on.

Ten of those 18 performance indicators were assigned dollar values: cost per error. How did the training department decide that? It didn't. The safety department, engineering, finance, and other groups supplied the figures. ("You may find," said Addicott, "that these departments want to get involved with you on something like this. Our finance people actually formed teams to come up with some of these figures.")

In the category of accidents (meaning accidents involving vehicles), for instance, the average cost per incident was $1600, according to the safety department. Given that figure and the data on the checklists turned in by supervisors at the end of the 90-day period, projecting the annual cost of accidents for couriers in each of the three groups becomes a simple exercise in arithmetic: Cost per error × number of errors = total cost of errors. Total cost of errors ÷ number of people in group = total cost per person. Multiply cost per person by four (because this was a 90-day study) and you have total cost per courier per year.

For everyone except the five-year veterans, Addicott subtracted 25 percent from that total, reasoning that in the course of a year performance would improve somewhat with experience on the job. In other words, both the trained and untrained couriers would probably get better at avoiding accidents (and at completing waybills and manifests and delivery records) if they simply stayed on the job for a year. The training course should not get undue credit for producing performance differences that are apparent for 90 days but might diminish within six or nine months.

The cost of accidents per employee per year? For a recently trained courier, $399. For an untrained courier, $1920. For a veteran courier, $428.

Using the same formula with all 10 performance indicators that had dollar figures attached, Federal Express determined the annual cost of all errors per courier for each of the three groups. Recently trained: $2492. Untrained: $4833. Veteran: $4064.

What did this tell the company? For one thing, something was very fishy about those veterans. Addicott knew which performance indicators were out of whack (veterans in this study made a lot of domestic air bill errors, for example), but this data alone didn't confirm a need for reoccurrence training: maybe the problem wasn't that the vets didn't know how to fill out air bills; maybe something else was wrong. When the veterans were debriefed, however, it turned out that there were knowledge problems. For example, some company procedures had changed in the past few years but the veterans' way of doing things hadn't. They were still taking "shortcuts" that used to work under the old air bill system but now created errors. Reoccurrence training was launched.

The "value" of the two-week course? The difference in errors per year between a trained courier and an untrained one is worth $2341 ($4833 − $2492). The cost of the training program, per courier, is $1890 (including hotel, meals, airfare, mileage allowance, instructor salary, courier salary while training, and "coverage" for the courier while in training—somebody else has to deliver those packages while this person is being trained). The ROI for one courier during the first year on the job is $451. In fiscal year 1989, Federal Express sent 1097 new couriers through the training course. Total ROI for the program in 1989: $494 747.

Source: Gordon, J. (1991). Measuring the "goodness" of training. *Training* 27 (8), 19–25.

in the course of a year, performance would improve *somewhat* with experience on the job." Why a 25-percent reduction—why not 20 percent, or 15 percent, or 2 percent? Obviously in this situation, 25 percent was a believable figure. Perhaps 25 percent made intuitive sense, or perhaps Addicott's reputation is what makes this figure acceptable. The major point here is that benefits estimation is an inexact procedure, another reason why trainers should be concerned about professional credibility.

Credibility is a major issue, perhaps *the* major issue in cost–benefits analysis (Bedinham, 1998). The final example illustrates the use of what have been called soft data.

A large bank was experiencing an abnormally high turnover rate. A training program was designed to counter the turnover problem. The cost of employee turnover needed to be estimated to calculate an ROI. But actual cost calculation was difficult because of the many interacting variables—administrative costs, interviewing, testing, relocation, orientation, increase in supervisory time, initial less-than-optimal performance, on-the-job training—all make up the cost of replacing one person. As the bank did not want to devote the considerable resources necessary to developing a precise calculation, turnover was classified as a soft cost and a combination of approaches were used to derive an acceptable figure.

Initially, a literature search was used to determine that another institution in the same industry had calculated a cost of $25 000 per turnover. This figure, derived by an internal-audit unit and verified by a consulting specialist in turnover reduction, was used as a starting point. The application of this statistic to another (even though quite similar) organization was in question, however. HRD staff then met with senior executives "to agree on a turnover cost value to use in gauging the success of the program. Management agreed on an estimate that was half the amount from the study, $12 500. This was considered very conservative because other turnover studies typically yield statistics of greater value. Management felt comfortable with the estimate, however, and it was used on the benefits side of program evaluation. Although not precise, this exercise yielded a figure that was never challenged" (Phillips, 1991, p. 337).

The term "never challenged" is significant. Trainers must perform cost–benefit analyses, but they must do so from a position of strength. In this example, senior managers were brought on side when they were used as experts. It mattered little that the turnover cost was set at $12 500 rather than $25 000, because the benefit estimation produced from these data was credible and accepted by those with the power to make investment decisions.

Thus, despite the appearance of quantitative rigour, virtually all but the simplest cost–benefit designs are dependent to a greater or lesser extent on assumptions and expert opinion (Geroy & Wright, 1988; Wright, 1990). As with training, cost–benefit design must fit into the organization's culture. The arithmetic must be believable so that investors who are accustomed to thinking in terms of present value on future returns and liabilities will allocate appropriate funding.

UTILITY ANALYSIS

In a typical training evaluation study, the performance of a training group is compared to a control group that did not receive the training to determine how effective the training program was for improving job performance. While the results of this comparison might tell us that there is a significant statistical difference in the job performance between the two groups, it doesn't tell us the dollar value associated with the training program. Utility analysis, however, can do just that.

utility analysis a method to forecast the net financial benefits that result from human resource programs such as training and development

Utility analysis is a method for forecasting the net financial benefits that result from human resource programs such as training and development (Saks, 2000). Utility analysis involves procedures in which the effectiveness of a training program can be translated into dollars and cents.

To calculate the utility of a training program, several key factors must be considered. One of the most important factors is the effectiveness of a training program. In other words, what is the difference in job performance between employees who are trained and those who are not? This is sometimes referred to as the *effect size*. The larger the effect size, the more effective a training program is and the greater its utility will be.

A second key factor is what is known as the standard deviation of job performance in dollars of untrained employees. This factor has to do with how much of a difference there is in the job performance of untrained employees and what the monetary value of this difference is. The standard deviation of job performance in dollar terms is an important factor because in jobs in which the contribution of individual employees to the organization is widely different, an effective training program will improve the performance of a greater number of employees and will, therefore, result in larger dollar gains. When individual contributions are relatively similar, an effective training program is less likely to result in large dollar gains. Therefore, it is necessary to know or estimate the value of the standard deviation of job performance of untrained employees to make estimates of utility. The larger the standard deviation of job performance of the untrained group, the greater the utility of a training program will be.

A third factor is the number of employees trained. The more employees who are trained, the greater the utility. A fourth factor is the expected length of time that the training benefits will last. The longer the effects of training will last, the higher the utility of the training program.

Utility is equal to the multiplication of all of these factors minus the cost of the training program (cost per employee × number of employees trained). The following formula is used to estimate the utility of a training program (Schmidt, Hunter, & Pearlman, 1982):

$$\Delta U = (T)(N)(d_t)(SDy) - (N)(C)$$

where

ΔU = utility, or the dollar value of the program

T = the number of years the training has a continued effect on performance

N = the number of people trained

d_t = the true difference in job performance between the average trained and untrained employee in standard deviation units (effect size)

SD_y = the standard deviation of job performance in dollars of the untrained group

C = the cost of training each employee

Consider a simple example. To increase the number of widgets produced in a factory, a training program is implemented, which 50 of the plant employees attend. Compared to a group of workers who did not attend the training program, the performance of the 50 trained employees is found to be twice as high (e.g., they produce 100 widgets per day compared to 50 produced by untrained workers). We will assume that this equals an effect size of 2. We also assume that the standard deviation of job performance of the untrained employees is $100. The expected length of time that the training will last is estimated to be five years. The cost of the training program is $300 per employee. Using the utility equation above, we can calculate the utility of the training program as follows:

ΔU = 5 (50) (2) ($100) − 50 ($300)

ΔU = $50 000 − $15 000

ΔU = $35 000

Thus, the expected return on the training program for each 50 employees trained is $35 000.

This amount might be even greater if the training program lasts longer than five years or if the untrained employees learn how to improve their performance just working with and observing the trained employees.

An interesting extension of the use of the utility formula is conducting a break-even analysis or finding the value at which benefits equal costs and utility is equal to zero (Cascio, 1991). This analysis can be done for any of the terms in the utility equation; however, it is most meaningful to conduct a break-even analysis for the effect size or the standard deviation. For example, what is the break-even effect size for the example presented on page 253? This figure can be calculated simply by dividing the cost of the training program ($15 000) by the multiplicative function of the other factors; that is, $(N)(T)(SD_y)$ or (50)(5)(100). The calculations are as follows:

$$d_t = 25\ 000/15\ 000$$
$$d_t = 1.6$$

Thus, a training program with an effect size of 1.6 will result in a utility of zero, and an effect size greater than 1.6 will result in a utility that is greater than zero. Therefore, a training program that is considerably less effective than the one in our example would still be likely to result in a financial gain so long as the effect size is greater than 1.6. Break-even analysis can be very useful because it helps reduce the uncertainty associated with the estimates of the various parameters used to calculate utility. For example, to the extent that the break-even effect size is far below the actual effect size used to calculate utility, the greater the confidence in the results one can have (Mathieu & Leonard, 1987).

SUPPORTING THE COSTING FUNCTION

COST–BENEFIT TRACKING SYSTEMS

One of the most important facets of a costing system is a database that can be used to measure the progress an organization is making toward meeting its objectives. In particular, historical data can be invaluable when costing new proposals or in negotiating for new funding.

The major weakness in past training design has been the inability to show its contribution to profits. Without a method of collating and reporting successes in financial terms, the HRD professional is reduced to a minor supporting role in the corporate enterprise (Phillips, 1992).

COST-REDUCTION SYSTEM

One way to support the HRD function is to constantly reduce training costs and to show that the training system is becoming more effective and efficient (Wright & Kusmanadji, 1993). There may be many other costs that can be reduced:

1. Company commitment:
   - pressure for in-company or on-the-job development leading to reduced reliance upon:
     a) outside consultants
     b) prestige trainers
     c) off-site training
   - Instructor costs:
     - use company staff and trainers where possible
     - use one instructor where one instructor will suffice
     - reduce preparation costs by using or reusing standard sessions and using course-member discussion
     - reduce travel time off the job
     - develop in-company skills and training talent
     - consider technology-based training
     - keep good records
     - develop Web-based training courses
3. Material costs:
   - use reusable training materials
   - let the client or company print the papers, provide the files, and so on
   - adapt commercial materials
4. Course design costs:
   - brief course members before and after courses
   - assign work before and after courses
   - reduce set-up costs by using standard courses and company facilities
   - evaluate off-the-shelf computer-based training and distance-learning courses
5. Course direction costs:
   - use company office staff for administrative support
   - use the lecturer/instructor/trainer as course director
   - use in-house directors

6. Course member costs:
   - reduce travel costs and bed and meal costs through in-company short courses
   - reduce off-the-job costs with short courses
   - counsel trainees on the need for training—don't send employees to courses automatically or in rotation as perks
7. Accommodation costs:
   - reduce visible accommodation costs by using client or company teaching and residential accommodation
   - use shorter courses to reduce overnight accommodation costs
   - use local community college facilities
   - use Web-based training

ACCOUNTING TREATMENT OF TRAINING COSTS

Once training costs have been identified, they have to be incorporated into the accounting system so that they can be included in the total cost of production or service rendered. There are three ways to administer training accounts.

1. *Allocation of costs.* Costs can be shared with other departments and may, for example, be allocated according to the number employed in a department and its labour turnover or output. The main advantage of this method is its simplicity. Because of that simplicity, it is the most widely used method. However, this method has disadvantages:
   - It is contrary to the principle that managers should not be held accountable for costs they do not control.
   - It does not relate to actual use of the training facilities or services.
   - It gives no incentive to the training unit or professional to reduce costs and to improve efficiency.
2. *Selling the service.* Under this system, the training unit is required to sell its services at competitive rates to the other departments, the aim being to cover the cost of the training department (Long, 1990; Phillips, 1992). The main advantages of this method are:
   - control over training costs (training costs have to remain reasonable or the training function will price itself out of the reach of consumer departments)
   - a check on the relevance and efficiency of the training offered (training is carefully evaluated by the departmental managers who are required to pay for it)
   - The disadvantages arising from a fluctuating demand for training services and the consequent planning difficulties seem to outweigh the advantages of this method.

3. *Policy costs.* Under this system, training costs are regarded as company policy costs and are stated as such in the accounts. Training costs are accumulated and shown as a deduction from the gross profit of the business. This approach is simple but can mean that control over training expenditures is less rigorous than it should be. Use of the method can, however, be justified when training is designed to keep human resources available, irrespective of individual departmental needs, such as in a company-wide, management-development scheme, for example.

Some form of joint responsibility for, or division of, costs appears to be the best solution. A fixed charge can be made to the departments according to the number of staff undergoing training and the duration and type of training given. This charge should be fixed in advance and be a realistic estimate of the expected cost of training an average employee. The departments utilizing the services know the amount in advance. The training department is treated as a profit centre in its own right; it is expected to show a profit on the fixed charges levied. In the company accounts, the training department's profit or loss is credited or debited, respectively, to the training account in the ledger, to which the total of the charges levied on the departments using the service is also debited. The balance on this training account is then incorporated in the final profit and loss account in the usual way.

RECORD KEEPING

Record keeping is not done for its own sake, but as a communication tool. Evidence needs to be presented that a contribution from training is being made on a day-to-day basis, rather than at a once-a-year review before the next year's training plan is written (Brown, 1992). In addition, historical and comparative data can be useful in the identification of opportunities. Even the humble flow chart can be used to advantage, to discourage "duplicate efforts and unnecessarily complicated procedures," and to prevent bottlenecks (Kaydos, 1991, pp. 132, 133).

Haislip's (1987, p. 66) comment still is valid: "Remember to record, record, record. The progress reports you submit will keep the pump primed for future interest in new training proposals. They will help keep management's attention on training as a means to greater efficiency in planning, production, sales, and service. Eventually, you may even be invited to real, live staff meetings, where your sage advice on all sorts of matters will be highly regarded."

REPORTING AND SELLING COST–BENEFIT ANALYSIS

Reporting and selling cost–benefit analysis are concepts that will be familiar to those who have read Chapters 2 and 3, but they are important enough to be reiterated briefly here. Remember that trainers have clients. In most cases, although these clients are internal members of the same organization, they will react favourably to any business initiative only if it fills a need. As there are often alternative methods of meeting any given need, the training professional must understand how decisions are made within an organization and build alliances that can support the view that human resources development (HRD) is a priority investment area.

This widening of the power base is possible only if the trainer can speak the language of business (e.g., quantitatively based decision parameters) and if a broad range of stakeholders at all levels are involved. As in our previously cited example, the senior executives who decided that turnover costs their bank $12 500 per person did not question this figure again; it was theirs, they owned it. The involvement of other interests in the development of cost–benefit analyses will obtain the same results. Note that the original bank's internal-audit function had prepared the $25 000 cost estimate. If this figure had been developed in cooperation with the training function, both groups (owners) would vouch for its validity. The primary strategy for selling cost–benefit analyses should be to involve as many potential clients as possible in the cost–benefit analyses preparation.

The reporting function is even more culture sensitive in that how a trainer gets a hearing with the real decision makers depends on how the organization works. What is certain is the necessity of ensuring that training data and results are integrated into the business reporting system, yet remain separate enough to give them visibility. An individual or a training unit that is combined or lumped into an overall personnel department budget is unlikely to have much impact on senior decision makers. Training or HRD needs to be highlighted. The actual format of this reporting process should vary by organization, according to the manner in which training is handled by the accounting system and according to established feedback mechanisms.

SUMMARY

The old adage that trainers are "last hired and first fired" is fast becoming obsolete as the amount of money invested in training continues to increase (Bassi & Van Buren, 1999). The credibility issue, however, is still extremely important. All training activities must be costed because training professionals need to compete for investment funding. As resources are always scarce, trainers must convince senior managers that funds spent on training will produce an acceptable return.

This chapter discussed how to measure both direct and indirect costs, estimate net benefit and utility, and support these activities with cost–benefit tracking systems, cost-reduction systems, and appropriate accounting treatment. As well, the client concept and the necessity to sell the costing system to them were discussed in detail. Finally, the idea that senior management must own the firm's costing methods is illustrated by using an example that showed that once a cost (in this case for turnover) was accepted, the figure was never questioned again.

Thus, trainers must be culturally sensitive when selling cost–benefit analyses. There are no set formulae or fool-proof methods for calculating training costs.

KEY TERMS

EXERCISES

As the housing market began to heat up, the Renswartz Realty Company decided to capitalize by increasing the number of listings and sales on a monthly basis. In order to do this, the company president believed they would have to do two things. First, they would have to better market the company's superior customer service. Second, they would have to train all agents to improve their sales and customer service skills. Choosing an advertising company turned out to be much easier than choosing a training program. Two consulting firms were contacted to provide a proposal to design and implement a training program that would be attended by all 200 of the company's sales agents.

The first consulting firm offered a five-day program that would consist of lectures on "how to get more listings," "how to improve your service," and "making the sale," and would involve videos and behavioural modelling. According to the consulting firm, research has shown that the sales performance of those who have attended the training is significantly better than those who have not; the effect size of the program is .35. The training is expected to last for two years and will cost $1500 per employee.

The second consulting firm offered a similar program with the exceptions that it would be for only two days and would consist of sessions on "how to improve your sales" and "providing excellent service." Research on the training program has found it to be highly effective with an effect size of .25. The effects have been found to last for one year at which time follow-up sessions are required. The cost of the training program is $450 per employee.

Based on the current sales performance of all 200 sales agents at Renswartz Realty, the standard deviation of sales is $15,000.

a. Calculate the utility of the training programs offered by each of the consulting firms.

b. Calculate the breakeven effect size for both training programs.

c. What are the advantages and disadvantages of each training program?

d. Which training program should the company purchase?

e. What are the advantages and limitations of this approach for calculating the benefits of a training program?

CASE: A THOUSAND MISTAKES A WEEK

Herritta Humbolt, marketing manager for a large mail-order jewellery firm, looked over the error sheets: 5 percent—not bad when you're 95 percent right! A second look, however, pinpointed the problem. Her shipping department mailed out 20 000 orders every week. Five percent of 20 000 is 1000, that's 1000 unhappy customers every week, 4000 every month, 48 000 every year. If everyone told 10 friends about Herritta poor service, 480 000 people could be struck off her potential customer list yearly. Obviously, Herritta had a big problem, especially since mail-order customers are a special breed. They get hooked on the bargains, each one tending to place at least three orders per year.

A thousand mistakes every week! What kind of mistakes? A quick analysis showed Herritta that wrong addresses and wrong picks (the wrong jewellery) made up 95 percent of the errors.

Herritta checked the stocking systems and the mailing procedures. Satisfied that nothing much could be done to improve shipping methods—a major systems analysis had been completed last year—she turned her thoughts to training.

A meeting of her three shift supervisors (the experts) set out the following performance criteria:

1. *Keyboarding* (order entry, inventory control) with no more than two errors per day
   - three shifts each with three shippers (266.6 orders per day per person)
   - 4000 orders per week
   - 800 orders per day; 2 errors = 0.025 percent error rate

2. *Picking* correct goods to ship
   - 0 percent error rate acceptable
   - Proper order *packing* (no tangles, breakage)
   - 0 percent error rate acceptable

3. Proper *shipping* (directly related to keyboarding as address labels were produced automatically from order-entry document)
   - 0 percent error rate acceptable

Again, using her panel of experts, Herritta calculated that each error cost:

$ 1.00	wasted postage
$ 1.00	labour wasted shipping original order
$10.00	labour (management/shippers) to correct original mistake
$ 4.00	phone/fax charges
$ 9.50	to send replacement order by courier
$ 5.00	restocking inventory
$30.50	

Herritta wanted to add in a large amount for lost goodwill, but the general manager vetoed the idea, telling her to stick with the hard figures.

Herritta contacted a local consultant who agreed to design a training program. She estimated that 15 hours of specialized keyboard training, followed by 5 hours in-house training in picking, packing, and shipping should be supported by 10 hours of general customer-service training. Her rate would be $160/contact hour for the initial training plus 10 hours at $100/hour for the evaluation. Additional costs would be $500/day for software rental (15 hours), and $16 per trainee for materials.

Although the training would take place at work on three consecutive weekends, seven computers would have to be rented at $80 per computer per weekend. Wages would have to be added in; average yearly wage was $25 000 + $12 000 in benefits. The shippers were promised time and a half (i.e., 1.5 times their regular wages). Salary costs for managers were set arbitrarily at $2000.

Additional costs included: record keeping in the personnel unit, invoicing, and extra payroll costs: $500 (an estimate); insurance on each of the rented computers at $12.50/day; lunch for 80 (three lunches) at $11.50 per person; coffee: $75 flat cost (three weekends); overhead (extra heat, lights, and so on): $500 (estimated for the entire course).

Assuming that the objective of no more than two errors per day is reached, calculate the return on investment for this proposed training program.

RUNNING CASE PART 6:
VANDALAIS DEPARTMENT STORES

Several months following the structured employment interview training program for Vandalais Department Stores (refer to Chapter 5 for details on the training program), the director of human resources contacted the two professors who designed and delivered the training program. She was upset because management did not receive the results of the evaluation very positively and she was concerned that they might not fund future training programs. The director thought that it would be a good idea to demonstrate the value of the training program in terms of its costs and benefits, and asked the two professors if they would help her to determine the various costs and benefits of the structured employment interview training program.

Keeping in mind that the most important issue when costing a training program is not to leave out items that are critical to the calculation of costs, identify all of the costs associated with the structured employment interview training program, and develop a costing sheet that includes all of the direct and indirect costs. In addition, indicate how you will calculate the monetary benefits of the training program. What are the indicators of the training benefits, and how can they be translated into dollars and cents?

REFERENCES

Agresta, R.J. (1992). Renaissance in human resources development: Can we afford it? *The Public Manager: The New Bureaucrat 21* (1), 33–37.

Baird, L., & Meshoulam, I. (1992). Getting payoff from investment in human resource management. *Business Horizons 35* (1), 68–75.

Bassi, L., & Van Buren, M. (1999). Sharpening the leading edge. *Training & Development. 53* (1), 23–33.

Bedinham, K. (1998). Proving the effectiveness of training. *Education & Training 40* (4), 166–167.

Blanden, M., Timewell, S., Laurie, S., Lewis, V., Robins, B., Miller, J., & Simon, L. (1998). Back to basics. *Banker 141* (779), 22, 24.

Brown, M.G. (1992). The Baldrige criteria—Better, tougher, and clearer for 1992. *Journal for Quality and Participation 15* (2), 70–75.

Cascio, W.F. (1991). *Costing human resources: The financial impact of behavior in organizations.* Boston, MA: Kent.

Commanducci, M. (1998). Revenue Canada revises employer-paid training rules. *Canadian HR Reporter 11* (11), 1.

Flynn, G. (1998). Training budgets 101. *Workforce 77* (11), 91–92.

Geroy, G.D., & Wright, P.C. (1988). Evaluation research: A pragmatic program-focused research strategy for decision makers. *Performance Improvement Quarterly 1* (3), 17–26.

Gordon, J. (1991). Measuring the 'goodness' of training. *Training 27* (8), 19–25.

Haislip, O.L. (1987). How to treat training as an investment. *Training 24* (2), 63–66.

Head, G.E. (1987). *Training cost analysis.* Denver: Marlin Press.

Kaydos, W. (1991). *Measuring, managing, and maximizing performance.* Cambridge, MA: Productivity Press.

Long, R.F. (1990). Protecting the investment in people—Making training pay. *Journal of European Industrial Training 14* (7), 21–27.

Mathieu, J.E., & Leonard, R.L., Jr. (1987). Applying utility concepts to a training program in supervisory skills: A time-based approach. *Academy of Management Journal 30*, 316–335.

Saks, A.M. (2000). *Research, measurement, and evaluation of human resources.* Toronto: Nelson Thomson Learning

Schmidt, F.L., Hunter, J.E., & Pearlman, K. (1982). Assessing the economic impact of personnel programs on workforce productivity. *Personnel Psychology 35*, 333B47.

Spencer, L.M., & Spencer, S.M. (1993). *Competence at work.* New York: John Wiley & Sons.

Trussel, J., & Bitner, L. (1998). Strategic cost management: an activity-based approach. *Management Decision 36* (7), 441–447.

Vander Linde, K., Harney, N., & Koonce, R. (1997). Seven ways to make your training department one of the best. *Training & Development 51* (8), 20–22+.

Warren, M.W. (1979). *Training for results.* Menlo Park, CA: Addison-Wesley.

Willyerd, K. (1997). Balancing your evaluation act. *Training 34* (3), 52–58.

Wright, P.C. (1990). Validating hospitality curricula within associated-sponsored certification programs: A qualitative methodology and a case study. *Hospitality Research Journal 14* (1), 117–132.

Wright, P., & Geroy, G.D. (1990). An investigation of qualitative planning techniques acceptable to owners/managers of small business." *Journal of Small Business and Entrepreneurship 8* (4), 41–50.

———. (1999). *Changing the mindset: The training myth and the need for world-class performance.* BRC working paper WP 99013, Dept. of Management, Hong Kong Baptist University.

Wright, P.C., & Kusmanadji, K. (1993). The strategic application of TQM principles in human resources management. *Training for Quality 1* (3), 5–14.

11

....

TRAINING
PROGRAMS

CHAPTER GOALS

By now you should be familiar with the training and development process. We have covered all of the major steps in the development of a training program: needs assessment, training objectives, program design, training methods, transfer of training, and the evaluation and costing of training programs. At this point, you might be asking yourself, "What type of training programs do organizations design and deliver to their employees?" Obviously, the type of training program depends on the organization's training needs and objectives. However, we can still understand and describe training programs within a number of broad categories. The purpose of this chapter is to describe the major types of training programs that are designed and delivered by organizations today.

After reading this chapter, you should be able to

- discuss the major types of training provided by organizations and employee reactions to training programs
- describe basic and technical skills training and why organizations need to offer this type of training to their workforces

....

- describe the orientation and training of new hires and the effect they can have on job attitudes and behaviour
- describe information technology training and why is it important
- understand the importance of health and safety training and describe the type of information that should be provided in these training programs
- describe total quality management and the type of training that quality programs require to be successful
- discuss the different types of nontechnical skills and why they are important
- describe team training and team building and its role in the implementation of teams
- describe the new approach to sales training
- discuss customer service training
- define sexual harassment and describe sexual harassment training
- describe the goals and content of cultural diversity and cross-cultural training

OVERVIEW

During the past three decades, training and development has experienced a dramatic growth. In the United States, where 15 million employees participate in 17.6 million courses, one out of every eight American workers attends a formal training course each year (Swanson & Falkman, 1997). In 1997, more than $60 billion was spent on formal workplace training in North America (Industry Report, 1998). As indicated in Chapter 1, Canadian organizations spend approximately $4 billion a year on training and development. This figure translates into about 5.8 million Canadian adults enrolled in education and training activities, $850 spent per employee, and the average Canadian worker receiving about seven hours of training annually. As well, those companies rated as the 100 best to work for in Canada spend the most per employee on training, and half of Canadian companies expect training budgets to increase.

With so much money and effort being spent on training, you might be wondering what type of training employees are receiving and what they think about the training. A recent study asked employees these and other related questions (Schaaf, 1998). The results may surprise you. First, nearly 80 percent of the employees reported that they had received some type of training in the past year. The most common types of training were job-specific and technical skills training followed by the use of new technology. Common types of soft skills training included teamwork, communication, problem solving, and customer service training. When asked if additional training would be useful to them, 99 percent of the respondents said yes; however, most indicated they wanted more of the same type of training they were already receiving. The exception to this was technology. In terms of training that is not provided by their organization but would be of value, 25 percent indicated computer training or some other type of current technology. If their organization offered it, nearly 75 percent said they would sign up for training on the use of new technology, communication skills to help them work better with other people, job-specific and technical skills, and management training.

Does training make a difference to employees' attitudes and work behaviour? The survey indicated that most employees value the training they receive. That is, they believe the training makes a difference in the way they perform their jobs, their attitudes toward their organization, and their intentions to remain employed at their organizations. In other words, the majority of respondents indicated that the training provided by their organizations is an important factor in their decisions to stay with the organizations or to leave. The *amount* of training was also found to be important. Trainees who received more training were more satisfied with their training and their organizations. On a more negative note, the majority of the respondents felt that the training they receive is marginal or irrelevant to preparing them for higher-level jobs (Schaaf, 1998). Now let's take a closer look at the types of training that employees receive.

TRAINING PROGRAMS

During the last decade, organizations have made dramatic changes in response to an ever-changing work environment. New work arrangements combined with new technologies have led to a demand for skilled employees in both the manufacturing and service sectors. Whether it's learning how to operate a new computer system on the factory floor or how to provide customers with excellent service, some type of training program is invariably required.

Among manufacturing companies, more than 60 percent of employees receive training in specific job skills, followed next by quality and statistical analysis, group decision making, team building, multiple jobs, and leadership skills. During the past decade, the number of manufacturing organizations that have trained a majority of their workers in each training category has doubled or tripled (Baker & Armstrong, 1996).

According to a 1991 survey conducted by the Canadian Labour Market and Productivity Centre of 9.3 million employees, Canadian employees are more likely to receive health and safety training than any other kind of training, followed by new employee orientation. Surprisingly, only 11 percent of employees received computer training; one-quarter of the companies surveyed said they would like to provide it but did not have the funds (*The Globe*

TABLE 11.1 GENERAL TYPES OF TRAINING

TYPES OF TRAINING	% PROVIDING*
Computer Applications	95
Communication Skills	88
Management Skills/Development	85
Customer Service	83
Supervisory Skills	82
Computer Systems/Programming	81
Executive Development	78
Technical Skills/Knowledge	77
Personal Growth	67
Sales	57

*Percent of all organizations with 100 or more employees that provide these types of training.

Source: Industry Report (1999, October). Where the training dollars go. *Training 36*, p. 56.

and Mail, 1992). Professional and technical workers receive the most training days per year and clerical workers received the least (McIntyre, 1994).

Table 11.1 shows the general types of training provided by organizations. As shown, more than 80 percent of organizations provide training in computer applications, communication skills, management skills/development, customer service, supervisory skills, and computer systems or programming. Table 11.2 provides a breakdown of more specific types of training programs. Notice that new employee orientation tops the list with 92 percent of organizations indicating that they provide this type of training. Recall that this is also the second most common type of training received by Canadian workers. In the remainder of this chapter we will review the most common types of training programs.

BASIC-SKILLS TRAINING

At one time, it was possible to find a job that paid well and that did not require a high-school education. Those days are gone. The ability to read, write, and understand mathematics is now required for an increasing number of jobs. The number of factory workers who have a college education has been steadily rising over the past decade (Baker & Armstrong, 1996). For young people, this means that a high-school diploma is the minimum amount of education they must have to acquire a good job in today's workplace.

But what about the workers who don't have a high-school education and whose jobs are changing and will require them to read, write, and understand arithmetic? Consider the literacy gap in Canada: A recent survey by Statistics

TABLE 11.2 SPECIFIC TYPES OF TRAINING

TYPES OF TRAINING	% PROVIDING THIS TYPE OF TRAINING
New-Employee Orientation	92
Leadership	81
Sexual Harassment	81
New-Equipment Operation	80
Performance Appraisals	80
Team-Building	77
Safety	77
Problem-Solving/Decision-Making	76
Train-the-Trainer	74
Product Knowledge	72

Source: Industry Report (1999, October). Where the training dollars go. *Training 36*, p. 58.

Canada found that 48 percent of Canadian adults have some trouble with everyday reading, writing, or arithmetic, and for 22 percent the problem is severe (Calamai, 1999). Literacy and numeracy are not only issues for immigrants or seniors. Forty percent of native-born Canadians between the ages of 16 and 65 have problems reading and 15 percent are in the lowest literacy category, meaning that they have serious difficulty with any printed material, including understanding a newspaper article or using a bus schedule (see Table 11.3 for literacy levels). It is estimated that there are 4.5 million Canadian adults in the lowest literacy category. This statistic is particularly alarming when you consider that these people will make up the bulk of the labour force for decades to come. The survey also found that the literacy skills of 20 percent of recent high-school graduates were too low for entry-level jobs. Statistics Canada concluded that the literacy problem in Canada is so serious that it threatens Canada's economic future and global competitiveness (Calamai, 1999).

The problem is just as serious in the United States, where it is estimated that up to 20 percent of the workforce is functionally illiterate (Hays, 1999). In a recent survey, 63 percent of the respondents indicated that their employees have serious basic-skills deficiencies. The skill deficiencies, beginning with the highest percentage of respondents indicating a deficiency, were basic job skills, basic math skills, basic written skills, understanding of diagrams or drawings, technical skills, verbal communications skills, computer skills, and teamwork skills. In addition, it has been reported that many job applicants for manufacturing jobs have inadequate reading, writing, and communication skills, and a deficiency in employee skills is the reason why one in five manufacturing companies are unable to expand (Hays, 1999).

The implications of the skills gap are enormous. For example, "In everyday work life, this deficiency translates into secretaries who can't write

TABLE 11.3 LEVELS OF LITERACY

Statistics Canada slots adults into five levels of literacy skills based on how well they handle everyday tasks that range from locating plant-care information in an article about impatiens to checking out a newspaper weather chart.

Level 1: Nonreaders who have serious difficulty with any printed material.

Level 2: Poor readers who can read only simple printed material containing no complex tasks.

Level 3: Average readers who can handle everyday printed material. This level of skill is needed for entry-level jobs.

Levels 4 and 5: High-end readers, from managers through professionals to academics. The passing grade to move up a level is 80 percent, meaning someone with a 75 percent probability of successfully completing the average Level 3 task is still slotted into Level 2 and labelled as having low literacy.

Faced with criticism that 80 percent is unrealistically high, Statistics Canada and other participants are seriously considering a 70 percent passing grade for the next international survey, planned for 2002.

Source: Calamai, P. (1999, August 28). The literacy gap. *Toronto Star*, p. J2. Reprinted with permission by The Toronto Star Syndicate.

letters free of grammatical errors, workers who can't read instructions that govern the operation of new machinery, and bookkeepers who can't manipulate the fractions necessary to compute simple business transactions" (Hays, 1999, p. 71).

It is estimated that the lack of basic skills in the workforce costs American organizations $60 billion in lost productivity as a result of mistakes, workplace accidents, and damage to equipment (Hays, 1999). Organizations will have difficulty implementing new programs and new technology and staying competitive if their workforce does not have a basic education. Many companies are discovering this. They implement a new program such as statistical-process control and then discover that employees do not have the ability to synthesize the information.

It is becoming increasingly clear that organizations must provide their workforces with basic-skills training if they are to compete and survive in a global and high-tech workplace. Evidence suggests that without first providing trainees with basic-skills training, other programs and initiatives will not succeed (Kuri, 1996). Consider the following example in which managers did not feel that basic-skills training had any value for their organization:

> These managers soon found that when hourly employees, many of whom spoke little English, were put through quality or team training without first receiving basic-skills training, nothing on the manufacturing floor changed—no up-line communication, no con-

sensus decision making, no team meetings. The managers who opposed basic-skills training were unable to comprehend what had gone wrong. (Kuri, 1996, p. 77)

As Kuri (1996) also notes, "What these companies failed to recognize was that improved literacy skills among the workforce could reduce waste and improve productivity—and increase earnings" (p. 77). Many companies have met the rigorous quality standards of the International Standards Organization and received ISO 9000 certification only after implementing basic-skills training programs (Kuri, 1996).

Basic-skills training programs are designed to provide employees with critical literacy skills and improve their ability to read things such as change orders, to make numerical calculations, to enter data for tracking, and to use the correct technical vocabulary (Kuri, 1996). **Literacy** has been defined as "an individual's ability to read, write, and speak English, compute and solve basic math problems, and develop one's knowledge and potential through listening skills" (Hays, 1999, p. 71).

As shown in Figure 11.1, there are four primary types of basic skills or remedial training: reading, basic math or arithmetic, English as a second language, and writing. Reportedly, the most popular way of teaching basic skills to manufacturing employees is on-the-job training. An increasing number of organizations are realizing that it is imperative that employees receive basic-skills training. Motorola Inc., for example, spent $40 million dollars to train 8000 of its employees in basic skills (Hays, 1999).

Organizations that have implemented basic-skills training have not only experienced an improvement in productivity, efficiency, and quality, but some also report a decrease in absenteeism and the number of workers' compensation claims made, and an improvement in cross-cultural communication and morale (Kuri, 1996). Basic-skills training also has several other advantages for employees. Not only does the training improve their skills, self-esteem, and self-efficacy, but it also improves their chances of remaining employed. The percentages of employees who receive basic-skills training and remain employed or are promoted are higher than employees who do not receive training (Kuri, 1996).

In the banking and financial services industries, meeting math requirements has become a major problem for career advancement. The major banks have become involved in more complex lines of business that require employees to provide financial counselling; employees must understand more than just adding, subtracting, multiplying, and dividing. This so-called math gap means that employees throughout the financial services industry must upgrade their math skills ("Bankers grapple," 1999).

Organizations cannot expand their services or implement new technologies if their employees do not have basic literacy skills. Providing basic-skills training is a critical requirement for surviving in an increasingly competitive and global environment.

basic-skills training training programs that are designed to provide employees with critical literacy skills such as reading and arithmetic that are required to perform their job

literacy an individual's ability to read, write, and solve basic math problems

FIGURE 11.1 REMEDIAL TRAINING BY ORGANIZATION SIZE

Number of Employees	% of Organizations Sponsoring Remedial/Basic Education
100–499	17
500–999	14
1,000–2,499	24
2,500–9,999	33
10,000 or More	36
All Sizes*	18

Types of Remedial Training Provided†

Reading ◢ 40%

Basic math/arithmetic ◢ 50%

English as a second language ◢ 51%

Writing ◢ 52%

*Refers to U.S. organizations with 100 or more employees.
†Of organizations that do some type of remedial training, percent that teach these topics.
  Based on 803 responses.

Source: Industry Report (1997, October 10). Training technology. *Training 34*, p. 58. Reprinted with permission of *Training* magazine. Copyright © 1997, Bill Communications Inc. Minneapolis, MN. All rights reserved.

TECHNICAL SKILLS TRAINING

technical skills training
training in specific job skills that all employees need to perform their jobs

Technical skills training is training for job specific skills that all employees need to perform their jobs. As noted previously, among manufacturing firms, specific job skills was the category for which the largest percentage of firms provided training to more than 60 percent of employees. As well, note that in Table 11.1 technical skills development was provided by 77 percent of organizations. These figures should not be surprising given the changes that have occurred during the past two decades. With increasing global competition, organizations have had to find new ways to stay competitive and to survive, typically through an increase in technology and a redesign of work arrangements and systems. As a result, employees have had to undergo a considerable amount of technical skills upgrading and training. Nowhere is this more apparent than in the manufacturing sector, where low-skilled employees have had to become highly skilled employees to keep their jobs and for their organizations to survive (Baker & Armstrong, 1996).

During the mid-1980s, companies such as Corning, Motorola, and Xerox began a trend toward high-skills manufacturing (Baker & Armstrong, 1996). Rote assembly-line workers were replaced with workers who needed to learn new skills to operate new technology and think while they worked. These innovative practices became mainstream in the 1990s as they spread throughout the manufacturing sector. Not only did these organizations realize that investments in training can boost productivity, but that training employees to improve their skills was essential to being competitive. As a result, factory workers in North America are now being trained to improve their technical skills to the level Japanese and German workers have already attained.

Consider the case of Acme Metals Inc., a speciality steel maker in the United States. Faced with increased competition, the company spent $400 million to redesign their mill with a new high-tech German caster that converts molten steel into two-inch thick bands. Employees took an exhaustive battery of exams to test for reading, math, technical, and communication skills. Based on the results, 750 employees were chosen to be part of a new team-oriented system. However, this selection was just the beginning. Employees then spent nine months in training to upgrade their skills, doing everything from studying metallurgy, math, and computers to completing a piece-by-piece study of the new machinery, at a cost of $8 million (Baker & Armstrong, 1996).

As organizations continue to change and compete in a global economy and to increase their use of new technologies, technical skills upgrading will become a way of life for manufacturing workers.

Technical training to upgrade specific job skills is the most common type of technical training, but let's look now at some other types of technical training, including new employee orientation and training, information technology training, health and safety training, and quality training.

New Employee Orientation and Training

As previously indicated, the second most common type of training received by Canadian workers is orientation. Formal orientation and training programs have become the main method used by organizations to socialize new employees (Feldman, 1989). As noted in Table 11.2, new employee orientation is the most common type of training provided by organizations, with 92 percent indicating they provide it. This finding is consistent across a number of studies in different countries.

For example, Nelson and Quick (1991) examined the availability and helpfulness of 10 socialization practices in a study of employees in the United States. They found that formal orientation was rated as one of the most available practices, whereas offsite training sessions were rated as one of the least available. Anderson, Cunningham-Snell, and Haigh (1996) found that an overwhelming majority of 100 major British organizations provided new hires with formalized, off-the-job induction training within four weeks of entry. Most of the organizations provided standardized programs that were designed and conducted by in-house personnel practitioners. The content of induction training was general in nature and pertained mostly to health and safety, terms and conditions of employment, organizational history and structure, specific training provisions, and human resource management policies and procedures.

An example of an organization with a comprehensive orientation and training program for new employees is Starbucks. New employees receive 24 hours of training in their first 80 hours of employment (Gruner, 1998). First CEO Howard Schultz greets them via video and then they learn about the company's history and obsession for quality and customer service (Gruner, 1998). This first phase is followed by classes during the next six weeks on topics such as "Brewing the Perfect Cup," "Retail Sales," "Coffee Knowledge," and "Customer Service." Employees are also taught relaxation techniques and guidelines for on-the-job interpersonal relations (Reese, 1996). According to CEO Howard Schultz, "For people joining the company we try to define what Starbucks stands for, what we're trying to achieve, and why that's relevant to them" (Gruner, 1998, p. 126).

Research has shown that orientation and training have a positive effect on the attitudes and adjustment of new hires. According to Feldman (1989), "the overall training program plays a major role in how individuals make sense of and adjust to their new job settings" (p. 399). Nelson and Quick (1991) did not find evidence that the availability of formal orientation was related to newcomers' adjustment; however, the availability of offsite training was related to psychological distress symptoms. Newcomers for whom offsite training was not available reported greater psychological distress.

Saks (1996) examined the training of entry-level accountants in Canadian accounting firms and found that the amount of training received was positively related to their ratings of training helpfulness, and both the amount and helpfulness of training were positively related to job attitudes and negatively related to turnover. Not surprisingly, the turnover rate at Starbucks is around 60 percent, which is considerably less than the average rate of 150 percent in the speciality-coffee industry (Gruner, 1998).

Tannenbaum, Mathieu, Salas, and Cannon-Bowers (1991) studied the training fulfillment of military trainees. They defined fulfillment as "the extent to which training meets or fulfills a trainee's expectations and desires" (p. 760). They found that training fulfillment was positively related to post-training organizational commitment, training motivation, and self-efficacy.

In summary, the orientation and training of new employees is one of the most common types of training. For new hires to learn their jobs and adjust to the organization, they require knowledge and information about their job-related tasks, work roles, group processes, and organizational attributes (Ostroff & Kozlowski, 1992). Research by Ostroff and Kozlowski (1992) demonstrated that newcomers' knowledge in these areas was positively related to their job satisfaction, organizational commitment, and adjustment. Knowledge about one's tasks and role was found to be especially important for successful socialization. Thus, orientation and training programs should be designed to provide new hires with information and knowledge about their job, role, work group, and organization. The orientation and training received by new hires can have a lasting effect on their job attitudes and behaviours.

INFORMATION TECHNOLOGY TRAINING

Information technology training refers to computers and computer systems training. As shown in Table 11.1, 95 percent or organizations indicated that they provide computer applications training and 81 percent provide computer systems or programming training (Industry Report, 1999). Information systems training has been ranked as one of the top 10 issues of critical importance and is known to be a key factor in the successful implementation of information systems technology (Harp, Taylor, & Satzinger, 1998). Research has shown that technological failures in the workplace are most often the result of training issues rather than the technology (Martocchio, 1992).

information technology training   training programs that focus on the use of computers and computer systems

Information technology training usually involves either introductory computer training programs in which trainees learn about computer hardware and software, or applications training in which trainees are instructed on specific software applications to be used within the organization (DeSimone & Harris, 1998). Applications training is required whenever an organization upgrades its computer systems.

With the growing use of computers and computer technology in the workplace, workers are increasingly in need of training in applications. For example, factory workers must now learn to use computer controls to operate new equipment and to read computer-generated information in areas such as inventories, suppliers and customers, costs and prices (Baker & Armstrong, 1996). It is not surprising that many computer users need training for computer-related job skills (Harp et al., 1998).

One of the most common types of information technology training is computer software training. "Computer software training refers to the planned, structured, and formal means of delivering information about how to use a specific computer software application" (Harp et al., 1998, p. 271). Computer software training has been shown to increase trainees' ability to use the system and their motivation to use software (Harp et al., 1998).

Information technology training is likely to continue to be a critical area of training given the rapid pace of change in computer technology and the increasing use of computers in the workplace. This means that trainers will have to increasingly provide computer-related training to employees. As discussed in the Training Today 1 box, trainers must pay special attention when the trainees are older employees.

In recent years, an increasing number of mature adults have been re-entering the workforce in unprecedented numbers. Older workers offer employers advantages such as strong work ethic, high productivity, a wealth of experience, and low absenteeism and turnover rates. But seniors usually are not regarded as computer savvy enough to help ease the high-tech labour shortage.

In fact, many employers and trainers assume that older workers can't—or won't—learn to use computers at all. But those who specialize in teaching older learners contend that this impression is dead wrong. Training departments attempting to teach computer applications to older learners often fail to consider their special needs.

For example, an insurance company decided to hire some older workers for its call centre because, it believed, its many elderly customers would relate better to a voice that had some years behind it. So the company recruited and trained a group of mature adults, and then ran them through the same computer training everyone else received. The company's new "old" workers had a high attrition rate during training and substandard performance afterward. The company concluded that hiring seniors was a mistake and that older people couldn't do the job.

But the fault didn't lie with the employees or the material but with the trainers. Trainers often do not think about how to accommodate the needs of an older audience. After adjusting the time allotted for its computer training, the same insurance company tried the experiment again and found that older employees' performance after training was on par with younger employees.

Those who specialize in training seniors suggest teaching them in smaller classes of people roughly the same age. A few seniors may find it a challenge to try to keep up with younger trainees, but most will be left behind and won't ask questions if the rest of the class seems to be faster on the uptake. Most experts recommend teaching seniors in small classes of six to ten. Computer training for older employees can also be improved by slowing it down; using mature trainers from the same peer group as the trainees who can allude to experiences they understand; conducting the training in a learning environment that is comfortable for older learners; and understanding that older learners have some particular problems with computers such as how to use a mouse and line-of-sight problems caused by bifocals. Most importantly, the trainer must adjust his/her instructional style to the needs of an older audience.

Excerpted from Filipczak, B. (1998, May). Old dogs, new tricks. *Training, 35* (5), 50–58.

HEALTH AND SAFETY TRAINING

Workplace health and safety has become an increasing concern in Canadian organizations. The costs of work-related injuries and illnesses are on the rise and present a serious threat to employees and their organizations (Montgomery, 1996). Approximately 423 000 workers in Canada are injured on the job each year. Workplace injuries result in 15 million lost workdays per year at a cost of $4 billion in compensation payments. The cost rises to between $8 and $10 billion when indirect costs are included (Montgomery, 1996).

Preventing accidents and injuries and improving workplace health and safety is an important concern of workers, governments, unions, and organizations. Occupational health and safety should begin with preventative and corrective actions that eliminate or reduce accidents and injuries. Safety training is one of the most important ways to deal with accidents before they occur by educating employees in safe work methods and techniques. Employees should also be trained to recognize the chemical and physical hazards in the workplace so that they are prepared and capable of taking corrective action in the event of an accident.

According to Montgomery (1996), an effective health and safety training program should include the following:

- the organization safety rules, practices, and accident and injury reporting procedures
- the duties of the employer, supervisor, and the worker as specified in the Occupational Health and Safety (OHS) legislation
- the importance of strict compliance with warning and emergency signs and signals
- the types and use of emergency equipment (e.g., extinguishers or spill retainers)
- the use, care, and acquisition of personal protective equipment
- the organization benefits
- the known hazards and safeguards against them
- the importance of reporting other hazards (e.g., defective equipment) and the mechanism for doing so
- the emergency and evacuation procedures for dealing with things such as fires and explosions, spills, toxic exposure, and so on
- the need for good housekeeping
- courses in first aid, CPR, and defensive driving where applicable

An important component of health and safety training involves the handling of hazardous materials and chemicals. The Workplace Hazardous Materials Information System (WHMIS) legislation is designed to ensure that workers across Canada are aware of the potential hazards of chemicals in the workplace and are familiar with emergency procedures for the clean-up and disposal of a spill. An important component of WHMIS legislation is employee training. Training in WHMIS is designed so that employees can identify WHMIS hazard symbols, read WHMIS supplier and workplace labels, and read and apply the information on material safety data sheets (MSDS), which outline the hazardous ingredient(s) in a product and the procedures for the safe handling of that product (Montgomery, 1996).

Besides including health and safety education as part of the orientation and training of new employees, organizations should provide it on an ongoing basis, such as through safety meetings during working hours, especially when new procedures or equipment are introduced into the workplace. In addition, all levels of management and supervision should receive training in health and safety. As Montgomery (1996) notes, "Well-trained and dedicated employees are the greatest deterrent to injuries, material damage, and health problems in the plant or institution" (p. 271).

QUALITY TRAINING

In the 1980s, North American manufacturing organizations found themselves challenged by the high quality of foreign goods. Given the emphasis on quantity and economies of scale in North America, quality was viewed as simply an inspection of goods at the end of the line (Kuri, 1996). To remain competitive, however, this approach had to change. In response, organizations in North America began to invest in new programs aimed at building quality into the production process. Today, quality programs can be found in many organizations (Murray & Raffaele, 1997). The best example of this is total quality management (TQM).

total quality management (TQM) a systematic process of continual improvement of the quality of an organization's products and services

Total quality management is a systematic process of continual improvement of the quality of products and services. In addition to an emphasis on quality and continual improvement, TQM also involves teamwork and a customer focus (Dean & Bowen, 1994). Because TQM requires the involvement of all stakeholders in an organization, the concept moves far beyond piecemeal approaches to quality improvement, which often are limited to inspection and quality-control methods carried out by a specialized department. Although this search for quality is not a new concept, TQM can require major organizational changes (Fine & Bridge, 1987; Armitage, 1992).

TQM places the training function in a pivotal position, as the process often requires significant changes in employees' skills and the way employees work. TQM literature, however, typically contains only superficial information about new approaches to training and development. Fortunately, some training professionals have had to become involved in TQM, and have provided some guidance on how to transform traditional practices into TQM (e.g., Cocheu, 1989; Rossett & Krumdieck, 1992).

For example, employees are empowered by having the decision-making power driven down to those who can do the most for quality improvement. TQM requires that employees at lower levels share managerial responsibility, moving away from conventional command-and-control procedures to a more participative style of management. With empowerment, the roles of employees change and they assume more responsibility. In addition, they are required to work in teams that share decision-making and problem-solving responsibilities.

Most TQM advocates emphasize the importance of training and development (e.g., Oakland, 1989; Schonberger, 1992; Tenner & DeToro, 1992). Without proper employee training, the act of empowerment in TQM is meaningless (Gandz, 1990). Training and development are primary methods of reinforcing employee commitment to the consistent delivery of high-quality products and services. Accordingly, leading TQM companies invest heavily in training and development at all levels. In the absence of proper training, many TQM systems that are excellent at identifying and quantifying the cost of performance problems are ultimately unsuccessful because there is no way of changing the behaviours that caused the deficiencies in the first place (Kiess-Moser, 1990; Regalbuto, 1992).

Because quality initiatives such as TQM involve substantial changes to employees' work roles and responsibilities, comprehensive and extensive training is required in a number of areas. Harper and Rifkind (1994) have provided the following outline for TQM training.

1. *Overview of the state of the organization.* This overview provides information about the health of the organization and why it is planning to implement TQM.

2. *Statement from the head of the organization.* The best way to communicate the support of top executives for TQM is for a statement by the head of the organization to be delivered in person as part of training.

3. *Overview of TQM.* Employees need to be informed about what TQM involves including the use of teams, continual improvement, customer focus, employee empowerment, and plans for implementation.

4. *Team training.* Employees need to be trained on how teams function, such as the difference between a team and a committee, rules for team formation, the composition of teams, and team responsibilities.

5. *Training in the use of tools.* TQM involves the use of a number of statistical tools such as Pareto charts, fishbone diagrams, affinity programs, and interrelationship diagrams as part of the problem-solving and decision-making processes. Employees will need to be trained on how to use each of these tools.

Although the name of quality programs might change from time to time, a focus on quality will continue to be one of the major initiatives critical to organizational competitiveness and survival. This focus on quality will require training programs to provide employees with the knowledge and skills required to function in a quality-oriented work system. Quality training has been found to be related to quality outcomes and is considered to be a critical factor in an organization's strategy and its ability to achieve a competitive advantage (Murray & Raffaele, 1997).

NONTECHNICAL SKILLS TRAINING

Although a great deal of emphasis has been given to technical skills, soft or nontechnical skills have also become increasingly important. **Nontechnical or soft skills** are those skills required to work and interact effectively with other people, such as communication skills, interpersonal skills, conflict resolution skills, negotiation skills, problem-solving solving, and so on. Many of the changes taking place in organizations lead to an increased awareness of the importance of these types of nontechnical skills.

For example, in addition to the technical skills upgrading required for factory workers, new work arrangements often require employees to work in teams. As a result, they require skills to be able to work with other people and

nontechnical skills (soft skills) skills that are required to work and interact effectively with people, such as communication and interpersonal skills

to make decisions and solve problems as part of a group. In addition to technical skills training, many factory workers also receive training in areas such as conflict resolution, problem solving, and customer and supplier relations (Baker & Armstrong, 1996).

As we saw in Table 11.1, several nontechnical skills training programs are at the top of the list of training programs provided by organizations, such as programs in supervisory skills, communication skills, and customer service. Although there are many types of nontechnical skills training, some of the most common are team training or team building, sales training, customer service training, sexual harassment training, cultural diversity training, and cross-cultural training.

TEAM TRAINING AND TEAM BUILDING

In recent years, many organizations have implemented team-based work systems such as GM's Saturn Plant, Rubbermaid, Xerox, Federal Express, and General Electric to name just a few. An estimated 80 percent of organizations with 100 or more employees now use some form of teams, and more than 50 percent of all organizations in the United States are exploring team-based work systems (Banker, Field, Schroeder, & Sinha, 1996; Guzzo & Dickson, 1996). The reasons for this vary but in many cases it is an attempt to improve efficiency, quality, customer satisfaction, innovation, and the speed of production, or in the case of Compaq Canada, to bring people together following the merger with Digital Equipment Corp ("Compaq Canada," 1999).

Because cultural differences are often the source of merger failures, Compaq Canada has begun sending its managers to a corporate "wilderness" training centre located in an industrial building in Toronto to learn team-building skills. In one exercise, managers must cross a toxic river painted on the floor. Success requires the team to learn to communicate with each other and to work together. Compaq is currently sending teams from all areas in the organization and is also planning to have sessions with client companies ("Compaq Canada," 1999).

Levi Strauss & Co. explored team-based work systems in 1992 as part of a solution for dealing with overseas, low-cost competitors and the need to increase productivity and reduce costs (King, 1998). Levi's employees had previously worked on their own, operating machines on which they performed a single, specific, and repetitive task such as sewing zippers or belt loops on jeans, and were paid a set amount for each piece of work completed. Once the teams were implemented, groups of 10 to 50 workers shared the tasks and were paid for the total number of trousers that the group completed.

However, top performers began to complain that their less skilled and slower teammates caused their wages to decline while the wages of lower skilled workers increased. Threats, insults, and group infighting became a regular part of daily work as faster workers tried to rid their group of slower workers. Top performers responded to their lower wages by reducing their productivity and employee morale began to deteriorate.

Because the groups had limited supervision, they had to resolve group problems on their own, and they also divided up the work of absent members themselves. In some plants, team members would chase each other out of the bathroom and nurse's station. Slower teammates were often criticized, needled, and resented by their group. Some couldn't take the resentment and simply quit. In one group, a member was voted off of her team because she planned to have hand surgery.

Unfortunately, the team system did not help Levis accomplish its objectives. Profit margins declined as competitors began offering private-label jeans at two-thirds the price of Levis, and Levi's market share of men's denim-jeans in the U.S. fell from 48 percent in 1990 to 26 percent in 1997. In 1997, the company closed 11 factories in the United States and laid off 6395 workers. In February of 1999, the company let go another 5900 employees, or 30 percent of its workforce of 19 900 in the U.S. and Canada, and announced that it will close 11 of its remaining 22 plants in North America (Steinhart, 1999).

What went wrong with the team approach at Levis? Certainly, the team system failed for several reasons. However, the reasons most relevant to us involve training. Employees who had worked alone for most of their working lives and who had no experience working in a group were given only brief seminars and training on team building and problem solving. Although workers were given time to learn unfamiliar machines, many felt that they had inadequate training on issues such as balancing workflows and spotting quality problems. Furthermore, although workers were now part of a team system, management was not given guidance on how to implement the system (King, 1998). The lack of training was an important factor in the failure of teams at Levi Strauss.

As this example illustrates, team training and building are critical for teams to function effectively. **Team training and building** programs are used to improve the effectiveness of teams in areas that are known to distinguish effective from ineffective teams, such as communication, coordination, compensatory behaviour, mutual performance monitoring, exchange of feedback, and adaptation to varying situational demands (Tannenbaum & Yukl, 1992). According to Bottom and Baloff (1994), team building is an "attempt to improve a group's process through the use of interventions targeted at specific aspects of process such as effective communication" (p. 318). Group processes are usually the focus of team building interventions; however, because team members are often expected to perform a variety of the group's tasks, they often must also receive technical training to become multiskilled.

Team building is one of the most popular types of human resource development interventions (Bottom & Baloff, 1994). However, such interventions have not always been effective primarily because of a lack of a diagnosis of all relevant variables. For team building to be effective, a comprehensive diagnosis must first be conducted on group input, task, and process variables to

team training and building training programs to improve the processes, functioning, and effectiveness of teams in areas such as communication and coordination

determine the appropriateness of team building and to tailor interventions to the needs of the group (Bottom & Baloff, 1994).

Training is a critical factor in the successful implementation of teams. In addition to providing team members with both technical and nontechnical training, managers and supervisors must also receive training on how to implement teams and on their new role as a team coach and facilitator rather than as a traditional manager. When team-building interventions are based on a comprehensiveness diagnosis, there is evidence that they can improve group processes and effectiveness (Bottom & Baloff, 1994).

SALES TRAINING

If you have ever seen the movies *Tin Men* or *Glengarry Glen Ross* then you have a good idea of what salespersons used to do. That is, they aggressively sold their wares by telling customers what they needed and their training focused on the hard sell approach. Today, shorter product cycles, finicky customers, more complex sales channels, and global competition has changed the sales profession and made it much more demanding and challenging (Stamps, 1997).

Sales professionals have to do much more than just sell. They need to develop relationships with their customers by listening to them, understanding their needs and problems, and helping them develop solutions. This process involves changing from an order-taking mentality, in which an organization competes primarily on price, to more of a business-partnership mentality, in which organizations compete by selling service rather than just commodities (Stamps, 1997). General Electric's CEO Jack Welch recently stated that GE is going to start to focus on customers by providing lower costs and more consistent service, and that the company-wide goal is to transform GE from a products provider to a provider of "productivity solutions" ("GE's Welch," 1999).

Sales professionals must develop a different set of skills to be successful in today's competitive sales environment. They need to be more knowledgable about their products and their business, as well as their customers' business. As a result, sales training has become something more than simply sending the sales troops off to a motivational pep rally (Stamps, 1997).

Today, sales training programs are being designed to upgrade sales professionals' skills and help them deal with new competitive challenges. At the centre of these new training initiatives is an emphasis on "relationship-based" sales training. Sales professionals are being trained to develop more strategic and complex relationships with clients and to create relationships across client functions. They are also being trained to become knowledgable about their customer's business needs and to develop customized sales strategies. Rather than just selling a commodity, integrated teams of people from sales, support, and service are learning to sell solutions that combine support and service agreements.

Unlike more traditional sales training, these new approaches require a high level of management support and commitment since they represent a cultural change in the way an organization conducts its business. However, there is evidence that this new approach can increase sales effectiveness. For example, Sprint Canada attributes an increase in revenues to its new sales training program that trains its sales force on developing strategic relationships with their clients (Stamps, 1997). If a change in an organization's approach to sales is required to remain competitive, than sales training will become a critical part of that strategy.

CUSTOMER SERVICE TRAINING

An organization's front-line employees play a key role in representing the organization to its customers. Good customer service and customer satisfaction are the keys to ensuring that customers return, so it is critical that front-line or customer-contact employees have the skills and abilities necessary to interact and communicate effectively with customers and provide them with excellent service. For many organizations, this requires extensive training in customer service.

Companies with a strong commitment to customer service such as L.L. Bean, Federal Express, Marriott, and Disney invest heavily in training their employees (Schneider & Bowen, 1995). For example, employees at L.L. Bean receive 40 hours of training before they deal with customers and at British Airways all employees attend two days of training called "Putting People First" (Schneider & Bowen, 1995). At Delta Hotels and Resorts, employees are trained and empowered to provide customers with excellent service such as settling a disputed minibar charge or offering a complimentary room if a guest has a reasonable complaint. According to Bill Pallet, Delta's senior vice president of people and quality, "The name of the game isn't customer satisfaction, it's customer loyalty. It costs more to go out and get new customers than retain your current customers." As part of its training program, Delta has produced an award-winning training video and promises employees a certain amount of training every year. Delta's employee turnover rate has dropped, morale has improved, and occupancy rates have risen without having to drop prices to be competitive. As well, Delta is talking with other service companies and the medical sectors about its program ("Delta promotes," 1999).

According to Schneider and Bowen (1995), "The fundamental issue in training, whether it be training of individuals or training of teams, is to ensure that when customer meets employee, the encounter unfolds in ways that yield a sense of seamlessness for the customer" (p. 132). Schneider and Bowen (1995) describe the experience this way: "By seamlessness, we mean that the service, in all of its dimensions and characteristics, is delivered without a hitch. It is *simultaneously* reliable, responsive, competent, courteous, and so forth, and the facilities and tools necessary for it are all put into play smoothly and without glitches, interruptions, or delay. The same applies to responses to system failures and special requests. Seamless service is something all customers expect" (p. 8).

Customer service training can be either informal or formal. Informal training can involve pairing new hires with the organization's best employees in terms of customer service behaviour and philosophy. The kind of formal training required will depend on the type of service business that an organization is in and its service strategy. In other words, the training program must be tailored to an organization's strategy and characteristics as well as its customers (Schneider & Bowen, 1995).

We can nonetheless get some idea of the type of content that service training must provide when considering the required behaviours of customer-contact employees. According to Schneider and Bowen (1995), such employees must be motivated and able to meet the following customer expectations for service quality, as first noted by Parasuraman, Zeithaml, and Berry (1985):

1. *Reliability:* dependability and consistency of performance (e.g., performing the service at the designated time).
2. *Responsiveness:* the willingness and readiness of employees to provide service (e.g., giving prompt service).
3. *Competence:* the required skills and knowledge to perform the service (e.g., research capability of the organization).
4. *Access:* approachability and ease of contact (e.g., convenient hours and location).
5. *Courtesy:* politeness, respect, consideration, and friendliness (e.g., clean and neat appearance).
6. *Communication:* keeping customers informed and listening to them (e.g., assuring customers that a problem will be handled).
7. *Credibility:* trustworthiness, believability, and honesty (e.g., personal characteristics of employees).
8. *Security:* freedom from danger, risk, or doubt (e.g., confidentiality).
9. *Understanding or knowing the customer:* making an effort to understand the customers' needs (e.g., providing individualized attention).
10. *Tangibles:* physical evidence of the service (e.g., appearance of personnel).

In addition to these quality expectations, employees must be able to deal with service failures, perform beyond customer expectations, and satisfy customer expectations for special requests. Employees must also ensure that customers feel secure, have their self-esteem enhanced, and are treated justly. Finally, service employees must also be able to act as supervisors or co-workers in those situations in which they are involved with customers in co-producing a service (Schneider & Bowen, 1995).

According to Schneider and Bowen (1995), service employees must have both the *ability* and *motivation* to perform effectively. Because you cannot always hire people with the required abilities or motivation, you must be able to train them. Many organizations that have reputations for superb customer service are successful because of their commitment to training. Organizations that provide the best service also provide the most training (Schneider & Bowen, 1995). The key to service quality and competitiveness is service training.

SEXUAL HARASSMENT TRAINING

In recent years, several high-profile sexual harassment cases have made the news headlines and brought increased attention to this problem. In addition to the numerous cases of sexual harassment reported in the military, many organizations, including Mitsubishi, Astra, Sears & Roebuck, and Del Laboratories have found themselves in costly litigation cases (Peirce, Smolinski, & Rosen, 1998). The failure of these organizations to effectively respond to charges of sexual harassment has cost them millions of dollars in settlements and in lower productivity, and increased absenteeism and turnover. Sexual harassment in the U.S. army is reported to cost $250 million a year in lost productivity, absenteeism, and the replacement and transfer of employees (Seppa, 1997). The effects of sexual harassment on employees can include decreased morale and job satisfaction, as well as negative effects on psychological and physical well being (Schneider, Swan, & Fitzgerald, 1997). Men who perceive their workplace as hostile toward women and minorities also report lower job satisfaction and trust for their employer (Murray, 1998).

Sexual harassment is any "unwelcome sexual advances, requests for sexual favours, and other verbal or physical conduct of a sexual nature ... when submission to requests for sexual favours is made explicitly or implicitly a term or condition of employment; submission to or rejection of such requests is used as a basis for employment decisions; or such conduct unreasonably interferes with work performance or creates an intimidating, hostile, or offensive work environment" (Schneider, Swan, & Fitzgerald, 1997, p. 401). There are two kinds of sexual harassment. *Quid pro quo* refers to explicit requests for sexual favours as a condition of employment. A *hostile environment* refers to a work environment in which language or actions or both create an uncomfortable and offensive work environment that interferes with job performance (Ganzel, 1998).

With the number of litigation cases and costly settlements growing, organizations have become more concerned about sexual harassment. The most effective way for organizations to deal with sexual harassment and to increase

sexual harassment
unwelcome sexual advances, requests for sexual favours, and verbal or physical conduct of a sexual nature that is a condition of employment, interferes with work performance, or creates a hostile work environment

their responsiveness is to, first, develop sexual harassment policies and procedures that include clear reporting procedures for filing complaints, and, second, to provide training programs that educate employees about sexual harassment and the organization's policies and procedures (Ganzel, 1998; Peirce, Smolinski, & Rosen, 1998). Training is especially important because the definition of what constitutes sexual harassment is not always clear or understood, and problems have occurred in situations in which employees and managers were unaware of an organizations' sexual harassment policy or did not know how to report it and proceed with a complaint (Ganzel, 1998). In the United States, sexual harassment training programs have become a popular way to ward off lawsuits (Ganzel, 1998). As indicated in Table 11.2, sexual harassment training is close to the top of the list, with 81 percent of the organizations providing this type of training.

Organizations that are responsive to complaints of sexual harassment not only have policies and procedures in place, but, among other things, they have comprehensive education and training programs (Peirce et al., 1998). For example, E.I. Du Pont de Nemours has developed a sexual harassment awareness program called "A Matter of Respect" that includes interactive training programs, peer-level facilitators who are trained to meet with employees who want to talk about sexual harassment, and a 24-hour hotline. As the company has become more international, so has its training on sexual harassment, which is now provided in Japan, China, Mexico, and Puerto Rico (Flynn, 1997).

With increasing concerns of sexual and racial harassment in the workplace, organizations will need to develop policies to deal with these problems and will also need to provide adequate training.

CULTURAL DIVERSITY TRAINING

During the last several decades, there has been a rapid rise in the percentage of ethnic, cultural, language, and religious minorities in Canada that has resulted in a considerable change in the ethnic and racial origins of employees working in Canadian organizations. Visible minorities now represent approximately 11.2 percent of the Canadian population and are expected to increase to 18.3 percent by the year 2006 (Employment and Immigration Canada, 1994). As a result, the composition of the Canadian workplace is changing and becoming more diverse. Because of this diversity and differences in attitudes and values across cultures, it has become increasingly important for organizations to provide training in cultural diversity. The effective management of these changes in the workplace can have economic and competitive consequences for organizations and is becoming part of many organizations' business strategies (Wentling & Palma-Rivas, 1998).

diversity training
training that focuses on differences in values, attitudes, and behaviours of individuals with different backgrounds

Diversity training is one of the most widely used strategies for managing diversity in the workplace (Wentling & Palma-Rivas, 1998). Such programs are designed to address the differences in values, attitudes, and behaviours of individuals with different backgrounds, in an effort to increase awareness and understanding of cultural diversity and to improve interaction and communication among employees with different backgrounds. According to Noe and Ford (1992, p. 357), "The goal of diversity training programs is to eliminate barriers such as values, stereotypes, and managerial practices which constrain employee contribution to organizational goals and personal development."

Some diversity training programs are designed to change people's attitudes by creating an awareness of diversity and an understanding of differences in values and behaviours. The expectation is that, by creating an awareness and understanding of these differences, people will change their behaviour and overcome any stereotypes they might hold. Another approach to diversity training is to change behaviour. This approach emphasizes learning new behaviours that might then lead to changes in attitudes (Noe & Ford, 1992). Diversity training has three main objectives: (1) increase awareness about diversity issues, (2) reduce biases and stereotypes, and (3) change behaviours to those required to work effectively in a diverse workforce (Hanover & Cellar, 1998).

A recent study on diversity in the workplace found that diversity experts rated training and education programs as one of the best strategies for managing diversity (Wentling & Palma-Rivas, 1998). According to the experts, training and education were considered to be important for the following reasons:

1. building awareness and skills

2. helping employees understand the need and meaning of valuing diversity

3. providing education on specific cultural differences and how to respond to those differences

4. providing the skills required to work on diverse work teams

5. improving employee understanding of the cultural diversity within the organization

6. learning about the culture and community that the organization serves

7. providing skills and activities to assist diverse groups to integrate within the organization, perform their jobs effectively, and increase opportunities for advancement (Wentling & Palma-Rivas, 1998)

In addition, the study noted that diversity training should focus on increasing *awareness* of what diversity is and why it is important; providing *skills* required to work effectively in a diverse workforce; and *application* strategies to facilitate the use of diversity awareness and skills to improve work performance, interactions, and communication. The study also indicated that effective diversity training programs have the following components: commitment and support from top management, inclusion as part of the organizational strategic plan, programs that meet the specific needs of the organization, qualified trainers, association with other diversity initiatives, mandatory attendance, inclusive programs (i.e., include all individuals and groups), and evaluation (Wentling & Palma-Rivas, 1998).

In one of the most comprehensive studies on diversity training, human resource professionals responded to questions about diversity programs in their organizations (Rynes & Benson, 1995). The results indicated that the majority of diversity programs last one day or less and use less than 10 percent of the training budget. As well, more than 80 percent reported that they evaluate participants' reactions immediately after training, but less than one third conduct any long-term evaluation. In terms of success, half of the programs were described as having a neutral effect, 18 percent were described as largely or extremely ineffective, and slightly more than 30 percent judged their training to be quite or extremely effective. The adoption and success of diversity training was strongly influenced by top management support as well as other organizational context factors such as organizational size and diversity-supportive policies (Rynes & Benson, 1995).

With the increasing diversity in the Canadian workplace, managing diversity and diversity training are likely to become more relevant and important than ever. For example, as part of their commitment to become more diversified, the Toronto Police Force has implemented a new recruitment strategy to hire more minorities (Duncanson, 1999). The Bank of Montreal has a Workplace Equality Program that includes training courses on the benefits of a multicultural workforce (Workforce, 1997). Organizations are realizing that managing cultural diversity and its effect on organizational success and competitiveness is important, and that diversity training is one of the most effective strategies for providing employees with the skills required to perform effectively in a diverse workplace. As noted by Wentling and Palma-Rivas (1998), "Organizations need to provide employees with the most important skills for operating in a multicultural environment so that they understand their own as well as others' cultures, values, beliefs, attitudes, behaviours, and strengths and weaknesses. Employers must invest constantly in all employees by providing training and improving competencies if they are to work most effectively in a diverse workplace" (p. 243).

CROSS-CULTURAL TRAINING

One of the implications of international business and a global marketplace is that workers, or *expatriates* as they are called, must work in different countries around the globe and interact with people from different cultures. Although middle managers are sent on overseas assignments most often, senior managers, sales staff, engineers, IS programmers, scientists, and HR professionals are also sent (Halcrow, 1999). Canada sends hundreds of technical advisors each year to developing countries as part of its international development assistance programs (Kealey, 1990). A foreign assignment can last for years and involve contact and interactions with persons who differ from Canadians in terms of culture, values, and language (Kealey, 1990). For an organization to succeed in its international business operations, it requires individuals who can function and work effectively in different cultures.

Unfortunately, both Canadian and American expatriates have typically not performed very well on such assignments. During the past two decades, North American expatriates who were assigned to work overseas for their organizations have tended to have a much higher failure rate than European or Japanese expatriates (Noe & Ford, 1992). In other words, these expatriates either perform poorly or return home early. In the United States, it is estimated that 20 percent of U.S. expatriates fail in their global assignments (Black, Gregersen, & Mendenhall, 1992). A study on Canadian technical advisors working in developing countries found that only about 20 percent were highly effective in terms of their ability to transfer skills and knowledge to counterparts in the host country, 65 percent had little impact, and 15 percent were highly ineffective (Kealey, 1990). The cost of failure is high, costing multinational companies millions of dollars each year. In North America, an estimated $2 to $2.5 billion is wasted when overseas postings fail.

One of the main reasons cited for the high failure rate of North American expatriates is the culture shock they and their families experience living in a foreign culture. The study of Canadian technical advisors working in developing countries found that more than 50 percent experienced culture shock, and a major reason for their lack of effectiveness was the inability to interact effectively with their counterparts in the host country (Kealey, 1990). In addition, a major reason for failure is the inability of the expatriate's spouse and family to adjust to the foreign culture (Black et al., 1992). This inability to adjust stems in large part from a lack of cross-cultural training or pre-departure training for the expatriates and their families. "**Cross-cultural training** is designed to prepare employees for overseas assignments by focusing on developing the skills and attitudes necessary for successful interactions with persons from different backgrounds" (Noe & Ford, 1992, p. 355).

cross-cultural training training that prepares employees for working and living in different cultures

Despite increasing awareness of the importance of cross-cultural training, only a minority of firms (30 to 45 percent) provide this training for expatriates (Dunbar & Katcher, 1990) or their families—a major contributing factor in expatriate assignment failure (McEmery & DesHarnais, 1990). Furthermore, in those few organizations that do provide some cross-cultural training, it tends to not be very rigorous (Black et al., 1992). In other words, cross-cultural training usually involves viewing films and reading books rather than on building cross-cultural skills. This choice of methods is unfortunate because research has shown that cross-cultural training can improve an expatriate's job performance, cross-cultural skills, and cultural adjustment (Black et al., 1992).

A critical factor in the success of cross-cultural training is *training rigour*. According to Black et al. (1992), training rigour refers to "the degree of mental involvement and effort that must be expended by the trainer and the trainee in order for the trainee to learn the required concepts" (p. 97). Training rigour also refers to the length of time spent on training. Generally, cross-cultural training programs that are high on training rigour tend to be more effective. Cross-cultural training programs that are considered to have a high degree of rigour include interactive language training, cross-cultural simulations, and field trips. Programs with a moderate degree of training rigour include role plays, cases, and survival-level language. Cross-cultural training programs that are considered to be the lowest in terms of training rigour include lectures, films, books, and area briefings. More rigorous cross-cultural training programs require trainees to be much more active and involved in practising cross-cultural skills (Black et al., 1992).

According to Black et al. (1992), the degree of cross-cultural training rigour required by an expatriate for a particular foreign assignment depends on three dimensions: cultural toughness, communication toughness, and job toughness. Cultural toughness refers to how difficult it is to adjust to a new culture. Generally speaking, cultural toughness will increase the greater the difference or distance between one's own culture and the foreign culture. For example, cultural toughness will be much higher for a Canadian expatriate in the Middle East than one in the U.S. The Canadian expatriate on assignment in the Middle East will require more rigorous cross-cultural training. An exception to this is the degree of past experience that an expatriate has had living in a foreign culture. For example, a Canadian expatriate with considerable experience living in the Middle East will require less cross-cultural training than one who has never lived there.

Communication toughness is a function of the extent to which the expatriate will have to interact with the locals of the host country. When an expatriate will be required to have frequent interactions with host nationals that will involve face-to-face, two-way, and informal communication, the level of communication toughness will be high, and more rigorous communication training will be required. Job toughness refers to how difficult the tasks will be for the expatriates compared to what they are used to doing. If the expatriate will be working in a new area and the demands of the job will be different and will require new responsibilities and challenges, then the degree of job toughness will be greater. As a result, the expatriate will require more rigorous job-specific training (Black et al., 1992).

An expatriate will have the most difficulty adjusting to foreign assignments that have a high degree of cultural, communication, and job toughness. As the levels of these three dimensions increase, the type of cross-cultural training required will need to be more rigorous. In addition to pre-departure training, it is important that the expatriates and their families also receive follow-up or in-country cross-cultural training in the host country (Black et al., 1992).

With the increasing pace of change and the ever-expanding global marketplace, more and more Canadian workers will be sent on overseas assignments that require them to work and interact with persons in different cultures. Given that an organization's competitive success in the global marketplace depends to a great extent on its people (Black et al., 1992), it is crucial that expatriates perform effectively and adjust to foreign cultures. Research on Canadian expatriates has found that interpersonal and intercultural adaptation skills as well as knowledge of the local culture and participation in that culture are important predictors of overseas effectiveness (Kealey, 1990). Kealey (1990) also found that among Canadian technical advisors, learning the local language was a major factor in overseas effectiveness. To be successful, expatriates require cross-cultural training that not only informs them of the history and politics of a country, but also teaches them the language, values, and appropriate patterns of behaviour. Cross-cultural training helps employees withstand the culture shock of working abroad and improves job performance and adjustment (Black et al., 1992).

SUMMARY

This chapter has provided an overview of the different types of training programs that are being designed and delivered by organizations today. These training programs are a direct result of the many challenges and issues facing organizations in today's rapidly changing environment. Many of these training programs have become critical components of the organizations' corporate strategy and are major factors in their efforts to remain competitive. While many organizations provide these types of training programs, it is important to remember that their relevance and effectiveness will depend on how well the program is designed and the extent to which it is based on training objectives and a rigorous needs assessment.

KEY TERMS

basic-skills training   271

cross-cultural training   289

diversity training   286

information technology training 275

literacy   271

nontechnical skills (soft skills)   279

sexual harassment   285

team training and building   281

technical skills training   272

total quality management (TQM) 278

EXERCISES

1. The extent to which organizations provide certain types of training programs is often driven by external and internal changes. In other words, social, political, and economic changes in the work environment, as well as internal

changes to organizational systems and work arrangements, have a substantial influence on training activities. For each of the following training programs, discuss the role of external and internal factors and how these factors might influence the need and importance of each type of training:

a. basic-skills training
b. technical skills training
c. orientation and newcomer training
d. information technology training
e. health and safety training
f. quality training
g. nontechnical training
h. team training and building
i. sales training
j. customer service training
k. sexual harassment training
l. cultural diversity training
m. cross-cultural training

2. Assume that you are a training director for a large retail organization. To increase your training budget for next year, you have to make a persuasive argument to convince other members of the organization of your need for an increase in resources. An important part of your argument will involve proving the need for and importance of several training programs. For each of the 13 types of training programs listed in exercise #1, describe how you will argue that each type is important, the impact it will have on employee attitudes or behaviour, the benefits it will have for the organization, and how it can help the organization gain a competitive advantage.

3. Design a training program for one of the types of training discussed in this chapter. In designing your program, specify each of the following:

a. the training content
b. the trainer for the program

c. the trainees that should attend the program
d. the training methods to be used
e. the required training materials and equipment
f. the training site
g. the schedule for the training program
h. the lesson plan

4. One way to find out more about the training programs discussed in this chapter is to ask trainers or people in HR and employees about training in their organization. Contact a human resource professional and ask the following questions for each of the 13 types of training described in this chapter:

a. Does your organization provide this type of training?
b. What are some of the reasons why you do or do not provide this type of training?
c. What is the basic content of this type of training?
d. What effect does this type of training have on employees' attitudes and behaviours?
e. What effect does this type of training have on the organization?

In addition, contact several employees who work in different organizations and ask them the following questions:

a. Have you ever received this type of training?
b. If yes, what was the reason why you attended the training program?
c. What was the basic content of the training you received?
d. What effect did the training have on your attitudes and behaviours?
e. What effect did the training have on the organization?

Summarize your results in a report and discuss the availability or frequency, purpose, content, and effects of each type of training program.

5. Human Resources Development Canada has an interactive training directory at <**www.trainingiti.com**>. Select a training course in an area that interests you (e.g., career exploration) and conduct a search for available courses in your area. Then refer to the page on "How to Screen Training Providers and Courses" and answer the questions for each of the programs you have located. How effective is the guide for assessing the quality of a training program?

REFERENCES

Anderson, N.R., Cunningham-Snell, N.A., & Haigh, J. (1996). Induction training as socialization: Current practice and attitudes to evaluation in British organizations. *International Journal of Selection and Assessment 4*, 169–183.

Armitage, H.M. (1992, January). Quality pays. *CGA Magazine 96* (1), pp. 30–37.

Baker, S., & Armstrong, L. (1996, September 30). The new factory worker. *Business Week*, pp. 59–68.

Banker, R.D., Field, J.M., Schroeder, R.G., & Sinha, K.K. (1996). Impact of work teams on manufacturing performance: A longitudinal field study. *Academy of Management Journal 39*, 867–890.

Bankers grapple with math gap. (1999, March 5). *The Globe and Mail*, p. B25.

Black, J.S., Gregersen, H.B., & Mendenhall, M.E. (1992). *Global assignments*. San Francisco, CA: Jossey-Bass.

Bottom, W.P., & Baloff, N. (1994). A diagnostic model for team building with an illustrative application. *Human Resource Development Quarterly 5*, 317–336.

Calamai, P. (1999, August 28). The literacy gap. *Toronto Star*, pp. J1, J2.

Cocheu, T. (1989). Training for quality improvement. *Training and Development Journal 41* (1), 56–62.

Compaq Canada climbs the training wall. (1999, August 23). *The Globe and Mail*, p. B8.

Dean, J.W., Jr., & Bowen, D.E. (1994). Management theory and total quality: Improving research and practice through theory development. *Academy of Management Review 19*, 392–418.

Delta promotes empowerment. (1999, May 31). *The Globe and Mail*, p. C5.

DeSimone, R.L., & Harris, D.M. (1998). *Human Resource Development* (2nd ed.). Fort Worth, TX: Dryden Press.

Dunbar, E., & Katcher, A. (1990). Preparing managers for foreign assignments. *Training and Development Journal 44* (9), 45–47.

Duncanson, J. (1999, March 6). Mostly while, mostly male: Why police are reaching out again. *Toronto Star*, pp. A1, A25.

Employment and Immigration Canada. (1994). *Employment equity availability data report on designated groups*. Ottawa: Author.

Feldman, D.C. (1989). Socialization, resocialization, and training: Reframing the research agenda. In I.L. Goldstein (Ed.), *Training and development in organizations* (pp. 376–416). San Francisco: Jossey-Bass.

Fine, C.H., & Bridge, D.H. (1987). Managing quality improvement. In Sepehri, M. (Ed.), *Quest for quality: Managing the total system* (pp. 66–74). Norcross, GA: Institute of Industrial Engineers.

Flynn, G. (1997). Respect is key to stopping harassment. *Workforce 76* (2), 56.

Gandz, J. (1990). The employee empowerment era. *Business Quarterly 55* (2), 74–79.

Ganzel, R. (1998). What sexual harassment training really prevents. *Training 35* (10), 86–94.

GE's Welch focuses on customers. (1999, March 5). *The Globe and Mail,* p. B25.

The Globe and Mail. (1992, September 15), B26.

Gruner, S. (1998). Lasting impressions. *Inc.*, p. 126.

Guzzo, R.A., & Dickson, M.W. (1996). Teams in organizations: Recent research on performance and effectiveness. *Annual Review of Psychology 47,* 307–338.

Hanover, J.M.B., & Cellar, D.F. (1998). Environmental factors and the effectiveness of workforce diversity training. *Human Resource Development Quarterly 9,* 105–124.

Harp, C.G., Taylor, S.C., & Satzinger, J.W. (1998). Computer training and individual differences: When method matters. *Human Resource Development Quarterly 9,* 271–283.

Harper, L.F., & Rifkind, L.J. (1994). A training program for TQM in the diverse workplace. *Human Resource Development Quarterly 5,* 277–279.

Halcrow, A. (1999). Expats: The squandered resource. *Workforce 78* (4), 42–48.

Hays, S. (1999). The ABCs of workplace literacy. *Workforce 78* (4), 70–74.

Industry Report (1997, October). Training technology. *Training 34,* p. 58.

Industry Report (1998, October). Training budgets. *Training 35,* p. 47.

Industry Report (1999, October). Where the training dollars go. *Training 36,* p. 56 and 58.

Kealey, D.J. (1990). *Cross-cultural effectiveness: A study of Canadian technical advisors overseas.* Hull, QC: Canadian International Development Agency Briefing Centre.

Kiess-Moser, E. (1990). International perspectives on quality. *Canadian Business Review 17* (3), 31–33.

King, R.T., Jr. (1998, May 20). Levi's factory workers are assigned to teams and morale takes a hit. *The Wall Street Journal,* pp. A1, A6.

Kuri, F. (1996, September). Basic-skills training boosts productivity. *HRMagazine 41* (9), 73–79.

Martocchio, J.J. (1992). Microcomputer usage as an opportunity: The influence of context in employee training. *Personnel Psychology 45,* 529–552.

McEmery, J., & DesHarnais, G. (1990). Culture shock. *Training and Development Journal 44* (4), 43–47.

McIntyre, D. (1994). *Training and development, 1993: Policies, practices, & expenditures* (pp. 128–194). Toronto: Conference Board of Canada Report.

Montgomery, J. (1996). *Occupational health and safety.* Toronto: Nelson Canada.

Murray, B. (1998, July). Workplace harassment hurts everyone on the job. *APA Monitor 29* (7), p. 35.

Murray, B., & Raffaele, G.C. (1997). Single-site, results-level evaluation of quality awareness training. *Human Resource Development Quarterly 8,* 229–245.

Nelson, D.L., & Quick, J.C. (1991). Social support and newcomer adjustment in organizations: Attachment theory at work? *Journal of Organizational Behavior 12*, 543–554.

Oakland, J.S. (1989). *Total quality management*. Oxford: Butterworth-Heinemann Ltd.

Ostroff, C., & Kozlowski, S.W.J. (1992). Organizational socialization as a learning process: The role of information acquisition. *Personnel Psychology 45*, 849–874.

Parasuraman, A., Zeithaml, V.A., & Berry, L.L. (1985). A conceptual model of service quality and its implications for future research. *Journal of Marketing 49*, 41–50.

Peirce, E., Smolinski, C.A., & Rosen, B. (1998). Why sexual harassment complaints fall on deaf ears. *Academy of Management Executives 12*, 41–54.

Reese, J. (1996, December, 9). Starbucks: Inside the coffee cult. *Fortune*, pp. 190–200.

Regalbuto, G.A. (1992). Targeting the bottom line. *Training and Development 46* (4), 29–38.

Rossett, A., & Krumdieck, K. (1992). How trainers score on quality. *Training and Development 46* (1), 11–16.

Rynes, S., & Rosen, B. (1995). A field survey of factors affecting the adoption and perceived success of diversity training. *Personnel Psychology 48*, 247–270.

Saks, A.M. (1996). The relationship between the amount and helpfulness of entry training and work outcomes. *Human Relations 49*, 429–451.

Schaaf, D. (1998). What workers really think about training. *Training 35* (9), 59–66.

Schneider, B., & Bowen, D.E. (1995). *Winning the service game*. Boston, MA: Harvard Business School Press.

Schneider, K.T., Swan, S., & Fitzgerald, L.F. (1997). Job-related and psychological effects of sexual harassment in the workplace: Empirical evidence from two organizations. *Journal of Applied Psychology 82*, 401–415.

Schonberger, R.J. (1992). Total quality management cuts a broad swath— Through manufacturing and beyond. *Organizational Dynamics 20* (4), 16–28.

Seppa, N. (1997). Sexual harassment in the military lingers on. *APA Monitor 28* (5), 40–41.

Stamps, D. (1997). Training for a new sales game. *Training 34* (7), 46–52.

Steinhart, D. (1999, February 23). Levi to shut plants in Cornwall, U.S. *Financial Post*, pp. C1, C9.

Tannenbaum, S.I., Mathieu, J.E., Salas, E., & Cannon-Bowers, J.A. (1991). Meeting trainees' expectations: The influence of training fulfillment on the development of commitment, self-efficacy, and motivation. *Journal of Applied Psychology 76*, 759–769.

Tannenbaum, S.I., & Yukl, G. (1992). Training and development in work organizations. *Annual Review of Psychology 43*, 399–441.

Tenner, A.R., & DeToro, I.J. (1992). *Total quality management, three steps to continuous improvement.* Reading, MA: Addison-Wesley.

Wentling, R.M., & Palma-Rivas, N. (1998). Current status and future trends of diversity initiatives in the workplace: Diversity experts' perspective. *Human Resource Development Quarterly 9*, 235–253.

Workforce staff. (1997). Bank of Montreal satisfies customers by satisfying employees. *Workforce 76* (2), 46–47.

12

....

MANAGEMENT DEVELOPMENT

CHAPTER GOALS

In the rapidly evolving global economy, "top management learning is one of the biggest challenges facing organizations" (MacLachlan, 1998). Not only must business leaders see into the future, they must "feel it [the instant, innovative economy] through direct exposure." Until senior managers are exposed to experiential learning, they are unlikely to start the systematic dismantling of old methods and practices that hinder company survival (Hamel, 1998). Given the influence that management can have on an organization's success and even its survival, it is not surprising that the training and development of managers is a multibillion dollar business (Tannenbaum & Yukl, 1992). Corporate expenditures on management education and training are estimated at $45 billion annually, with approximately $12 billion spent on executive education, and one-fourth spent on university business schools. The average cost of executive education for an organization today is reported to be about $2 million annually (Fulmer, 1997).

Management training and development programs focus not only on training in technical and human resource management skills, but also on creating corporate work environments within which all members of the organization direct their actions toward fulfilling the values and the vision set out by senior management (Trainor, 1996a; West, 1997). How organizations accomplish this most difficult of tasks is the focus of this chapter.

After reading this chapter you should be able to

- describe the strategy for management development and its purpose
- understand the meaning and role of climate for management development
- describe the skills needed in any management job in terms of core and discretionary tasks
- describe the differences between the roles of managers and leaders
- understand the meaning of culturally acceptable delivery systems and the most effective methods for learning of core and discretionary skills
- describe the role of the trainer in management development

INTRODUCTION TO MANAGEMENT DEVELOPMENT

management development the processes by which individuals grow, learn, and improve their abilities to perform managerial tasks

In the previous chapter, we described many types of employee training programs. In this chapter we focus on **management development**: "the process by which individuals learn, grow, and improve their ability to perform professional management tasks" (Wexley & Baldwin, 1986, p. 277). Management development is separated from employee training for a number of reasons: (1) the techniques tend to be different (e.g., coaching, mentoring), (2) in Canada, per capita training expenditures have tended to be higher for managers than for other employees, (3) management work is less predictable and less (directly) measurable than many other jobs, and (4) incompetent managers can have a catastrophic effect on an entire organization's ability to survive. Of all the human resource development (HRD) functions, however, management development is perhaps the most misunderstood and poorly implemented. Yet the single characteristic that distinguishes a successful organization, large or small, from others is the calibre of the management team (McCallum, 1993; Brown, 1995).

management education the acquisition of a broad range of managerial knowledge and general conceptual abilities

management training activities designed to impart specific managerial skills

The development of managers has typically involved management education and management training. **Management education** refers to "those activities traditionally conducted by colleges and universities that focus on developing a broad range of managerial knowledge and general conceptual abilities" (Wexley & Baldwin, 1986, p. 278). In contrast, "**Management training** differs from management education in that training covers those activities designed to impart specific managerial skills (e.g., time management, delegation) which would be immediately applicable in a particular organizational setting. Training may also focus on a manager's level of self-awareness or motivation" (Wexley & Baldwin, 1986, p. 280).

The problems associated with program design and delivery are many, ranging from the changing nature of managerial work to organizational politics. Lees (1992), who regards management development as "the socio-political domain of management," lists 10 reasons why organizations invest in their managers.

1. *Functional—performance:* the most common superficial rationale, this concept is aimed at improving direct managerial functioning and, by implication, improving corporate performance.

2. *Agriculture:* the desire to "grow" managers.

3. *Functional—defensive:* the perceived need to acquire a reserve of skills and knowledge for some undefined future.

4. *Socialization:* to develop a common ethos or culture.

5. *Political reinforcement*: to initiate cultural redesign toward norms as defined by senior management.

6. *Organizational inheritance:* enhancement of the ability to climb the corporate ladder.

7. *Environmental legitimacy:* attempts to gain favour with outside stakeholders by giving out politically correct signals about the environment and other social issues.

8. *Compensation:* management development is used as a form of payment or compensation.

9. *Psychic defence:* training is seen as a defensive mechanism, protecting the manager from subordinates so they will continue to cooperate.

10. *Ceremonial:* the legitimization and conformation of the social order and the progression through the social order.

A management development program based solely on one or any combination of these concepts will create confusion and in Lees's (1992) words "pose massive problems," because the results of investing in management development cannot be evaluated adequately against other more tangible opportunities. Thus, a substantial percentage of the development programs fail to meet either senior management's or the participants' expectations (Whetten & Cameron, 1995). For management development to be successful, an organization must first have a strategy.

THE STRATEGY FOR MANAGEMENT DEVELOPMENT

Despite, or perhaps because of, the many failures, a new model of management development is emerging. Those using the new paradigm link the process closely to strategy formation (Sullivan, 1993) and are adamant that "the only legitimate reason to put in place an executive development program is that it

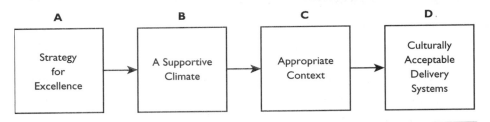

FIGURE 12.1 A MODEL FOR MANAGEMENT DEVELOPMENT

A	B	C	D
Strategy for Excellence	A Supportive Climate	Appropriate Context	Culturally Acceptable Delivery Systems

is integral to the business strategy. Any other reason will result, at best, in a series of interesting training programs tangentially related to the business or, at worst, in a variety of expensive activities conveying irrelevant or contradictory messages" (McCall, 1992, p. 25).

The focus of management development is not on the individual but toward the cultivation of collective managerial talents, capabilities, and perspectives that will allow the organization, as a whole, to cope with the future by creating innovative products and services (Bolt, 1993; Hamel, 1998).

Based on the general concepts outlined in Chapter 2, the practical application of this ideal requires an in-depth understanding of two factors: the characteristics of excellent companies and the nature of managerial work. Without a firm grounding in both these concepts and a commitment to re-engineer current processes, an organization is unlikely to have appropriate strategies in place to support effective management development (Vogl, 1993).

As discussed in Chapter 4, training must fit into the organization's culture, and conscious cultural formation begins with strategy (Geroy & Wright, 1994) in that employees use exhibited corporate values in making career-oriented decisions (Isaac, Cahoon, & Zenbe, 1994). A major purpose of management development activity, then, is to build commitment to strategic intent (McClelland, 1994) so that strategy-formation activities and management development processes support one another as both aim to create excellence (see Figure 12.1).

Managers who embark on an excellence-development strategy are more likely to create successful management development programs, as they know which behavioural characteristics they want to instill in employees. In these organizations, there often is an intentional effort to expose employees to multiple functions within the enterprise. The success or failure of a management development program seems to be closely tied to the presence of a sustainable business strategy capable of coping with change (Bencivonga, 1997).

Although difficult to achieve, this picture of a strategically driven company is not hard to describe. Eight management principles combine to foster the excellence concept.

1. Leadership is seen as a renewable resource that is not easily copied or stolen.

2. Managers are given autonomy appropriate to their expertise and position.

3. The act, or the art, of management is viewed as a process of interpretation, not as a process of control.

4. Involvement, or ownership, is seen as crucial.

5. Market orientation is strong, with a focus on customer care and satisfaction.

6. The concept of human capital formation is understood and practised.

7. Controlled chaos is accepted, fostering innovation and change.

8. Integrity or sound business ethics are part of a cultural orientation that leads to respect in the community and enhanced customer relations.*

Indeed, if a corporation is to thrive in the long term, management must ensure it contributes to the quality of community life (Masloche & Leiter, 1997). These eight factors fit into the model as shown in Figure 12.2.

After devising strategies aimed at creating excellence, management development structures are put in place to socialize employees into the orga-

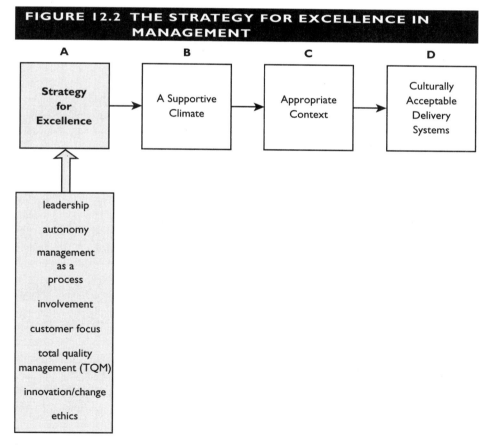

FIGURE 12.2 THE STRATEGY FOR EXCELLENCE IN MANAGEMENT

A	B	C	D
Strategy for Excellence	A Supportive Climate	Appropriate Context	Culturally Acceptable Delivery Systems

leadership

autonomy

management as a process

involvement

customer focus

total quality management (TQM)

innovation/change

ethics

*Holt's 1989 concepts are supported by a variety of sources including: McCall, 1992; McCallum, 1993; Vicere, 1992; Fargular, 1990–91; Crosby, 1993; Wright and Kusmanadji, 1994.

nization and its culture. The application of these structures—training, job rotation, coaching, and so on—will be discussed in detail later in this chapter, but the key issue here is that they be viewed as symbols of culture in which the rites and rituals of the management role are enacted through design, content, and process (Preston, 1993). Any management development program must be designed with the knowledge that the format will send a message to managers and employees alike. For example, if the programs are used as rewards for those who do not disturb the status quo, all innovation is likely to cease, as managers will find their greatest rewards in the application of established systems and procedures (Stewart & Fondas, 1992).

As suggested previously by Lees (1992), the rationale for conducting development activities can be flawed, creating management rites and rituals that are self-serving and counterproductive, especially when practised within a poorly functioning or ineffective culture. More current research supports Lees's work (Heraty & Morley, 1998). Truly effective management development is unlikely to be practised in poorly managed organizations, especially those that are not strategy-driven. To reiterate, of all the HRD functions, management development is perhaps the most misunderstood and poorly implemented. For an example of how management development is strategically based, see the Training Today 1 box.

THE CLIMATE FOR MANAGEMENT DEVELOPMENT

The concept of linking management development to strategy within the context of creating a well-managed company has a practical purpose: management development will flourish only if the climate or culture is supportive (see Figure 12.3). Management development activity must be institutionalized into the cultural fabric of the organization; it is a particularly vulnerable activity, because programs can be costly and often are directed toward those whose status and salary may make them think they need no more training (Sherwood, 1992). As well, the development of people is rarely given first priority. It is "difficult to make a good case that development should be a first priority. With no shot at top priority, development must still compete with other compelling issues to make the priority list" (McCall, 1992). The key activities that create an organization's supportive structure fit into that part of the management development model illustrated in Figure 12.3.

Although nonparticipants should not be completely left out, the results of participating should lead to obvious rewards. This approach takes time, as the development program needs to build a track record or history. Remember that it takes 10 to 20 years to develop general managerial talent (Kotter, 1988) and that length of tenure is directly related to high performance. Participation in development activity must be given sufficient long-term encouragement so that the program comes to be regarded as an essential part of both executive

The goal of most corporate training and executive education programs these days is to help employees in the rest of the company deal with issues such as downsizing, re-engineering, and increased competition in the marketplace. But at Bell Canada, it seems that the shoe is on the other foot.

When Bell took a good look at its Institute for Professional Development, it didn't like what it found: An organization that was fat, unaccountable, and unable to prepare employees for the new world of telecommunications competition.

Now Bell is drastically cutting the Institute's budget, shifting its training and development programs to outside providers, remaking its instructors and course designers into counsellors and consultants, and looking to cut the staff of 400 to a slim 60 people.

The Bell Institute for Professional Development was formed in 1990 by the amalgamation of training efforts in 19 different areas, which included 2000 different courses, from the highly technical to those aimed at upper management. Most were offered inside the Institute, which was made up of 400 training designers as well as deliverers or instructors and administrative staff.

But by the early 1990s, the company, like many others, was questioning the cost and effectiveness of such massive in-house training efforts, especially as it geared up for com-petition. The internal departments that paid to use the Institute felt there was little rationale for sending particular employees on courses (they were alternatively considered a reward and a punishment) and it was difficult to measure their benefit in the long run.

Now there is a desire to teach employees how to learn as well as give them specific skills or philosophies. Almost all training will be done outside Bell at myriad specialized training institutes, with the Institute acting as consultant to the 47 000 employees. Much of the emphasis will be on executive development and the reinvigoration of the management team.

One-on-one sessions will ensure executives have the right skills for the future as well as leadership programs, coaching, and opportunities to investigate the future of telecommunications technology.

The only courses that Bell will still offer internally are competitive business programs, which are considered highly sensitive and strategic. The rest of the staff of the Institute will become consultants offering information on how training needs can be best met, either in traditional classroom settings, university courses, through reading or video presentations.

Source: Excerpted from Gooderham, M. (1996, August 20). Private, public utilities give new life to learning. *The Globe and Mail*, p. C3.

career plans and the firm's strategic intent (Vicere & Graham, 1990; Trainor, 1996b).

A common example of failure to institutionalize management development is the use of an overseas assignment. In many organizations, the promise of foreign service is not realized, since the managers are forgotten while they are abroad and no suitable position is made available upon their return (Guzzo, 1996). What could be a sought-after opportunity for career enhancement can also be regarded as a dead end. Senior managers should be aware that every posting, every transfer sends a message to employees. If a technique like job rotation (or any other method) is to be used in a developmental sense, it must be a planned activity that fits into an organization-wide, learning-from-experience paradigm.

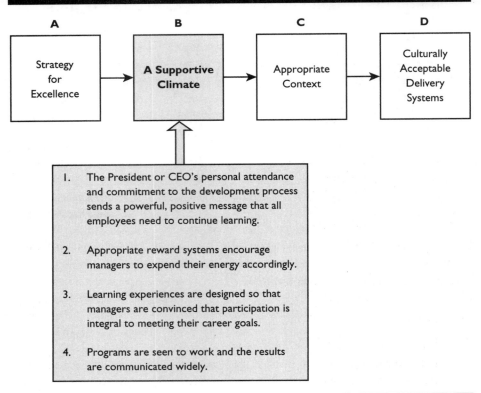

FIGURE 12.3 CREATING A SUPPORTIVE CLIMATE FOR MANAGEMENT DEVELOPMENT

A — Strategy for Excellence

B — A Supportive Climate

C — Appropriate Context

D — Culturally Acceptable Delivery Systems

1. The President or CEO's personal attendance and commitment to the development process sends a powerful, positive message that all employees need to continue learning.

2. Appropriate reward systems encourage managers to expend their energy accordingly.

3. Learning experiences are designed so that managers are convinced that participation is integral to meeting their career goals.

4. Programs are seen to work and the results are communicated widely.

THE NATURE OF MANAGEMENT WORK

Having described the environment in which management development programs must operate, let's look now at the work managers do; how managers are developed is closely linked to the importance placed on the various aspects of the manager's role. Stewart's (1984) address to the World Congress on Management Development contained a model of management work that, with some modification, has continued to prove useful for many years, in a wide variety of situations. Her concept is based on the analogy that a job is a flexible space surrounded by constraints, enclosing basic, often routine job demands or functions (the core) and an area of choice, or discretion (see Figure 12.4).

Jobs are dynamic, so the lines are wavy, representing change. Managers have choices within the job parameter to do or not do some tasks, but no two managers would make identical choices. The choices any individual makes may emphasize some aspects of the job at the risk of neglecting others, since there are competing demands from:

- *peers:* consulting, planning, and so on

FIGURE 12.4 THE MANAGER'S JOB

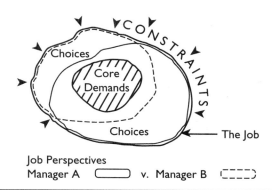

Job Perspectives
Manager A ⊂⊃ v. Manager B ⊏╌╌╌⊐

- *the boss:* accepting responsibility for long-term objectives
- *subordinates:* coaching, communicating, providing feedback, organizing, and so on
- *the system:* paperwork, routine obligations
- *external forces:* accepting or avoiding innovation, change, fear, insecurity in self or in others
- *new technology:* re-engineering, change, employee reactions

At the core of this concept are basic, sometimes routine, job demands or tasks originating from the need to maintain day-to-day activity. Again, these arise from interactions with peers (for assistance or advice), the boss (for effective short-term performance), subordinates (providing guidance, training, and so on), the system (conforming with work regulations), external forces (customers, suppliers, the public), and self (meeting personal standards). Depending on the situation, these core activities can be the most visible aspect of the manager's role (Broadwell, 1993).

This whole invariably is surrounded by constraints (see Figure 12.4). As might be expected, constraints are factors in the internal and external environments that influence the job holder:

- financial limitations
- company policies
- economic and market conditions
- government legislation
- technological advances and limitations
- demographic considerations
- union activities
- free-trade opportunities and threats

These largely uncontrollable issues form parameters within which every manager must work. They construct the limitations or emerging opportunities that shape long-term organizational strategy.

It has been predicted that, to survive, most private-sector organizations will need to be re-engineered, in whole or in part, during the next decade, reducing the middle-management workforce by approximately 75 percent. The managerial responsibilities of those who remain will change dramatically, so that two new types of managers—process managers and employee coaches—will emerge. Process managers will oversee a re-engineered process from beginning to end. For example, a process manager might be responsible for managing order fulfillment or product development. Employee coaches will be responsible for supporting and nurturing employees (Hammer & Champy, 1993; Hogarty, 1993; Shandler, 1996; Hammer, 1998).

Even if this drastic scenario is not realized, it is certain that the era of the specialist manager is ending. A new generation of generalists will need to be trained to understand not only finance, accounting, or marketing, but economic trends, political issues, and human resources (Zeidenberg, 1993; Spitzer, 1995; Ulrich, 1997).

Stewart's (1984) model fits well with the management (core) versus leadership (discretionary) dichotomy. At the core, individuals are taught how to operate within systems that are more or less established. This activity is defined as management. The discretionary portion of the model describes leadership in that a leader takes the organization in directions or into performance parameters never before attempted. Obviously, there is some overlap, but for our purposes the two functions will be treated separately.

As before, our model takes into account the nature of management work. A management development program should encompass both core and discretionary elements (see Figure 12.5).

THE MANAGEMENT DEVELOPMENT PROCESS

CHOOSING A METHOD FOR MANAGEMENT DEVELOPMENT

As illustrated previously, when creating a method for management development, three major factors must be considered: (1) the firm's long-term strategies as they relate to the development of the work environment or culture, (2) the role of the manager within that culture, (3) and the changing external environment (constraints and opportunities) that inevitably will transform both the organization and the nature of managerial work. The only alternative is to maintain the status quo and to continue offering traditional, course-based, individually oriented learning experiences.

Revolution is underway, however, in the way North American companies use education to improve managerial performance. The shift was caused, in

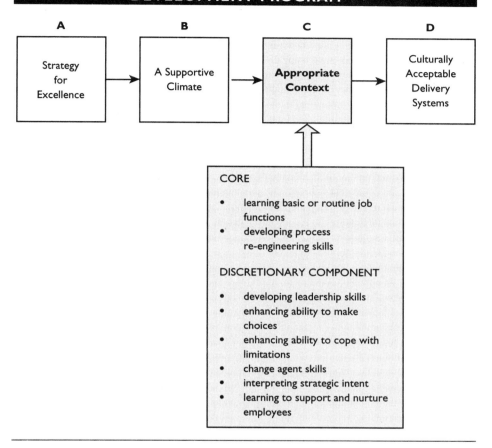

FIGURE 12.5 THE CONTEXT OF A MANAGEMENT DEVELOPMENT PROGRAM

A
Strategy for Excellence

B
A Supportive Climate

C
Appropriate Context

D
Culturally Acceptable Delivery Systems

CORE

- learning basic or routine job functions
- developing process re-engineering skills

DISCRETIONARY COMPONENT

- developing leadership skills
- enhancing ability to make choices
- enhancing ability to cope with limitations
- change agent skills
- interpreting strategic intent
- learning to support and nurture employees

part, by the recent increase in the number of MBAs, many of whom proved to be poor managers despite their impressive credentials (Pfeffer & Sutton, 1999). Senior managers are now looking for programs that give their managers the skills to be effective in the emerging nonhierarchical corporate structure, hence the focus on creating a supportive climate, carefully defining what managers do, and developing "imagination-intensive industries" (Hamel, 1998).

Within this context, Stewart's (1984) analogy has proven useful because two major forces are at work. The first is the need to teach the specific skills required by each level of management (the core); the second is the much broader imperative of cultivating strategic leadership and innovative skills (discretionary activity).

In essence, management development must contribute to business success and add value to the organization. The questions that must be asked include the following:

1. Are management development strategies, technologies, and resources aligned with company goals?

2. Is a clear, fact-based understanding of business needs driving the organization's management development strategy?

3. Is the management development program providing excellent service to the participants at a competitive cost (Shoulder, 1996)?

The answers to these questions will determine in large measure whether the program will be successful.

THE CORE: DEVELOPING MANAGERS

Since all management jobs contain routine functions that must be mastered (see Figure 12.5), efficient learning processes need to be in place within the organization. The subject matter can range from computer-systems manipulation to more sophisticated concepts like those covered in General Electric's business management course. Here, basic concepts such as business strategy, economics, finance, and marketing are taught to potential general managers. The bulk of the core, however, is usually transmitted through localized in-house training focusing on the specific skills required by each level of management. For example, at the supervisory level, the program might cover basic personnel and company procedures, along with interpersonal problem solving (Digman, 1986; Noel & Charon, 1992). Participants learn the company way. There is little need for theory-based course work that cannot be applied to day-to-day management. The manager's task is to develop sufficient skill to meet minimum performance levels.

Traditionally, most of the literature and theory concerned with training has focused on the needs and experiences of large-company managers. Yet it is often managers in smaller firms who require the most training. The core skills are most important in this context; managers in many smaller businesses are learning that rejuvenating their organizations hinges on the application of basic principles of good business practice—always with the understanding that there are no panaceas (Trainor, 1996c). Stewart's (1984) model (see Figure 12.4), then, can be adapted to both large and smaller businesses, although the smaller firm may, of necessity, devise a more informal management development system.

core skills identifiable, tangible, and basic managerial competencies required by all levels of management

Core skills often are identifiable, tangible competencies. The how-to aspect of acquiring these basic competencies begins with a well-developed orientation program and continues throughout the manager's career as part of the performance-review process. Although the effectiveness of current appraisal systems has been questioned, one-on-one reviews still play an important role in the mentoring procedure that provides a platform for discussion of achievements.

The advent of 360-degree feedback systems of appraisal, however, has created new opportunities for management development. Using this multi-source feedback approach, an individual receives comment or ratings from a variety of sources, for example, supervisors, colleagues, customers, and subordinates. Because each of these stakeholders views the individual from a different perspective, provided the feedback isn't seen as a threat, the potential to identify developmental needs is enormous (Brillinger, 1996).

Tornow and M. London and Associates (1998) have refined this process to create a culture of continual learning that links individual goals to company strategy. Using their system, 360-degree feedback gives insights (for example) into whether or not individuals seek to take advantage of new challenges, or whether they might be good managers but poor learners. Using this broader view, feedback items on appraisal surveys are linked to the organization's long-term, strategic needs, not the specific, short-term requirements of a manager's day-to-day work.

Aside from formal orientation packages, the learning methods employed in the core may vary. In-house courses in larger firms, outside courses, MBA programs, self-directed learning, CD-ROMs, and even board games have been tried (Gunsch, 1993; Lewis, 1996; Filipczak, 1997).

One study on the percentage of companies that use various methods of management training and development found that when used as part an overall management training and development program, 93 percent use on-the-job training, 89 percent use formal training and education programs, 80 percent use special projects or task forces, 57 percent use mentoring, 40 percent use job rotation, and 32 percent use career planning. In more formal management training and education approaches, 90 percent use external short-course programs, 75 percent use company-specific programs, 31 percent use university residential programs, and 25 percent use executive MBA programs for at least some of their managers (Saari, Johnson, McLaughlin, & Zimmerle, 1988).

One review of research in the area of the effectiveness of managerial training methods concluded that "different methods of managerial training are on the average moderately effective in improving learning and job performance" (Burke & Day, 1986, p. 243). Among the various methods, behavioural modelling, sensitivity training, lecture, lecture with discussion, role playing or practice, and leader match (awareness of one's leadership style) methods were found to be effective (Burke & Day, 1986).

A key method, however, and one that bridges the core and discretionary concepts, is coaching (see Chapter 7). Coaching has two distinct functions: (1) to improve performance and skill level and (2) to establishing relationships that allow the coach to enhance the trainee's psychological development and ability to accept assignments of ever-increasing complexity and difficulty (Popper & Lipshitz, 1992; Elliott, 1993). At senior levels, executive development counselling or coaching by an outsider is an alternative with a high success rate, because the consultant can assess needs objectively and provide practical developmental support and training techniques (Commanducci, 1998b). This process provides personal guidance that would be difficult to find through any other method. One senior executive, for example, thought he was being flattered by his staff and not receiving honest feedback. By using an executive coach, he was able to get the brutally honest advice he needed. Using this new knowledge, the executive successfully modified his firm's strategic plan (Bentley, 1997a). Learning can come in many forms, ranging from acquiring essential knowledge, to learning how to control anger (Bentley, 1997b).

Coaching is ineffective if the organizational culture does not allow the intense person-to-person interaction necessary to devise individual learning projects that do not threaten the trainee. We previously emphasized the type of climate necessary to support development.

When developing basic managerial skills (the core), the key issue is ensuring direct transfer from the learning venue to the work venue. Passive learning is unlikely to be sufficient. Whatever method is used, participants must engage in activities that require decision making and actually deal with the consequences of their decisions. If the training does not provide for direct, hands-on experience (e.g., a coaching assignment), then the timeframe between learning and application must be kept to a minimum (Hoberman & Mailick, 1992; Trainor, 1996c).

THE DISCRETIONARY FACTOR: DEVELOPING LEADERS

discretionary skills
leadership and change management competencies

Excellent companies are built primarily on innovation and change. This requires **discretionary skills** and the development of strategic leadership. Leadership development takes place within the context of strategically linked, change-management activity (Stewart, 1997). Without an organization-wide commitment to continual improvement, leadership training is unlikely to flourish—if it exists at all (Colledge & March, 1993; Finigin & Walsh, 1998).

Within this context, Shandler (1996) has adapted Bennis's (1990) well-known differentiation checklist that illustrates the differences between management and leadership roles:

1. A manager administers, a leader innovates.
2. A manager maintains, but a leader develops.
3. A manger's focus is on structure and systems; a leader is preoccupied with people.
4. A manager relies on controlling, but the leader develops trust.
5. A manager works in the short-term; a leader has a long-term view.
6. A manger accepts what is; a leader is an individualist.
7. A manager does the job right, but a leader does the right job.

While these phrases may seem trite, they explain the essential differences between managers and leaders. Of course, no organization would want to hire someone who was either a total manager or a total leader—there must be some overlap (i.e., managers must have some leadership skills and leaders need to know how to manage). These essential differences, however, need to be understood before a leadership development program can be designed.

Within the appropriate setting, much can be accomplished. Firms that enhance leadership potential invariably "focus on a broad range of activities (including training), but emphasize on-the-job training as the primary vehicle for development" (McCall, 1992). This learning-from-experience approach is based on action-learning theories, suggesting that exposure to rich development opportunities provides the optimum conditions for executive development. Learning by doing—through wilderness survival trips, interactive team training, even exposure to humanities courses dealing with values central to leadership—is all part of the action design. Business simulations, however, seem to have become more popular, especially in Europe. Not only are they being used to evaluate skills, but also recent developments in computing technology are allowing for a more sophisticated approach (Fripp, 1997; Commanducci, 1998a; Fowler, 1998).

Job rotation, however, is still the main activity that links education and training with reforms in the workplace (Raskas & Hambrick, 1992; Rothwell, 1992). Exposure to many functions within the firm as part of an ongoing career-development program broadens individuals, providing them with multiple perspectives and possibly even multiple areas of expertise. Indeed, the practice of line managers temporarily taking staff jobs has met with some success (Zemke, 1987). A variety of cross-job and project-based experiences can be devised to create a pool of leadership talent capable of responding to emergencies and to rapidly changing business environments while making the constant incremental changes necessary for corporate survival (McCall, 1992; Miller, 1993).

Some organizations benefit from job rotation more than others. In highly technical environments, for example, it may be difficult for some employees to be productive in areas for which they are untrained. "The professional rigors of the field [may be] just too great" (Raskas & Hambrick, 1992, p. 13). Here, short-term assignments and planned observations may prove useful, so that nontechnical managers gain familiarity with technical processes without actually managing the unit or division (Rothwell, 1992).

A practical management development process, however, revolves around coaching. As detailed in Chapter 7, the effective coach works one-on-one with managers at all levels to increase their abilities to lead. Presuming that the organization is committed to excellence, that the climate is conducive to learning, and that the strategic intent of the management development program is known to both coach and participant, they work together to (1) identify the changes required in particular areas, (2) provide the perspective necessary to be effective, and (3) develop a plan to try out new behaviours (McDermatt, 1996).

Working from a confidential individual-development needs analysis provides managers with opportunities to learn and to grow through intelligent risk taking and identifies how they should divide their careers between expe-

job rotation
exposure to many functions within the firm as part of an ongoing career-development program

riences within their own networks (where they might have the most visible impact) and other assignments (that help them rise above their functional experience and training). The nature and the scope of acceptable projects and assignments are unlimited (even including temporary residence at an important customer's work site), but they must be chosen carefully—they should be neither too easy nor too difficult (Elliot, 1993; Gilley & Boughtom, 1996).

Job assignments must be challenging and must be chosen with considerable input from the participants. The goal is to create a pool of excellence, made up of individuals that can be selected for assignments as organizational needs arise (Hammer, 1997).

Goals should be specific and well understood. Furthermore, participants need to be protected from backlash, especially if they try to change the corporate culture. Criticism should be kept to a minimum, but feedback must be intensive. Finally, more formal program assessment and subsequent refinements should occur at fixed intervals (Harris & Field, 1992; Gilley & Boughtom, 1996). The key is to create a greater stake in the organization through the expansion of roles, authorities, and responsibilities by recognizing that empowering people produces excellence in a wide variety of situations (Gilbert & Whiting, 1993; Bridges, 1998).

Two final elements arising from the coaching process are the sometimes elusive assumption that management development is an ongoing process, not a program, and the vital concept of self-development (Smith, 1991). The idea that personal and professional learning is a lifelong activity has permeated our society. Coaching as a developmental method is no exception. Vicere (1992) suggests that leadership enhancement is a cyclical process in which an organization is engaged in "continuous" effort to identify, develop, and integrate a team of strategic leaders. Whittaker (1993) describes coaching as a "continual" transfer of skills, while Yager (1993) and Gaines (1993) also stress the need for "continuous" encouragement. Finally, Wolff (1993) indicates that coaching should become a regular part of a manager's routine. As strategy formation is an ongoing, dynamic phenomenon (Graham, 1996), and as coaching is linked to strategy, similarly, management development must remain flexible and sensitive to both internal and external environmental change.

Just as a coach in sports cannot play the game, in business the coach cannot personally manage every subordinate's career development. Indeed, an increasing number of organizations are creating systems that encourage employees to enhance both skills and leadership capabilities through self-development (Lewis, 1996). As self-development is described fully in Chapter 6, the topic will not be treated in detail here. Note, however, that this model of personal development is not confined to professional life, but includes social and recreational activities. This holistic approach becomes a conscious model for planned achievement (Alder, 1992).

At this point, a final look at our model (see Figure 12.6) is appropriate. The methods (delivery systems) we choose must fit into the organization's culture, encourage innovation (Simon, 1996), and be able to transfer or develop

FIGURE 12.6 THE DELIVERY OF A MANAGEMENT DEVELOPMENT PROGRAM

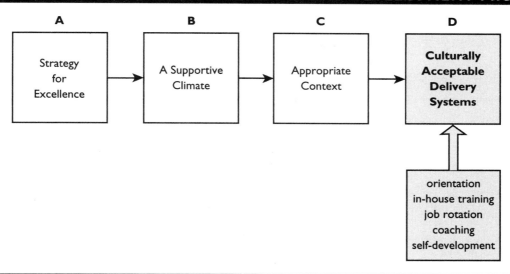

appropriate skills, knowledge, and attitudes directly related to the core and to the discretionary parts of the manager's job (Figure 12.5). This system is not likely to work well unless the organization's climate is supportive (Figure 12.3), but a supportive climate will not necessarily grow spontaneously. A well-designed strategy for excellence is the best starting point (Figure 12.2). Working backward through the model (Figure 12.1), therefore, illustrates how each function (strategy through delivery) acts as a foundation that supports the next step.

THE TRAINER'S ROLE IN MANAGEMENT DEVELOPMENT

Having outlined a two-pronged (skills versus leadership) approach to management development that includes very few traditional, course-based learning experiences, we now examine the role of the trainer. Again, tied to the previous assertion that excellent companies are characterized by their capacity to foster innovation and to manage change, the trainer's emerging role is that of change agent and internal consultant. As early as 1979, Lippitt and Nadler forecast three roles for trainers: (1) as learning specialists and instructors, (2) as program administrators, and (3) as contributors to organizational problem solving. Their predictions have been accurate, especially the suggestions concerning how trainers might work as internal consultants:

* by providing expert advice to management, usually about the appropriateness and value of training options
* by advising management as to what environmental changes are necessary to support and to maintain training

- by providing a range or a continuum of alternatives
- by taking part in a wide variety of problem-solving processes

In addition, the following must be added:

- by developing value by increasing the intellectual assets of the organization (Hope & Hope, 1998).

As the focus of organizational development (OD) is shifting increasingly toward measuring productivity and performance and creating revenue, to these roles can be added the need for an increased emphasis on the OD model as follows: (1) problem identification, (2) consultation with experts, (3) data gathering and preliminary diagnosis, (4) feedback to stakeholders, (5) joint diagnosis, (6) action, (7) follow-up evaluation and feedback (Svantet, O'Connell, Baumgardner, 1992).

This approach should mesh with current research in adult development that (1) amalgamates personal and institutional needs into a framework that combines modes of learning into a process of irreversible qualitative change using planned stages, leading toward new personal and professional perspectives; (2) develops a global outlook that broadens these life perspectives; (3) accounts for organizational environment or culture, stressing that a supportive climate is a critical factor that allows a manager to continue along a developmental path (Morris, 1992); and (4) recognizes that the best leaders are the ones who teach, either by coaching or by deliberately embodying personal values and aggressively encouraging employees to use these values in their own decision making (Ticky, 1998).

In specific terms, at the corporate level, the trainer focuses on the development of mechanisms that allow for talent to be matched with opportunity (e.g., succession planning, executive review committees, appraisal systems), as well as policies and procedures concerning special assignments, responsibility enhancement, staff assignments, job rotation, and reward systems (McCall, 1992). To this high-level developmental activity is added an individual thrust that includes many things: assessing leadership potential; assessing strengths and weaknesses; assessing previous experience (McCall, 1992); assisting managers to review their jobs and their potential choices; discussing (with both superior and subordinate) what learning experiences would help an individual to become more innovative; designing career paths; advising on an appropriate mix of learning experiences; managing the learning process to integrate learning with work; creating learning communities and learning groups, both face-to-face and virtual (Bank, 1997); developing peer learning modules; consulting with both superiors and subordinates on the self-directed learning process; advising on ISO quality standards (Scicchitano, 1997); identifying and cataloguing sources of assistance, both internal and external; identifying areas where assistance would be accepted and valued; relating learning experiences to individual learning styles and suggesting appropriate changes in direction; and helping to create appropriate networking systems (Knight, 1997).

This list must be augmented by carefully targeted training that includes coaching potential coaches, evaluating the training, and creating ethical standards (Korton, 1997).

Finally, evaluation deserves special mention because few companies do it (Saari et al., 1988). At the very least, patterns should be noted (both successes and problems) and refinement made in any of the critical variables, such as, who is to conduct management development? How? At what point in their careers? Who should coach? Only if the company has the capacity for systematic reflection and reassessment can management development programs achieve their full potential (Raskas & Hambrick, 1992, p. 16).

The challenge for trainers, then, is to respond to changing economic and social climates by creating customized, strategically linked, needs-driven processes designed to meet both individual and organizational goals. They will have to "understand fully the competencies required in the global business environment and the most effective methods for developing these competencies," designing learning experiences, both informal and formal, in "a more conscious and reflective way." The ideal would be to form a "learning partnership" in which all the stakeholders—top management, managers, professionals, employees, customers, suppliers—share responsibility for defining the need and then for designing and implementing the best possible management development experiences (Mann & Staudenmier, 1991).

SUMMARY

Management development is a process stemming from a strategic plan that creates a supportive climate or environment. Only within this context can appropriate content be designed and delivery systems developed. The strategic-planning and supportive-climate concepts are more likely to be in place when management fosters the excellence concept by creating an organization in which leadership is regarded as a renewable resource and managers are given autonomy and encouraged to view their craft as a process of interpretation, while fostering innovation and change. Within this type of environment, trainers can use Stewart's (1984) model of management work to design programs that develop core skills and the ability to make decisions within the context of constraints and choices. This discretionary portion of the job presents problems for the trainer, as no two managers will react exactly the same way when faced with a complex business situation, so management development tends to revolve around coaching, self-development, and networking. More traditional techniques, like course work, do not have the flexibility to deal with highly individualized work situations.

The trainer's role in this process is to work as an internal consultant, solving organizational, individual, and ethical problems through a wide variety of HRD initiatives. Personal and institutional needs are combined into a framework that leads, through planned stages, toward a shared image of excellence.

KEY TERMS

core skills   308

discretionary skills   310

job rotation   311

management development   298

management education   298

management training   298

EXERCISES

1. In a recent article called "The smart-talk trap," Jeffrey Pfeffer and Robert Sutton (1999) described a phenomenon in organizations that they call the "knowing-doing gap." According to the authors, many managers are knowledgable and very good at talking but not very good at doing or action. In other words, talk substitutes for action. An especially dangerous form of talk is "smart talk" where the speaker is particularly good at sounding confident, articulate, and eloquent. Unfortunately, smart talk tends to focus on the negative and is often unnecessarily complicated. As a result, it tends to result in inaction or what the authors call the "smart-talk trap." Problems are discussed and plans for action might be formulated, but in the end nothing is done. This can have serious negative consequences for organizations. The authors suggest that one of the main reasons for the knowing-doing gap and the smart-talk trap is that managers have been trained to talk.

   i.   What do you think about the knowing-doing gap and the smart-talk trap? Do you think that this is a serious problem in organizations?

   ii. The authors argue that one of the reasons for the existence of the knowing-doing gap and the smart-talk trap is because of the training that managers receive. Do you agree with this assertion? How can management training result in so much knowing and talking and so little doing?

   iii. Discuss the knowing-doing gap and the smart-talk trap with somebody you know in a managerial position. Find out what they have to say about the prevalence of it in their organization, why it might or might not be a problem, and what can be done to avoid it.

   iv. What advice would you give organizations about how to develop managers in order to avoid the knowing-doing gap and the smart-talk trap?

2. To find out more about management development, contact a human resource professional and ask about management development in their organization. To guide your discussion, consider the following issues:

i. Describe the organization's business strategy and the role it plays in management development. What is the organization's strategy for excellence and is it linked to management development?

ii. Describe the climate of the organization in terms of management development. How supportive is the climate of management development and what does the organization do to provide support?

iii. Describe the context of management development with respect to the core and discretionary activities. What is the content or focus of management development programs?

iv. Describe the delivery systems or methods of management development. What methods are used, why, and how effective are they?

v. What is the role of the trainer in management development?

vi. How effective is management development for improving managerial and organizational effectiveness?

In addition, contact several managers who work in different organizations and ask them questions about their own management development along the following lines:

a) Describe the extent to which they have been involved in management development programs in their organization. How often and to what extent have they participated in management development?

b) To what extent is management development linked to their organization's strategies?

c) How supportive is the organization's climate for their management development and how does the organization support their development?

d) What has been the content or focus of their management development programs in terms of the core and discretionary activities?

e) What delivery systems or methods have been used as part of their management development and how effective have they been?

f) Has their participation in management development activities improved their managerial effectiveness? Why or why not?

Summarize your results in a report in which you discuss the extent and nature of management development in organizations; the use of the management development model presented in the text; and the effectiveness of management development in terms of managerial and organizational effectiveness.

CASE: MIND GAMES

"We hire about six new managers a year into this outfit," stormed Mr. Big. "They don't seem to stay very long and they certainly don't show as much dedication to the job as I'd expect in this competitive world! I want you," said Mr. Big, nodding toward the vice president of human resources, "to develop some sort of mind-bending orientation that really puts them through the wringer. When they finish, they'll know they work for a company that means business and expects total dedication!"

"The old man certainly is on the warpath over this one," thought the vice president. "I'd better come up with something good!"

Later that evening, the vice president began to think about what he should do. Here is his preliminary program.

1. We should pay more attention to our recruiting process, perhaps lengthening it to include two or three interviews and a full battery of tests—we now know what we want (dedication and longevity of tenure), so why not seek these sorts of people?

2. Let's turn to the military for a model here. We'll break down their personalities and substitute our own. We'll give them lots and lots of routine work to begin with, more than any one person can be expected to handle. They'll have no social life, no outside contacts. To survive they'll have to lean on each other (other newly hired young managers)—that will form a team spirit. They'll all be pushed to the limit of endurance.

3. Then just before they crack (we'll have to be careful here), we'll back off (their egos will be in our hands by then)—we'll send them to be trained in one of the firm's branch offices, to learn the business from the bottom up. Remember that the recruit has been socialized to think the company way— if we supervise closely, we should be able to solidify our values. As well, we'll ensure that they all start from roughly the same career stage, so they'll begin to think of themselves as the "class" or the "intake" of the year 200X; that should start them networking.

4. We (this firm) have to become more results oriented. Any reward our new managers receive should be based on results. This practice should continue throughout their careers.

5. The company should continually reinforce those values that enhance corporate success (e.g., hard work, dedication to the firm, the drive for profit above self-interest). The new recruits must know how they'll be measured, when they'll be measured, and what the penalties are for poor performance. There can be no surprises. Everything must be laid out in advance.

6. The good ones will get publicity, both internally and, when we can, in the press. Everybody should be told about successes, so our winners can act as role models for the rest. To be ignored will show our displeasure! In addition, we'll attach these new people to some of our older managers as assistants. Not as assistant managers—they might get the idea they're good—but some time as an assistant will cement the behaviour, values, attitudes, and beliefs we want into their psyche. Then they'll be ours in both thought and deed!

"That should please the old man," he thought, "I'll get this typed up in the morning as a draft proposal; that way the final report will look like it comes from the old man, not me."

QUESTIONS

1. Do you feel that employers have the right to develop career plans like this one? Support your answer.

2. Is it fair to socialize managers to suit the company's purposes. Why or why not? How far should this intense character destruction and build up (in the firm's image) be allowed to go?

3. Would you be willing to go through the vice president's six steps, even if the rewards were substantial? Discuss.

4. Discuss the advantages and the disadvantages of the vice president's career-management program.

5. Is this an ethical way to train employees?

REFERENCES

Alder, H. (1992). A model for personnel success. *Management Decision 30* (3), 23–25.

Bank, D. (1997, June 16). All together. *The Wall Street Journal,* p. R26.

Bencivonga, D. (1997, June). Employees and workers come to terms. *HR Magazine,* pp. 91–97.

Bennis, W. (1990). Leadership in the twenty-first century. *Training* (May), 16–24.

Bentley, T. (1997a). Executive coaches say what others can't. *Canadian HR Reporter* (November 3), p. 15.

———. (1997b). Coaching puts a shine on rough CEO. *Canadian HR Reporter* (June 3), p. 9.

Bolt, J. (1993). Achieving the CEO's agenda: Education for executives. *Management Review 82* (5), 44–48.

Bridges, W. (1998). *Creating you and co.* Reading, MA: Addison-Wesley Longman.

Brillinger, R. (1996). The many faces of 360-degree feedback. *Canadian HR Reporter* (December 16), 20–21.

Broadwell, M. (1993). How to train experienced supervisors. *Training 30* (5), 61–66.

Brown, T.L. (1995). Leadership is everyone's business. *Apparel Industry Magazine 56* (9), p. 14.

Burke, M.J., & Day, R.R. (1986). A cumulative study of the effectiveness of managerial training. *Journal of Applied Psychology 71,* 232–245.

Chaykowski, R.P. (1997). *Fostering human resources in the "new" economy: Challenges to the way ahead.* Kingston: IRC Press.

Colledge, M., & March, M. (1993). Quality management: Development of a framework for a statistical agency. *Journal of Business & Economic Statistics 11* (2), 157–165.

Commanducci, M. (1998a). Training can be fun. *Canadian HR Reporter* (May 4), 15–16.

———. (1998b). Executives turn to personal coaches in growing numbers. *Canadian HR Reporter* (May 4), 1–2.

Crosby, P. (1993). Quality leadership. *Executive Excellence 10* (5), 3–4.

Digman, L. (1986). How well-managed organizations develop their executives. In Rynes, S., & Milkovich, G. (Eds.). *Current Issues in Human Resources Management* (pp. 248–257). Plano, CA: Business Publications Inc.

Elliot, K. (1993). Managerial competencies. *Training and Development 11* (11), 14–15.

Farquhar, C. (1990–91). Total quality management: A competitive imperative for the '90s. *Optimum 21* (4), 30–39.

Filipczak, B. (1997). Soft skills on a hard platter. *Training Magazine* (June), 93–94.

Finigin, K., & Walsh, E.K. (1998). Companies need strategy to develop leaders. *Capital District Business Review 24*(43), 7–13.

Fowler, A. (1998). Role rehearsal. *People Management 4* (12), 52–55.

Fripp, J. (1997). A future for business simulations? *Journal of European Industrial Training 21* (4), 138–142.

Fulmer, R.M. (1997, summer). The evolving paradigm of leadership development. *Organizational Dynamics*, 59–72.

Gaines, H. (1993). Ten ways you can help your employees succeed. *Supervising Management 38* (2), 8.

Geroy, G.D., & Wright, P.C. (1994). *Using skills needs assessment in support of economic development strategies*. Bradford: MCB University Press.

Gilbert, N., & Whiting, C. (1993). Empowering professionals. *Management Review 82* (6), 57.

Gilley, J., & Boughtom, N. (1996). *Stop managing, start coaching*. Burr Ridge: Irwin Professional Publishing.

Graham, J. (1996). How to outsmart, outmarket, outsell and outdistance the competition. *Supervision 96* (57), 11–13.

Gunsch, D. (1993). Games augment diversity training. *Personnel Journal 72* (6), 78–83.

Guzzo, R.A. (1996). The expatriate employee. In Cooper, C.L., & Rousseau, R.M. (Eds.), *Trends in organizational behavior* (Vol. 3) (pp. 123–137). Chechester: John Wiley & Sons.

Hamel, G. (1998). [As quoted in] *People Management 4* (10), 16.

Hammer, M. (1997). *Beyond reengineering*. London: Mayor Collins.

Hammer, M., & Champy, J. (1993). *Re-engineering the corporation: A manifesto for business revolution*. New York: Harper Collins.

Harris, S., & Field, H. (1992). Realizing the "potential" of "high-potential" management development programmes. *Journal of Management Development 11* (1), 61–70.

Hoberman, S., & Mailick, S. (1992). *Experiential management development: From learning to practice*. New York: Quorum Books.

Hogarty, D. (1993). The future of middle managers. *Management Review 82* (9), 51–53.

Holt, L. (1989). Project management excellence: The Shell Stanney case. *Construction Management and Economics 7* (3), 217–234.

Hope, J., & Hope, T. (1998). *Competing in the third wave*. Boston: Harvard Business School Press.

Isaac, R.G., Cahoon, A.R., & Zenbe, W.J. (1994). In Jain, H.S., & Wright, P.C. (Eds.), Values in corporations—who is in charge? *Trends and challenges in human resources management* (pp. 251–261). Scarborough, ON: Nelson Canada.

Kanter, R. (1997). *On the frontiers of management.* Boston: Harvard Business School Press.

Korton, D. (1997). A new focus: corporate cost internalization. *Business Ethics* (July/Aug), 16.

Kotter, J. (1988). *The leadership factor.* New York: Free Press.

Lees, S. (1992). Ten faces of management development. *Management Education and Development 23* (2), 80–105.

Lewis, J. (1996). Self-directed learning making inroads. *Canadian HR Reporter* (June 17), 22–23.

Lippitt, G., & Nadler, L. (1979). Emerging roles of the training director. *Training and Development Journal 21* (6), 26–30.

MacLachlan, R. (1998). An imaginative loop from serendipity to capability. *People Management 4* (10), 16.

Mann, R., & Staudenmier, J. (1991). Building transactional partnerships in executive learning through applied research. *Training and Development 45* (7), 37–40.

Masloche, C., & Leiter, M. (1997). *The truth about burnout.* San Francisco: Jossey-Boss.

McCall, M. (1992). Executive development as a business strategy. *Journal of Business Strategy 13* (1), 25–31.

McCallum, J. (1993). The manager's job is still to manage. *Business Quarterly 57* (4), 61–67.

McClelland, S. (1994). Gaining competitive advantage through strategic management development. *Journal of Management Development 13* (5), 4–13.

McClelland, S., Harbaugh, N., & Hammett, S. (1993). Improving individual and group effectiveness. *Journal of Management Development 12* (3), 48–58.

McDermatt, L. (1996). Wanted: chief executive coach. *Training and Development 50* (5), 67–71.

Miller, F. (1993). Management development. *Training and Development 11* (8), 16.

Morris, L. (1992). Research capsules: A focus on development. *Training and Development 46* (11), 25–28.

Noel, J., & Charon, R. (1992). G.E. brings global thinking to light. *Training and Development 46* (7), 28–33.

Pfeffer, J., & Sutton, R.I. (1999, May–June). The smart-talk trap. *Harvard Business Review*, 135–142.

Popper, M., & Lipshitz, R. (1992). Coaching on leadership. *Leadership and Organization Development Journal 13* (7), 15–19.

Preston, D. (1993). Management development structures as symbols of organizational culture. *Personnel Review 22* (1), 18–30.

Raskas, D., & Hambrick, D. (1992). Multifunctional managerial development: A framework for evaluating the options. *Organizational Dynamics 21* (2), 5–17.

Rothwell, W. (1992). Issues and practices in management job notation programs as perceived by HRD professionals. *Performance Improvement Quarterly 5* (1), 49–69.

Saari, L.M., Johnson, T.R., McLaughlin, S.D., & Zimmerle, D.M. (1988). A survey of management training and education practices in U.S. companies. *Personnel Psychology 41*, 731–743.

Scicchitano, P. (1997). Warning: dangerous curve. *Quality Digest* (May), 21.

Shandler, D. (1996). *Reengineering the training function.* Delray Beach, CA: St. Lucie Press.

Sherwood, F. (1992). Institutionalizing executive development and attendant problems. *Public Productivity and Management Review 15* (4), 449–461.

Simon, H. (1996). *Hidden champions*. Boston: Harvard Business School Press.

Smith, K. (1991). Measuring your managers' skills. *Folio: The Magazine for Magazine Management 21* (9), 106–107.

Spitzer, D.R. (1995). *Supermotivation*. New York: AMACOM Books.

Stewart, R. (1984). *Management development and implications for managerial choice*. Excerpt from an address to the World Congress on Management Development in London, England, as reported by Cawthray, B. (c. 1988). (Outline 2.14). Marsfield: Marsfield Publications Ltd.

Stewart, R., & Fondas, N. (1992). How managers can think strategically about their jobs. *Journal of Management Development 11* (7), 10–18.

Stewart, T.A. (1997). *Intellectual capital: The new wealth of organizations*. New York: Currency/Doubleday.

Sullivan, P. (1993). Nine best practices. *Executive Excellence 10* (3), 3–4.

Svantet, D., O'Connell, M., & Baumgardner, T. (1992). Applications of Bayesian methods to OD evaluation and decision making. *Human Relations 45* (6), 621–636.

Tannenbaum, S.I., & Yukl, G. (1992). Training and development in work organizations. *Annual Review of Psychology 43*, 399–441.

Ticky, N. (1998). *The leadership engine*. New York: Harper-Business.

Tornow, W.W., & M. London and Associates (1998). *Maximizing the value of 360-degree feedback*. San Francisco: Jossey-Bass.

Trainor, N.L. (1996a). Management training: no magical formulas. *Canadian HR Reporter* (June 3), 9.

———. (1996b). Dialogue: An essential learning tool. *Canadian HR Reporter* (January 15), 7.

———. (1996c). Re-engineering training departments for performance accountability. *Canadian HR Reporter* (December 2), 11.

Ulrich, D. (1997). *Human resource champions: The next agenda for adding value and delivering results*. Boston: Harvard Business School Press.

Vicere, A. (1992). The strategic leadership imperative for executive development. *Human Resource Planning 15* (1), 15–23.

Vicere, A., & Graham, K. (1990). Crafting competitiveness: Toward a new paradigm for executive development." *Human Resource Planning 13* (4), 281–295.

Vogl, A. (1993). The age of re-engineering. *Across the Board 30* (5), 26–33.

West, D. (1997). Management training: why bother? *Accountancy—International Edition* (July), 37.

Wexley, K.N., & Baldwin, T.T. (1986). Management development. *Journal of Management 12*, 277–294.

Whetten, D.A., & Cameron, K.S. (1995). *Developing management skills* (3rd ed.). New York: Harper Collins College Publishers.

Whittaker, B. (1993). Shaping the competitive organization—managing or coaching. *CMA Magazine 67* (3), 5.

Wolff, M. (1993). Become a better coach. *Research-Technology Management 72* (17), 10–11.

Wright, P., & Kusmanadji, K. (1994). The strategic application of TQM principles in human resources management. *Training for Quality 1* (3), 5–14.

Yager, E. (1993). Coaching models. *Executive Excellence 10* (3), 18.

Zeidenberg, J. (1993). The boss goes back to school. *Canadian Business 66* (4), 51–53.

Zemke, R. (1987). Bill Yeomans: Making training pay at J.C. Penney. *Training 24* (8), 63–64.

13

....

EQUITY IN TRAINING

CHAPTER GOALS

Trainers within organizations face an increasingly diverse workforce. This chapter documents that diversity, identifies access and treatment barriers to the full participation of designated groups in training activities, and suggests ways to increase their participation.

After reading this chapter, you should be able to

- understand the diversity issues in training
- discuss the access and treatment issues in training
- describe the nature of discrimination in the classroom
- outline ways in which the trainer can increase participation in the classroom
- suggest some ways in which trainers can accommodate people with special needs

ACKNOWLEDGING DIVERSITY

Canadian immigration policies and a political strategy that promote a cultural mosaic have resulted in a rapid rise in ethnic, cultural, language, and religious minorities working in Canada. The variety of ethnic origins of employees in Canada has expanded considerably over the past two decades. The change in the workforce is indeed dramatic.

According to census figures, visible minorities represent about 11.2 percent of the Canadian population. Their representation is expected to increase to 18.3 percent by the year 2006. Their labour-force participation rate (in 1991) was 9.1 percent (Employment and Immigration Canada, 1994). Any growth in the labour force will come from the four designated groups and about two thirds of new entrants to Canada are from the designated groups: women, aboriginals, visible minorities, and people with disabilities (Heritage Canada, 1996).

This diverse labour force reflects the realities of the world, in which Caucasians are a small numerical minority. To illustrate this concept, consider the world as a global village made up of 1000 citizens. The population demographics would be 60 North Americans, 80 South Americans, 564 Asians, 86 Africans, and 210 Europeans. Seven hundred people in this village would not be white. Given that visible minorities are truly the majority, the term will no longer be used in this chapter and will be replaced by "persons of non-European descent."

Learning to understand and connect with a diversity of experiences will enable Canadians to understand the nature of intercountry differences in a global marketplace.

diversity within an organization, the multicultural mix of employees

Valuing **diversity** matters because 85 percent of all workforce entrants in the year 2000 will not be white males. This labour pool also reflects the customers and clients of organizations. Today, most trainers and educators will have classrooms of students from many nations. In some cases, students will belong to more than one ethnic group. For example, one human resource management (HRM) student was born in China (and identified with the Asians), raised in Jamaica (and spoke with a Jamaican accent), and as a teenager moved to South America, where he learned Spanish and became assimilated in the South American cultural mosaic. Now an adult, he is a highly valued employee in an international marketing department of a Canadian firm. His differences are prized by his employer, and illustrate the positive aspects of acknowledging a diverse workforce.

Many well-meaning trainers claim not to see diversity. Their refrain is "I do not see men or women, blacks or whites. I see students." Being colour blind may mean being nondiscriminatory, but it may also mean not taking into account the differences that do exist or not using these differences to enhance learning. For example, female business students, who receive the same education as male business students, rarely study cases in which the CEO is a woman or in which a key player in a business decision is a competent women. In this case, equal ends up perpetuating the inequality that already exists.

Attitudes such as "I see all my trainees the same way," or "I don't see my students as black, white, purple, or green" are not based on reality. Students as well as trainers have social identities, formed by their location in gender, ethnic, class, and myriad other hierarchies (Lee, 1985). These identities have an effect on the teaching and learning environment.

Bigots who harbour racist or sexist attitudes will rarely say that they do not wish to work with blacks or women. The new racist will rationalize that a predominantly white (or male) customer base will be more responsive to a white employee. These business justifications are part of a new racist ideology, and contemporary executives speak in terms of attitudes, styles or fit, which have the same outcome as racist attitudes—the systemic exclusion of designated groups (Brief et al, 1997).

As experts in behavioural change, most trainers acknowledge the need to understand the behavioural expectations of diverse groups. Acknowledging diversity means being aware of the differences in background that students have, understanding that these differences may influence how students learn, and accommodating these learning styles and preferences (Nieto, 1992). These types of accommodations with students are part of a trainers' professional repertoire. Trainers already acknowledge and respond to differences among students based on levels of experience or learning preferences. Most trainers realize that some students prefer working in groups, others learn best through films and discussion, others prefer clear learning objectives to be achieved independently, and so on. Likewise, affirming diversity means regarding the students as individuals and respecting their differences and preferences. Indeed, the best approach is the individual one, because classifying trainees according to culture or gender to make provisions for them would be over-generalizing and would result in a different kind of stereotyping.

THE MEANING OF EQUITY

Equity does not mean that everyone can, for example, become the Prime Minister of Canada. This statement overlooks the fact that some people may not be intelligent enough or motivated enough to take advantage of available resources or opportunities (education, contacts, and so on) to become prime minister. **Equity** means that no one should be denied access to resources or opportunities based on irrelevant grounds like ethnicity or gender (Wilson, 1991).

equity the treatment of employees in a fair and nonbiased manner

Equity does not mean that everyone assimilates into the mainstream culture. Unlike previous generations of immigrants to Canada who "Canadianized" their names, perfected their English, and consciously buried symbols of their roots, immigrants today challenge assumptions about assimilation. Funding programs and attitudes encourage officially sanctioned pluralism. The bottom line is that trainees must be given equitable treatment because it is illegal to do otherwise.

HUMAN RIGHTS

The Canadian Charter of Rights and Freedoms states that every person is entitled to be treated without discrimination based on certain enumerated grounds: race, colour, religion or creed, sex, marital status, physical disability, and age (within a range of 18 to 65). All provinces have enacted similar legislation and some have included other grounds, such as sexual orientation. Large employers are familiar with this legislation, particularly regarding hiring. The legislation is not limited to employee selection but also covers selection for training.

ACCESS ISSUES

designated groups
females, persons of non-European descent, aboriginal peoples, and people with disabilities who have been disadvantaged in employment

access equitable opportunity to undertake training and development

People in the four **designated groups** (females, persons of non-European descent, aboriginal peoples, and people with disabilities) must not only have access to jobs but equitable access to quality training. Discrimination does not end when a person is hired. **Access** to the supervisor, the orientation program, the coaching and mentoring process, and formal training also must be distributed fairly.

Discrimination in training does exist. According to the Canadian Congress for Learning Opportunities for Women, during 1992–93, Canadian women received only 34 percent of federal training dollars, even though they make up 44 percent of the labour force and represent more than 60 percent of new entrants to the labour market (Suderman, 1993). The training they do receive is typically for jobs that are low-paying and becoming obsolete.

The most extreme form of access discrimination is withholding training from individuals who are members of certain groups. Women management trainees, for example, may not receive an out-of-city developmental assignment because it is assumed that their husbands will not let them go or that some day the women will become pregnant and quit. If fewer target-group members enter or successfully complete training (thus triggering an adverse impact), then the training may be viewed as discriminatory under Canadian human rights legislation (Cronshaw, 1991). Women report less support for graduate training in business than men, but these women also had shorter employment periods with their current organizations, which also tended to be smaller than those employing men (Keaveny & Inderrieden, 1999).

This access discrimination may not be conscious at an individual level, but may be systemic. Discrimination may not be the result of individual acts of bigotry but may stem from the traditional or historical operating methods of an organization. For example, management training courses may be held only in the evenings or weekends, so the effect is that women, who are usually the primary caregivers in families, cannot attend without great difficulty or expense.

Less obvious than discrimination in selection for training are the more subtle ways trainees from the designated groups are treated during training.

TREATMENT ISSUES

Employers are not only responsible for ensuring a workplace free of discrimination, but also a workplace free of harassment. **Harassment** occurs whenever an individual is subjected to mental or physical abuse because that individual is considered different in some way (Jain, 1989). Courts have ruled almost universally that the employer is required to provide a workplace free of harassment as a condition of employment. These rulings mean that the training environment must not be adversely affected by negative comments or actions by managers or instructors.

harassment unwelcome behaviour, often based on a person's differences

Treatment of students has been found to differ based on gender and ethnicity. Women are expected to be quiet, attentive, and passive, receiving less attention from teachers for either good or bad behaviour. Asian women have reported that faculty expected them to fit the model of the quiet, subservient woman, and so they participated less in class (Jenkins, 1990). Teachers give white students more academically challenging work, as well as more encouragement and praise (Nieto, 1992).

treatment the equitable handling of trainees

In addition, expectations of performance have a profound effect on student achievement. In a classic study, Rosenthal and Jacobson (1968) gave students a nonverbal intelligence test purported to identify intellectual growth. Their teachers were told that certain students (randomly picked by the researchers) were intellectual bloomers. The subsequent year, these students showed considerable IQ gain and were rated much higher in positive personality traits than other equally intelligent children. Expectations about abilities to learn have a dramatic effect on learning. Trainers who assume that persons of non-European descent cannot handle quantitative material illustrate this effect in training.

The next section examines some of the dynamics that result in differences in treatment in the training setting.

THE ISOLATION OF THE CLASSROOM

From the time of Socrates, the classroom has been idealized as pure: the one place where students and teachers come together in the free pursuit of knowledge (Marcroft, 1990). Learning is condensed to one neutral, autonomous, ahistorical site: the classroom. Separated from outside influences and connected only to each other, students and teachers learn in the isolation of the classroom (Hancock, 1990). Truth is discovered and legitimated as knowledge.

But classrooms are full of students who arrive with connections to the external world, and to the historical world of their own cultures. All cultures are built upon conceptual systems—a pattern of beliefs and values that define how people act, judge, decide, and so on (Mathews, 1973). These systems are transmitted to members of that culture through socialization practices. But these socialization practices, which teach an individual how to behave, also teach members how to learn in particular ways. In other words, different cultures produce different learning styles (Wilson, 1991).

In addition to cultural conditioning, different groups bring their own experiences of school into the training classroom. Typically, women and persons of non-European descent receive less attention from teachers and so learn that the learning process requires them to become passive receivers of knowledge (Wright, 1987); before trainers enter the classroom, certain assumptions and beliefs about learning are waiting for them.

For example, in general, the non-Western world values group cooperation, group achievement, harmony with nature, the relativity of time, holistic thinking, the pervasive influence of religion, the acceptance of affective (emotional) expression, and the perspectives of other cultures. Students with this orientation do best on verbal tasks and materials that have a human social content, which are perceived as part of a larger picture. Their performance is influenced by the opinions of those in authority (Wright, 1987).

Because Canadian education and training departments are dominated by Caucasians, the dominant educational philosophies are guided by Western world views. These views emphasize individual competition, individual achievement, the mastery and control of nature, adherence to a rigid time schedule, religion distinct from other parts of culture, task orientation with a limit to affective expression, and a feeling of a superior world view (Anderson, 1988). Students who succeed in this environment do best on analytical tasks, learn impersonal material easily, and their performance is not dependent on others' opinions.

Most trainers have been educated and trained in the Western world view. They see themselves as knowing more than the students. Their role is to fill students with knowledge and skills. Trainers come into the classroom with one world belief, students with a variety of world perspectives. Beliefs may underlie specific and probably unconscious acts of discrimination in the training situation.

Many research studies demonstrate that a diverse team is more creative and solves problems more effectively than teams that are homogeneous (Jehn, 1995). In a training situation, this means that these teams will look at a problem from different perspectives, generate more alternatives, and more critically evaluate the proposed solutions.

The Nature of Discrimination in the Classroom

Discrimination refers to actions and a belief system, both personal and institutional, directed against individuals or groups based on their gender (sexism); ethnic group (ethnocentrism); social class (classism); age (ageism), and so on (Nieto, 1992). Discrimination always helps somebody and hurts somebody else. Rewards and opportunities are distributed (or withheld) based on whether a person belongs to a certain group, regardless of individual merits or weaknesses.

Society, and citizens within that society, classify people according to visible characteristics and then deduce personality and behavioural traits. Stereotypes are the result: "Boys are not as smart as girls; the lower classes need instant gratification; Germans are clean." Note that stereotypes can be both positive and negative (e.g., Asians are perceived to be "good at math, but not good with people"). These stereotypes, when present in the classroom, affect instruction. Stereotypes block learning in organizations (Friedlander, 1983). A learning organization must treasure differences in perception, values, preferences, and so on because these differences may benefit the organization. For example, the "feminine" values of emotional support and nurturance are valuable for teamwork and mentoring.

The dominant instructional model in North America, the one under which most trainers learned to learn, is the transmission model (Barnes, 1976; Wells, 1982). The task of the trainer in the transmission model is to impart knowledge and skills—which the trainer possesses—to the students who do not yet have these skills. The trainer controls the content (knowledge) and the pedagogical process. Training from this dominant model often excludes minorities, as illustrated next.

discrimination actions and a personal and institutional belief system that result in inequitable treatment of certain groups of employees

Content

Knowledge and truth, content and subject matter, are perceived to be universal, but curriculum is ethnocentric (Sarup, 1986). Adding material from different cultures and perspectives by searching for models and practices from other situations is less valuable than infusing and integrating this material into the core curriculum. Trainees appreciate material that appeals to different groups.

Most students interviewed in Jenkins's (1990) study participated more when instructors included materials pertinent to their ethnic group. These students were afraid to introduce this kind of material into classroom discussions because they felt that the trainer would not understand the value of these cultural contributions.

However, asking students to speak for their culture is inappropriate. Women and persons of non-European descent may become very uncomfortable when asked by an instructor to give, for example, the black perspective, or to discuss how a woman manager would have handled a certain situation.

The balancing strategy for instructors is to encourage participation by responding positively, allowing time for responses, but avoiding asking individuals of visible groups to act as spokespersons for these groups (Jenkins, 1990). The cognitive development of other students can only benefit from learning about different perspectives (Kitching, 1991).

PEDAGOGY

Considerable research data suggest that when persons of non-European descent are in a subordinate group, teaching that takes into account their languages and cultures will significantly increase academic success (Campos & Keating, 1984; Cummins, 1989; Rosier & Holm, 1980). Trainees are more likely to learn with the inclusion of instructional strategies that take into account culturally conditioned learning styles.

Studies of gender and language confirm that men and women speak differently. Men speak more often and for longer periods than women (Phillips, Steele, Tanz, 1987). Male parents and teachers interrupt more often and give more direct commands than female parents and teachers.

Social class affects style of language more than does gender. Differences in the choice of words, forms of politeness, hesitations, and so on tend to reflect power differences. Less powerful people (regardless of gender) tend to use more tag questions ("Do you want to hear something interesting? Well … "). Men, who typically hold more powerful positions in society, control the content and rhythm of conversations. Those in subordinate positions have to work harder to maintain the conversation by asking more questions, and by supporting and encouraging responses. Thus we have the stereotype that women are good at interpersonal skills such as sympathetic listening, careful questioning, and sustaining flagging conversations (Thorne, Kramarae, & Henley, 1983, Cheshire & Jenkins, 1991).

In a seminar or discussion group, these conversational patterns persist, based on who holds power both within the group and between groups. Thus, men often ignore the comments of previous speakers, make more frequent declarations of fact and opinion than women, and talk more often and at greater length than women. Men use taboo words more often than women (Hall & Sandler, 1982; Smith, 1985), and women interpret this verbal aggression as personal, negative, and disruptive.

Are women more comfortable taking training courses, such as assertiveness or leadership, with other women? Many organizations offer this segregated training for their female employees. These special training programs are designed to allow women the opportunity to practise skills in a safe environment, and discuss their real perceptions and feelings, without the fear of ridicule and dominance by males. This approach has risks. One obvious concern is that because women and men work together, women must learn to express ideas and use skills in the real world, not in an artificial world of training.

Furthermore, evidence suggests that female candidates for jobs who have participated in gender-based training are perceived as less desirable than other females who have not had segregated training (Reavelly & Naughton, 1993).

A large part of information is not communicated via language but through nonverbal actions. These nonverbal behaviours are culture specific and learned at a very young age. Confusion and misreading of intentions may result from misinterpreting actions that have different meanings for different groups. For example, children in some cultures are taught that looking an adult in the eye is a sign of disrespect; North American white children are socialized to believe that looking away from an adult who is talking is a sign of disrespect (Byers & Byers, 1972). The decoding of these communication patterns influences instructor reaction to the student.

Research has shown that other variables in interracial interactions are the amount of distance between the communicators, the amount of eye contact, and tone of voice (Feldman, 1985). These findings are summarized in Table 13.1. All of these studies underline the need for trainers to consider the training environment in terms of the learning styles and communication patterns from the perspective of participants.

Despite the fact that practices and belief systems are deeply ingrained, trainers can adopt certain techniques to lessen discriminatory treatment.

DISCRIMINATION OUTSIDE THE CLASSROOM

Mentoring is seen as particularly useful for women and visible minorities. Employers believe that a senior employee may be able to coach and counsel a junior employee in the ways of the organization more effectively than any training course. Should these mentor–protégé relationships be same-sex, or same ethnic group? Those in same-ethnic-group mentoring relationships have reported more psychosocial support than those in cross-ethnicity relationships (Ragins, 1997). But there may not be enough senior women, for example, to mentor all the junior women. Mentors also learn from their protégés and perhaps a junior member of a designated group could sensitize a senior manager to diversity issues. The biggest impediment may be that these same-sex, same-ethnic-group mentoring relationships may contravene the principle of equity.

Sexual harassment and diversity training programs were discussed in Chapter 11, and may serve as a starting point for ending discrimination outside the classroom.

A MODEL OF MULTIPERSPECTIVE TRAINING

The quality of the interaction between the trainer and the student is the centre of the developmental process. This process can only be enhanced by the elimination of discriminatory behaviour.

TABLE 13.1 BODY LANGUAGE IN CULTURES WORLDWIDE

Acceptable interpersonal distance in various countries:

0 to 18 inches	Middle Eastern males, Eastern and Southern Mediterraneans, and some Hispanic cultures.
18 inches to 3 feet	Americans and West Europeans.
3 feet or more	Asians (Japanese the farthest) and many African cultures.

It is inappropriate behaviour to touch Asians on the head.

Acceptable length of eye contact in various countries:

0 to 1 second	Native Americans, East Indians, and Asian cultures (least in the Cambodian culture, which believes that direct eye contact is flirtatious).
1 second	Americans (to continue direct eye contact beyond 1 second can be considered threatening, particularly between Anglo- and African-American persons).
1 second or more	Middle Eastern, Hispanic, Southern European, and French cultures generally advocate very direct eye contact.

Variations of handshakes in various countries:

Firm	Americans, Germans
Moderate grasp	Hispanics
Light	French (not offered to superiors).
Soft	British
Gentle	Middle Easterners
Gentle	Asians (for some cultures, though not Koreans, shaking hands is unfamiliar and uncomfortable).
Pointing	Generally poor etiquette in most countries, except in Asian countries where it is considered rude and in poor taste. If pointing is necessary, in Hong Kong you use your middle finger, in Malaysia it is the thumb, and in the rest of Asia it is the entire hand.
Beckoning	The American gesture of using upturned fingers, palm facing the body, is deeply offensive to the Mexicans, Filipinos, and Vietnamese. For example, this gesture in the Philippines is used to beckon prostitutes.
Signs of approval	The use of the "okay" sign, the "thumbs-up" signal, and the "V" for "victory" are among the most offensive to other cultures.
Signaling "no"	This can be confusing. In Mexico and the Middle East, a "no" is indicated by a back-to-forth movement of the index finger.
The left hand	Gesturing or handling something with the left hand among Muslims is considered offensive because they consider this the "toilet" hand.

Crossing legs is in poor taste among most Asians and Middle Easterners. The Russians find it distasteful to place the ankle on the knee.

Adapted with the permission of Lexington Books, an imprint of The Free Press, a Division of Simon & Schuster, from *Bridging Cultural Barriers for Corporate Success: How to Manage the Multicultural Work Force* by Sondra Thiederman, Ph.D. Copyright © 1991 by Sondra Thiederman.

Merely presenting trainers with research that documents discrimination and its effects on minority students will not bring about equality. Instead, the reactions of trainers may be defensive. Asking trainers to police their own behaviour (most of which is socialized and unconscious) is difficult. The act of monitoring behaviour may make the trainer less able to instruct, as energies are concentrated on how things are being said and done. Some leakage of this unconscious behaviour may still occur, but it appears that some conscious control is possible.

The following suggestions may prove helpful to trainers who are motivated to reduce discriminatory behaviour.

- *Use neutral words:* Words that have negative connotations for some groups can be eliminated from the vocabulary, and others can be introduced that are more acceptable. For example, the use of "flight attendant" instead of "stewardess" was an easy transition for most airline personnel and clients.

- *Mirror effective and ineffective behaviours:* Another technique is to mirror trainer behaviour in the classroom. Showing videotapes of individual teaching behaviours will enable educators to become participant observers of their own dynamics.

- *Overcompensate*: Teachers have been able to compensate for their lack of attention to women in class by deliberately soliciting more contributions from women and reinforcing these comments nonverbally and verbally (Corson, 1992). In this way, women and minorities can be brought in from the margins of the classroom. (More suggestions for increasing the participation of minorities are contained in Figure 13.1).

Some managers and trainers attend diversity training workshops to sensitize them to language and behaviours that might be biased. Although many of these workshops are very effective, this type of diversity training does have some risks, which are outlined in the Training Today 1 box.

TRAINEES WITH SPECIAL NEEDS

As employers meet targets within an employment-equity program, more employees with special needs will be regular participants in the training and development process. **Persons with disabilities** are described as those with a physical or mental impairment limiting one or more major life activity. The range of disabilities includes sensory impairment (such as vision or hearing loss), motor-skill impairment (such as paralysis or loss of limbs), and learning impairment (including difficulties reading, writing, and using numbers). Information on the representation of persons with disabilities is very hard to collect. We estimate that they represented about 3 percent of the employed labour force in 1991.

persons with disabilities those individuals with a physical or mental impairment limiting one or more major life activity

FIGURE 13.1 MANAGING PARTICIPATION

Here are some practical suggestions to facilitate the equitable treatment of women and minorities in the classroom.

Elicit participation from all

Participating in group discussions is normal for Canadians, but for people who have been socialized in Asian cultures, like the Japanese, it is normal to listen to the instructor or teacher (Hanamura, 1989). Listening *is* participating; perhaps those who prefer to listen could provide a written summary or reaction at the end of the class.

Hand-raising and turn-taking are culture specific. Some students are more comfortable speaking out in class without waiting for permission. There are ways to manage participation in the classroom through controlling turn-taking and through the design of the seating arrangements. One alternative to the trainer allowing students to speak by acknowledging their raised hands is to let the students determine who is next (perhaps by throwing a soft ball to the next speaker). Students will monitor their own and others' participation. Give students strips of coloured paper or beans, each entitling them to one comment or question. Another strategy is to have students answer in groups. Students can discuss answers in small groups before responding to the trainer. Another approach is to have every student write down the answer to the question, and then call on a student to read the written answer.

Responses to comments and questions also determine the level of equitable participation in a training room. Examples of discrimination by response include sounding surprised when a minority student responds well, praising or criticizing men's comments and ignoring women's comments, asking whites analytical questions and asking blacks fact-based questions.

Seventy percent of classroom interaction exists between the teacher and the immediately available students—those at the front of the room (Jackson & Lahderne, 1967). This action zone excludes everyone at the rear of the room. The physical seating arrangements in the classroom can affect the behaviour of the students (Hood-Smith & Leffingwell, 1983). Instead of having students in rows facing the trainer, students can be seated in a circle, in tables of four or five, or in two rows along the side walls, each facing the centre, or in herringbone patterns with a wide centre aisle. All these designs increase the level of student comfort, facilitate interaction among everyone, and allow the trainer to monitor participation. Part of the effectiveness of the learning experience is the ability to interact with the instructor and other students.

Use cross-cultural material

Use source materials that appeal to the diverse backgrounds of the class. (If you have no time to do this, invite students as a group to contribute their perceptions; build a file). Explain why you are (or are not) using material from a multicultural perspective. Refer to your own experience as one that has shaped your perspective (e.g., "As a woman executive, I ..." or "My grandparents, who were ... lived at a time when workers did what they were told.")

FIGURE 13.1 MANAGING PARTICIPATION (continued)

Use nondiscriminatory language

The use of language that assumes that men are the only actors silences women. Words such as *executive* or *manager* and *humanity* can replace *businessman* and *mankind*. Sexist humour should not be used to lighten up a dull subject. Sexist language, humour, and remarks should be labelled as such if someone is behaving in this way in a class.

Another effective strategy involves teaching people to decode behaviour; in other words, people can be trained to be sensitive to cues and miscues in communication, and more accurately interpret their meaning from the other's perspective (Rosenthal, Hall, Archer, Di Matteo, & Rogers, 1979). As illustrated earlier, the recognition that eye contact has different meanings for different ethnic groups may allow trainers to accommodate variations rather than negatively evaluate them.

Trainers might alter their training methods to adapt to different learning styles. A highly successful premedicine program with a large population of persons of non-Europeans descent moved from an instructor-focused format of theory first, labs second (with each student competing), to a format of building an environment of family in which students cooperate. Bonding occurred between students and faculty in a highly supportive atmosphere. Lessons that progressed from practical experiences in the lab to theoretical concepts resulted in greater student retention and learning (Brown, 1986). The teaching model that embraces these concepts has been termed "reciprocal interaction" (Cummins, 1986). The trainer acts not as a transmitter, but as a facilitator. This model works particularly well with adults, who are guided in a collaborative effort to learn meaningful material. Internally motivated students assume greater control over the learning process. This technique empowers the student to continue to learn outside the classroom and back on the job.

The presence of minority trainers also directly affects the amount and extent of learning among minority students. The minority instructor serves as a role model, as an advocate, ensuring the equitable application of policies and directly influencing the quality of the educational experience (Massey, Scott, & Dornbusch, 1975; Meier and Nigro, 1976; Saltzstein, 1979; Fraga, Meier, & England, 1986).

Perhaps because of the dynamics within the traditional classroom, ethnic minorities and women have turned to other centres for learning. Nonmainstream settings have a rich history of group participation. Organizations such as churches, community centres, women's organizations, and voluntary organizations have provided educational opportunities for centuries. Participation of black Americans in voluntary organizations is higher than any other ethnic group (Florin, Jones, & Wandersman, 1987). The network of farm wives in Quebec has provided training for rural women since the nineteenth century.

These informal settings enhance discussion opportunities for women and minorities. When less formal instructional opportunities exist in a formal teaching setting (such as in laboratories or discussion groups), interaction patterns change and there appears to be a more just distribution of interactive opportunities than in the dominant training model.

Often the disability is the principal focus of attention by managers who are not able to see abilities. Contrast this attitude with that of McDonalds, which has hired and trained more than 10 000 people with mental and physical disabilities in North America, focusing on the abilities of workers and ensuring that they have equal opportunity. Managers undergo sensitivity training to dispel myths about disabilities (McMichael, 1992).

The tools and techniques used to assist special-needs workers to learn vary from the simple and inexpensive to the highly sophisticated. Moving a classroom to the ground floor increases accessibility for everyone, as does providing audio cassettes or lecture notes. Braille printers can be used to produce training manuals. Sound can be amplified within the classroom. Sign-language interpreters can be provided (Reid, 1992). During testing, extra time may be allowed for written tests. Tests may also be given orally, with the answers recorded on tape.

Frequently, funding is available to help employers accommodate workers with special needs. For example, the Ontario Ministry of Community and Social Services supports 1500 workers with mental and physical disabilities by providing work-support assistants who coach trainees until an acceptable level of proficiency is attained (Goodson, 1991).

Computer manufacturers have developed technology designed to serve trainees with special needs. Adaptive equipment has paralleled the rapid growth of personal computers. Examples of this equipment include software that recognizes speech and eye movements, and keyboards with large customized keys for sticks and wands. One researcher estimates that, given the proper equipment, people with special needs can function proficiently in 80 percent of the jobs listed in the *Dictionary of Occupational Titles* (Acosta, 1991).

More information on accommodation strategies and funding is available from provincial training departments and offices of human rights and employment equity. A particularly good reference book is *Training Employees with Disabilities* (Tracy, 1995).

The situation does appear to be improving. One study of the federal (U.S.) workforce analyzed five types of training and development (management training, professional conferences, employer subsidized university and college courses, mentoring and development assignments), which were provided at substantial cost to the employer, required absence from the work site, and prepared the recipient for organizational (rather than job-specific) training. Black women and white women received less management training and attended more professional conferences. However, among employees with the same amount of education and experience, black men were most likely to receive management training and white women were more likely to attend conferences. Access to mentoring and developmental assignments did not appear to differ among groups (Smithey & Lewis, 1998).

SUMMARY

Trainers should be aware of practices and policies that systematically discriminate against women and persons of non-European descent, including factors that reduce access to training and development programs and treatment within these programs. Conscious efforts must be made to include content and methods that elicit participation on an equitable basis.

KEY TERMS

access   326

designated groups   326

discrimination   329

diversity   324

equity   325

harassment   327

persons with disabilities   333

treatment   327

EXERCISES *

SCENARIO 1

During a human resources training session, one of your participants points out that all the material you have used during the workshop has portrayed situations involving only white male and female employees. A white participant counters

*These exercises were developed by Dale Hall, advisor, Sexual Harassment Education and Complaint Centre, and Cheet Singh, former advisor, Centre for Race and Ethnic Relations at York University.

this claim by saying that the other person is being too sensitive and goes on to suggest that the problem with minorities is that they want to change Canadian culture, when they should be listening and learning how to get along here.

QUESTIONS

1. As a trainer, how do you respond to the claim that your material is biased and does not really portray the diversity of the Canadian workforce?
2. Is the white participant voicing a racist view? How do you respond to the claim?
3. How can you use this situation in a way that will be constructive and educational for all the participants?

SCENARIO 2

"I am a woman who has participated in a series of quality control workshops. I have felt very uncomfortable in these workshops. It's nothing that I can really put my finger on, but I do not seem to participate very much. The trainer is really nice and helpful but does not seem to ask the female participants any questions when a point needs to be illustrated or elaborated on. The other amazing thing is that the trainer seems to always know the names of the men but never refers to the women by name. I always have to remind the trainer what my name is. When we are paired off into groups to work on projects, the men dominate the discussion, either interrupting us or ignoring us. They just don't seem to take our opinions seriously. I end up just sitting there, or taking notes. I do not think this is fair, but I do not know how to get the men to let me participate equally."

QUESTIONS

1. The trainer is most likely unaware that unequal treatment is being given to male and female trainees. Why do you think the trainer is not aware of this different treatment?
2. How would you respond if this participant came to you with this problem about your session?
3. Why do you think this woman did not speak up during the session about this problem?

REFERENCES

Acosta, T.M. (1991). CBT opening doors. *CBT Directions 4* (2).

Anderson, J.A. (1988). Cognitive styles and multicultural populations. *Journal of Teacher Education 39* (2), 2–9.

Barnes, D. (1976). *From communication to curriculum.* New York: Penguin.

Brown, M. (1986). Calculus by the dozen: A retention program for undergraduate minority students in mathematics-based majors. Paper presented at the second annual conference of Black Student Retention, Atlanta, GA.

Brief, A.P., Buttram, R.T., Reizenstein, R.M., Pugh, S. D., Callahan, J.D., McCline, R. L, & Vaslow, J.B. (1997). Beyond good intentions: The next steps towards racial equality in the American workplace. *Academy of Management Executives 11* (4), 59–70.

Byers, P., & Byers, H. (1972). Nonverbal communication and the education of children. In Cazden, C.B., John, V.P., & Hymes, D. (Eds.), *Functions of language in the classroom* (pp. 3–31). New York: Academic Press.

Campos, J., & Keating, B. (1984). *The Carpinteria preschool program: Title VII second year evaluation report.* Washington: Department of Education.

Cheshire, J., & Jenkins, N. (1991). Gender differences in the GCSE oral English examination, Part II. *Language and Education 5*, 19–40.

Corson, D.J. (1992). Language, gender, and education: A critical review linking social justice and power. *Gender and Education 4* (3), 89–101.

Cronshaw, S. (1991). *Industrial psychology in Canada.* Waterloo, ON: Waterloo Academic Press.

Cummins, J. (1986). Empowering minority students: A framework for intervention. *Harvard Educational Review 56* (1).

———. (1989). *Empowering minority students.* Sacramento, CA: California Association for Bilingual Education, 18–36.

Employment and Immigration Canada. (1994). *Employment equity availability data report on designated groups.* Ottawa: Author.

Feldman, R.S. (1985). Nonverbal behaviour, race, and the classroom teacher. *Theory into Practice 24* (3), 45–49.

Florin, P., Jones, E., & Wandersman, A. (1987). Black participation in voluntary associations. *Journal of Voluntary Actions Research 15* (1), 65–68.

Fraga, L., Meier, K., & England, R. (1986). Hispanic Americans and educational policy: Limits to equal access. *Journal of Politics 48* (3), 851–876.

Friedlander, F. (1983). Patterns of individual and organizational learning. In Srivasta, S. (Ed.), *The executive mind.* San Francisco: Jossey-Bass.

Goodson, L. (1991). People who need people. *Human Resources Professional 8* (3).

Hall, R., & Sandler, B.M. (1982). *The classroom climate: A chilly one for women?* Washington: Project on the Status and Education of Women, Association of American Colleges.

Hanamura, S. (1989). Working with people who are different. *Training and Development Journal 44* (4), 110–114.

Hancock, L. (1990, July 24). Teacher comforts. *Village Voice*, p. 75.

Heritage Canada. (1996). *Annual report 1994–5 on the operation of the Canadian Multiculturalism Act*. Ottawa: Author.

Hood-Smith, N., & Leffingwell, R.J. (1983). The impact of physical space alteration on disruptive classroom behaviour: A case study. *Education 104* (3), 224–230.

Jackson, P.W., & Lahderne, H.M. (1967). Inequalities of teacher–pupil contacts. *Psychology in the Schools 3*, 204–211.

Jain, H. (Ed.). (1989). Human rights: Issues in employment. In *Human resources management in Canada*. Scarborough, ON: Prentice-Hall Canada.

Jehn, K.A. (1995). A multi-method examination of the benefits and determinants of intra-group conflict. *Administrative Science Quarterly 40* (2), 256–282.

Jenkins, M. (1990). Teaching the new majority: Guidelines for cross-cultural communication between students and faculty. *Feminist Teacher 5* (1), 8–14.

Keaveny, T.J., & Inderrieden, E.J. (1999). Gender differences in employer-supported training and education. *Journal of Vocational Behavior 54*, 71–81.

Kitching, K.W. (1991). A case for a multicultural approach to education. *Education Canada 27* (4).

Lee, E. (1985). *Letters to Marcia: A teachers' guide to anti-racist education*. Toronto: Cross Cultural Communication Centre, 8.

McMichael, C. (1992). Focus on ability. *Employee Assistance* (July).

Marcroft, M. (1990). The politics of the classroom: Towards an oppositional pedagogy. *New Directions for Teaching and Learning 44*, (Winter), 61–71.

Massey, G., Scott, M., & Dornbusch, S. (1975). Institutional racism in urban schools. *Black Scholar 7* (3), 10–19.

Mathews, B. (1973). Black cognitive process. Unpublished paper, Howard University, School of Social Work, Washington, DC.

Nieto, S. (1992). *Affirming diversity—the sociopolitical context of multicultural education*. New York: Longham Publishing Group.

Phillips, S., Steele, S., & Tanz, C. (Eds.). (1987). *Language, gender, and sex in comparative perspective*. Cambridge: Cambridge University Press.

Ragins, B.E. (1997). Diversified mentoring relationships in organizations: A power perspective. *Academy of Management Review 22* (2), 482–521.

Reid, RL. (1992). On target: Tools to train people with disabilities. *Technical and Skills Training* (July).

Reavelly, M.A., & Naughton, T.J. (193). The effect of gender-based training on selection decisions. *Women in Management Review 8* (4), 16–21.

Rosenthal, R., & Jacobson, L. (1968). *Pygmalion in the classroom*. New York: Holt Rhinehart & Winston.

Rosenthal, R., Hall, J.A., Archer, D., Di Matteo, M.R., & Rogers, P.L. (1979). Measuring sensitivity to nonverbal communications: The PONS test. In Wolfgang, A. (Ed.), *Nonverbal behaviour: Applications and cross-cultural implications*. New York: Academic Press.

Rosier, P., & Holm, W. (1980). *The Rock Point experience: A longitudinal study of a Navajo school*. Washington: Center for Applied Linguistics.

Saltzstein, G.H. (1979). Representative bureaucracy and bureaucratic responsibility. *Administration and Society 10* (2), 465–475.

Sarup, M. (1986). *The politics of multiracial education.* London: Troutledge & Kegan Paul.

Smith, P. (1985). *Languages, the sexes, and society.* Oxford: Blackwell.

Smithey, P.N., & Lewis, G.B. (1998). Gender, race, and learning in the federal civil service. *Public Administration Quarterly 22,* (2), 204–228.

Suderman, B. (1993, November 10). Women get short shrift. *The Globe and Mail,* p. A20.

Thorne, B., Kramarae, C., & Henley, N. (Eds.). (1983). *Language, gender, and society.* Rowley, MA: Newbury House.

Tracy, R. (1995). *Training employees with disabilities.* New York: Amacom.

Wells, G. (1982). Language, learning, and the curriculum. In Tikunoff, W. J. (Ed.), *Language, learning, and education* (pp. 205–226). Bristol: Centre for the Study of Language and Communication, University of Bristol.

Wilson, J. (1991). Education and equality: Some conceptual questions. *Oxford Review of Education 17* (2), 223–230.

Wright, C. (1987). The relations between teachers and Afro-Caribbean pupils: Observing multi-racial classrooms. In Weiner, G., & Arnot, M. (Eds.), *Gender under scrutiny.* London: Hutchinson.

14

ORGANIZATIONAL LEARNING

CHAPTER GOALS

A smart organization knows what it knows. **Organizational learning** refers to the process of creating, sharing, diffusing and applying this knowledge. A learning organization supports the individual learning of every employee. However, organizational learning is not simply the sum of individual employee learning. Thus far, we have approached performance management through a training system that enables employees to learn and apply that learning. Now our focus is on the systems used to create and distribute new knowledge on an organization-wide basis.

After reading this chapter, you should be able to

- define a learning organization
- describe the strategic advantages garnered by a learning organization
- explain what is meant by knowledge, and give examples of explicit and tacit knowledge
- outline the four types of intellectual capital
- define knowledge management

organizational learning
the process of creating, sharing, diffusing, and applying knowledge in organizations

- list several ways organizations can facilitate the creation of new knowledge
- explain what is meant by a learning culture
- discuss the importance of knowledge interpretation
- give examples of how organizations can disseminate knowledge
- outline some ways that employee knowledge can be captured and stored
- discuss several methods for measuring knowledge, and briefly explain the problems in assessing knowledge in financial terms
- discuss how the managers' and trainers' roles change in a learning organization

THE NEED FOR ORGANIZATIONAL LEARNING

The traditional perspective of learning has always been strongly associated with the training function. The goals of training have been viewed from a traditional perspective, the strengthening of employees' knowledge, skills, and abilities (KSA). Employees can learn, and this process of training and learning can be managed. This has been the focus of the text. An organization can't learn unless individual employees learn. As Senge (1990), the originator of the concept of learning, states, "Organizations learn only through individuals who learn. Individual learning does not guarantee organization learning. But without it, no organizational learning occurs" (p. 139).

The training of employees for tomorrow is effective when that future is relatively predictable. However, in a turbulent environment, some organizations feel the need to supplement the traditional training model, and they attempt to do more than just train employees for the current state of affairs. In a learning organization, employees are trained to learn how to learn. To survive and develop, organizations must learn to manage by managing learning—the capacity to learn and change, consciously, continually, and quickly. A company's knowledge, including that contained in its employees' brains, has always been a source of competitive advantage. The ability to learn faster than the competition is a source of sustainable advantage. The executives at Nortel say that their success depends on their ability to market new product solutions faster than their competitors, and this ability depends entirely on Nortel's intellectual capital (Edwards, 1997). Simply put, organizational learning is a dynamic process of creating and sharing knowledge.

This chapter moves our perspective of performance management from the role of the trainer in the training department whose job it is to increase skills and knowledge, to that of the chief learning officer whose job it is to manage the learning to reshape organizational vision. The learning organization does not represent another management fad; it signifies a strategic orientation that can result in a critical capability to compete.

THE LEARNING ORGANIZATION

If knowledge is a resource, then learning is the way to create and use it (Baets, 1998). A **learning organization** is one that consciously gathers, organizes, shares, and analyzes its knowledge to further its goals. Consider it an art in which value has to be created from intangible assets. A learning organization is able to transform itself by acquiring new knowledge, skills, or behaviour. A learning organization is one that has an enhanced capacity to learn, adapt, and change its culture (Bennet & O'Brien, 1994). Embedded in this concept is the ability to make sense of and respond to the surrounding environment. Organizational values, policies, systems, and structures support and accelerate learning for all employees. This learning results in continual improvements in work systems, products, services, teamwork, management practices—a more successful organization. Organizational learning is learning that actually results in improvements.

Organizational learning is a cycle of:

- experience
- observation and reflection
- formation of understanding and generalization of that experience
- testing new ideas that in turn generate more experiences (Baets, 1998)

One company used this process to lower its scrap rate. Employees of this laser drive manufacturer were trained to use their brains when they identified a defective product. In the past, they rejected a defect by placing it in the scrap pile. After training, they knew how to identify the cause of the problem and develop solutions so that it would not happen again (Kapp, 1999).

Organizational learning depends on leveraging employee knowledge. But first we have to understand what we mean by knowledge.

> **learning organization** an organization that consciously gathers, organizes, shares, and analyzes its knowledge to further its goals

KNOWLEDGE

Employee knowledge is a synthesis of information: all the facts, theories, and mental representations employees know about the world and, in the context of work, about their jobs and the organization. **Knowledge** is the sum of what is known: a body of truths, information, and principles. Knowledge can be found in the heads of employees or transferred and stored in systems in the organization.

Knowledge is more than information, which we have in abundance, represented by dusty books filling shelves and facts floating across the Internet. Knowledge, on the other hand, is information that has been edited, put into context, and analyzed in a way that makes it meaningful, and therefore valuable to an organization (Tapscott, 1998). This knowledge can be grouped in two ways: explicit knowledge and tacit knowledge.

> **knowledge** the sum of what is known; facts or procedures

Types of Knowledge

explicit knowledge
information that can be
codified and formalized

Explicit knowledge refers to those things that you can buy or trade, such as patents or copyrights and other forms of intellectual property. The formula for making Coca-Cola and the brand name Coke are examples of intellectual properties that are extremely valuable. These tangible assets can normally be codified or formalized. Explicit knowledge can be written into procedures or coded into databases and is transferred fairly accurately. However, less than 20 percent of corporate knowledge is explicit (Stamps, 1998).

tacit knowledge
wisdom gained from
experience and insight
that is difficult to codify

The other 80 percent of corporate knowledge is implicit (Stamps, 1999) and is difficult to quantify or even describe accurately. Implicit or **tacit knowledge** refers to the valuable wisdom learned from experience and insight, and has been defined as intuition, know-how, little tricks, and judgment. (Seasoned executives with tacit knowledge of a situation make million-dollar decisions.) Tacit knowledge is used by employees but is almost impossible to transfer. To grasp the concept of explicit knowledge and tacit knowledge, imagine describing the physical characteristics of your best friend; now try to describe the methods your friend would use to influence a supervisor. The latter involves your tacit knowledge of your friend.

A well-known example of tacit knowledge is that of the decision-making behaviour of dealers in financial markets. That behaviour appears to be instinctual, but it is based on their past experience, what they read and hear, and the climate of the market. Extracting this knowledge from these dealers and then training others in this winning behaviour is extremely difficult (Baets, 1998).

The transfer of tacit knowledge requires personal contact. The personal contact must be extensive and built on trust. The types of personal contact that facilitate the transfer of tacit knowledge are partnerships, apprenticeships, and mentoring.

Knowledge is different from intellectual capital.

Intellectual Capital

Intellectual capital is more than knowledge; intellectual capital is more like intelligence. Intelligence is the ability to create knowledge, and includes the ability to learn, to reason, to imagine, to find new insights, to generate alternatives, and to make wise decisions (Miller, 1999). By increasing the general level of intelligence of employees, organizations hope to create new knowledge that will result in new products, services, and processes.

intellectual capital
cognitive knowledge,
advanced skills, motiva-
tion, and commitment of
employees

Intellectual capital refers to an organization's knowledge, experience, relationships, process discoveries, innovations, market presence, and community influence. Intellectual capital is the source of innovation and wealth production—it is knowledge of value (Miller, 1999). Intellectual capital has to be formalized, captured, and leveraged to produce a more highly valued asset (Stewart, 1994).

Intellectual capital is not like other assets; it grows with use. When an employee learns and uses that learning, she usually learns even more, and is motivated to learn again. She can share her learning and not deplete it or use it up, like other assets. Sharing results in the acquisition of even more knowledge, as you probably learned when you worked on projects with other people.

Intellectual capital is often divided into four types: human capital, renewal capital, structural capital, and relationship capital.

Human capital: This capital is the knowledge, skills, and abilities of employees. Included in this type of capital are some basic components of intelligence, such as the ability to learn, to reason, to analyze. Interpersonal skills, such as the ability to communicate with others and work in teams to generate better work methods, would also be part of an organization's human capital.

Renewal capital: This type of capital refers to what we have labelled intellectual property, which consists of patents, licences, copyrights, and marketable innovations including products, services, and technologies.

Structural capital: Organizations are not amoebas; they need a skeleton or structure to function. Although the organizational chart captures some of the concept of structure, what we really mean are the formal systems and informal relationships that allow employees to communicate, solve problems, and make decisions. Structural capital is the set of structures, routines, and information systems that stay behind when employees go home. Sometimes these structures are represented by policies and procedures. For example, a company might require you to obtain the approval of the vice president of marketing before launching an innovative but costly advertising campaign. Another part of structural capital can be stored in databases and knowledge documents. For example, a consultant at IBM developed a high-quality analysis of the forest industry, which predicted nearly perfectly the rise and fall of timber prices. A consultant in the same firm, but located in Japan, had access to this document to prepare an impressive bid for a contract for a Thai forestry company (Tapscott, 1998).

Relationship capital: Organizations, like individual employees, do not exist as islands. Organizations have relationships with suppliers, customers, and even competitors that influence how they do business. These relationships, particularly if they are based on trust and integrity, can be a source of competitive advantage.

Customer capital is a subset of relationship capital. Customer capital is the value of an organization's relationships with its customers. For example, many small businesses enjoy high degrees of customer capital. Neighbours

human capital knowledge, skills, and abilities of employees

renewal capital intellectual capital that can be codified and bought and sold

structural capital the formal systems and informal relationships that allow employees to work

relationship capital the value of an organization's relationships with suppliers, customers, and competitors

will shop at the local milk store even though the milk is more expensive because they know the owner and her family. In larger organizations, customer capital refers to all the efforts that a company makes to keep customers returning to buy their products or services.

This chapter will focus on human capital: the sum and synergy of employee knowledge. Companies want to grow this intellectual capital, and one way to do it is to create an environment in which learning is valued and actively managed. The term "learning organization" refers to the programs and culture required to increase an organization's capacity to learn and create intellectual capital. Creating and leveraging that knowledge has become a goal of many organizations. Training and performance specialists must understand that the creation, capture, and transfer of knowledge are strategic imperatives. Learning organizations have to actively manage this knowledge. We will discuss ways to acquire, interpret, disseminate, and store this knowledge in the next section.

KNOWLEDGE MANAGEMENT PRACTICES

knowledge management
the creation, collection, storage, distribution, and application of compiled "know what" and "know-how"

The value of knowledge occurs only when it is put into action. **Knowledge management** consists of the creation, collection, storage, distribution, and application of compiled "know what" and "know-how" (Miller, 1999). We will look at the four processes through which organizations manage knowledge: acquisition, interpretation, dissemination, and retention (Garvin, 1998). The ability to create and use knowledge is what characterizes a learning organization and the practices organizations engage in to actively manage knowledge under these four categories are discussed next.

KNOWLEDGE ACQUISITION

Companies acquire or create new knowledge in many ways. Some focus on well-respected creative processes such as brainstorming. Others may benchmark competitors or the best companies in the world. Others engage in simulations or scenario planning to stimulate new ideas. Most scan the environment looking for new ideas or changing conditions.

Because culture is the most important part of managing knowledge, it tops our list of knowledge management practices.

A LEARNING CULTURE   Experts (i.e., those with experience in creating and managing knowledge), claim that the biggest obstacle in creating a learning organization is culture. Remember that culture can be defined as an organizations' beliefs, knowledge, attitudes, customs, and values as articulated by senior managers and employees. The attitudes and beliefs of people in an organization can encourage, discourage, or even prohibit learning. If employees view training as a waste of time (because the supervisor does not like new methods or because there is no time to practise new skills), then they will be discouraged from learning.

Some firms have an innate advantage in that they are knowledge-intensive firms that attract a workforce committed to advanced education and lifelong learning. Other companies must create this passion for new knowledge, but first they must understand what a learning culture is. In a new fad, some consultants and suppliers are willing to sell ideas and tools that lead to the appearance of a culture in which knowledge is valued. For example, establishing an Intranet does not mean that employees are exchanging and applying new knowledge. Appointing a chief learning officer does not mean that employees will risk sharing their knowledge.

Recall from Chapter 8 that a learning culture can be described as one in which knowledge and skills acquisition are highly valued and are considered to be responsibilities of every employee. Employees are given challenging job assignments that promote personal development. Social networks support new learning. Employees who do learn new things are rewarded. In a learning culture, managers expect employees to want to be the best and to be innovative. Simply put, a learning culture values learning and its application.

The first step in creating a learning culture is to conduct a culture audit to assess the values, behaviours, and outputs of a learning culture. See the Training Today 1 box for a checklist against which you can compare your organization to determine if a learning culture exists.

As with most organizational change efforts, the creation of a learning organization begins at the top with an active commitment to the principle that building employee skills leads to organizational survival and prosperity. The challenge is to encourage informal learning and direct that to organization goals.

What is ironic is that despite all these tools and techniques to create a culture in which employees value learning, we still are critical of the employee who sits at his desk reading a book, or suspicious of employees who seem to be wasting company time talking around the coffee pot. We expect reading and conversations to take place on the employee's time and off site. Despite all attempts to create a learning organization, managers sometimes send mixed messages. The research team that studied Motorola and discovered the incredible amounts of informal learning that took place there also studied Siemens Power Transmission and Distribution in Raleigh, North Carolina. Siemens had created a learning environment, except for one aspect that worked against informal learning. Management was concerned that workers were spending too much time socializing in the cafeteria, so they walled off part of the room believing that the small cramped space would no longer be attractive. But, as it turned out, employees were using the company cafeteria as a meeting place to discuss work issues. Three-quarters of the employees interviewed said that

TRAINING TODAY 1 Checklist for a Learning Culture

Conduct a cultural audit to determine if there is an organizational value for learning. For each statement below, indicate whether you

   1. strongly disagree   2. disagree   3. neither agree nor disagree
   4. agree   5. strongly agree

1. Job assignments are challenges that stretch employees' knowledge to the limit.
    1   2   3   4   5

2. Supervisors give recognition and credit to those who apply new knowledge and skills to their work.
    1   2   3   4   5

3. Employees are able to provide reliable information about ways to improve job performance.
    1   2   3   4   5

4. There is a performance appraisal system that ties financial rewards to technical competence.
    1   2   3   4   5

5. Job assignments consistently expose employees to new technical information.
    1   2   3   4   5

6. Supervisors can match an employee's need for personal and professional development with opportunities to attend training.
    1   2   3   4   5

7. Employees tell each other about new information that can be used to increase job performance.
    1   2   3   4   5

8. There is excellent on-the-job training.
    1   2   3   4   5

9. Job assignments are created in an employee's area of interest and designed to promote personal development.
    1   2   3   4   5

10. Supervisors encouraged independent and innovative thinking.
    1   2   3   4   5

My organization ...

11. is highly innovative
    1   2   3   4   5

12. expects continuing technical excellence and competence
    1   2   3   4   5

13. has a progressive atmosphere
    1   2   3   4   5

14. attempts to be better than its competitors
    1   2   3   4   5

15. expects high levels of work performance
    1   2   3   4   5

Adapted from: Tracey, J. B., Scott, I. T., & Kavanagh, M. J. (1995). Applying training on the job: The importance of the work environment. *Journal of Applied Psychology 80* (2), 239–252.

they talked about work issues away from the job, on lunch or coffee breaks (Stamps, 1998).

Sharing knowledge is still risky in some organizations because knowledge in bureaucratic organizations is power. If the best ideas are published, other teams or competitors may steal them. Someone who came up with a good idea that was used successfully by another employee may not be given credit for the idea. Other contextual factors also send a negative message about the value of learning. When the workload or production schedule is overwhelming, employees have no time to learn or to transfer their learning to others.

Another mistake that many organizations make when empowering employees to risk innovation and creativity is punishing them for mistakes. Learning is not always successful, and few employees will risk innovation if they are punished for failures. Mistakes happen and managers must learn to distinguish between bad judgment and bad luck. Sometimes failures are really successes when viewed from another perspective. For example, floating soap came from a production mistake in which too much air was injected into the bar. The toughest challenge for most managers is to tolerate mistakes. At Ciba Ceigy, a pharmaceutical company, a lab technician noticed severe side effects with a drug that was supposed to be hugely profitable. The executive of the cancelled-project team congratulated the department for creating a climate in which the lowest status person could raise an issue that could cancel a major project and that encouraged them to publish their learning in professional journals (Miller, 1999). Managers interested in fostering a learning culture must be careful not to undermine their efforts by sending mixed signals. A second way to increase the acquisition of new knowledge, is of course, by training employees.

TRAINING EMPLOYEES   Formal training is an integral and complementary part of the knowledge-acquisition process. Xerox, one of the first companies to transform itself into a learning organization, trains all its employees in a six-step problem-solving process that must be used at all meetings and that is used for virtually all decisions. Royal Bank has established a worldwide network of self-development programs, easily accessed from home or work, and promotes a philosophy of lifelong learning. Royal Bank's learning centre manager believes that access to learning is the first step in creating a learning organization (Trainor, 1998).

INFORMAL LEARNING   Employees know a lot. The empowered employee knows a lot about customers and about their current problems and emerging needs. Customers are demanding increased responsiveness and shorter turnaround times. Employees who work daily with these customers may have developed ways to be responsive. Organizations need to tap into that deep knowledge in a systematic way.

Employees, indeed most people, have always learned without being taught. Some employees learn how to handle client problems by trial and error. Some learn by being taught but not in a formal (i.e., classroom) setting: perhaps another employee demonstrated a way to save time by combining two steps in customer complaint handling. Employees learn how to work together effectively, perhaps by learning meeting rules, or how to deal with conflicting points of view. Sometimes learning occurs when an employee returns from a formal training session and teaches others what she has learned. When a research team studied informal training at Motorola, they discovered that every hour of formal training yielded four hours of informal training (Stamps, 1998). Learning does happen in organizations, and managers who value this learning will learn to interpret and capture this knowledge.

KNOWLEDGE INTERPRETATION

Learning occurs when individual employees form their views of the organization and its environment. These views are often called mental models. Senge (1990), the guru of organizational learning, describes **mental models** as "deeply ingrained assumptions, generalizations, or images that influence how we understand the world and how we take action" (p. 8). For example, if we have a mental model of managers as manipulators, then we will see all their actions as politically motivated and act accordingly. Much new knowledge will not be accepted because we cannot recognize and change our mental models. As one researcher noted, the acceptance of new knowledge can be likened to an organ transplant—the possibility of rejection is highly probable (Stamps, 1999). Even when employees are aware of best practices in other companies or units, it might take more than two years for the information to be understood in a way that can be acted on.

> **mental models** the perceptions that influence how we understand the world and take action

An effective way to develop shared mental models is to establish teams. The most valuable and innovative work-related learning occurs in these real work teams, solving real problems (Stamps, 1997). At Chevron Corporation, based in San Francisco, best-practice teams save the companies millions of dollars annually by improving processes (Neely Martinez, 1998). These groups, learning by doing, are sometimes given a formal name of "communities of practice." Communities of practice are networks of people who work together and regularly share information and knowledge.

Knowledge cannot be valued unless there is a shared understanding of its importance. Learning is social, and as teams work together, they not only learn, but they develop a common way of thinking about things and a common identity emerges. These common perspectives are termed mental maps and are vitally important to the interpretation of the work environment and any lessons it contains. New learning is difficult to accept and apply without this shared perspective.

The creation and sharing of knowledge often occurs when people can talk with each other, and over time, develop a relationship. As we noted earlier, these long-term relationships, such as those that occur with apprentices or protégé's, are excellent vehicles for the transfer of knowledge. North Americans generally do not appreciate the importance of the social and emotional context of learning. We see learning as information transfer. Yet, even the youngest student will tell you that he learns more from a teacher he likes.

The higher your position in an organization, the more likely you are to learn about events in face-to-face conversations. Chief executives spend about 95 percent of their time in conversations and discussions. Workers at the entry level spend less time, but still need to interface to solve problems. For example, people working on the assembly line at Motorola had no chance to even talk with co-workers—they discussed work problems and solutions as the shifts changed (Stamp, 1998). Perhaps a good way to start creating a learning organization is to build on what is already working at the grassroots level. Other organizations can help employees interpret knowledge by creating networks in which individual learners and teams can share information and insight. In learning organizations, employees need to value talking time.

North Americans also do not appreciate the value of reflection, "the process of stepping back from an experience to ponder, carefully and persistently, its meaning" (Seibert, 1999, p. 56). In Japan, when a person sits quietly, no one will interrupt, because the assumption is that the person is thinking. When the person is moving, then interruptions are allowed. Exactly the reverse practice occurs in North America (Senge, 1990). Managers need time to reflect on their actions, to examine their choices, and to interpret the information they are receiving. Providing tools for reflection and even coaches to ask the right questions can help employees make sense of what they are experiencing and learning.

The next step in knowledge management is the sharing of these insights and experiences.

KNOWLEDGE DISSEMINATION

Moving products, services, and money through, and between organizations is a standard process for most organizations. Moving ideas requires a different set of skills and even different norms. At times, it feels like capturing a snowflake and passing it to a friend.

Companies must design systems or ways of sharing knowledge so that others can improve their work practices. You might say that information has always been shared between employees, and knowledge management is just a new way of describing communication. Although employees have always passed on new ideas by talking with each other, the difference is that these informal systems can be replaced by formal mechanisms grounded in technology.

ICTs (information and communication technologies) allow for increased codification of knowledge; that is, its transformation into information that can easily be transmitted. Today, most organizations have electronic bulletin boards, libraries, virtual conference rooms, or connected knowledge bases. Through technology, employees can exchange proposals, presentations, spreadsheets, specifications, and so on. For example, the CEO of Memphis-based Buckman Laboratories, a manufacturer of industrial chemicals, noticed this informal sharing when he toured the plants and labs in 20 countries. He and his executive team accumulated case histories of best practices developed in one country, and passed on this information in the next country. Obviously, some dilution of information occurred at each stop, because the executive team did not actually do the work. This experience led Buckman Laboratories to ask "How can we transfer our company's best practices in a better way?" They actually set up a knowledge transfer department, with more than 40 employees in information management and training. As early as 1988, Buckman Laboratories, the winner of the Optimas award for competitive advantage had established a series of private forums in which employees could share their insights 24 hours a day. Buckman Laboratories credits these online forums with an increase of $300 million in revenues, because they reduced the amount of time it takes for new ideas to reach the marketplace (Sunoo, 1999).

There is a growth in benchmarking best practices. Normally, benchmarking implies that organizations study the best in the field and then attempt to replicate the best practices in their own companies. But as seen with the Buckman Laboratories example, benchmarking can also occur within organizations. For example, the branch in Regina may have the lowest rate of returns and it would benefit other branches to understand why.

An Intranet is a critical component for managing knowledge. An employee who posts a question or seeks advice can receive that information in hours, not weeks. Just as we use the little help icons (or wizards) for our software, we could use a company expert or subject-matter specialist who would pop up on the monitor while we are working on a new project—an instant coach!

KNOWLEDGE RETENTION

As noted earlier, knowledge resides in the brains of employees or in systems created to store that knowledge. To capitalize on these sources of knowledge, organizations must build tools to quickly compile, store, and retrieve this knowledge, a kind of intellectual inventory. These are called knowledge repositories. Knowledge repositories should not be seen as sacred libraries in which great books are stored and never read. The system has to be designed to encourage its use, to facilitate interaction. One reason for the growth of interest in this area is that the cost of managing it has been significantly lowered through technology.

There are ways to capture and store knowledge in information systems for later use. Some of these are highly structured databases. Digitalized knowledge can be more easily and cheaply processed, indexed, searched, converted, and transmitted.

Some knowledge repositories are more informal lists of lessons learned, white papers, presentations, and so on. Others are more actively stored in discussion groups. Most have links to the originators of the documents or at least to those who tend to access the repositories, thus signalling who is actively interested in that area. These collaborative filters monitor databases and Intranet sites, and can tell you which sites others with interests similar to yours have found useful. Another useful idea is that of online mentors. Hughes Space & Communications Co. share knowledge and best practices using just-in-time mentoring. Hughes has an index of mentors who can be called for advice on various aspects of any project. For example, a mentor with experience preparing a business case for a project might be asked to coach an employee who is facing a similar task (Stuller, 1998).

Not all knowledge repositories are based on computer technology. Some knowledge is tacit and not easily codified. So more traditional means of storing knowledge might include transcripts or audiocassettes from strategic planning sessions, consultants' reports in text or multimedia formats, videotaped presentations, market-trend analyses, and any number of information-rich resources. IBM, whose core competence is knowledge, maintains dozens of knowledge repositories that consist of project proposals, work papers, presentations, and reports. IBM says that these repositories have reduced project time by as much as two thirds (Tapscott, 1998).

Oral histories are another way to capture knowledge, particularly when organizations suffer the memory loss associated with departures and downsizing. For example, in the United Kingdom, Rothschild PLC used an exit interview to capture the vast amount of knowledge that its departing head of public relations held. A professional with HR and PR experience interviewed the executive, for an entire afternoon, and the conversation was recorded. Information that would not normally be transmitted to the successor was uncovered, edited, and indexed (Kransdorff, 1997). Other companies record oral histories of retiring managers. At Kraft General Foods, the brand manager of Cracker Barrel Cheese was facing declining sales. She consulted the archives where the interview transcripts with the manager who had launched the brand were recorded. Based on these insights into the original goals for the cheese, the current brand manager was able to re-invigorate the brand.

You have just read descriptions of the various practices used by some companies to manage the acquisition, interpretation, dissemination, and retention of knowledge. A survey of knowledge management practices found that the most frequently used method was the Intranet. See Table 14.1 for a list of other methods used.

Few organizations engage in the management of knowledge in a systematic way using all the practices outlined in Table 14.1. Those that do practise knowledge management typically formalize the job by appointing a senior

TABLE 14.1   KNOWLEDGE MANAGEMENT PRACTICES

PROJECT	PERCENTAGE USING
Creating an Intranet	47
Repositories	33
Decision support tools	33
Groupware to support collaboration	33
Networks of knowledge workers	24
Mapping sources of internal expertise	18
Establishing new knowledge roles	15

Source: Executive perspectives of knowledge in the organization. Ernst & Young Center for Business Intelligence [as cited in] Bassi, L., Cheney, S., & Lewis, E. (1998). Trends in workplace learning: Supply and demand in interesting times. *Training and Development* (November).

executive who is responsible for this important work. This formalization signals the importance of knowledge management to the success of the company.

KNOWLEDGE MANAGEMENT JOBS

If knowledge management is a source of competitive advantage, then it makes sense to appoint someone in the organization who has specific responsibility for leveraging that knowledge. Some organizations have taken this path and appointed a chief knowledge officer or a director of intellectual capital or a chief learning officer. This executive level position, reporting directly to the president, signals to the rest of the organization that organizing and distributing knowledge is a valuable activity. The title given is important, as outlined in the Training Today 2 box. Those learning organizations that value knowledge often wish to put a price tag on its value. How can they do this? The next section examines some methods that organizations have used to measure the value of knowledge.

THE MEASUREMENT OF KNOWLEDGE

What does a high IQ company look like? We know how to create and manage the knowledge, but would we know an effective learning organization from an ineffective one? Knowledge assets can only have value if they contribute to organizational strategy and performance. The head of the Securities and

TRAINING TODAY 2 Chief of Corporate Brains

Although most organizations call those who are responsible for learning (via training) directors of training, many are turning to different titles to signal the importance of learning creation and diffusion. The holders of these new titles must develop and deploy corporate brainpower. The fact that such positions exist is recognition that intellectual capital (the ideas, knowledge, and experience of employees) is the firm's chief asset. Hubert St. Onge has held the titles of vice president of learning organization at CIBC, and senior vice president for strategic capabilities at The Mutual Group.

The title is important. The label, chief knowledge officer, seems to imply that the position is responsible for coordinating, cataloguing, and keeping databases and reports. Compare this to chief learning officer, someone who helps employees to develop their own expertise, and helps the organization develop processes to create and share knowledge. Chief training officer is a title that comes with a vision of classrooms and rigid curriculum, so many organizations don't use it to describe the new vision of increasing knowledge and skills. Technology is so important in a learning organization that many executives who are the knowledge managers for their organizations come from a technology background. They are given titles such as Director, Information Systems. Many argue that even the title chief or director should be dropped as it implies a hierarchical relationship that doesn't exist.

The job descriptions vary widely but usually include the ability to manage culture, collaboration, communication, and business strategy. Managers of corporate knowledge build knowledge networks and computer infrastructure.

Exchange Commission states the measures of intellectual capital will be the main features in annual reports within a decade, while financial statements will become supplemental information (Miller, 1999). But measurement is a problem.

If intellectual capital is tacit (i.e., we cannot sense it with our five senses), how can we measure it? How do we know it is there and how much it is worth? Companies that are committed to the concept, such as Skandia, the Swedish insurance company, and Dow Chemical have conducted most of the research in this area (Bassi, Cheney, & Lewis, 1998). We will look at the approaches these companies use.

MEASUREMENT OF VALUE

Skandia focuses on the measurement of value, using 164 variables including education and skills. For example, Skandia reports that by managing knowledge, they were able to reduce start-up time for launching a new facility from seven years (the industry average) to three years. Other companies followed Skandia's lead and express the value of knowledge management through anecdotes and stories. For example, at one automotive supplier, 30 percent of the design engineers' time was wasted solving problems that had already been solved in the company (Kransdorff, 1997). Companies know that knowledge isn't being shared when work is duplicated, or expertise was available but hidden in the company and opportunities were lost, or needless staffing took place. Platinum Technology saw a $6 million return on an investment of $750 000 in a Web system that allows its sales staff to find product data (Stahl, 1999).

MEASUREMENT OF HARD ASSETS

Knowledge at Dow Chemical is managed like a hard asset. Dow Chemical tries to assess the hidden value of patents and licences that have not been used. Dow manages its portfolio of more than 30 000 patents by assigning them to individual managers who are then responsible for converting them into profitable businesses (Neely Martinez, 1998). CIBC tracks the number of new ideas generated, new products created, and percentage of income from new revenue streams.

Accountants have been struggling with the challenges of measuring the worth of employees and have tried several ways to put a dollar value on employees, including HR accounting, HR valuation, and a balanced performance measurement system.

HUMAN RESOURCE ACCOUNTING

Human resource accounting is the activity of assigning, budgeting for, and reporting the *costs* of human resources incurred by an organization. Thus, the cost of an employee to an organization consists of the costs of acquisition, training, orientation, coaching, and development. These expenses are amortized over the expected working lives of employees. But these costs are difficult to measure, and employees are not assets that can be sold or traded. The major problem is that a firm can spend the same amounts of money hiring and training two employees, but receive very different returns from them, with one being highly productive, and the other a marginal worker.

HUMAN RESOURCE VALUATION

Human resource valuation is the assignment of value to employees in their positions within an organization based on the future economic services those employees are expected to render.

Under this model, *contributions* are measured, not costs. Accountants try to determine what an employee will contribute to an organization over the employment period. However, this model has problems. The main failure is that these models cannot account for differences in employee effectiveness. A complete discussion of these measurement issues can be found in Belcourt and McBey (2000).

Balanced Performance Measurement System

In this system, intellectual capital (the product of a learning organization) is the sum of a company's intangible assets.

Market value equals book value plus intellectual capital:

$$MV = BV + IC$$

For example, Nortel paid $450 million dollars for a company that had never produced a single product; they bought brainpower (i.e., 150 telecommunication specialists in high-speed networking equipment at Cambridge Systems Corporation, in Kanata, Ontario). They paid three million dollars per brain (Pezim, 1999).

Microsoft is a good example of a company in which investors are putting a price tag on intellectual capital, because the total market value of the company exceeds its books value. Investors must believe in the future earnings potential, based not just on goodwill, but on the intellectual potential of the company. The four types of capital (human, renewal, structural, and relationship) work in a cycle to increase intellectual capital. As more investments are made in human capital, the employees are more capable and committed to increasing renewal and structural capital, leading to more productive relationship capital, resulting in better financial performance (Knight, 1999). The money can then be recycled to increase intellectual capital.

While many acknowledge that capturing and leveraging intellectual capital is crucial for survival, some argue that attempting to measure it will ensure its demise. Indeed, researchers who have attempted to track and assign value to employees as assets have abandoned the effort, claiming it is simply too difficult. But measurement is an accepted way to manage. What implications does this inability to measure human capital have for managers?

Implications for Management

For more than a century, organizations have survived by using a command-and-control style of management. The advocates of scientific management divided the job tasks into thinkers and doers. Managers were the thinkers, and employees were dissuaded from contributing at this level. But the current corporate world is complex, with international operations, alliances, changing technologies, empowered clients, and virtual companies. The CEO is no longer all knowing, all seeing. Managing by compliance has been replaced by managing by commitment. Individual employees must share responsibility for envisioning and shaping the future of the organization. They can only do this in an environment that values the creation of ideas and the sharing of this knowledge.

Rather than one top-down boss, Senge (1997) suggests that the new paradigm is a community of leaders in which there are three important roles:

1. *Research*—the deliberate pursuit of discovery and understanding that forms the theory that can guide the practice.
2. *Capacity building*—increasing employees' capabilities and knowledge
3. *Practice*—employees working together to not only achieve results but to understand why this occurs.

Previously, these three roles were the responsibilities of various and separate units. Research was done by universities or labs or consultants. Capacity building was the job of the training department. Practice was just every day work, with no method to capture what worked and why. In the learning organization, these roles are combined and diffused throughout the organization. Organizations that do this deserve the label of learning organizations.

The shift has had an impact on the way in which organizations structure the learning experiences of their employees. Obviously, every organization still retains the methods to teach employees new KSAs. But some organizations are using tools to enable employees to create and share new knowledge. The movement from training to learning is captured in Table 14.2.

TABLE 14.2 THE TRAINING ORGANIZATION VERSUS THE LEARNING ORGANIZATION

FOCUS	TRAINING	LEARNING
methods	formal	informal
knowledge	explicit, codified	tacit, embedded
location	off site	integrated with real work
learning role	instructor	facilitator
goal	knowledge transmission	development of new practices
evaluation	testing	changed practices

Source: *From training to learning: Preparation for success in the digital world—final report.* (1997, February). Menlo Park, CA: Institute for Research on Learning, Xerox Education and Learning Organization, Xerox Corporation.

The role of the trainer is a necessary, but not sufficient, condition in the creation of a learning organization. Trainers and performance management experts can work closely with those in information technology and communications in the creation of a learning organization.

In our examination of the management of performance, we have looked at both the individual and the organization for models to increase the knowledge, skills, and abilities of employees, and the effectiveness of organizations.

SUMMARY

We described a learning organization, and the strategic advantages associated with it. The ultimate goal of a learning organization is to adapt and survive by creating new knowledge. We defined knowledge, and compared explicit and tacit knowledge. Examinations of the methods organizations use to acquire, interpret, diffuse, and store knowledge were provided. Some ways of valuing the worth of intellectual capital were given. We concluded by looking at the implications of creating a learning organization for managers and trainers.

KEY TERMS

explicit knowledge   346

human capital   347

intellectual capital   346

knowledge   345

knowledge management   348

learning organization   345

mental models   352

organizational learning   343

relationship capital   347

renewal capital   347

structural capital   347

tacit knowledge   345

EXERCISES

1. Consult these Internet sites: <www.knowledge.inc>, <www.trainingsupersite.com>, and <www.brint.com/orgLrng> to locate articles about the evolution of the learning organization. Find the most recent articles and list some new ideas that have occurred since this chapter was written in late 1999.

2. The International Federation of Accountants (IFAC) publishes articles on its Web site, <www.ifac.org>, about the measurement of intellectual capital. These articles describe the challenges and opportunities inherent in an intellectual capital approach to management accounting. Consult the Web site and prepare a summary of the most recent articles for class discus-

sion. You can access a test developed by The Canadian Institute of Chartered Accountants to measure intellectual capital by going to <www.cica.ca>. The Montague Institute has developed 12 ways to measure intellectual capital, and you can read their list at <www.montague.com>. Develop a list based on all of these sources.

3. Using the learning culture checklist in Table 14.2, assess the learning culture of the organization in which you work. Can you provide a specific example to support your assessment of each of the 15 items?

4. Using the information contained in this chapter, develop a checklist to

determine if the organization in which you work is a learning organization. How many of the knowledge management practices does it use? What would you recommend to the CEO to support efforts to manage knowledge?

CASE: FROZEN ROCK-SOLID

At General Motors of Canada Ltd., Nick Vanderstoop is in charge of implementing a system that he created to prevent the "erosion of knowledge." He loves to scare the daylights out of GM executives and managers by telling them a true story about the company.

The story goes something like this: Several years ago a worker at the head office of General Motors of Canada Ltd. in Oshawa retired. Among the many tasks that were performed by him, one was particularly important. Every fall he would spend about an hour sending messages to inform others that certain freezable chemicals like upholstery cleaners must be shipped in heated trucks during the winter.

A few months after he retired, the parts distribution centre in Woodstock, Ontario, began to receive calls from angry customers across Canada who were upset because the chemicals that they were receiving were frozen rock-solid. The reason: Nobody in the company knew enough about the retiree's job to make sure that the chemicals were properly transported during the winter. A minor oversight? Not quite. It cost the company $1.5 million.

Other incidents at GM have also been reported. For example, 400 perfectly good carburetors were accidentally destroyed at a cost of $300,000 because the worker who kept them off the scrap list retired. It has also been reported that a $250,000 car prototype was crushed into scrap metal because the employee who was responsible for it was transferred. Incidents like these are known to occur at other companies.

Source: Livesey, B. (1997, November). Glitch doctor. *Report on Business Magazine*, pp. 96–102.

QUESTIONS

1. Why do you think this is an important story to tell company executives and managers?
2. What is the main point of the story?
3. Organization mishaps like those reported in the case appear to be common occurrences. A traditional organization might blame or attribute the causes of them to a number of different sources. What reasons might be given for such mishaps?
4. What could GM and other companies do to solve the problems reported in the case?

5. What would a learning organization do to identify and solve the types of incidents described in the case? What knowledge management practices would you recommend and why?

6. In Chapter 1, three models of training and development were described: the performance model, strategic model, and learning model. Discuss how the three models relate to the incidents described in the case and provide potential solutions for each of them.

References

Baets, W.R.J. (1998). *Organizational learning and knowledge technologies in a dynamic environment.* Boston: Kluwer Academic Publishers.

Bassi, L., Cheney, S., & Lewis, E. (1998). Trends in workplace learning: Supply and demand in interesting times. *Training and Development* (November), 51–77.

Belcourt, M., & McBey, K. (2000). Strategic human resources planning. Toronto: Nelson Thomson Learning.

Bennet, J.K., & O'Brien, M.J. (1994). The building blocks of the learning organization. *Training Magazine* (June).

Edwards, S (1997). The brain gain. *CA Magazine* (April), pp. 21–25.

Garvin, D.A. (1998). The processes of organization and management. *Sloan Management Review* 39 (4), 33–50.

Kapp, K.M. (1999). Moving training to the strategic level with learning requirements planning. *National Productivity Review* (Spring), 15–21.

Kransdorff, A. (1997). Fight organizational memory loss. *Workforce* (September), 34–39.

Miller, W. (1999). Building the ultimate resource. *Management Review* (January), 42–45.

Neely Martinez, M. (1998, February). The collective power. *HRM magazine*, pp. 88–94.

Pezim, S. (1999, January 11). Fishing in the knowledge pond. *Canadian HR Reporter*, pp. 15–16.

Seibert, K.W. (1999). Reflection in action: Tools for cultivating on-the-job learning conditions. *Organizational Dynamics* 27 (3), 54–65.

Stamps, D. (1997). Communities of practice: Learning is social, training is irrelevant? *Training* 34 (2), 34–42.

———. (1998). Learning ecologies. *Training Magazine* 35 (1), pp. 32–38.

———. (1999). Is knowledge management a fad? *Training* 36 (3), 36–42.

Senge, P. M. (1990). *The fifth discipline.* New York: Double Day.

———. (1997). Communities of leaders and learners. *Harvard Business Review* 75 (5), 30–32.

Sunoo, B.P. (1999). How HR supports knowledge sharing. *Workforce* 78 (3), 30–34.

Stahl, S. (1999, April 5). Knowledge yields impressive returns. *Information Week*, p. 115.

Stewart, T. (1994, October 3). Intellectual capital. *Fortune*, pp. 68–74.

Stuller, J. (1998). Chief of corporate smarts. *Training 35* (4), 28–37.

Tapscott, D. (1998). Make knowledge an asset for the whole company. *Computerworld 32* (51), p. 32.

Trainor, N.L. (1998, April 20). Learning creates value for organizations. *Canadian HR Reporter*, p. 9.

INDEX

Job specification, 52
Johnson Controls, 25

Knowledge
    acquisition of, 348–52
    defined, 345
    dissemination of, 353–54
    as domain of learning, 83–85
    explicit, 346
    interpretation of, 352–53
    measurement of, 356–59
    retention of, 354–56
    tacit, 346
Knowledge management, defined, 348
Knowledge management jobs, 356, 357
Knowledge management practices, 348–56
Knowledge of results, 113
KPMG, 161
Kraft General Foods, 355

Labour. See Unions
Language, nondiscriminatory, 335
Learning
    action, 148–49
    affective, levels of, 87–88
    defined, 80, 106
    distance, 137, 139
    domains of, 83–89, 106
    informal, 351
    measuring, 219–21
    organizational, 343–60
    and practice, 199–200
    principles, 112–14, 115
    self-directed, 172–73
    taxonomy of, 219
    theories of, 106–11
    vs. training, 360
Learning culture
    checklist for, 350
    defined, 16
    and knowledge management, 348–51
    and transfer of training, 196–97
Learning model, defined, 14–15
Learning objectives. See Objectives
Learning organization, 345
Learning outcomes, categories of, 106
Lectures, 134–35
Legal considerations, in needs analysis, 45
Lesson plans, 120–23
Levi Strauss & Co., 280–81
Line professionals, trainers as, 26
LINK performance management system, 78–79
Liquor Control Board of Ontario, 79

Literacy, 268–71
    defined, 271
    levels of, 270
L.L. Bean, 283

Macrotraining needs, 49
Mager and Pipe's decision tree, 60–63
Management development
    choosing method for, 306–308
    climate for, 302–304
    context of, 307
    and core skills, 308–10
    defined, 298
    and discretionary skills, 310–13
    introduction to, 298–99
    model for, 300
    and nature of management work, 304–306
    process of, 306–308
    strategy for, 299–302, 303
    trainer's role in, 313–15
Management education, 298
Management training, 298
Managers
    core skills for, 308–10
    discretionary skills for, 310–13
    and employee analysis, 58
    maintenance strategies after training, 204–206
    process, 306
    support for training programs, 195
Managing the training function, 27–28
Marketing the training function, 34–35
Marriott, 283
Massed vs. distributed training, 112
Math skills, 271
McDonald's, 13, 336
McMaster University, 192
Measurement techniques, 35
Mechanism, 88
Mental models, 352
Mentoring, 169–72, 196, 331, 355
Metaphors, 51
Microsoft, 359
Microtraining needs, 49
Ministry of Transporation, 45
Mission, training, 35
Mitsubishi, 285
Mnemonics, 199
Moral obligations, in needs analysis, 45–46
Motivation, 190–91
Motorola Inc., 172, 206, 271, 273, 349, 352, 353
Motorola University, 15

Motor skills, 106
Multimedia, 138–40. *See also* Computer-
based training
Multiperspective training, model of,
331–33

National Cash Register (NCR), 24
Native Women's Association, 33
Need assessment checklist, 63
Needs analysis, 17
    advantages/disadvantages of tech-
        niques, 64–65
    comparison of methods, 66–67
    data-collection issues, 68–69
    data-collection methods for, 63
    decision tree for, 60–63
    defined, 44
    and diagnostic process, 46–48
    documentation for, 63–66
    importance of, 45–46
    information sources, 67–68
    and organizational analysis, 48–63
    and training programs, 101
Net benefits, estimating, 248–52
Net benefit value calculation worksheet,
    249
Nike, 144
Nilson, Carolyn, 36
Nondiscriminatory language, 335
Nontechnical skills training, 279–80
Normative approach, to grading, 198
Nortel, 344, 359

Objectives
    advantages of, 80–81
    cautions about, 89–90
    defined, 80
    and domains of learning, 83–89
    objections to use of, 90–93
    suggestions for preparing, 93
    types of, 83
    writing of, 81–83
Observation
    as needs assessment technique, 64
    and social learning theory, 110
Observation rating form, 222
Off-the-job training methods
    choosing, 149–52
    described, 133–49
On-the-job training (OJT) methods
    defined, 158
    described, 157–75, 181–85
    requirements for instructors, 159
Ontario Hydro, 49, 149

Ontario Institute for Studies in Education,
    172
Ontario Ministry of Community and Social
    Services, 336
Ontario Workplace Health and Safety
    Agency, 45
Operational consulting, 141
Opportunity, after training program,
    204–205
Oral histories, 355
Organization, as level of affective learning,
    87
Organizational analysis
    and benchmarking, 50
    and culture, 50–51
    defined, 48
    and employee analysis, 56–63
    and environment, 49–50
    and job analysis, 52–56
    and strategy, 49
Organizational development (OD), 173–75
Organizational learning
    defined, 343
    need for, 344
Organizational restructuring, and training, 10
Organizational strategy, linked with
    training, 78–79
Organizers, 199
Organizing training function, 24–27
Orientation, 273–75
Origination, 89
Outsourcing training, 30–31
Overlearning, 113

Pallet, Bill, 283
Participation, managing, 334–35
Pedagogy, and diversity, 330–31
Pepsi Cola, 49
Perception, 88
Performance
    base line of, 45
    defined, 82
    vs. learning, 80
    obstacles to effective, 58–59
    standards of, 91
Performance aids, 159–60
Performance contracts, 202
Performance culture, 16–17
Performance management, 2–4
    defined, 3
    models, 15
Performance model, defined, 12–13
Performance problems, 44
    determining solutions to, 60–63

Performance-support systems, electronic, 160–61
Persons with disabilities, 333–37
Platinum Technology, 358
Policy costs, 257
Politics, organizational, 27
Positioning, training function, 24
Practice
    active, 112
    conditions of, 112–13
    defined, 199–200
    massed vs. distributed, 112
Pressure point, 47
Pre-tests, 193–94
Print media, as needs assessment technique, 64
Problems/solutions, in delivery of training programs, 124–27
Process managers, 306
Professional associations
    and coaching, 169
    as stakeholders in training, 33
Proficiency tests, 58
Programs, defined, 80. *See also* Training programs
Psychomotor abilities, 189
Psychomotor domain, 88–89
Punishment, 200

Quality control, and training, 4
Quality training, 278–79
Questionnaires
    as needs assessment technique, 64
    reaction, 217–19

Rating form, 218
Reaction, as level of evaluation, 216–19
Receiving, 87
Record keeping, 257
Records, as needs assessment technique, 65
Reinforcement
    after training, 205–206
    during training, 200–201
Relapse prevention, 203–204
Relationship capital, 347–48
Renewal capital, 347
Reports, as needs assessment technique, 65
Responding, 87
Restructuring, organizational, 10
Results, as level of evaluation, 223
Return on expectations, as level of evaluation, 223–26
Return on investment (ROI), 248–52

Revans, Reginald, 148
Rewards, 200
Role plays, 145–46
Rothschild PLC, 355
Royal Bank, 34, 144, 351
Rubbermaid, 280

Sales training, 282–83
Sample size/depth, in surveys, 67
San Diego County, 25
Sask Tel, 94–95
Scheduling, for training programs, 119–20
Schultz, Howard, 274
Sears Roebuck & Co., 225, 285
Self-assessment, 68
Self-directed learning (SDL), 172–73
Self-efficacy, 110–11, 191
Self-management, 111, 202–203
Set, 88
Sexual harassment training, 285–86
Shaping, 107–108
Siemens, 349
Similarity effect, 58
Simulations, 144–45
    business, 311
Six sigma, 233–34
Skandia, 357
Skills
    basic, 268–72
    core, 308–10
    discretionary, 310–13
    as domain of learning, 88–89
    intellectual, 106
    math, 271
    motor, 106
    nontechnical, 279–80
    soft, 279–80
    technical, 272–73
Skinner, B.F., 107
Slides, 137–38
Social learning theory, 110–11
Soft data, 223, 224
Soft skills, 279–80
Solutions to performance problems, determining, 60–63
Sony Technology Centre, 12
Sprint Canada, 78, 283
Staff, trainers as, 26
Stakeholders, managing, 32–33
Standard deviation of job performance in dollars, 252
Standards of performance, 91
Starbucks, 274

Statistical analysis, in job analysis, 55
Stentor, 138
Stereotypes, 329
Stimulus variability, 114, 200
Stories, 51
Strategic model, defined, 13–14
Strategy
    defined, 13
    and organizational analysis, 49
Structural capital, 347
Student's return quotient, 28
Subject-matter experts, as trainers, 104–105
Summative evaluation, 214
Surveys
    for evaluation, 222–23
    in job analysis, 54–55
    sources of information for, 67–68
Synthesis, 84
Systems approach, to performance
    management, 16–17

Tacit knowledge, 346
Target, 14
Task, defined, 52
Task sequencing, 113
Taxonomy of Educational Objectives, 83
Taxonomy of learning, 219
TD Bank, 214
Teams, and knowledge interpretation, 352
Team training and building, 280–82
Technical skills training, 272–73
Technology, and training, 10, 136–40, 148,
    160–61
Tests
    as needs assessment technique, 65
    cognitive, 190
    to evaluate learning, 219–21
    as feedback, 198
    pre-, 193–94
    work-sample, 190, 191
Texas Instruments, 56
360 degree appraisals/feedback, 67,
    308–309
Toronto Police Force, 288
Total quality management (TQM), 175,
    278–79
Trainability, 189–92
Trainees
    involvement in learning experience,
      192
    reaction to training, 216–19
    selecting, 114–16, 189–92
    with special needs, 333–37

    strategies for, 202–204
    treatment of, 327
Trainers
    and acknowledging diversity, 324–25
    and avoiding discrimination, 331–33
    as consultants, 26, 28–30
    as line professionals, 26
    role in management
      development, 313–15
    selecting, 104–105
    as staff, 26
Training
    administration, 121
    basic-skills, 268–72
    benefits of, 4–7
    budget, 33–34
    in Canada, 8–9
    centralized, 25
    computer-based, 136, 138–40, 148,
      160–61
    computer software, 275
    cross-cultural, 288–91
    customer service, 283–85
    decentralized, 25
    defined, 3
    discrimination in, 326–27, 329–31
    diversity, 286–88, 336
    environmental influences on, 9–11
    equity in, 323–37
    establishing need for, 194
    and ethics, 36–37
    evaluating, 213–32
    experiential, 146
    health and safety, 276–77
    importance of, 4–7
    information technology, 275–76
    and knowledge management, 351
    vs. learning, 360
    and management development,
      297–315
    massed vs. distributed, 112
    materials and equipment, 117–18
    methods, 116–17. *See also* Training
      methods
    models of, 12–15
    multiperspective, 331–33
    for new employees, 273–75
    nontechnical skills, 279–80
    organizational context of, 11–12
    organizational strategy linked with,
      78–79
    outsourcing, 30–31
    plans, 116
    quality, 278–79

To the owner of this book

We hope that you have enjoyed *Managing Performance through Training & Development,* by Monica Belcourt, Philip Wright, and Alan Saks (ISBN 0-17-616648-3), and we would like to know as much about your experiences with this text as you would care to offer. Only through your comments and those of others can we learn how to make this a better text for future readers.

School _____ Your instructor's name _____

Course _____ Was the text required? _____ Recommended? _____

1. What did you like the most about *Managing Performance through Training & Development?*

_____
_____
_____

2. How useful was this text for your course?

_____
_____
_____

3. Do you have any recommendations for ways to improve the next edition of this text?

_____
_____
_____

4. In the space below or in a separate letter, please write any other comments you have about the book. (For example, please feel free to comment on reading level, writing style, terminology, design features, and learning aids.)

_____
_____
_____

Optional

Your name _____ Date _____

May Nelson Thomson Learning quote you, either in promotion for *Managing Performance through Training & Development,* or in future publishing ventures?

Yes _____ No _____

Thanks!

You can also send your comments to us via e-mail at
college@nelson.com

PLEASE TAPE SHUT. DO NOT STAPLE.

TAPE SHUT

TAPE SHUT

- - - FOLD HERE - - -

MAIL ⮞ POSTE

Canada Post Corporation
Société canadienne des postes

Postage paid   Port payé
if mailed in Canada si posté au Canada
Business Reply   **Réponse d'affaires**

0066102399   01

Nelson
Thomson Learning.™

0066102399-M1K5G4-BR01

NELSON THOMSON LEARNING
HIGHER EDUCATION
PO BOX 60225 STN BRM B
TORONTO ON M7Y 2H1

TAPE SHUT

TAPE SHUT